CHALLENGE

Challenging the Market

The Struggle to Regulate Work and Income

Edited by
JIM STANFORD
AND LEAH F. VOSKO

McGill-Queen's University Press
Montreal & Kingston · London · Ithaca

© McGill-Queen's University Press 2004
ISBN 0-7735-2726-5 (cloth)
ISBN 0-7735-2727-3 (paper)

Legal deposit third quarter 2004
Bibliothèque nationale du Québec

This book has been published with the help of a grant from
the Canadian Federation for the Humanities and Social Sciences, through
the Aid to Scholarly Publications Programme, using funds provided by
the Social Sciences and Humanities Research Council of Canada. Funding
has also been received from the Centre for Research on Work and Society,
York University.

McGill-Queen's University Press acknowledges the support of the Canada
Council for the Arts for its publishing program. It also acknowledges the
financial support of the Government of Canada through the Book
Publishing Industry Development Program (BPIDP) for its publishing
activities.

National Library of Canada Cataloguing in Publication

Challenging the market : the struggle to regulate work and income /
edited by Jim Stanford and Leah F. Vosko.

Includes bibliographical references.
ISBN 0-7735-2726-5 (bnd)
ISBN 0-7735-2727-3 (pbk)

1. Labour market.   2. Labour policy.   3. Labour costs.   I. Stanford, Jim
II. Vosko, Leah F

HD5706.C44 2004   331.12   C2004–901848–5

Typeset in 10/12 Baskerville by True to Type

Contents

Acknowledgments

This volume is the product of an International Working Group on Labour Market Regulation and Deregulation, which operated from 1998 to 2003 through the Centre for Research on Work and Society at York University in Toronto, Canada. The Working Group consisted of approximately 30 academics and policy researchers from several countries, each pursuing research critical of the assumptions, practices, and social and economic consequences of labour market flexibility. The group's activity included a conference in Toronto in June 2001 ("Challenging the Market") that saw presentation and discussion of most of the chapters in this volume. The Working Group, the conference, and this volume all provided opportunities for an international, interdisciplinary exchange of ideas and findings by researchers with diverse interests and methods, but a common interest in preserving and advancing a more emancipatory vision of labour market regulation. The co-editors of this volume were also the co-chairs of the Working Group.

As co-editors of this volume, we are indebted to many individuals and organizations for their support of the Working Group, the conference, and the preparation of this book. First and foremost, we thank staff members of the Centre for Research on Work and Society at York University for their consistent support of the Working Group and all of its activities, including this collection. The centre is a unique institution that aims to facilitate closer co-operation and collaboration among academics, labour unions, and labour advocates, and the success of this Working Group is testimony to the centre's proven ability to accomplish that goal. The past director, Carla Lipsig-Mummé, played an essential role in envisioning and planning the Working Group, organizing the conference, and helping to raise money for the conference and for this publication. We also gratefully acknowledge the continuing involvement of the centre's current director, Norene Pupo, and the efforts of the former associate director, Robert Drummond. Others at the centre, especially Russell Janzen, Robin Smith, and Steven Tufts, offered invaluable assistance to the Working Group, the conference, and the volume. Without this active and ongoing participation by the centre's staff, the networking and research that have culminated in this volume would never have occurred.

Several people – Kristine Vendrame, Kim O'Neil, and Gary Perlmutter, of the Canadian Auto Workers; Susan Wessels, from the School of Social Sciences, Atkinson Faculty, York University; Rochelle Goldberg, research projects administrator, York University; and Krista Johnston from the Graduate Programme in Women's Studies, York University – provided invaluable logistical and technical assistance in the preparation of the manuscript.

We are also grateful to the various granting agencies and other organizations that donated generously to both the conference and this publication. The Social Sciences and Humanities Research Council of Canada provided direct financial support for the conference and additional assistance through "Training Matters: The Labour Education and Training Research Network" (under its Strategic Network Programme). Additional funding for the conference came from several labour unions (including the Canadian Auto Workers, the Canadian Labour Congress, the Canadian Union of Postal Workers, the Communication Energy and Paper Workers' Union, the Public Service Alliance of Canada, the United Food and Commercial Workers, and the United Steelworkers of America), and several labour studies departments (including those at McMaster University, the University of Windsor, and York University). The dean of the Faculty of Arts of York University and the Canadian Auto Workers financially supported the publication of this volume. Leah Vosko also thanks the Canada Research Chairs Programme for enabling her to co-chair the Working Group and co-edit this volume. The financial commitment of all the sponsors made possible the creative and critical research activity reflected in this book.

Philip Cercone of McGill-Queen's University Press provided his whole-hearted support for this project from the inception of the Working Group to the completion of the manuscript. John Parry's copyediting was extraordinary. We also thank contributors for their committed and timely work on their chapters, the various discussants at the conference for their incisive commentaries on earlier versions of these chapters, and all members of the Working Group for their contributions to the creation of a research network that was uniquely co-operative and stimulating.

Finally, our heartfelt thanks go to our own families, friends, and colleagues, especially Donna, Gerald, Maxine, and Thea, for their interest and their encouragement. We are grateful not only for their support for this particular project, but for their comradeship in our shared efforts to build a better and more just world.

Jim Stanford and Leah F. Vosko
January 2004

CHALLENGING THE MARKET

1

Challenging the Market:
The Struggle to Regulate
Work and Income

JIM STANFORD and LEAH F. VOSKO

REGULATING WORK AND INCOME

Most people must work in order to meet the material requirements of their lives, and hence work is a central feature of human existence. That work occurs in many different forms, in a variety of places and settings, incorporating various techniques and tools, and in the context of differing relationships with others. Work can be both a necessary evil – something that people do mostly because it provides the material basis for other, more enjoyable activities – and a meaningful and worthwhile activity in its own right. But in either case, one's work is an essential and central feature of one's life.

In a capitalist, or market economy, much work takes the form of paid employment. Indeed, the employment relationship is so dominant (both materially and normatively) within this type of economy that the terms "employment" and "work" are often used synonymously, reflecting the hegemony of neoclassical conceptions of the labour market (Picchio, 1992). Yet these terms are by no means equivalent (Fudge and Tucker, 2000: 251; Pahl, 1988). Rather, *employment* is a subset of the broader category of *work*, referring to a socioeconomic relationship symbolized by some form of labour contract between a worker and an employer. *Work*, in contrast, refers to the much broader set of productive human activities, including notably unpaid labour (performed largely by women) within households. The terms and conditions of paid employment under capitalism obviously constitute matters of intense interest to social scientists and social activists alike, as do the relationships and connections between paid employment and the other forms of work that still carry on within and alongside the market system. Understanding *employment* thus requires a broader understanding of *work*, and vice versa.

In developed capitalist economies, most people perform a large portion of their lifetime work activity engaged in paid employment. The income thereby generated is typically a primary determinant of the material standard of living of the worker and his or her household. Individuals' physical and mental well-being also depend centrally on the environment of the workplace: the safety and security of that environment, the choice and power that employees are able to exercise there, and the opportunities (or lack thereof) that employment provides for their overall personal development. At the same time, the relationship between paid employment and unpaid work is fundamental to the well-being and happiness of both individual workers and other members of their households.

The practice and experience of employment are defining features of modern capitalist society, and they are the focus of our collection of essays, where we define "employment" broadly, to encompass all forms of paid work. Yet our broad goal is to disclose the inherently social character of the labour market (Armstrong and Armstrong, 1994; Seccombe, 1973), in the course of considering recent changes in the nature of employment and employment relationships; changes in the social, political, and economic structures and institutions that regulate those relationships; and the evolving links between employment and other forms of work.

The processes that establish the terms and conditions of paid work are hugely important and fraught with potential for conflict and controversy. At the micro- level, individuals invest vast amounts of energy and creativity in negotiating employment relationships, attempting to better their terms and conditions, and in many cases simply trying to survive the experience with as much of their physical well-being and emotional integrity intact as is possible. At the social level, these challenges and conflicts play out with amplified political and economic repercussions.

Indeed, historical trends in politics, in labour relations, in social policy, and in economic development have been centrally shaped by changing attitudes towards, and the realities of, paid work. In a capitalist society, those developments reflect the particular nature of labour relationships in an economy in which profit-seeking, privately owned firms carry on most production of goods and services. These firms hire workers in return for wages, to perform the bulk of required work. Capitalism thus required the emergence – or more precisely, the deliberate creation – of a free labour market: an amorphous socioeconomic space in which propertyless workers "offer" their labour services for sale to prospective property-owning employers.

The relationships between the "supply" and the "demand" sides of this labour market are simultaneously symbiotic and conflictual. In late capitalist society, individuals increasingly work for wages; the paid labour market encompasses a larger and larger share of the total working population. Firms need workers to perform this labour and hence have a considerable stake in the creation and maintenance of a healthy and disciplined workforce. Thus the terms and conditions of paid work are subject to strongly competing interests. Workers would obviously prefer to be paid more, in return for less work (or less demanding work, or more comfortable work, or safer work), and with greater recognition and allowance for the often unpaid work of social reproduction. Meanwhile, firms typically desire exactly the opposite. Naturally, both the supply and demand sides of the labour market try to strike the best "bargain" possible, from their contrasting perspectives. At the same time, each side also attempts to influence the rules of the game within which the bargain is struck – that is, determining and enforcing the formal and informal policies and practices that make it easier for one side or the other to attain a more desirable employment relationship. This ongoing and contested process, making and remaking the rules that guide and structure the employment relationship, is the process of labour market regulation.

By "labour market regulation," therefore, we mean the complex of formal and informal laws, institutions, policies, and cultural attitudes that organize and constrain the relationships and practices of paid work. That complex of structures and practices is extremely broad, diverse, and heterogeneous. The realm of labour market regulation includes the decisions and actions of governments, employers, civil society institutions (such as labour unions, professional associations, and community development agencies), and households. The subject matter of labour market regulation includes everything from explicit labour market policies (such as minimum-wage laws and other forms of direct pay regulation), through broader forms of social policy and regulation (such as pension, health care, and income security policies), to policies oriented to the supply side of the labour market (such as "family policies" or education and training programs).

Fittingly, this breadth and diversity shape the scope of the contributions in this volume. Chapters address a range of topics – macroeconomic policy, regional development, "race" and gender inequality in employment, and new strategies for labour organizing. What unifies them is a common interest in the changing ways of organizing and regulating the employment relationship. Contributors also share a common concern with the historic challenge to egalitarian social goals posed by the recent general trend of labour market regulation.

LABOUR MARKET REGULATION
AND THE EVOLUTION OF SOCIOECONOMIC REGIMES

The changing patterns and directions of labour market regulation naturally reflect the broader economic and political context, which helps to determine the expectations and the forcefulness with which parties to the employment relationship can articulate and promote their respective interests. At the same time, trends in labour market regulation exert their own influence back onto broader social, economic, and political trends – since paid work is so central to both the individual and the collective consciousness of groups, to the creation and maintenance of a healthy and productive workforce, and to the productivity and development of the entire economy. Therefore trends in regulation simultaneously reflect and reinforce the broader political-economic tides of society (Boyer, 1990). It is in this sense that we understand and critique the deregulatory thrust that has characterized global labour market policy in the past two decades.

The long postwar economic expansion – the so-called "Golden Age" that lasted from 1945 until the mid-1970s – underwrote a historic but particular expansion in the scope and effectiveness of labour market regulation throughout the developed capitalist economies and in many developing countries as well. In some aspects, that regulatory structure was progressive and egalitarian, enhancing economic security and equality for some groups of workers. The growth of unions and collective bargaining, the expansion of the welfare state and its network of income security and public programs, and the growth of relatively well-paying public-sector employment all helped increase incomes and economic security for millions of workers. But the particular, peculiar nature of postwar labour market regulation skewed distribution of the economic gains of the postwar expansion. Since labour market structures assumed the existence of a "standard" employment relationship (characterized by full-time hours, stable tenure, and extensive non-wage benefits), workers who fell outside that assumed template did not attain the same material and social gains. Thus while the largely white, male industrial workforces of developed countries made substantial progress, followed by some white-collar categories, other groups – including especially women, immigrants, and racialized groups – did not (Armstrong and Armstrong, 1994; Finkel, 1995; Guard, 1995; MacDonald, 1991; Vosko, 2000).

In retrospect, this era of progressive yet fundamentally flawed labour market intervention was dependent on a unique historical conjuncture of economic and political circumstances. Investment by private firms was strong, creating millions of new jobs. Technological and structural change, facilitated by rapid business investment, generated rising productivity. This underlying dynamism of private accumulation was reinforced by expansionary government policy during most of this time, including macroeconomic, labour market, and social policy measures that amplified and supplemented the growth in employment and earnings. But postwar expansion, so crucial to social and economic gains and to consolidation of the welfare state, also contained the seeds of its own demise.

On the demand side of the labour market, the broad shift in labour relations eventually took a toll on the investment-driven capitalist economy. Spurred on by tight labour market conditions and supportive regulatory and social structures, workers' movements in most countries stepped up their campaigns for economic and political progress. Strikes became more frequent, and other symptoms of industrial conflict became more common. Other economic and political factors (such as the oil-price shocks of the 1970s, student and youth protests, global financial instability, and the political and military challenges posed by national liberation movements in the "Third World") contributed to general instability and crisis. Initially, the scale of business profits had helped to spur early postwar economic vibrancy (by stimulating strong investment spending) and also helped finance the increasingly intrusive (and expensive) demands of workers and communities. Eventually, however, business profits became somewhat squeezed: by workers' collective strength, by regulatory constraints on business activities, by the growth of the non-profit sphere, and by increasing competition from other companies (including global competition through international trade). Business investment declined in response, and the whole postwar expansion began to sputter (Bowles, Gordon, and Weisskopf, 1990; Epstein and Gintis, 1995). Since labour market interventions generally assumed that business would continue to take primary responsibility for production and for employment (which then became a target for progressive regulatory intervention), sagging private-sector growth "stranded" this regulatory agenda.

Indeed, business began to experience (and react against) gradual but forceful challenges to its dominant role in economic growth and to its role in society in general. By the mid-1970s corporate and political elites (representing both businesses and the individuals who own them) identified a coming near-crisis in the economic and political structure of capitalism. Profits on real production were eroding. High inflation produced negative real returns on most financial assets. The demands of a more confident and empowered workforce for better treatment on the job in turn sparked employers to seek ways of subverting and/or sidestepping the standard postwar employment relationship in material and normative terms. For employers, one of the most dangerous elements in this volatile mix was an increasingly anti-business political and cultural tone in society – visible most obviously in the rebelliousness of youth, but also in a myriad of other ways. A resulting slowdown in private-sector investment and job creation, and a general weakening of conditions on the demand side of the economy, began to undermine the legitimacy and sustainability of the postwar order.

On the supply side of the labour market, too, two main factors further limited the liberating dimensions of postwar labour market regulation. First, the entire regulatory regime continued to rely on households as the principal site of social reproduction, and hence on the unpaid work of household members (largely women). Second, the rise of precarious employment – a strategy that employers used to erode workers' collective empowerment and to construct a supply of more vulnerable workers and that demonstrates a persistently gendered and racialized character – also undermined the effectiveness of the postwar regulatory regime for women, immigrants and racialized groups. Postwar welfare-state and labour market policies assumed a male-breadwinner–female-caretaker household; it extended few protections and benefits to so-called secondary breadwinners, especially those in non-standard forms of employment and work arrangements. In labour law, this bifurcated approach produced minimalist employment standards legislation, compared to the historically more expansive character of collective-bargaining law (Fudge and Vosko, 2001a, 2001b). In social policy, the contrasting character of unemployment insurance versus social assistance policies exemplified the same dualistic approach (Neis, 1993; Porter, 2003; Pulkingham, 1998; Vosko, 1996).

In this era, the "standard" employment relationship was the normative model around which states designed and delivered labour and social policy. While Canada and other industrialized countries eventually extended some formal protection to women and other equity-seeking groups, largely through formal equality policy, only "standard" workers received the full benefits of this later extension of labour market regulation (Fudge, 2002; MacDonald, 1999; Ursel, 1992). Thus the emancipatory expansion of labour market regulation failed to generate a movement from "segmentation to solidarity" (Cameron, 1995), but instead helped perpetuate segmentation and the spread of racialized and gendered precariousness (Krahn, 1995; Ornstein, 2000; Vosko, 2002; Zeytinoglu and Muteshi, 1999). As a means of escaping state policies designed to promote equity and fairness and, more specifically, of abdicating work-related responsibilities, employers increasingly adopted "flexibility-enhancing" strategies in the 1970s and 1980s, contracting out jobs and relying on non-standard forms of work in order to shrink their core staff (Jenson, 1989; Walby, 1997). Ironically, therefore, the rise of precarious employment accompanied "emancipatory" labour market regulations, which assisted primarily people in standard employment relationships.

After an unstable period of grappling with all these pressures on both the supply and the demand sides of the labour market, and groping for an internally consistent policy response, neoliberalism emerged, reflecting a new bargain between organized capital and nation-states (Bowles, Gordon, and Weisskopf, 1989). Neoliberalism denotes a new form of political-economic governance, premised on the extension of markets and tied to specific political projects in particular countries. Its general aim is to protect and restore the former dominance of private businesses and investors in the economy, as well as in broader society (Larner, 2000: 5; McBride and Shields, 1997). Numerous specific policy thrusts, most applied in the majority of developed capitalist economies beginning in the early 1980s (and imposed more violently in many industrializing countries at about the same time), were consistent with this general goal. The broad neoliberal agenda includes at least four main elements:

1 *Controlling inflation and restoring financial profitability.* The 1970s was a bitter decade for financial investors, who incurred negative real returns because of rising inflation and the eroding real profitability of corporations. The consistently tough monetary and financial policies imposed ever since can be interpreted as a "revenge of the rentiers" (Smithin, 1994), anxious to prevent a repeat of this experience (Epstein and Schor, 1992). Indeed, the arrival of tight-money policies (starting with the Volcker disinflation in the United States in the late 1970s) signalled the onset of the neoliberal era. Full employment ceased being the pre-eminent goal of economic policy, replaced by inflation control and the attempted stabilization of financial returns. This lasting shift in macroeconomic policy has carried numerous consequences for labour markets, income distribution, and the relationship between the real and the financial spheres of the economy (Palley, 1998; Stanford, 1999).

2 *"Leaning" and refocusing government programs.* One overarching goal of neoliberalism is to downsize and reorient the state's economic and social interventions – making them more supportive of, and less disruptive to, the requirements of private investors and employers. The state remains a strong and active player, so it is a mistake to equate neoliberalism with a general trend to "less government" (Cohen, 1996; Panitch, 1998). Many forms of powerful state intervention – such as the anti-inflation actions of central banks, the active protection of increasingly abstract forms of intellectual property, and the design and enforcement of free-trade agreements – are entirely consistent with the neoliberal project. Nevertheless, the downsizing or elimination of government activities considered unfavourable to business has been a major feature

of neoliberal restructuring. Moreover, this retrenchment has produced
demonstrably gendered consequences (Bashevkin, 1998; Little, 2001;
McKeen, 2001; Sheldrick, 1998).

Relatively rare government experiments with the direct public ownership of productive firms were an obvious first target (sparking a wave of
privatizations beginning in the 1980s and continuing today), as were
income-security programs that enhanced the economic position of
current or potential workers, especially those belonging to marginalized
groups. The fiscal problems that faced most governments in the wake of
the economic slowdown of the 1980s and 1990s provided an additional
(and convenient) rationale for the scaling back of government programs, particularly in income security. But there is ample evidence – not
least, continued fiscal restraint in many countries, including Canada,
that now enjoy dramatically improved budgetary situations – that fiscal
prudence was not the main motivation for the downsizing (Stanford,
2001).

3 *Restoring "discipline" to labour markets.* High-interest-rate macroeconomic
policies and the deliberate recreation of long-term unemployment went
a long way to reimposing a sense of permanent insecurity in the minds
of workers. But this thrust has been further reinforced by structural
efforts to deregulate labour markets (or, in the neoliberal discourse, to
make them more "flexible") and to strengthen the links between labour
market success and material security. In this sense, the global trend to
labour market deregulation that gathered steam through the 1980s and
1990s, and which is the focus of this collection, appears to be a fundamental plank in the broader neoliberal restructuring of capitalist
society.

4 *Privatizing social reproduction.* The flip-side of the disciplining of paid
labour markets has been the growing expectation among employers and
the state that private households and/or third-sector organizations will
absorb the increasing insecurities experienced by households (Bakker,
1998; Elson, 1998). With the state and employers withdrawing from
responsibility for the overall security of workers and their dependants,
an increasing burden of responsibility for social reproduction – understood to encompass a range of activities related to the daily and inter-
generational maintenance of people – falls to families and communities
(Aronson and Neysmith, 2000; Picchio, 1992). Feminist scholars point
out that this privatizing impulse – defined broadly, a realignment
between production and social reproduction in capitalist labour
markets, and, more narrowly, the marketization and/or reprivatization
of formerly public sector services – is a centrepiece of neoliberalism

(Fudge and Cossman, 2002).[1] It involves the institutionalization of a new division of responsibilities between states, markets, families, and the voluntary sector in developed capitalist economies and a deepening absence of public services in developing ones (Armstrong and Armstrong, 1997; Beneria, 2003; O'Connor, Orloff, and Shaver, 1999).

It is in this longer-run political-economic context, then, that we describe the overall reorientation of labour market regulation that has taken place in most countries over the past two decades. The new doctrines of deregulation, "flexibility," and discipline represent just one stream of a broader, powerful political and economic trend. Neoliberalism emerged from the petering out of postwar expansion and the resulting economic and political instability. Its concern with labour market deregulation and discipline is consistent with its overall effort to re-establish the dominance of private firms (and the individuals who own them) in economic and political life.

UNDERSTANDING LABOUR MARKET "FLEXIBILITY"

Many specific elements of labour market deregulation were implemented piecemeal by neoliberal governments – such as the rollback of collective-bargaining rights and income-security programs, which were early priorities of the neoliberals who took power in the United Kingdom and the United States in the early 1980s (Baskevkin, 1998). It was not until the mid-1990s, however, that a more unified and intellectually coherent policy agenda took form, most forcefully and influentially in the *OECD Jobs Study* (Organization for Economic Cooperation and Development, 1994). The new agenda claimed to increase labour market "flexibility" – a carefully chosen euphemism that disguises and makes palatable a more controversial underlying vision (McBride and Williams, 2001; Vosko, 1995). After all, who could be in favour of "inflexibility"? The apparently successful economic performance of the United States, which clearly possesses by far the most deregulated labour market of all industrialized countries, became a powerful example of the "flexibility agenda."[2] The broad policy orientation flowing from the *OECD Jobs Study* suggests a range of specific policy recommendations: income-security reform (reducing benefit levels and eligibility and tying benefits more closely to work experience and job search); the relaxation of direct regulation over pay and other aspects of work (including collective-bargaining coverage and employment-security provisions); the de facto expansion of precarious employment (including various forms of part-time and self-employment); and a reorientation of training and education to respond more quickly and effectively to the skills requirements of private employers.

This evolution of labour market policy at the governmental level has a natural analogue in the evolution of employment practices at the level of the firm. From the perspective of individual firms, "flexibility" implies the rise of a new set of employment practices in which employers are able to alter their employment decisions more readily to accommodate fluctuations in demand, while avoiding responsibilities related to the provision of benefits and entitlements (Atkinson, 1988). While this shift in employment practices – visible in the dramatic expansion of precarious employment – takes advantage of new openings in regulation, it also requires a new managerial philosophy and practice. Hence scholarship on labour market flexibility needs to consider trends in policy and in practice, while remaining sensitive to racialized, gendered, and age-based inequality (Jenson, 1989; Pollert, 1988). In this volume, for example, while numerous chapters analyse the deregulatory trend in broader labour policy, several (including those by Whittal; Grant; and McFarland and Good) examine its impact on employment and production practices in particular firms and industries.

While analysts commonly use "deregulation" and "flexibility" as short hand for neoliberal labour market policy, such policy does not necessarily imply withdrawal or weakening of government regulatory powers and interventions or allowing employment relationships to respond quickly to change. Orthodox free-market economic analysis dismisses attempts – no matter how well-intentioned – by governments or non-governmental institutions (such as unions) to interfere with competitive labour market outcomes as distorting and inefficient and ultimately more harmful than beneficial. The classic example (learned by rote in virtually every introductory economics course) indicates how minimum-wage laws supposedly create unemployment, by raising wage levels above some efficient, market-clearing level;[3] similar, more elaborate critiques denounce other forms of interventionist labour or social policy. This perspective sees the deregulation of labour markets as equivalent to a cessation or relaxation of government interventions, leaving the market better able to match supply with demand autonomously and flexibly.

In practice, however, even the neoliberal "free" market still leaves plenty of scope for active and powerful labour market interventions by government and continues to demonstrate more rigidity than flexibility. Consider, for example, neoliberal monetary policy. Modern central banks continue to assume (at least implicitly) a minimum, or "natural," rate of unemployment, and if actual unemployment falls below that level inflation will accelerate (driven first and foremost by rising wage demands and unit labour costs), with ultimately disastrous effects. Central banks therefore set interest rates in order to maintain that assumed equilibrium unemployment rate, which corresponds, they believe, to the potential output of the aggregate economy.[4] The aggregate behaviour of labour markets is therefore still subject to regulation by a powerful (albeit unelected) governmental entity willing deliberately to restrict employment growth (with corresponding economic and social consequences) in the pursuit of discrete policy goals (sustaining unemployment, and hence controlling inflation, at "acceptable" levels). Surely this is active labour market regulation writ large, yet it grounds the supposed neoliberal emphasis on deregulation and flexibility.

Other policy measures also reflect the continuing influence of often-rigid regulatory mechanisms and structures. Neoliberal labour market policy propounds an active role for government in training and education. Restrictions on union organizing, union security arrangements, and work stoppages are increasingly intrusive in many jurisdictions, backed up with growing legal penalties (including far-reaching restrictions on secondary picketing, seizure of union funds, and new powers for affected employers to sue offending unions).[5] And many collective-bargaining relationships (where unions do exist) have become more rigid. Ironically, Alan Greenspan (head of the U.S. Federal Reserve) once praised long-term collective agreements, which now commonly extend six years or more; he interpreted this seemingly rigid relationship as a symptom of a *desirable* underlying insecurity on the part of U.S. workers and their unions (Greenspan, 1997). Similarly, many business analysts see a longer-run decline in employee turnover (another seeming manifestation of diminished flexibility) as evidence that employers can more easily retain workers, given the now-limited options for exit. Meanwhile, the privatization of health care and other forms of social security, celebrated by neoliberals, can further restrict individual employment decisions, if such job-linked benefits are not portable (Armstrong and Armstrong, 2001; Townson, 2000).

Clearly the underlying goal of such labour market policy is not flexibility – the ability to respond quickly and effectively to change. Indeed, its real, observed impact seems rather different: a more disciplined, hard-nosed labour market, with employers better able to hire and fire as they wish, with workers who are committed to being compliant, and with strict limits on compensation levels. This type of policy exhibits a particular flexibility, but also grim rigidity. Flexible for whom? Even where greater flexibility emerges, it is typically very one-sided. For example, firms now rely on a stable of workers in precarious employment to respond to prevailing market conditions and/or to changes in the production process. Yet we could imagine, in contrast, worker-centred flexibility, which might feature greater ability to combine paid work with unpaid responsibilities (such as child rearing); this vision, however, is clearly not compatible with the neoliberal vision of flexibility (Bruegel, 1998; Cook, 1998). Instead, many workers now must accept precarious employment, in order to earn an

income while caring for others. This situation implies continuing insecurity and increased inequality in several dimensions, including wages, job
security, and social benefits, and removal of protections from the weakest
(Deakin and Wilkinson, 1991; Fudge and Vosko, 2001b; Rosenberg, 1989:
397).

The broad economic and social consequences of neoliberal labour
market policies – which have been implemented in most developed and
developing countries, by governments of virtually every political stripe –
are clear and, in many cases, painful. Economic growth has been much
slower than in the early postwar era, often barely sufficient to increase real
income for the majority of the employed population. Most countries have
experienced growing income inequality, resulting in large part from precarious and informal forms of paid work (practices limited – though never
eradicated – under the previous, more egalitarian regulatory regime).[6] At
the global level, of course, the growth of inequality has been even more
extreme (Caffenztsis, 1999; Dalla Costa, 1999). The economy has become
more reliant on private, profit-seeking business.

Governments are leaner, accepting (and in some cases applauding)
social problems that were unacceptable in earlier decades, their interventions more focused on facilitating private accumulation. Policies of
restraint, deregulation, and privatization have transferred an increasing
burden of reproductive labour from social programs and agencies onto
unpaid labour performed in households, further polarizing work and
income opportunities between the sexes and among women of different
classes and races (Luxton and Corman, 2001; Ornstein, 2000; Vosko,
2002; Zeytinoglu and Muteshi, 1999). The multidimensional agenda of
labour market deregulation has helped make these changes possible.

Yet despite its seeming dominance in labour market and social policy,
the neoliberal vision has not attained a complete or permanent victory.
Consider our earlier argument that deregulation is basic to the neoliberal
response to the economic instability of the 1970s. Did this broad policy U-
turn, implemented to reverse a challenge to business's authority, which (in
retrospect) peaked thirty years ago, in fact re-create an internally consistent and sustainable regime of business-led growth and accumulation?[7]
There have been pro-business changes in the economies, societies, and
cultures of most countries. Private business is dominant again in economic
and social development. Business profits, employment, and economic
growth rebounded in some countries in the 1990s (most notably in the
United States), but that rebound has not proven lasting or sustainable.
The high-tech financial meltdown and subsequent recession of 2000 and
2001 quickly took much of the shine off the U.S. model. In many other
countries, including Canada, business profits and other economic indicators never even recovered to levels of the 1970s – when economic and

financial instability motivated the subsequent radical change in policy direction. As evidenced by the chapters in this volume (by Clarke; Patroni; and Bienefeld, Tchetvernina, and Lakounina), broader social contradictions are also growing in developing countries.

To be sure, if macroeconomic conditions can be stabilized, then business can hope to exploit a "playing field" that has been tilted markedly in its favour. In the United States the combination of pro-business structural features and an expansionary macroeconomic stance allowed for very substantial profits, growth, and job creation through most of the 1990s.[8] Other countries have not so easily found that macroeconomic "sweet spot": an economy vibrant enough to generate sizeable profits, but not so hot as to rekindle rising expectations, workers' militancy, and policy intervention. Few developing economies, in particular, experienced sustained economic expansion, despite (or perhaps because of) widespread and painful neoliberal restructuring. The economic crisis in Argentina, which followed the neoliberal recipe as closely as any other, is sure to damage permanently the allure of that model in the global South.

From the perspective of the system's elites, then, global capitalism after two decades of neoliberalism reflects an improved but still uncertain dynamic. The structural position of business is clearly stronger, and the internal logic of the system has become perhaps more vibrant. Yet business sees itself as still too much constrained politically and economically by continuing labour market regulation, not to mention workers' demands for better and more secure lives. And the system's internal economic logic is still fragile, prone to financial crisis and continuing macroeconomic instability.

On balance, then, it is not at all clear that labour market deregulation will stimulate more employment, productivity, and income – as its adherents and advocates continue to claim. In response, as several chapters in this collection show (especially those in part IV), researchers and organizers alike are developing and campaigning for policies that would allow hard-working people around the world a better chance to enjoy a share of the wealth that they produce, with more security and more dignity.

That human beings have agency – an inherent and unstoppable willingness to oppose social arrangements that they see as unfair or exploitive – should rekindle our hope that the labour market policy pendulum will swing back, sooner rather than later, towards measures emphasizing fairness and equality. So while the widespread adoption of neoliberal labour market policy is obviously disheartening to those who do not trust that competitive labour markets produce socially acceptable employment opportunities and living standards, more broadly the triumph of deregulation may not be nearly as complete as some people have concluded.

OVERVIEW OF THIS COLLECTION

The goal of *Challenging the Market: The Struggle to Regulate Work and Income* is to contribute to the theoretical and policy critique of labour market deregulation, often billed as labour market "flexibility," and hence to encourage development of alternative and more humane approaches. Interdisciplinary in its approach, the volume combines pieces that examine the policies and practices of labour market deregulation, the use of the concept of flexibility in the dominant policy discourse, its role in exacerbating racialized and gendered labour market segmentation, and alternative visions for regulating work and income.

Several common understandings frame the collection. First, contributors recognize that the postwar regulatory vision, associated with the creation of the redistributive welfare state and a diverse array of labour rights and protective legislation, is declining. Second, they identify the common symptoms (such as sustained mass unemployment) and critique the perceived causes (such as the assumed link between progressive labour market regulation and high levels of structural unemployment) of the decline of the postwar regulatory model. Third, they question fundamentally the dominant view that policies of labour market flexibility, modelled on the U.S. experience, reduce long-run unemployment and promote economic stability. They thus seek to explore alternative methods of regulating labour markets.

Reflecting the multidimensional nature of the broad project of labour market deregulation, we organize the collection into four parts, addressing various aspects and contexts of labour market policy and its social and economic effects. We position deregulation in the context of the evolving political economy of global capitalism, and hence part I focuses on the macroeconomic context of neoliberal policy-making. As we note above, however, labour market deregulation direction finds expression in particular countries and sectors. So part II considers more specific case studies of regulation and deregulation in action. The differential effects of labour market policies and structures on various segments of the labour market are the topic of part III, while part IV looks at initiatives and projects aimed at rekindling a more egalitarian and interventionist approach. Together, these four parts paint a composite picture of the roots of neoliberal labour market policy, its effects, and potential alternatives to it.

Each chapter pivots around the collection's central, organizing theme: challenging the market. Each also explores intersections between race, class, gender, age, and region in analysing policies and practices linked to labour market deregulation. Documenting the effects of labour market deregulation on marginalized workers is a key objective. Yet our goal is also to move beyond questioning the dominant model, to advance a range of alternatives for regulating work and income in a manner that redresses (rather than exacerbates) persisting inequality and hardship.

Part I (chapters 2–4), "The Changing Economics of Labour Market Regulation," contains three chapters that critique the economic underpinnings of neoliberal labour market policy. Collectively, they also serve as a foil for the rest of the collection, since these authors advance their arguments primarily through a macroeconomic lens. In chapter 2, "The NAIRU, Labour Market 'Flexibility,' and Full Employment," Malcolm Sawyer analyses the non-accelerating inflation rate of unemployment (NAIRU). This concept has been influential both in monetary policy, where it argues for deliberately maintaining unemployment at levels sufficient to restrain inflation, and in setting the framework for labour market, welfare-to-work, and labour-relations policies. Sawyer highlights NAIRU's shaky foundations, by demonstrating that its acceptance is ultimately a matter of faith (since it can never be directly observed); empirical estimates are so inconsistent and unstable that they have no use in real-world policy purposes.

Thomas Palley's chapter 3, "The Causes of High Unemployment: Labour Market Sclerosis versus Macroeconomic Policy," compares recent macroeconomic and labour market performance within the OECD and similarly challenges the standard claim that superior U.S. economic performance is the result of the structural deregulation of domestic labour markets. Palley argues forcefully that differences in macroeconomic policy are the dominant explanation for differences in labour market performance between the United States and Europe in the 1980s and 1990s. Differences in labour market structures play a secondary and inconsistent role; in particular, the claim that high European unemployment rates are the result of "rigid" or "inflexible" labour markets finds no support in the empirical data. Challenging conventional economic wisdom along lines similar to Saywer's, Palley shows that it was not the "tough-love" structural features of the labour market that explain U.S. economic success in the 1990s, but rather a much easier and more pragmatic stance by monetary authorities.

Peter Auer uses a very different approach with his comparative study of labour market and economic institutions in several smaller European countries. Yet he ends up reinforcing the central finding of Sawyer and Palley – namely, that low unemployment is not inherently incompatible with price stability. Chapter 4, "Institutions and Policies for Labour Market Success in Europe," highlights the cases of Austria, Denmark, Ireland, and the Netherlands, which all experienced strong labour market performance in the 1990s. Active labour market policies and measures there aimed at social dialogue, Auer argues, contributed to sustainable lower unemployment. His analysis demonstrates that the preservation of core labour market institutions and regulations, alongside the development of macro-level "corporatist" institutions regulating key macroeconomic and labour market outcomes in an economically efficient manner, helped produce success in these interesting cases. Testing the hypothesis advanced by Sawyer and Palley, Auer reinforces the conclusion that strong unions and interventionist governments can solve labour market problems, without dismantling the welfare state and other features of progressive labour market regulation.

Part II (chapters 5–8), "National and Sub-National Developments in Labour Market Structure," provides a range of case studies of shifting labour market regulation. Its chapters take up broader questions linked to the changing economics of labour market regulation but do so through case studies. Two contributions focus on the national level, and two offer sub-national case studies. Together, they give a sense of the variety of labour market experience that persists despite the seemingly universal dominance of the flexibility paradigm.

Marlea Clarke's chapter 5, "Challenging Segmentation in South Africa's Labour Market: 'Regulated Flexibility' or Flexible Regulation?," explores labour market restructuring in a country that is pursuing racial and gender equality while integrating itself into the global economy, by promoting privatization, government downsizing, and "flexibility-enhancing" employment policies. Her review of these contradictory tendencies reveals the international dominance of the U.S. model of labour market regulation and the profound influence of neoliberalism in a country struggling to remedy major problems inherited from the apartheid regime. The South African government has enacted legislative changes aimed at remedying these problems; it is revamping collective bargaining, overhauling minimum labour standards, and introducing employment equity and skills-training. These new laws are equity-oriented; they aim to reduce working hours and increase maternity provisions, overtime rates, and annual leaves. Yet emergent legislation addresses neither the erosion of employment norms nor the rise of precarious employment, which is gendered and racialized. Consequently, the growing numbers of workers excluded from new laws are precisely those marginalized under apartheid. Clarke notes a dual and contradictory process that is both reregulating and resegmenting the South African labour market.

The Russian labour market has undergone changes as dramatic as South Africa's, within an equally historic transition. Yet Russian policy-makers have seemingly not even attempted to moderate the human and social effects of the shift towards a market-oriented and globally integrated economy. In chapter 6, "The Russian Reforms and Their Impact on Labour: A Transition to What?" Manfred Bienefeld, Tatyana Tchetvernina, and Liana Lakounina describe how Russia's shocking labour market transition has resulted in a dramatic expansion of the informal economy, a precarious polarization in income and opportunity across gender, generation, and region, and the waste of the accumulated skill and capacities of tens of millions of Russians. They show that the Russian economy, in suddenly embracing a neoliberal model, has produced a bizarre situation in which the majority of workers in large parts of the economy receive no wages at all. The gendered nature of Russia's neoliberal "shock therapy" has been especially striking. Prospects for labour market development look gloomy indeed.

The effects of deregulation on specific sectors of the North American and western European economies have not been as spectacular as the changes in South Africa and Russia. Yet Michel Grant's chapter 7, "Deregulating Industrial Relations in the Apparel Sector: The Decree System in Quebec," shows that these diverse processes and outcomes reflect the same underlying global economic forces. The decree system, unique in North American industrial relations, enables the Quebec government to extend collective agreements to non-unionized workers in a given region or industrial sector. Decrees represent an innovative sub-national regulatory strategy, which uses legislative means to decrease the wage gap between unionized and unorganized workers in a region or sector. However, this regulatory approach faces considerable threat. Grant contends that the disappearance of the four decrees that formerly covered the garment industry reflects a larger strategy to abolish the system altogether.

Michael John Whittal's chapter 8, "European Labour Market Regulation: The Case of European Works Councils," also examines a specific industry: the automobile sector. Whittal wonders whether European workplace-based institutions, such as the European Works Councils (EWC), can function as catalysts for international worker solidarity. He examines BMW's EWC, the first such council to be formed in the European auto industry. He first describes two factors that prompted BMW to institute the EWC voluntarily: competition between Germany and Britain over productivity, wages, and hours, and a "host-factor" process whereby BMW's German employee representatives determine key aspects of agenda-setting throughout the company's continental operations. Second, through an examination of various crises in the BMW Rover Group in the United Kingdom, Whittal explores the EWC's brokerage role. His findings disclose both merits and shortcomings of the EWC model. For Whittal, the strength of the EWC approach lies in its perceived endorsement of core trade-union values, including independence and equity. Yet he cites numerous structural hindrances, including a lack of effective democracy and the risk that EWCs might evolve into compliant "company unions." Accordingly, the EWC's development of political and regulatory weight will require greater political commitment by labour to the idea of transnational trade unionism.

The contributions in part III (chapters 9–13), "The Differential Effects of Labour Market Deregulation," focus on the devastating effects of labour market deregulation on marginalized groups, while emphasizing the continuing agency of working people. Its chapters address the general question "Who's 'flexible' and who isn't?" on a number of levels.

Grace-Edward Galabuzi's chapter 9, "Racializing the Division of Labour: Neoliberal Restructuring and the Economic Segregation of Canada's Racialized Groups," examines the impact of labour market deregulation on the work experience and quality of life of members of racialized groups. Using data from Canada's most recent census, as well as other surveys, Galabuzi profiles the labour market situation of workers belonging to racialized groups. After describing the income gap between racialized Canadians and non-racialized Canadians, as well as the racialized and gendered character of precarious work in Canada and continued occupational segregation by race, he analyses the persistence of racialized, gendered labour market division in Canada. His provocative explanation is that, despite the introduction of employment equity policies and other remedial legislation in Canada in the 1980s and 1990s, the labour market continues to be racialized largely because of the rise of precarious jobs, themselves fuelled by deregulation. Mirroring the South African case, even egalitarian policies such as employment equity address only the situation of standard workers, yet workers belonging to racialized groups represent a disproportionate percentage of workers falling outside this eroding norm (Cranford, Vosko, and Zukewich, 2003).

Stephen McBride's chapter 10, "Towards Perfect Flexibility: Youth as an Industrial Reserve Army for the New Economy," argues that young people aged 15–30 are particularly vulnerable in unequal and insecure labour markets because of their perceived role as a highly flexible source of labour. McBride's data from OECD countries reveal their lower employment rates, their employment gap vis-à-vis adults, their greater likelihood of unemployment, their declining incomes, their growing dependency on adults, and the increasing inequality between young people. These employment conditions are not simply the product of employers' preferences associated with global competitive forces. Rather, McBride argues, they reflect policies that have emphasized "active labour market policies" centred on "individual responsibility" and "self-sufficiency," decreased state support, and increased stress on workfare and work experience. These policies echo strikingly the neoliberal social and labour market policy first advanced in the *OECD Jobs Study* of 1994.

"The Crisis in Rural Labour Markets: Failures and Challenges for Regulation," by Martha MacDonald (chapter 11), and "Technology, Gender, and Regulation: Call Centres in New Brunswick," by Tom Good and Joan McFarland (chapter 12), also find young people are disproportionately affected by accelerated labour market restructuring. Both pieces note the high rates of youth underemployment and unemployment in less developed regions of Canada. Both also illustrate how youth are increasingly compelled to migrate to more densely populated zones.

MacDonald's chapter centres on the crisis in rural labour markets, describing how reforms to federal labour market programs in Canada (such as Employment Insurance) have disproportionately affected workers outside urban areas. Focusing on Atlantic Canada, and taking the Atlantic Groundfish Strategy (TAGS) as a case in point, MacDonald examines the spatial dimensions of labour market restructuring and the failure of Canadian policy to assist non-urban workers. Her discussion of TAGS illuminates the relationship between gender, age, region, and deregulation. Ottawa initiated the TAGS program to facilitate labour market adjustment for unemployed ground-fishery workers and their families in response to labour market deregulation and declining fish stocks. Yet it effectively became an income-maintenance program, since policy-makers ignored displaced workers' (especially women's) needs for child care and locally based training. Moreover, it denied both spouses in a single household access to training.

In Atlantic Canada, service work is frequently the only employment option for young people who reject migration, as well as for other workers lacking mobility (such as those with employed spouses and/or dependent children). New Brunswick's government is investing considerable funds to subsidize telephone call centres. McFarland and Good describe the rise of the call-centre industry in the 1990s, probing both its causes and its effects. They show how changes in telecommunications have facilitated work in a call-centre format, while promoting geographical flexibility for employers. They describe the gendered labour process in call-centre work, as well as the feminized employment relationships that dominate the inbound–call centre industry in the province. In New Brunswick, sixty to eighty per cent of call-centre workers are women, reflecting the gendered content of the work, which requires "emotional labour," telephone skills, and routine clerical tasks. The work is also highly unstable. Characterized by part-time and shift work, non-permanent status, strict discipline, stressful working conditions and high rates of soft-tissue injuries, the industry is attracted to highly deregulated labour markets – making business-oriented New Brunswick a prime location. The ready availability of workers in the province's relatively depressed labour market is another obvious advantage.

As McFarland and Good report, subsidizing call-centre relocation was a pillar of the government's job-creation strategy during the 1990s. An extensive package of neoliberal workforce policies included collaborative relationships between NBTel (the public telephone company) and call centres; reduced non-wage payroll expenses for employers; cutbacks to social programs to increase effective labour supply; and a range of anti-union policies. The result, the authors contend, is the expansion of a highly gendered, precarious workforce.

Dave Broad, Della McNeil, and Sandra Salhani Gamble explore the growth of part-time work in chapter 13, "Neoliberalism, Social Democracy, and the Struggle to Improve Labour Standards for Part-time Workers in Saskatchewan." Their story centres on legislative developments, and hence provides a bridge to part IV of this book (on alternative visions). In the early 1990s, the social-democratic government of Saskatchewan undertook to revise labour standards to improve the working and welfare conditions of part-time workers. New provisions in 1994 provided greater job security and increased access to benefits. However, after considerable opposition from business, the government rescinded some provisions benefiting part-timers.

The authors' central finding is that "politics matter" in the struggle to improve conditions for all workers in precarious employment. Improving labour standards is a critical component of progressive reregulation. Yet recent events in Saskatchewan show the pressing need for an economic paradigm aimed at much more than simple redistribution of (low-wage, part-time) paid work. The writers propose reregulation that counters labour market and social polarization in all its dimensions: social, economic and political.

Most of the chapters in this volume work towards a critique of the dominant U.S. model of labour market deregulation, as applied in a range of contexts and at various levels, and with due attention to its differential effects. Concluding on a more hopeful note, however, part IV (chapters 14–18) introduces several "Alternative Visions" for regulating work and income. Stephanie Luce's chapter, "Labour Market Deregulation and the U.S. Living Wage Movement," describes the efforts of a constellation of social movements to improve workers' standards of living in several cities. While acknowledging the nearly eighty U.S. living-wage campaigns to date, Luce focuses on Los Angeles. She considers whether living-wage ordinances hurt or help low-wage workers and evaluates the movement's challenge to labour market deregulation. Are its positive features transportable beyond the United States? Luce's central finding is that in Los Angeles the campaign has been most effective at a political level – that is, in challenging the deregulation imperative among local politicians and business leaders.

The theme of alternative means of securing decent wages and working conditions is also central to Cynthia Cranford's chapter 15, "Gendered Resistance: Organizing Justice for Janitors in Los Angeles." Cranford examines how Mexican, Salvadoran, and Guatemalan women janitors are challenging flexible employment relationships. She provides an ethnography of Local 1877 of the Service Employees' International Union. She concentrates on Latina janitors' use of new spaces outside traditional labour law to press for immigrant workers' rights, emphasizing the importance of new forms of trade unionism and innovative organizing strategies among workers who lack a single worksite and/or employer. In Los Angeles, Latina janitors challenged employers' flexibility and its racialized and gendered expression, especially through the local's "Year 2000" campaign. This effort featured sit-ins and walk-outs, leaflet distribution, and street-theatre performances, all aimed at drawing attention to low wages and deteriorating conditions resulting from expanded subcontracting. Cranford credits its success – it helped achieve a new three-year collective agreement, including family medical and dental coverage, paid vacation, and sick days – to women's leadership in it, its urban focus, and its effective links to city-wide campaigns for living wages.

Viviana Patroni's chapter 16, "Labour's Current Organizational Strategies in Argentina: Towards a New Beginning?," is a case study of a new and innovative grouping of workers: the Central de Trabajadores Argentinos (CTA). Like Cranford, Patroni stresses the need to develop new organizing strategies in response to the challenging political and economic circumstances of neoliberalism. Focusing on workers' resistance to deregulation, and to the resulting casualization and entrenchment of the informal economy, she provides a timely tale of workers' agency in a country facing historic challenges and controversies. The CTA is a loose association of workers (both organized and unorganized) – "a social movement aimed at consolidating a new awareness of the sources of working-class problems and at presenting an alternative to dominant ideas about the primacy of markets and the incontestability of globalization." The CTA's unique contribution has been its use of direct forms of affiliation in response to the weakening structural position of the working class. Highly diverse in its membership, the CTA attempts to cultivate unity among workers throughout the country, including those who are unemployed or work under precarious conditions, and its program challenges the spectrum of neoliberal policies. The CTA not only organizes around wages and working conditions but also addresses more general issues, such as housing and landlessness, consistent with the spirit of social-movement unionism.

The trend towards more "flexible," employer-friendly labour market regulation has been a dominant but not a universal feature of policy-making in recent years. Sparked by continuing concern over the quality of work life and social conditions, advocates of a more egalitarian vision continue their efforts in numerous countries – sometimes with encouraging results. One of the most interesting attempts in the 1990s was the French experiment with legislation limiting working hours. Steve Jefferys's chapter 17, "Critical Times for French Employment Regulations: The 35–Hour Week and the Challenge to Social Partnership," outlines the intense political struggles that new labour market regulations are likely to spark. (In its emphasis on the complexities of political struggle, Jefferys complements Broad, McNeil, and Gamble on Saskatchewan's part-time regulations.) Unprecedented union mobilization pushed the French government to move forward with its 35–hour legislation, but a lack of political decisiveness opened space for employers' groups to oppose the legislation fiercely. The trade-union movement, politically divided and organizationally fragmented, mounted a defence of the legislation, and an intense conflict ensued. The legislation remained in effect, despite employers' opposition, and initial studies indicate that it has been effective in reducing working hours. The French conflict over working time, Jefferys argues, has tested the capacity of organized labour (and capital) to mobilize to shape the whole labour-relations system. And since the French example clearly swims against the global deregulatory tide, its outcome will have worldwide implications.

Of course the struggle to regulate work and income takes place in regions where labour market regulation is weak or non-existent and where investors and employers routinely circumvent regional and national controls. Don Wells's chapter 18, titled "How Credible Are International Corporate Labour Codes? Monitoring Global Production Chains," takes up these issues. Wells explores the growth of global supply chains in manufacturing and the prospects for regulating transnational production. Building on the theme of reregulation, which often accompanies or follows state-sanctioned labour market deregulation, Wells assesses new forms of voluntary or private labour regulation, which large transnational firms have supported. Wells provides a detailed, critical review of the codes of conduct and monitoring practices of the Fair Labor Association. This voluntary, U.S.-based association of manufacturers and non-governmental organizations has a mandate to monitor the labour practices of participating firms at their facilities in developing countries. Wells concludes that this new "labour code capitalism," rooted in a voluntarist, non-state model of regulation, compares poorly to more effective and compulsory monitoring systems. To the extent that transnational firms genuinely support these voluntary codes of conduct, Wells argues, they do so to undercut campaigns for more binding and effective global labour standards. Once again the political context for debates over labour standards and regulations appears to be the crucial factor in determining future policy trends.

Numerous authors in this collection emphasize this same point. The future prospects of a revival in egalitarian labour market regulation depend entirely on the strength with which working people and their organizations press for better treatment in the workplace, better supports and institutions for social reproduction, and enhanced economic and social security. It is these political struggles, not any prior evolution in the thinking of policy-makers, that will determine how long the current deregulatory trend in labour market policy continues and when and how that trend may be reversed. It is our hope that this collection makes a contribution to that shift in direction, sooner rather than later.

NOTES

1 Fudge and Cossman, 2002, cast the current privatization project in Canada as entailing six processes, which resonate with the national and sub-national trends in the developed capitalist economies considered in this volume: reprivatization, a process that reconverts public goods into private goods; commodification, which reconstitutes once-public goods and services on the basis of market delivery; familialization, which recasts public goods as naturally located in the family; individualization, which reconstitutes social issues as individual problems and challenges; delegation, which devolves decision-making from publicly accountable and visible agents to less-accountable agents; and, finally, depoliticization, which removes issues, goods, and services from the realm of public contestation.

2 Whether or not U.S. economic success in the 1990s had anything to do with labour market deregulation is an issue of continuing controversy; see the chapters by Sawyer and Palley in this volume for sceptical views.

3 The fact that mass unemployment has existed in virtually every capitalist economy, with or without minimum-wage laws, does not figure in this standard supply-and-demand picture, which simply assumes (and verifies by drawing supply and demand functions that cross in the middle) that in the absence of an artificial wage floor the labour market clears autonomously. A less sanguine analysis would incorporate the continuing existence of unemployment, even in deregulated labour markets. Card and Krueger, 1995, provide a fuller discussion of the issues encountered in analysing the impact of minimum-wage laws.

4 Economic events in the 1990s posed serious challenges to this traditional understanding of the natural rate of unemployment, or NAIRU, as described in this volume by Sawyer and Palley. While some national central banks (led by the U.S. Federal Reserve) have become more flexible in their interpretation of NAIRU doctrine as a result of that experience, they hold on to the underlying assumptions – that labour market developments ultimately drive inflation and that interest rates should be set to maintain some significant positive level of unemployment.

5 The (U.S.) Wagner Act model of regulating industrial relations explicitly

traded off some restrictions on work stoppages (especially during the term of contracts) in return for greater longer-run recognition and protection for union activity. Subsequent developments, however, have tended to accentuate restrictions (increasingly far-reaching and punitive), while stepping back from recognition and protection. The implicit trade-off is now quite one-sided.

6 Several chapters in this volume consider this rise in precarious employment, including the chapters by Broad, McNeil, and Gamble; McBride; and Mac-Donald.

7 Many analysts have considered and debated this open question; noteworthy interventions in recent years include Brenner (1998) and the vigorous debate that his commentary sparked.

8 Of course the economic and social benefits of that strong growth were muted by the continuing inequality of U.S. society.

REFERENCES

Armstrong, Pat and Hugh Armstrong. (1997). "Forms of Privatization." *Studies in Political Economy* 53 (Summer), 3–11.

Armstrong, Pat, Hugh Armstrong, and M. Patricia Connelly. 1994. *Theorizing Women's Work.* Toronto: Garamond Press.

Aronson, Jane, and Sheila Neysmith. 2000. "Valuing Unpaid Work in the Third Sector: The Case of Community Resource Centres," *Canadian Public Policy* 26 (2), 331–46.

Atkinson, John. 1988. "Recent Changes in the Internal Labour Market in the U.K.," in William Buitelaar, ed., *Technology and Work.* Aldershot: Avenbury.

Bakker, Isabella. 1998. *Unpaid Work and Macroeconomics: New Discussions, New Tools for Action.* Ottawa: Status of Women Canada.

Bashevkin, Sylvia. 1998. *Women on the Defensive: Living through Conservative Times.* Toronto: University of Toronto Press.

Beneria, Lourdes. 2003. "Markets, Globalization and Gender," in *Gender, Development and Globalization: Economics As If All People Mattered.* New York: Routledge.

Bowles, Samuel, David M. Gordon, and Thomas E. Weisskopf. 1990. *After the Waste Land: A Democratic Economics for the Year 2000.* Armonk, NY: M.E. Sharpe.

– 1989. "Business Ascendancy and Economic Impasse: A Structural Retrospective on Conservative Economics," *Journal of Economic Perspectives* 3 (1), 107–34.

Boyer, Robert. 1990. *The Theory of Regulation: A Critical Introduction.* New York: Columbia University Press.

Brenner, Robert. 1998. "The Economics of Global Turbulence," *New Left Review* 229, 1–265.

Bruegel, Irene. 1998. "The Restructuring of the Family Wage System, Wage Relations and Gender," in Linda Clarke, Peter de Gijsel, and Jorn Janssen, eds., *The Dynamics of Wage Relations in the New Europe.* London: Kluwer, 214–228.

Cameron, Barbara. 1995. "From Segmentation to Solidarity: A New Framework for Labour Market Regulation," in D. Drache and A. Ranikin, eds., *Warm Heart, Cold Country*. Toronto: Caledon Press.

Caffentzis, George. 1999. "On the Notion of a Crisis of Social Reproduction: A Theoretical Review," in M. Dalla Costa and G. Dalla Costa, eds., *Women, Development and Labor Reproduction: Struggles and Movements*. Trenton, NJ: Africa World Press.

Card, D., and A. Krueger. 1995. *Myth and Measurement: The New Economics of the Minimum Wage*. Princeton, NJ: Princeton University Press.

Cohen, Marjorie Griffin. 1996. "From the Welfare State to Vampire Capitalism," in P. Evans and G. Wekerle, eds., *Women and the Canadian Welfare State: Challenges and Change*. Toronto: University of Toronto Press.

Cooke, Joanne. 1998. "Flexible Employment: Implications for Gender and Citizenship in the European Union," *New Political Economy* 3 (2), 261–77.

Cranford, Cynthia, Leah F. Vosko, and Nancy Zukewich. 2003. "Precarious Employment in the Canadian Labour Market: A Statistical Portrait," *Just Labour* (Sept.), 6–22.

Dalla Costa, Mariarosa. 1999. "Development and Reproduction," in M. Dalla Costa and G. Dalla Costa, eds., *Women, Development and Labor Reproduction: Struggles and Movements*. Trenton, NJ: Africa World Press.

Deakin, S., and F. Wilkinson. 1991. "Labour Law, Social Security, and Economic Inequality," *Cambridge Journal of Economics* 15 (2), 125–48.

Elson, Diane. 1998. "The Political, the Economic and the Domestic," *New Political Economy* 3 (2), 189–207.

Epstein, Gerald A., and Herbert M. Gintis, eds. 1995. *Macroeconomic Policy after the Conservative Era: Studies in Investment, Saving and Finance*. Cambridge: Cambridge University Press.

Epstein, Gerald A., and Juliet B. Schor. 1992. "Corporate Profitability as a Determinant of Restrictive Monetary Policy: Estimates for the Postwar United States," in Thomas Mayer, ed. *The Political Economy of American Monetary Policy*. Cambridge: Cambridge University Press.

Evans, B. Mitchell, and John Shields. 2001. "The Third Sector: Neo-liberal Restructuring, Governance and the Re-making of State–Civil Society Relationships." Mimeo on file with authors.

Finkel, Alvin. 1995. "Trade Unions and the Welfare State in Canada, 1945–1990," in Cy Gonick, Paul Phillips, and Jesse Vorst, eds., *Labour Gains, Labour Pains: 50 Years of PC 1003*. Winnipeg: Society for Socialist Studies/Fernwood.

Fudge, Judy. 2002. "From Segregation to Privatization: Equality, the Law, the Canadian State and Women Public Servants, 1908–2001," in Judy Fudge and Brenda Cossman, eds., *Feminism, Privatization and the Law*. Toronto: University of Toronto Press, 87–127.

Fudge, Judy, and Brenda Cossman. 2002. "Introduction: Privatization, Law and the Challenge to Feminism," in Brenda Cossman and Judy Fudge, eds.,

Privatization, Law and the Challenge to Feminism. Toronto: University of Toronto Press, 3–40.

Fudge, Judy, and Eric Tucker. 2000. "Pluralism or Fragmentation? The Twentieth-Century Employment Law Regime in Canada," *Labour/Le Travail* 46 (fall), 251–306.

Fudge, Judy, and Leah F. Vosko. 2001a. "By Whose Standards? Re-regulating the Canadian Labour Market," *Economic and Industrial Democracy* 22 (3), 327–56.

– 2001b. "Gender, Segmentation and the Standard Employment Relationship in Canadian Labour Law and Policy," *Economic and Industrial Democracy* 22 (2), 271–310.

Fraser, N. 1997. *Justice Interruptus: Critical Reflections on the 'Postsocialist' Condition.* New York: Routledge.

Gill, S., and D. Law. 1988. *The Global Political Economy.* Baltimore: Johns Hopkins University Press.

Greenspan, Alan. 1997. "Testimony before the Committee on the Budget, United States Senate, January 21." Washington: Federal Reserve Board.

Guard, Julie. 1995."Womanly Innocence and Manly Self-Respect: Gendered Challenges to Labour's Postwar Compromise," in Cy Gonick, Paul Phillips, and Jesse Vorst, eds., *Labour Gains, Labour Pains: 50 Years of PC 1003.* Winnipeg: Society for Socialist Studies/Fernwood.

Harvey, David. 1989. *The Condition of Postmodernity.* Cambridge, Mass.: Blackwell Press.

Jenson, Jane. 1989. "The Talents of Women, the Skills of Men," in S. Wood, ed., *The Transformation of Work?* London: Unwin Hyman.

Jessop, Bob. 1993. "Towards a Schumpetarian Workfare State? Preliminary Remarks on Post-Fordist Political Economy," *Studies in Political Economy* 40 (spring), 7–41.

Krahn, Harvey. 1995. "Non-standard Work on the Rise," *Perspectives on Labour and Income* 7 (4), 35–42.

Larner, Wendy. 2000. "Neo-liberalism: Policy, Ideology and Governmentality," *Studies in Political Economy* 63 (autumn), 5–26.

Little, Margaret. 2001. "A Litmus Test for Democracy: The Impact of Ontario Welfare Changes on Single Mothers," *Studies in Political Economy* 66 (autumn), 9–36.

Luxton, Meg, and June Corman. 2001. *Getting By in Hard Times: Gendered Labour at Home and on the Job.* Toronto: University of Toronto Press.

McBride, Stephen, and John Shields. 1997. *Dismantling a Nation: The Transition to Corporate Rule in Canada.* Halifax: Fernwood.

McBride, Stephen, and Russell A. Williams. 2001. "Globalization, the Restructuring of Labour Markets and Policy Convergence: The OECD 'Jobs Strategy,'" *Global Social Policy* 1 (3), 281–309.

MacDonald, Martha. 1999. "Restructuring, Gender and Social Security Reform in Canada," *Journal of Canadian Studies* 34 (2), 57–88.

– 1991. "Post-Fordism and the Flexibility Debate," *Studies in Political Economy* 36 (autumn), 177–92.

McKeen, Wendy. 2001. "The Shaping of Political Agency: Feminism and the National Social Policy Debate, the 1970s and the Early 1980s," *Studies in Political Economy* 66 (autumn), 37–58.

Neis, Barbara. 1993. "From 'Shipped Girls' to 'Brides of the State': The Transition from Familial to Science Patriarchy in the Newfoundland Fishery Industry," *Canada Journal of Regional Science* 27 (2), 185–211.

O'Connor, Julia S., Ann Shola Orloff, and Sheila Shaver. 1999. *States, Markets, Families: Gender, Liberalism, and Social Policy in Australia, Canada, Great Britain, and the United States.* New York: Cambridge University Press.

Organization for Economic Cooperation and Development (OECD). 1994. *The OECD Jobs Study.* Paris: Organization for Economic Cooperation and Development.

Ornstein, Michael. 2000. *Ethno-Racial Inequality in Toronto: Analysis of the 1996 Census.* Prepared for the Chief Administrator's Office of the City of Toronto.

Pahl, R.H. 1988. *On Work: Historical, Comparative and Theoretical Approaches.* London: Oxford University Press.

Palley, Thomas I. 1998. *Plenty of Nothing: The Downsizing of the American Dream and the Case for Structural Keynesianism.* Princeton, NJ: Princeton University Press.

Panitch, Leo. 1998. "'The State in a Changing World': Social-Democratizing Global Capitalism?" *Monthly Review* 50 (5), 11–32.

Picchio, Antonella. 1992. *Social Reproduction: The Political Economy of the Labour Market.* Cambridge: Cambridge University Press.

Pollert, Ann. 1988. "Dismantling Flexibility," *Capital and Class* 34 (spring), 42–75.

Porter, Ann. 2003. *Gendered States.* Toronto: University of Toronto Press.

Pulkingham, Jane. 1998. "Remaking the Social Divisions of Welfare: Gender, Dependency and UI Reform," *Studies in Political Economy* 56 (summer), 7–48.

Rosenberg, S. 1989. "From Segmentation to Flexibility," *Labour and Society* 14 (4), 361–407.

Seccombe, Wally. 1973. "The Housewife and Her Labour under Capitalism," *New Left Review* 83, 3–24.

Sheldrick, Byron. 1998. "Welfare Reform under Ontario's NDP: Social Democracy and Social Group Representation," *Studies in Political Economy* 55 (spring), 5–36.

Shields, John, and Brian Evans. 1998. *Shrinking the State: Globalization and Public Administration "Reform".* Halifax: Fernwood Publishing.

Smithin, John. 1994. "Cause and Effect in the Relationship between Budget Deficits and the Rate of Interest," *Economies et Sociétés* 9 (Jan.–Feb.), 151–69.

Stanford, Jim. 1996. "Discipline, Insecurity and Productivity: The Economics behind Labour Market 'Flexibility,'" in J. Pulkingham and G. Ternowetsky, eds., *Remaking Canadian Social Policy.* Halifax: Fernwood.

– 1999. *Paper Boom: Why Real Prosperity Requires a New Approach to Canada's Economy.* Toronto: Lorimer.

– 2001. "The Economic and Social Consequences of Fiscal Retrenchment in Canada in the 1990s," *Review of Economic Performance and Social Progress* 1 (June), 141–60.

Townson, Monica. 2000. "Reducing Poverty among Older Women: The Potential of Retirement Incomes Policies." Working paper, Status of Women Canada Policy Research Fund.

Ursel, Jane. 1992. *Private Lives, Public Policy: 100 Years of State Intervention in the Family.* Toronto: Women's Press.

Vosko, Leah F. 1995. "Recreating Dependency: Women and UI Reform," in D. Drache. and A. Ranikin, eds., *Warm Heart, Cold Country.* Toronto: Caledon Press.

– 1996. "Irregular Workers, New Involuntary Social Exiles: Women and UI Reform," in J. Pulkingham and G. Ternowetsky, eds., *Remaking Canadian Social Policy: Social Security in the Late 1990s.* Toronto: Fernwood Press.

– 2000. *Temporary Work: The Gendered Rise of a Precarious Employment Relationship.* Toronto: University of Toronto Press.

– 2002. "Rethinking Feminization: Precariousness in the Canadian Labour Market and the Crisis in Social Reproduction," Annual Robarts Lecture, Robarts Centre for Canadian Studies.

Walby, Sylvia. 1997. *Gender Transformations.* London: Routledge.

Zeytinoglu, Isik Urla, and Jacinta Khasiala Muteshi. 1999. "Gender, Race and Class Dimensions of Non-standard Work," *Industrial Relations/Relations Industrielles* 55 (1), 133–67.

PART ONE

The Changing Economics
of Labour Market Regulation

2

The NAIRU, Labour Market "Flexibility," and Full Employment

MALCOLM SAWYER

The concept of the non-accelerating inflation rate of unemployment (NAIRU) has proved very influential, currently dominating much of macroeconomic analysis and feeding into and constraining economic policy-making in a number of countries. Macroeconomic analysis defines the NAIRU as that level of unemployment, determined on the supply side of the economy, that holds inflation steady. The NAIRU determines (in the long run) the level of economic activity, and so aggregate expenditure in the economy has to conform to that level, or inflation will escalate. At a policy level, the theory behind the NAIRU has been especially influential in the setting of monetary policy – and, so far as there still is such a thing, in fiscal policy. Deviations of unemployment below the NAIRU are believed to lead to accelerating inflation, and hence monetary and fiscal policies tolerate or even attempt to increase unemployment in order to restrain inflation.[1] But the NAIRU approach has also set the framework for labour market, welfare-to-work, collective bargaining, and similar policies. Explicitly or implicitly, a NAIRU-type analysis of the functioning of labour markets underpins the policy analysis and policy prescriptions associated with the OECD's *Jobs Study* (1994) and similar statements in favour of a deregulated, more "flexible" labour market. According to this approach, the only way to reduce long-run unemployment (i.e., to reduce the NAIRU) is through structural reforms that help the labour market behave more competitively and efficiently – rather than through demand-stimulating measures to increase output and employment.

The NAIRU is typically presented as a labour market phenomenon: the NAIRU is the level of unemployment that is effectively settled by what happens in the labour market. Hence it appears that measures to lower unemployment should focus on the labour market and on changing the ways in which people behave there. In contrast, I argue in this chapter that any "inflation barrier" limiting output and employment arises ultimately from a lack of general productive capacity, not solely or even especially from the labour market. In particular, the formation of productive capacity (especially fixed-capital formation) centrally affects the expansion of the economy's overall capacity – a factor ignored or under-emphasized in NAIRU-type models. Empirically and operationally, the acceptance of the NAIRU is inevitably a matter of faith, since it is never directly observable. The falling unemployment levels experienced in the 1990s in Canada, the United States, and Britain, consistent with a steady rate of inflation, has undermined the credibility of the NAIRU approach. At the same time, strong aggregate demand there clearly helps explain falling unemployment. The implication of the approach presented here is that the road to full employment lies through measures aimed at stimulating high levels of both aggregate demand and capacity creation – not through the further deregulation of labour markets.

THE EVOLUTION OF NAIRU THINKING

The concept of the NAIRU emerged from the earlier theory of the "natural rate of unemployment," developed first by Friedman (1968) and others. It viewed the "natural rate of unemployment" as an equilibrium position, characterized by labour market clearing (i.e., a position of equilibrium between effective labour supply and labour demand, despite apparent unemployment). The natural rate theory incorporated two ideas that have become very influential. First, the model proposed an "inflation barrier" – if unemployment fell below the natural rate, high and rising inflation would result, followed ultimately (if the situation was not reversed) by hyperinflation. Second, this "inflation barrier" was a labour market phenomenon, based on the interaction of demand for and supply of labour. The demand for labour is negatively related to the real wage, and supply, positively. The natural rate therefore corresponds to a particular real wage: any higher real wage reduces demand for labour and hence increases unemployment. The natural rate can be structurally influenced by taxation and social security benefits, through their influence on demand for and (effective) supply of labour. Any market "imperfection" that reduces demand for labour, or that hampers or interferes with labour market clearing, pushes observed unemployment above the "natural level," and clearly much economic policy in the past two decades has aimed at reducing or removing these so-called imperfections.

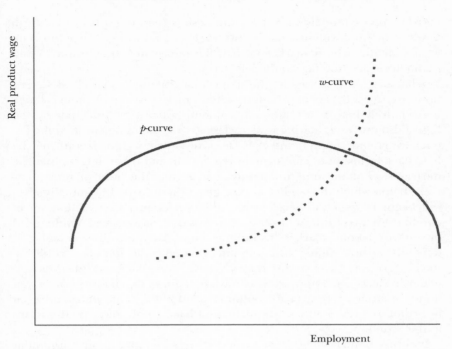

Figure 2.1   *p*- and *w*-curves

The concept of the NAIRU carries over from natural rate theory the ideas that the causes of unemployment lie within the labour market and that the labour market poses the ultimate constraint on the economy's productive capacity (or, in other words, that the inflation barrier is rooted in the labour market). The very phrase "non-accelerating inflation" implies an inflation barrier to full employment. Inflation would quickly accelerate if actual unemployment fell below the inflation barrier posed by the NAIRU. Standard presentations of the NAIRU approach (for example, Layard, Nickell, and Jackman, 1991) offer two equations relating real wages to the level of employment: one negative (a "demand for labour" function), and one positive (a relationship based on wage determination, which associates higher effective labour supply with higher real wages). The equilibrium intersection of these two equations determines the NAIRU (and a corresponding level of real wages). Figure 2.1 is a simple illustration of this approach: the downward-sloping *p*-curve indicates the employment offers made by business, and the upward-sloping *w*-curve reflects wage-determination considerations. The implications of this type of diagram (and of more complex models with the same basic structure) seem clear. High levels of unemployment (that is, low levels of employment) would occur, even with this labour market (strictly speaking) in "equilibrium," when both curves are "too far" to the left.

What structural factors might create that situation? The usual suggestions are that workers may be too militant or too powerful (hence claiming relatively high real wages), that unemployment benefits may be too high (also encouraging high wage claims, while simultaneously reducing effective labour supply), and that employers' demand for labour may be held back by taxation, employment regulation, and other anti-competitive measures. "Equilibrium" unemployment is thus the level of unemployment below which the labour market, given these structural impediments, will begin to generate accelerating inflationary pressures. This level of equilibrium unemployment – the NAIRU – is not constant and is influenced by various labour market institutions and structures. In particular, it depends on how willing and able unemployed individuals are to fill the stock of job vacancies at any time (Nickell, 2000). The NAIRU thus ultimately reflects the extent to which workers are compelled to work, even under unattractive terms and conditions, and in this sense indicates (even in orthodox presentations) the structural balance of power relationships in the economy.

In terms of the framework described in Figure 2.1, the central argument of this chapter is that the inflation barrier represented by the NAIRU is not solely or even primarily a labour market phenomenon, and hence the focus on the labour market in describing and analysing this barrier is misplaced. Other economic relationships underlie labour market supply and demand, and incorporating them leads to rather different policy conclusions.

Problems in Understanding and Operationalizing the NAIRU

The NAIRU falls into that category of concepts which are deemed to be a useful aid to analysis, but by their nature can never be directly observed. The underlying phenomenon may or may not actually exist, and to some degree the users of the concept may not be too concerned as to whether it does actually exist – although they would be concerned that events in the real world conformed to the predictions derived from the concept. The NAIRU can never be directly observed; it may be possible to observe whether events in the real world (in this case the rate of inflation) do or do not conform to the predictions based on the NAIRU, although even this task is difficult and controversial. Yet even conformity between observed real-world experience and the NAIRU predictions (namely, if inflation rises when unemployment is below a particular level and falls when it is higher), would not necessarily prove the existence of the NAIRU. In particular, we could not conclude that the level of unemployment for which inflation is constant is indeed a NAIRU (which we take here to be supply-side determined). Other factors being equal, the rate of inflation may demonstrate a simple inertial tendency to remain constant, whatever the unemployment rate. Indeed, empirical estimates of the NAIRU tend to follow the actual movement of unemployment. For example, Nickell (1990) estimated that the equilibrium rate of unemployment (equivalent to the NAIRU) in Britain rose over the postwar era, as summarized in Table 2.1. His estimates closely track the rise in the actual unemployment rate.

Similarly, see recent OECD estimates of the NAIRU for a wide range of countries in Table 2.2. Again, note the clear correlation between the NAIRU estimates and actual rates of unemployment (demonstrating a simple correlation coefficient of 0.95 in 1999, for example). There is also a substantial correlation (0.85) between *changes* in the NAIRU and changes in actual unemployment between 1985 and 1999. This could be evidence that the NAIRU is effectively and closely determining the actual rate of unemployment, but alternatively the estimates of the NAIRU may be following the actual experience of unemployment. NAIRU estimates, after all, are derived from econometric equations of price and wage determination, which explicitly impose the condition of constant inflation. That is equivalent to the condition that money wages rise in parallel with prices plus productivity, producing a constancy of the distribution of income between wages and profits. Given little overall trend in the distribution of income or in the rate of inflation, any successful estimate of the NAIRU will almost certainly lie in the range of observed unemployment.

Estimates of the NAIRU for any particular country vary widely according to the model specification. Moreover, for particular countries they vary greatly over time. A number of authors favourably disposed to the NAIRU (such as Gordon, 1997; Giorno, Richardson, Roseveare, and van den Noord, 1995) have produced time-varying NAIRU estimates. But this approach needs reinforcement with good reasons as to why the underlying parameters had changed.

A concept's unobservable nature, or its difficulty of operationalization, does not make it wrong or useless. However, it must be used carefully, and its assumptions and arguments require close consideration. The NAIRU approach generally assumes supply-side determination of the underlying equilibrium, which itself fulfils expectations, with wages rising in line with prices after adjustment for productivity changes.

Estimates of the NAIRU are derivable only indirectly from econometric models and their solution under certain conditions (namely, the imposition of constant inflation). The estimation itself may conflict with the basic assumptions (for example, many econometric models do not, unlike the

Table 2.1   Estimates of NAIRU and actual unemployment (percentage of labour force), Britain, 1956–1990

Years	NAIRU estimate (%)	Actual unemployment (% avg.)
1956–59	2.2	2.24
1960–68	2.5	2.62
1969–73	3.6	3.39
1974–80	7.3	5.23
1981–87	8.7	11.11
1988–90	8.7	7.27

Source: Nickell, 1990.

Table 2.2   Estimates of NAIRU and actual unemployment (percentage of labour force), selected OECD countries, 1985 and 1999

	NAIRU estimates		Actual		Change, 1985–99	
	1985	1999	1985	1999	NAIRU	Actual
Australia	6.0	6.8	8.2	7.2	0.8	–1.0
Austria	3.2	4.9	3.7	5.2	1.7	1.5
Belgium	6.8	8.2	10.4	9.1	1.4	–1.3
Canada	10.1	7.7	10.5	7.6	–2.4	–2.9
Denmark	5.9	6.3	7.1	5.2	0.4	–1.9
Finland	3.9	9.0	5.0	10.2	5.1	5.2
France	6.5	9.5	10.2	11.1	3.0	0.9
Germany	4.4	6.9	8.0	8.3	2.5	0.3
Greece	6.5	9.5	7.8	12.0	3.0	4.2
Ireland	13.2	7.1	16.5	5.6	–6.1	–10.9
Italy	7.8	10.4	8.6	11.5	2.6	2.9
Japan	2.7	4.0	2.6	4.7	1.3	2.1
Netherlands	7.5	4.7	9.2	3.2	–2.8	–6.0
New Zealand	5.1	6.1	3.5	6.8	1.0	3.3
Norway	2.6	3.7	2.6	3.2	1.1	0.6
Portugal	5.4	3.9	8.9	4.5	–1.5	–4.4
Spain	14.4	15.1	20.9	15.9	0.7	–5.0
Sweden	2.1	5.8	2.8	5.6	3.7	2.8
Switzerland	2.9	2.4	1.0	2.7	–0.5	1.7
United Kingdom	8.1	7.0	11.6	6.0	–1.1	–5.6
United States	5.6	5.2	7.2	4.2	–0.4	–3.0
Euro zone	7.1	8.8	10.2	9.9	1.7	–0.3

Source: OECD, 2000: Table V.1, Annex Table 21.
Note: Unemployment rates (actual and NAIRU) are measured via commonly used national definitions, except in Belgium and Denmark, which apply a standardized measure (which differs little from the common definition).

NAIRU theory, require that nominal wages respond one for one to nominal prices). Hence any estimates derived via econometric models are only as reliable as the models themselves.

A wide margin of potential error surrounds point estimates of the NAIRU and therefore undermine its usefulness as a guide to policy. As Staiger, Stock, and Watson (1997) and others have observed, estimates of the NAIRU are only that and hence are subject to possible error: the authors estimate that a 95 per cent confidence interval for the NAIRU in the United States lies between 4.3 per cent and 7.3 per cent. Numerous authors have commented on the unreliability of NAIRU estimates (for example, Setterfield, Gordon, and Osberg, 1992), and others, on the uncertainty surrounding them (for example, Madsen, 1998). Setterfield, Gordon, and Osberg (1992) "suggest that estimates of the NAIRU [for Canada] are extremely sensitive to model specification, the definition of variables and the sample period used. [Further] ... the final range of all NAIRU estimates ... is about 5.5 percentage points. Indeed, the size of this range is so great that it covers virtually the entire range of male unemployment rates in Canada since 1956" (134). Similarly, the Directorate-General for Economic and Financial Affairs of the European Commission concluded that the concept of the NAIRU is "unusable operationally" because "empirical studies on both sides of the Atlantic have shown that large variations in NAIRU may be caused by apparently small differences in sample, retained explanatory variables and analytical formulation. Furthermore, the confidence interval around these estimates is so large that it generally contains the whole historical range of unemployment rates observed in the last 15 to 20 years."[2] Nevertheless, as UNCTAD (1995: 172) observes, "natural rate estimates are still used to assess and guide macroeconomic policy, thereby contributing to rising unemployment."

Another weakness of the NAIRU approach is its general inability to analyse regional and sectoral differences in labour market performance. In essence, the NAIRU is an aggregate macroeconomic phenomenon. It is derived from the condition that the rate of inflation is constant, and it is usually assumed that a single economy's pace of inflation varies little across regions. No suggestion appears in the usual presentation of the NAIRU that the level of unemployment will vary significantly across regions, between urban and rural areas, and between genders or ethnic groups. A partial defence would be that the NAIRU model is an aggregated one that allows few differences between groups. Since the usual presentation focuses on labour market operations, variations in unemployment across regions or groups must depend on variations in labour market conditions. In so far as legal factors, hiring traditions, employment contracts, and other factors related to flexibility are similar across a country, there would be no implied mechanism to generate variations in unemployment between groups. In reality, however, the regional differences in unemployment arise more from differences in effective capacity and demand for a region's production than from differences in labour market flexibility, despite interdependence between a country's regions, such as labour mobility.

Aggregate demand is the "unmentioned guest" in the NAIRU analysis: there, but rarely discussed. As we see, for example, in Figure 2.1, the NAIRU is a supply-side equilibrium position. There is no particular reason to think that aggregate demand will be just enough to support such a level of unemployment. Aggregate demand may be more or less than the level of output corresponding to the NAIRU. But monetary policy and fiscal policy are acknowledged to affect aggregate demand.

The level of aggregate demand has a further role, as we see in the last section of this chapter. It (and associated variables, such as profitability, availability of funds for investment, and capacity utilization) help determine the level of investment. Low levels of investment lead to slow growth of productive capacity, which in turn generates "poor" positions of the p-curve in Figure 2.1 (since employers are not investing in new facilities, their employment does not grow or may decline with productivity growth, and hence the p-curve shifts leftward), reduced real wages, and lesser levels of employment and output. If demand remains weak, then investment stays weak (since firms have little incentive to invest), business employment stagnates, and the apparent NAIRU rises (since the unemployment caused by short-run demand becomes self-perpetuating as productive capacity remains stagnant).

The NAIRU approach attributes inflationary pressures to a "too low" level of unemployment (that is, below the equilibrium NAIRU). The policy implication is clear: increase unemployment to control inflation (first, stop its acceleration, and then decelerate it back towards a preferable, lower rate). Policy-makers currently tend to use interest rates to influence demand and thereby unemployment. In principle, the NAIRU analysis could incorporate other inflationary factors. For example, rising world commodity prices could increase domestic prices and costs, (represented as a downward shift in the p-curve in Figure 2.1). But those factors are essentially exogenous to the NAIRU analysis. This downplays the impact of these factors (notably commodity and energy prices) on domestic inflation. Further, current macroeconomic policies, especially monetary policy, deal poorly with those other inflationary factors. Central bankers probably do not possess the tools to target observed inflation rates, given the diversity of causes and sources of inflation. Monetary policy works towards an inflation target but can only change interest rates and seek thereby to influence overall demand.

To sum up, there are many difficulties with the estimation and operationalization of the NAIRU model of inflation and of its control. The unobservable NAIRU can only be imputed from econometric models. The resulting NAIRU estimates thus depend on those models' questionable assumptions, and their expected error throws even deeper into question their policy relevance. If inflation is inertial (such that a given rate will tend to continue, unless jolted by some exogenous force), then estimated NAIRUs will track actual unemployment rates – as they in fact do. Since the NAIRU approach imagines inflation as arising solely or primarily from the aggregate labour market, it does not allow for sectoral or regional differences or segmentations in labour markets. Moreover, NAIRU models are ill-suited to understanding or remedying inflation that might result not solely from an overheated labour market. NAIRU thinking is at best muddy on the role of aggregate demand conditions: it grounds the NAIRU in the structural, supply-side features of the labour market yet does not integrate the always-present influence of demand-side factors on the labour market and the overall economy.

RECENT EXPERIENCE IN CANADA, BRITAIN, AND THE UNITED STATES

Despite the theoretical and operational problems with the NAIRU approach, the model perhaps experienced its most serious damage from the failure of its predictions in the late 1990s. The U.S. economy seemed to combine very low unemployment – far below economists' estimates of the NAIRU – with stable and low inflation. Other countries (such as Britain and Canada) also experienced falling unemployment with stable inflation. This section briefly reviews inflation and unemployment in the three countries over the past decade. This experience casts doubt on the NAIRU's usefulness in explaining both labour market outcomes and overall macroeconomic performance. Further, this review shows the importance of investment spending in all three countries during that decade, both in increasing general aggregate demand and in creating productive capacity.

Unemployment in all three economies declined substantially during the 1990s. In Canada, it fell from a high of 11.4 per cent in 1993 to 7.6 per cent in 1999. U.S. unemployment fell from 7.5 per cent in 1992 to 4.2 per cent in 1999, and British, from 10.5 per cent in 1993 to 6.1 per cent in 1999 (in terms of the OECD standardized measure of unemployment in all cases). Some caveats apply: for example, the rapid rise in the U.S. prison population (excluded from labour-force statistics) and changes to the operation of Britain's unemployment-benefits system both reduced measured rates of unemployment.[3] Nevertheless, labour market conditions strengthened considerably in all three countries over the decade.

These declines in unemployment (along with the simultaneous generation of government surpluses in all three countries) may appear to vindicate neoliberal, free-market policies, which advocated often painful "reforms" and cutbacks in social policies and labour market regulations aimed at both making the labour market more "efficient" and reducing government expenditures. While unemployment has declined significantly in the three countries, it has remained at over 10 per cent in the euro zone since 1991. Many observers draw the implication that the "flexible" labour markets of the Anglo-Saxon economies have reduced unemployment, while the "inflexible" euro zone has suffered chronic high unemployment.[4] "Here is the received wisdom. The European job market is rigid and inflexible. Result: high unemployment. The North American job market is dynamic and flexible. Result: low unemployment. So Europeans had better do something about their labor markets unless they want permanent double digit unemployment" (Nickell, 1997: 55).

Inflation has remained low in all three countries, even as unemployment tumbled. In Canada, since falling from 5.6 per cent in 1991, consumer price inflation (CPI) has never exceeded 2.2 per cent and was just 1.7 per cent in 1999. U.S. CPI ranged between 2 and 3 per cent for most of the 1990s and dipped to 1.6 per cent in 1998. In Britain, inflation fluctuated at about 3 per cent for most of the 1990s (after starting at 9.5 per cent in 1990) and fell to 1.6 per cent in 1999.

At the beginning of the 1990s, most estimates of the U.S. NAIRU were in the range of 5.5 to 6.5 per cent,[5] and for the British, from 6 to 8 per cent[6]. The OECD (2000) estimated the NAIRUS in 1990 as 9.0 per cent for Canada, 8.6 per cent for Britain, and 5.3 per cent for the United States. These estimates had declined to 7.7 per cent, 7.0 per cent, and 5.2 per cent, respectively, by 1999. In each jurisdiction, actual unemployment declined far below what had, until recently, been considered the NAIRU; in fact, by 1999, unemployment was still lower in each country than the updated NAIRU estimates (which predictably tracked observed unemployment). Inflation's failure to rise in the face of unemployment below the previous NAIRU estimates challenges the validity of those estimates and their underlying theoretical and empirical logic. NAIRU's advocates, of course, maintain its validity: either the estimates were wrong, or the NAIRU moved over time in response to structural changes in labour markets (as argued, for example, by Gordon, 1997).

There are considerable similarities in the experience of Canada, Britain, and the United States over the past decade. In each country, an economic upswing began about 1992 or 1993 and on many counts lasted longer than any previous postwar upswing. Government budgets have moved from substantial deficit in the early 1990s (in 1992, 8.0 per cent of GDP in Canada, 6.5 per cent in Britain, and 5.9 per cent in the United States). By

Table 2.3   Gross fixed capital formation, average annual growth (%), selected OECD countries, 1972–1999

	1972–82	1983–91	1992–99
United States	1.2	3.7	7.3
Japan	2.2	5.9	–0.2
Germany	–0.7	3.6	0.8
France	1.0	2.9	1.0
Italy	0.9	1.6	0.8
United Kingdom	–1.0	4.1	4.3
Canada	4.8	4.1	4.2
Total OECD	1.9	7.0	4.1
Euro area	0.2	4.6	1.3

Source: Calculated from OECD, *Economic Outlook*, June 2000.

1999 the budgets were in surplus to the extent of 2.8 per cent of GDP in Canada, 1.1 per cent in the United Kingdom, and 1.0 per cent in the United States.[7] At the same time, however, personal savings ratios declined significantly. In Canada, the rate fell from 11.4 per cent of disposable income in 1992 to 7.5 per cent in 1995 and just 1.4 per cent in 1999; the U.S. rate dropped from 8.7 per cent in 1992 to 5.6 per cent in 1995 and 2.4 per cent in 1999; and the British figure, from 10.5 per cent in 1995 to 6.2 per cent in 1999. Meanwhile, businesses increased investment expenditure. Non-residential investment grew at close to 10 per cent per annum in the United States from 1994 onwards. In the five years 1994–99 it rose by nearly 60 per cent in the United Kingdom, and by 45 per cent in Canada (albeit after years of falling investment).

The differences in the growth rates of fixed capital across OECD countries revealed in Table 2.3 are striking. During the 1990s, investment in the euro zone grew on average just 1.34 per cent per annum, compared to well over 4 per cent in Britain and Canada and over 7 per cent in the United States. The expansion of investment adds to capital stock; in the terms of Figure 2.1, it is equivalent to a shift of the p-curve to the right since firms have more capacity to hire workers and (with strong aggregate demand) more need. U.S. capacity utilization tended to decline from 1995 to 1999 in the face of this strong capital expansion.[8]

A crude summary of the upswing in these three countries might suggest a consumer and investment boom, with saving rates falling and investment expenditure rising. In fact, the preceding data may understate investment growth in the three countries, as they refer only to tangible investment; intangible investment may now be central to expanding productive capacity (for example, in information technology industry). We do not attempt here to explain why investment rose so much in the three countries; rather, we wish to note that investment spending was much stronger there than in most of the rest of the OECD. Not only does investment stimulate aggregate demand, it also adds to productive capacity; ensuring that firms experience a growing demand, while increasing their capacity to meet that demand, is an obvious recipe for non-inflationary growth and employment.

The upswings of the 1990s in all three countries were relatively "smooth": in Canada annual GDP growth rates fell between 1.7 per cent and 4.7 per cent (1993–99); in Britain, 2.1 per cent and 4.4 per cent (1993–99); and in the United States, between 2.7 per cent and 4.4 per cent (1992–99). No country experienced the higher growth spikes characteristic of previous expansions. This relative "smoothness" has perhaps helped to restrain inflation, if it is *changes* in unemployment rates rather than the *level* of unemployment that stimulate inflation.[9]

NAIRU advocates have (at least) two possible responses to this apparently anomalous experience. First, the estimated equations for prices and wages often predict only a slow acceleration of wages and prices when unemployment falls below NAIRU. For example, Stiglitz (1997) argues that, "contrary to the accelerationist view, not only does the economy not stand on a precipice – with a slight dose of inflation leading to ever-increasing levels of inflation – but the magnitude by which inflation rises does not increase when the unemployment rate is held down for a prolonged period of time" (Stiglitz, 1997: 9). "In our regressions [at the Council of Economic Advisers], we find that keeping the unemployment rate one percentage point below the NAIRU for one year will result in the inflation rate increasing by between 0.3 and 0.6 of a percentage point. Finally our analysis indicates that at least 20 per cent of the variation in the inflation rate can be explained by unemployment alone" (Stiglitz, 1997: 5). This implies, of course, that unemployment cannot explain 80 per cent of inflation. NAIRU believers might therefore argue that observed low unemployment will only slowly affect inflation rates. Further, other influences (some of which may be treated as random) affect the rate of wage and price inflation, and these may have favoured low domestic inflation during the latter 1990s, for example, in Britain the strong exchange rate from 1996 on served to depress domestic inflation;[10] for all three countries, the generally low world inflationary climate, particularly in commodity prices, was also clearly helpful. Even if this defence of the NAIRU were sustained, the resulting policy conclusion would be clearly weaker than has traditionally been implied. Instead of concluding that the NAIRU is like a "cliff-edge," such that one step beyond it sparks rapidly and continuously accelerating inflation, at most it may be a kind of gentle "beach," against which various forces (wind, tides, exogenous storms) act in an uncertain and complex manner.

Second, perhaps the level of the NAIRU has itself fallen, as indicated in the estimates from OECD, 2000, reported above. The quote from the (British) Treasury, 1997, in note 6 is suggestive of this idea. The chancellor of the exchequer has argued that "the more our welfare to work reforms allow the long-term unemployed to re-enter the active labour market, the more it will be possible to reduce unemployment without increasing inflationary pressures. And the more our tax and benefit reforms remove unnecessary barriers to work, and the more our structural reforms promote the skills for work, the more it is possible to envisage long-term increases in employment, without the fuelling of inflationary pressures" (Brown, 1999). A leading exponent of the NAIRU has recently suggested that "equilibrium unemployment is considerably lower than it was in the 1980s and early 1990s partly because of changes in the operation of the benefits system, and partly because trade unions are both less adversarial and cover a much smaller proportion of the private sector. Precisely where unemployment is relative to the equilibrium rate today is not known" (Nickell, 2000: 21).

Only a more detailed inquiry into the experience of these three countries for the 1990s can determine its implications for the NAIRU – both in theory and in policy. But the summary indicators that we have assembled highlight two features that require further research. First, the idea of a constant NAIRU, departure from which quickly generates rising inflation, is very questionable. Even if one agrees that foreign exchange fluctuations and the generally low world inflation rate contributed to favourable macroeconomic performance in these three countries, domestic inflationary forces generated by unemployment below the NAIRU are demonstrably weak. Yet if one accepts the notion of a time-varying NAIRU, it then becomes crucial to explain precisely how it varies – and not just by citing pro-competitive changes in labour market and social policies. Our approach suggests that the growth of productive capacity was also important.

Second, the stimulus to aggregate demand in all three countries apparently derived largely from rising investment, falling savings by households, and (in the mid-1990s) exports.[11] The change in the balance between private savings and investment is not only a stimulus to aggregate demand, but also helps to explain the huge swing of government budgets from deficit to surplus.[12] Are the low savings rates and the trade deficit (see Godley, 2000) sustainable? What caused the rising investment share and the declining savings ratio? Although we do not address these broader questions here, it is certainly true that the stimulus to aggregate demand from these sources helps to explain falling unemployment in these three countries.[13]

The NAIRU approach concludes that inflation is the main barrier to the achievement of full employment and accelerates when unemployment falls below the NAIRU. In contrast, we argue here that inflationary pressures encountered as the economy expands are more complex and multifaceted than the NAIRU approach assumes. It is important to unravel those inflationary pressures and then to identify economic policies that may mitigate those pressures. High levels of employment would seem to require substantial aggregate demand, sufficient productive capacity to provide employment, and appropriate forms of work organization.

Figure 2.1 illustrates the role of productive capacity. In effect, the position of the p-curve depends on the capital stock and productive capacity of enterprises. The greater the productive capacity, the higher and more to the right the p-curve, reflecting firms' greater ability to provide employment (though only at the appropriate level of aggregate demand). The equilibrium rate of employment rises (and the apparent NAIRU declines).

Meanwhile, the w-curve in Figure 2.1 represents the outcome of wage determination. There are many ways in which the analysis can incorporate such a process (for further discussion, see Sawyer, 2001). Some approaches have used models of collective bargaining to determine wages. Others (generally now more popular) rely on notions of "efficiency wages," which deem employees' work effort to depend on the relationship between wages in their current employment and their alternative potential income (or, in other words, the cost of job loss). The alternative income depends on wages elsewhere, the level of unemployment benefits, and the perceived time spent unemployed in the event of job loss. This approach assumes that workers enhance their work effort only if there is a cost (of job loss) to not doing so. Full employment therefore removes the cost of job loss: under literal full employment, someone being sacked can immediately find another job. No cost of job loss means no pressure to work hard and not to slack or "shirk," to use the terminology of Shapiro and Stiglitz (1984). This puts the argument in its extreme form and would lead to the w-curve becoming vertical at or before full employment. Full employment would then become unreachable. A less extreme version would postulate that full employment substantially reduces the cost of job loss for an individual and reduces the "disciplining" effect of unemployment. Work effort and productivity would then decline at full employment, compared to conditions of significant unemployment.

The policy implications of this analysis are, in some respects, trivial: 30

years ago they would have stated the blindingly obvious, although prevailing orthodoxy has obscured them ever since. Full employment of labour requires a high level of aggregate demand and an appropriate level and distribution of productive capacity. At any point in time, with given productive capacity (and distribution thereof), some form of "inflationary barrier" exists, such that a level of demand beyond that productive capacity would tend to generate inflation. Periods of low investment will lead to relatively low productive capacity, and similarly major shifts in the composition of demand can render productive capacity unproductive. The NAIRU may then appear rather high, from which "believers" will conclude that stimulating the economy will accelerate inflation. Yet, in the absence of stimulation, investment will be insufficient and unemployment will remain chronically high. In this manner, NAIRU policy doctrine can become self-fulfilling.

It also seems clear that the achievement of full employment has little to do with labour market "flexibility." Workers can be very "flexible" – but that does not create employment in the absence of the necessary productive capacity and sufficient aggregate demand.

Kalecki argued nearly 60 years ago that "under a regime of permanent full employment, the 'sack' would cease to play its role as a disciplinary measure" (Kalecki, 1943). The "efficiency wage" approach suggests that full employment is impossible, because the cost of job loss falls to zero at full employment, and so work effort and productivity drop. Kalecki concluded his famous article by claiming that "full employment capitalism" will of course have to develop new social and political institutions that will reflect the increased power of the working class. "If capitalism can adjust itself to full employment, a fundamental reform will have been incorporated in it" (Kalecki, 1943). The design and implementation of alternative forms of work organization, workers' involvement, and regulation of income distribution are the greatest challenges in the achievement of full employment. High levels of aggregate demand and of productive capacity are certainly necessary components, but the *sustainability* of full employment also requires wage determination, work effort, and labour productivity to be compatible.

CONCLUSION

The central argument of this chapter is that any inflation barrier to full employment is primarily a problem of inadequate productive capacity, rather than of labour market inflexibility. Only policies that stimulate aggregate demand can motivate investment spending and ensure adequate capacity (not to mention employment levels as high as possible). Policies of restraint – whether in monetary and fiscal policy or in painful changes in social policy and labour market structures – not only under-mine employment in the short run but, by reducing investment and the formation of productive capacity, also harm future employment prospects.

NOTES

1 "Estimates of the NAIRU help to make more transparent the assumptions that lie behind policy analysis and recommendations" (OECD, 2000: 155).

2 *European Economy*, Supplement A, Jan. 1995, 2, as reported in UNCTAD, 1995: 172.

3 The many changes to the way Britain measured unemployment, which signifi-cantly altered the national measure, should not affect the OECD standardized measure.

4 The chapter by Palley in this volume similarly challenges this traditional dichotomy.

5 "Tightness in the labor market is measured by the excess of CBO's estimate of the non accelerating inflation rate of unemployment (NAIRU) over the actual unemployment rate. It is an indicator of future wage inflation" (Congres-sional Budget Office, 1994: 4). That office uses an estimate of 6 per cent for the NAIRU.

6 "The sustainable rate of unemployment, or NAIRU, is believed to have risen in the UK during the 1970s and 1980s, but there is broad agreement that this increase has been partly reversed since the late 1980s. Although the magni-tude of any fall is very difficult to estimate, most estimates of the current level of the NAIRU lie in the range of 6 to 8 per cent on the LFS measure of unem-ployment. However, considerably lower levels should be achievable in the long run through re-integrating the long-term unemployed back into the labour market, upgrading skills, and reforming the tax and benefit systems to promote work incentives" (Treasury, 1997: 82).

7 Figures from OECD, *Economic Outlook*, June 2000.

8 The figures on capacity use refer only to "total industry" (manufacturing, mining, and utilities), and fluctuated between 79.3 (1991) and 83.5 (1997), before falling back to 81.2 in 1999 (Council of Economic Advisers, 2001, Table B-54).

9 Vickrey, 1997, makes this argument.

10 In Canada, the currency weakened through most of the period, which should have made it even harder to maintain stable inflation in the face of falling unemployment.

11 The OECD figures indicate annual growth of over 7.5 per cent for real exports for both the United Kingdom and the United States in each of the four years from 1994 to 1997. In each case, the rate falls to under 2.5 per cent in 1998 and under 4 per cent in 1999.

12 Recall the national income identity that $(S-I) + (M-X) = (G-T)$, where S is

private savings, *I* investment, *M* imports, *X* exports, *G* government expenditure, and *T* tax revenue.

13 Palley, 1998, argues that "the superior job creation performance of the U.S. model was fool's gold in that it was accompanied by a tendency to generate wage stagnation and increased income inequality and poverty rates. [However], the U.S. economy's recent [1980s–mid-1990s] superior job creation performance has been driven by macroeconomic forces rather than by microeconomic considerations of greater labor market flexibility."

Palley, 2000, examines the OECD *Jobs Study* (1994), which had emphasized the role of labour market reform and flexibility in reducing unemployment. He concludes (based on regression analysis of changes in unemployment in the mid-1990s) that "actions taken to reform labour markets do not explain any of the reduction in the rate of unemployment. There is some evidence that reforms of the educational system may have lowered total employment growth, which could be the result of young people staying in school longer. There is also stronger evidence that business sector reforms have lowered total employment growth, and reduced the quality of employment by slowing the growth of full-time employment" (9). As Palley suggests, this is indirect support for the view that the cause of high European unemployment is macroeconomic in nature.

REFERENCES

Brown, G. 1999. "The Conditions for Full Employment," *Mais Lecture.* City University of London, 19 Oct.

Congressional Budget Office. 1994. *The Economic and Budget Outlook: Fiscal Years 1996–2000.* Washington, DC: Congressional Budget Office.

Council of Economic Advisers, 2001. *Economic Report of the President.* Washington, DC: United States Government Printing Office.

Friedman, M. 1968. "The Role of Monetary Policy," *American Economic Review* 58 (1), 1–17.

Giorno, C., P. Richardson, D. Roseveare, and P. van den Noord. 1995. "Potential Output, Output Gaps and Structural Budget Balances," *OECD Economic Studies* 24 (1), 167–209.

Godley, W. 2000. "Drowning in Debt," *Policy Notes (online).* Jerome Levy Economics Institute.

Gordon, R.J. 1997. "The Time-varying NAIRU and Its Implications for Economic Policy," *Journal of Economic Perspectives* 11 (1), 11–32.

Kalecki, M. 1943. "Political Aspects of Full Employment," *Political Quarterly* 14.

Layard, R., S. Nickell, and R. Jackman. 1991. *Unemployment: Macroeconomic Performance and the Labour Market.* Oxford: Oxford University Press.

Madsen, J. 1998. "The NAIRU and Classical Unemployment in the OECD Countries," *International Review of Applied Economics* 12 (2), 165–86.

Nickell, S. 2000. Evidence to the Treasury Committee: Seventh Report: The

Monetary Policy Committee of the Bank of England: Confirmation Hearings, vol. II, Minutes of Evidence, HC 520–II May 2000.

- 1997. "Unemployment and Labor Market Rigidities: Europe versus North America," *Journal of Economic Perspectives* 11 (3), 55–74.

- 1990. "Inflation and the UK Labour Market," *Oxford Review of Economic Policy* 6 (4), 26–35.

Organization for Economic Cooperation and Development (OECD). 2000. *Economic Outlook*. Dec. 2000.

- 1994. *The OECD Jobs Study*. Paris: Organization for Economic Cooperation and Development.

Palley, T. 2000. "Evaluating the OECD's *Job Strategy*: Has It Helped Lower Unemployment?" *AFL-CIO Technical Working Paper*. T024.

- 1998. "Restoring Prosperity: Why the U.S. Model Is Not the Answer for the United States or Europe," *Journal of Post Keynesian Economics* 20 (3), 337 – 53.

Sawyer, M. 2001. "Aggregate Demand, Investment and the NAIRU." *Metroeconomica*, 53 (1), 66–94.

Setterfield, M., D.V. Gordon, and L. Osberg. 1992. "Searching for a Will o' Wisp: An Empirical Study of the NAIRU in Canada," *European Economic Review* 36 (1), 119–36.

Shapiro, C., and J. Stiglitz. 1984. "Equilibrium Unemployment as a Worker Discipline Device," *American Economic Review* 74 (3), 433–44.

Staiger, D., J.H. Stock, and M.W. Watson. 1997. "How Precise Are Estimates of the Nature Rate of Unemployment?" in C.D. Romer and D.H. Romer, eds., *Reducing Inflation: Motivation and Strategy*. Chicago: University of Chicago Press.

Stiglitz, J.E. 1997. "Reflections on the Natural Rate Hypothesis," *Journal of Economic Perspectives* 11 (1), 3–10.

Treasury. 1997. *Pre Budget Report*, Cmnd. 3804, London: HMSO.

United Nations Conference on Trade and Development (UNCTAD). 1995. *Trade and Development Report*. New York and Geneva: United Nations.

Vickrey, William. 1997. "A Trans-Keynesian Manifesto," *Journal of Post Keynesian Economics* 19 (4), 495–510.

3

The Causes of High Unemployment: Labour Market Sclerosis versus Macroeconomic Policy

THOMAS I. PALLEY

The economies of western Europe remain afflicted by high and intractable rates of unemployment. European Union unemployment averaged 9.6 per cent between 1993 and 2000, while the rate in the smaller (eleven-country) euro zone was even higher (averaging over 10 per cent). In stark contrast, U.S. unemployment was much lower through the last decade, averaging barely 5 per cent from 1993 through 2000 and touching a thirty-year low of 3.9 per cent in September 2000.

This divergence has sparked a great debate. One side claims that Europe's rigid and sclerotic labour markets are incapable of adjusting to technological advance and change in the international economy. Unemployment benefits are too generous and last too long, unions are too strong, and employee protection discourages firms from hiring workers. This contrasts with the U.S. economy, which has flexible, dynamic labour markets that have adjusted to these developments and used them to create new jobs. This "labour market flexibility" hypothesis is represented forcefully by *The OECD Jobs Study* (OECD, 1994) and its subsequent policy applications.

The other side attributes Europe's unemployment to bad macroeconomic policy (Baker and Schmitt, 1998; Palley, 1998, 1999; Solow, 1994), mistakenly adhering to the theory of the natural rate of unemployment.[1] According to this "macroeconomic policy" hypothesis, policy-makers have adopted austere macroeconomic policies aimed at reducing inflation, regardless of the resulting unemployment or the underlying cause of inflation. Currency-market concerns also contributed to this austerity. In the 1980s and 1990s the persistent threat of currency speculation induced

European governments to raise interest rates to defend their currencies and guard against imported inflation. Subsequently, arrangements leading up to the introduction of the euro aggravated the problem, imposing strict criteria of fiscal convergence that called for austerity irrespective of economic conditions. The net result has been persistently contractionary policy, insensitive to the business cycle. In contrast, U.S. macroeconomic policy has been relatively flexible and counter-cyclical (Palley, 1999). Both the U.S. budget deficit and (U.S.) Federal Reserve monetary policy have exhibited clear counter-cyclical fluctuation, and in the recession of 1990–91 the Federal Reserve lowered short-term nominal rates so that the real rate (after inflation) equalled zero.

Moreover, this sharp difference in macroeconomic policy still persists. Thus, on one hand, in 2001, the Federal Reserve, facing an economic slowdown, slashed its interest rate, doing so a dozen times during the next 30 months, and lowering the rate from 6.5 per cent in January 2001 to just 1.0 per cent (an all-time low) by mid-2003. Side by side, fiscal policy became expansionary, with a significant tax cut (tilted towards the affluent). These aggressive policy shifts were undertaken even though unemployment was significantly lower than in Europe, and the inflation rate actually increased above 3 per cent for a time. The European Central Bank (ECB), on the other hand, lowered rates more modestly – by 2.75 points during the same period – despite significantly higher unemployment and slowing growth.

These two accounts of unemployment – labour market inflexibility and bad macroeconomic policy – have enormously different policy implications. If the first is correct, Europe should adopt the U.S. model and introduce labour market flexibility that renders wages downwardly flexible, reduces employee protection, and reduces unemployment benefits and other social protection. If the second is correct, Europe should adopt expansionary macroeconomic policies predicated on lower real interest rates. It also needs rules that ensure that monetary policy and fiscal policy exert a more powerful counter-cyclical influence.

The outcome of this controversy is germane not only to OECD countries, but to developing economies, which are experiencing a parallel debate. Thus the "Washington Consensus" – which represents the developing world's analogue of the "Euro-sclerosis hypothesis" – maintains that growth in employment and output requires labour market flexibility. Supporters counsel developing countries to resist calls for international labour standards, which would promote workers' rights of freedom of association and collective bargaining. Instead, they propose structural measures to make labour markets more reliant on market forces and competition.

These observations reveal the critical nature of the debate over the causes of unemployment. How it is resolved promises to affect policy in both developed and developing countries. This chapter provides some new statistical evidence on the relative contributions of macroeconomic factors and labour market institutions to unemployment in the OECD. The author's principal empirical innovation is the integration of macroeconomic time-series variables that capture the stance of macroeconomic policy, along with microeconomic labour market institution variables. The result is a comprehensive statistical examination – in the first section of this chapter – of the causes of international differences in unemployment rates that takes into account the effects of both labour market institutions and macroeconomic policy.

Several patterns emerge clearly. Macroeconomic-policy variables consistently and robustly affect national unemployment rates, and macroeconomic policy influences unemployment rates in the manner expected. High real interest rates and slow growth raise unemployment, as does a slowdown in export growth. As for the microeconomic labour market variables, the evidence is more problematic. Duration of unemployment benefits and union density are both consistently insignificant in explaining unemployment rates. The level of wage-bargaining co-ordination and the extent of union coverage matter consistently but need not raise unemployment if paired appropriately with other policies. Finally, the significance of other microeconomic variables (employment protection, the unemployment insurance wage-replacement rate, and the tax burden) is unstable and not robust to changes in the specification of the statistical models.

These findings suggest – as we see in the chapter's second section – that high unemployment in western Europe is the result principally of self-inflicted, dysfunctional macroeconomic policy. Disinflation, high real interest rates, and slower growth raised unemployment. Moreover, policy-makers all adopted this course at the same time, thereby generating a wave of trade-based, cross-country spill-overs that generated a continent-wide macroeconomic funk and further raised unemployment. The empirical evidence does imply that real interest rates have tended to be systematically higher in countries with high union density, despite the lack of evidence that such density raises inflation. This suggests, as the third section argues, that central banks have systematically adopted tighter monetary policy in countries with high union density. The conclusion presents some policy recommendations that would promote full employment and better income distribution.

EVIDENCE ON THE CAUSES OF DIFFERENT UNEMPLOYMENT RATES IN THE OECD

As we saw above, the current study incorporates both microeconomic and macroeconomic variables, thereby assessing the relative contributions of

Table 3.1 Macroeconomic data, by country, 1983–94

Country	Average standardized unemployment rate (%)		Average real GDP growth rate (% per yr.)		Average CPI inflation rate (% per yr.)		Average short-term interest rate (%)		Average short-term real interest rate (%)	
	1983–89	1989–94	1983–89	1989–94	1983–88	1989–94	1983–88	1989–94	1983–88	1989–94
Australia	8.40	9.05	4.43	2.65	7.60	3.78	12.62	9.79	5.02	6.01
Austria	2.86	3.43	2.09	2.76	2.87	3.30	5.36	7.78	2.49	4.48
Belgium	10.30	7.83	2.00	1.77	3.83	2.88	7.21	8.00	3.38	5.12
Canada	9.98	9.81	4.26	1.35	4.45	3.17	9.32	7.87	4.87	4.70
Denmark	6.41	8.51	2.71	1.49	5.02	2.53	10.47	10.48	5.45	7.95
Finland	5.68	9.90	3.41	-0.26	5.47	3.87	12.76	11.00	7.29	7.13
France	9.71	10.35	2.19	1.69	5.25	2.75	9.57	8.87	4.32	6.12
Germany	6.70	5.90	2.35	2.92	1.53	3.57	4.73	7.60	3.20	4.03
Ireland	15.98	14.70	2.77	5.44	5.60	2.90	11.42	9.13	5.82	6.23
Italy	8.88	9.76	2.73	1.29	8.30	5.43	14.52	11.67	6.22	6.24
Japan	2.68	2.35	3.98	2.61	1.27	2.05	5.15	4.90	3.88	2.85
Netherlands	8.51	6.36	2.47	2.84	1.40	2.57	5.47	7.63	4.07	5.06
New Zealand	4.48	8.85	1.81	1.98	10.70	3.08	17.31	9.38	6.61	6.30
Norway	2.78	5.58	3.35	2.91	7.17	3.02	13.22	10.06	6.05	7.04
Portugal	7.63	5.06	3.12	2.58	17.42	9.67	16.70	13.78	-0.72	4.11
Spain	20.13	19.21	3.22	2.08	8.52	5.77	13.75	12.58	5.23	6.81
Sweden	2.76	5.06	2.56	0.38	6.47	6.07	10.97	11.94	4.50	5.87
Switzerland	0.81	2.31	2.07	1.20	2.22	3.78	3.58	6.47	1.36	2.69
United Kingdom	10.75	8.90	3.95	1.07	4.68	5.17	10.32	9.94	5.64	4.77
United States	7.16	6.36	3.68	2.06	3.45	3.83	8.08	5.63	4.63	1.80

labour market institutions and macroeconomic policy to higher unemployment. This section describes the data, the empirical model, and the empirical findings.

Data

Data for the labour market institutional variables came from Stephen Nickell, who describes them fully in his widely cited study on the impact of labour market rigidities on unemployment (Nickell, 1997). Data for the macroeconomic variables came from the annex tables in the OECD's *Economic Outlook* (1999), from the World Bank's statistical CD-ROM, and from the International Monetary Fund's (IMF's) *International Financial Statistics* CD-ROM.[2] Further details regarding the data appear in the appendix.

The statistical analysis covers the twelve-year period from 1983 to 1994. It measures the macroeconomic variables with annual time-series data, with one observation per year for each variable for each country. In contrast, the labour market institution variables correspond to longer-lasting, fixed effects. Therefore for each type of institution the author constructed six-year average measures for each country covering 1983–88 and 1989–94. Thus for each institutional variable in each country there are two observations, for 1983–88 and for 1989–94. The regressions included the following OECD countries: Austria, Belgium, Denmark, Finland, France, Germany, Holland, Ireland, Italy, Norway, Portugal, Spain, Sweden, Switzerland, the United Kingdom, Australia, Canada, Japan, New Zealand, and the United States.

Table 3.1 summarizes the average macroeconomic data for these twenty countries for the two periods; Table 3.2 does the same for the microeconomic labour market indicators. The macroeconomic data reported include the average standardized unemployment rate (percentage), average real GDP growth (percentage per year), the average inflation rate (percentage), the average short-term nominal interest rate (percentage), and the average short-term real interest rate (percentage, defined as the difference between the short-term nominal interest rate and the inflation rate). Data on labour market institutions include the wage-replacement rate of the unemployment insurance system (percentage), the duration of unemployment benefits (years), an index of employment protection (on a scale of 1–20), union density (percentage), the overall tax rate (as a percentage of average labour income), an index of spending on active labour market programs, an index of union wage coverage (on a scale of 1–3), and an index of co-ordination in wage bargaining (on a scale of 2–6). Nickell, 1997, fully describes the rationale for and construction of these measures.

Table 3.2 Labour market institutional data, by country, 1983–94

Country	Unemployment-insurance benefit rate (% of wages)		Unemployment-insurance benefit duration (years)		Employment-protection index (scale 1–20)		Average union density (% non-agric. workers)	
	1983–89	1989–94	1983–89	1989–94	1983–88	1989–94	1983–88	1989–94
Australia	39	36	4	4	4	4	44.7	40.4
Austria	60	50	4	2	16	16	51.2	46.2
Belgium	60	60	4	4	17	17	53.6	51.2
Canada	60	59	5	1	3	3	35.9	35.8
Denmark	90	90	2.5	2.5	5	5	73.7	71.4
Finland	75	63	4	2	10	10	70.9	72.0
France	57	57	3.75	3	14	14	13.8	9.8
Germany	63	63	4	4	15	15	34.3	32.9
Ireland	50	37	4	4	12	12	53.4	49.7
Italy	20	20	0.5	0.5	20	20	44.1	38.8
Japan	60	60	0.5	0.5	8	8	28.3	25.4
Netherlands	70	70	4	2	9	9	30.4	25.5
New Zealand	38	30	4	4	2	2	50.4	44.8
Norway	65	65	1.5	1.5	11	11	56.5	56.0
Portugal	60	65	0.5	0.8	18	18	46.3	31.8
Spain	80	70	3.5	3.5	19	19	18.0	11.0
Sweden	80	80	1.2	1.2	13	13	81.1	82.5
Switzerland	70	70	1	1	6	6	28.6	26.6
United Kingdom	36	38	4	4	7	7	44.8	39.1
United States	50	50	0.5	0.5	1	1	19.0	15.6

Table 3.2 Labour market institutional data, by country, 1983–94 (continued)

Country	Overall labour income tax rate (%)		Active labour market spending (% potential gdp per unemployed worker)		Collective-bargaining wage coverage (scale 1–3)		Collective-bargaining co-ordination (scale 2–6)	
	1983–89	1989–94	1983–89	1989–94	1983–88	1989–94	1983–88	1989–94
Australia	30.8	28.7	4.1	3.2	3	3	3	3
Austria	54.5	53.7	8.7	8.33	3	3	6	6
Belgium	47.6	49.8	10	14.6	3	3	4	4
Canada	37.8	42.7	6.3	5.9	2	2	2	2
Denmark	48.8	46.3	10.6	10.3	3	3	6	6
Finland	59.6	69.5	18.4	16.4	3	3	6	5
France	62.8	63.8	7.2	8.8	3	3	4	4
Germany	52.6	53	12.9	25.7	3	3	5	5
Ireland	59.3	56.5	4	6.9	3	3	4	4
Italy	33.6	34.3	9.2	9.1	3	3	2	2
Japan	57.2	62.9	10.1	10.3	3	3	3	4
Netherlands	33.1	36.3	5.4	4.3	2	2	4	4
New Zealand	35.3	34.8	15.4	6.8	2	2	3	3
Norway	49.9	48.6	9.5	14.7	3	3	6	6
Portugal	33.5	37.6	5.9	18.8	3	3	6	4
Spain	50.1	54.2	3.2	4.7	3	3	4	3
Sweden	68.9	70.7	59.5	59.3	3	3	6	6
Switzerland	40	38.6	23	8.2	2	2	4	4
United Kingdom	44.6	40.8	7.8	6.4	3	2	2	2
United States	42.6	43.8	3.9	3	1	1	2	2

The data display interesting features. First, the U.S. unemployment rate is in the bottom half of the distribution, but many countries experienced even lower rates over the entire period (1983–94). In other words, it was not the only economy with low unemployment, contrary to the implicit assumption of the "labour market flexibility hypothesis" – that U.S.-style labour market structures are necessary for low unemployment. Second, inflation rates were much higher in Europe in the first half of the sample but fell significantly in the second half. Third, average short-term real interest rates have been very much lower in the United States than in the other OECD countries. These two features – disinflation and higher real interest rates in Europe – are indicative of the more difficult macroeconomic conditions in Europe.

The United States clearly has the most laissez-faire labour markets, as indicated by its low wage-replacement rate, benefit duration, level of employment protection, union density, union wage coverage, tax rate, spending on active labour market programs, and level of co-ordination of wage bargaining. Many of these features carry over to the other "Anglo-Saxon" countries (Australia, Canada, New Zealand and the United Kingdom), particularly their relatively low employment protection, tax rates, labour market spending, union wage coverage, and co-ordination of wage bargaining. However, despite deregulated labour markets, unemployment rates there tended to cluster in the top of the distribution.

An Empirical Model

The empirical model incorporates both macroeconomic and institutional variables to analyse differences in unemployment rates across the OECD.[3] Table 3.3 summarizes the factors incorporated into the statistical regressions. The dependent variable is the set of annual unemployment rates for 1983–94 in the twenty countries.

We can break down the explanatory variables into three sets. The microeconomic labour market variables consist of the employment-protection index, the unemployment-insurance replacement rate, the duration of unemployment benefits, union density, union bargaining coverage, the tax rate on labour income, the extent of wage-bargaining co-ordination, and the extent of active labour market programming. The effects of macroeconomic policy and conditions are captured by the change in the inflation rate (with reduced inflation corresponding to tighter monetary policy), the level of real interest rates (with high real rates corresponding to tight policy), and the rate of real GDP growth. Two variables that measure foreign trade flows in the economies of Europe and Canada also appear in the set of macroeconomic variables and capture the cross-country Keynesian multiplier effects in international trade. Within the

Table 3.3   Variables included in the empirical model

Symbol	Definition

DEPENDENT VARIABLE

$UNEMP_{j,t}$ — Standardized unemployment rate in country j in year t

LAGGED DEPENDENT VARIABLE

$UNEMP_{j,t-1,\,t-2}$ — Standardized unemployment rate in country j (lagged one and two periods)

MICROECONOMIC LABOUR MARKET EXPLANATORY VARIABLES

$EMPROT_{j,t}$ — Index of employment protection (1–20) in country j

$REPRATE_{j,t}$ — Unemployment-insurance wage-replacement rate (%) in country j

$BENDUR_{j,t}$ — Benefit duration (years) in country j

$UNIONDEN_{j,t}$ — Union density (%) in country j

$UNIONCOV_{j,t}$ — Extent that union wage coverage extends to non-union workers (1 = less than 25 percent, 2 = 25–70 percent, 3 = greater than 70 percent) in country j

$COORD_{j,t}$ — Extent of co-ordination (index = 2–6) of wage bargaining among unions and employers in country j

$TAXRATE_{j,t}$ — Total tax rate (sum of average payroll, income, and consumption tax rates) in country j

$ALMPROG_{j,t}$ — Measure of active labour market policy (spending per unemployed worker as a percentage of the potential output per worker) in country j

MACROECONOMIC EXPLANATORY VARIABLES

$DINFLATE_{j,t}$ — Change in the CPI inflation rate (%) in country j in year t

$REALINT_{j,t-1}$ — Real interest rate (%) in country j in year t-1 (lagged one period)

$GDPGROW_{j,t}$ — Rate of real GDP growth (%) in country j in year t

$GDPGROW_{j,t-1}$ — Rate of real GDP growth (%) in country j in year t-1 (lagged one period)

$EUROPEN_{j,t}$ — Measure of exposure of individual European countries to intra-European trade in year t (0 for non-European countries)

$CANUS_{j,t}$ — Measure of exposure of the Canadian economy to trade with the United States in year t (0 for all countries except Canada)

COUNTRY-SPECIFIC DUMMY VARIABLES

IREDUM — Dummy variable capturing effects specific to unemployment in Ireland

SPADUM — Dummy variable capturing effects specific to unemployment in Spain

---

European economy, these cross-country spill-over effects are critical because of tight economic integration. Just as developments in the U.S. economy help explain unemployment, for example, in Texas, so European events affect employment in, for example, France. This same approach also applies to Canada, which is highly dependent on foreign trade with the U.S. economy. These cross-country effects are noticeably absent from other studies of higher European unemployment (Blanchard and Wolfers, 1999; Nickell, 1997). Country-specific dummy variables for Ireland and Spain capture unique fixed effects in these two countries, quasi-developing, peripheral economies that experienced much higher unemployment.[4]

The empirical model also includes two lags of the unemployment rate itself as an explanatory variable, reflecting gradual adjustment in labour markets, as workers relocate and firms create new jobs. As a result, unemployment shocks exhibit considerable persistence in all economies. The appendix describes the construction of all the variables.

Empirical Findings

Table 3.4 reports several regression estimates of the empirical model, using a two-stage least-squares process, for the sample period 1983–94.[5] Column 2 reports a benchmark regression equation that contains just the lagged dependent variable itself (two lags of a country's unemployment rate). This model assumes absolutely no differences between countries and omits both micro institutions and macro policy and performance factors. None the less it has considerable explanatory power as measured by the adjusted R^2 – the model's goodness of fit with the data. Persistence of unemployment rates is common to all economies and should appear in all models of unemployment.

Column 3 expands the benchmark equation to include labour market institution variables. The coefficients of the unemployment-benefit replacement rate and the overall tax rate are both statistically significant at the 5 per cent level, and both variables raise unemployment. The extent of wage-bargaining co-ordination is significant at the 1 per cent level, but it results in lower unemployment. Employment protection and union coverage are both significant, but only at the 10 per cent level, and both raise unemployment. Unemployment-benefit duration, union density, and active labour market programs are all insignificant at the 10 per cent level.

Column 4 reports on the same regression after expansion of the model to include country-specific effects for Ireland and Spain – statistically significant and positive at the 1 per cent level – which transforms the significance of other explanatory variables. Now, both the employment-protection index and the replacement rate become statistically insignificant at the 10 per cent level, but union density and spending on active labour market programs now both become statistically significant at the 1 per cent level – indicating coefficient instability among the microeconomic, labour market institution variables.

Table 3.4 Time-series unemployment-rate regressions, pooled annual data, 20 OECD Countries, 1983–94

1	2	3	4	5	6	7	8	9
CONSTANT	0.359‡	-0.378	-0.049	0.695†	0.383	0.434	1.190‡	0.795‡
	(2.91)	(-0.95)	(-0.13)	(2.21)	(1.13)	(1.30)	(8.17)	(5.84)
UNEMP(-1)	1.522‡	1.475‡	1.392‡	1.273‡	1.237‡	1.142‡	1.204‡	1.287‡
	(28.49)	(27.99)	(27.11)	(23.26)	(22.01)	(20.76)	(21.82)	(22.72)
UNEMP(-2)	-0.564‡	-0.617‡	-0.644‡	-0.348‡	-0.313‡	-0.296‡	-0.271‡	-0.293‡
	(-10.29)	(-11.17)	(-12.39)	(-5.96)	(-5.30)	(-5.27)	(-4.88)	(-4.97)
EMPROT		0.034*	0.005	0.023‡	0.029*	0.007		
		(1.84)	(0.27)	(1.55)	(1.96)	(0.49)		
REPRATE		0.013†	0.005	0.007‡	0.013‡	0.007		
		(2.40)	(0.94)	(1.78)	(2.69)	(0.20)		
BENDUR		0.029	0.026	-4.610-5	0.016	0.007		
		(0.58)	(0.55)	(-0.01)	(0.42)	(1.47)		
UNIONDEN		0.008	0.016‡	-0.002	0.003	0.007		
		(1.37)	(2.84)	(-0.51)	(0.56)	(1.47)		
UNIONCOV		0.385*	0.556‡	0.381†	0.415‡	0.540‡		
		(1.86)	(2.81)	(2.46)	(2.69)	(3.64)		
COORD		-0.463‡	-0.520‡	-0.243‡	-0.298‡	-0.286‡		
		(-4.11)	(-4.85)	(-2.76)	(-3.24)	(-3.28)		
TAXRATE		0.020†	0.035‡	-0.005*	-0.003	0.012*		
		(2.57)	(4.42)	(-0.83)	(-0.40)	(-1.93)		
ALMPROG		-0.014	-0.029‡	-0.002	-0.006	-0.019‡		
		(-1.56)	(-3.23)	(-0.230)	(-0.81)	(-2.73)		
DINFLATE				-0.084‡	-0.077‡	-0.064‡	-0.080‡	-0.086‡
				(-3.54)	(-3.27)	(-2.86)	(-3.51)	(-3.58)
REALINT(-1)				0.070‡	0.061‡	0.046‡	0.046‡	0.040†
				(3.85)	(3.39)	(2.70)	(2.97)	(2.41)
GDPGROW				-0.263‡	-0.245‡	-0.225‡	-0.257‡	-0.274‡
				(-10.23)	(-9.30)	(-9.01)	(-10.65)	(-10.78)
GDPGROW(-1)				-0.055*	-0.067‡	-0.103‡	-0.079†	-0.040
				(-1.68)	(-2.08)	(-3.31)	(-2.48)	(-1.21)
EUROPEN					-0.227‡	-0.269‡	-0.167‡	-0.135†
					(-2.62)	(-2.97)	(-2.51)	(-2.00)
CANUS					-0.318	-0.031	-0.057	-0.288
					(-1.49)	(-0.15)	(-0.29)	(-1.44)
IREDUM			1.028‡			1.332‡	1.196‡	
			(3.07)			(4.84)	(4.87)	
SPADUM			2.440‡			1.536‡	1.229‡	
			(5.74)			(4.49)	(4.56)	
Adj. R^2	0.956	0.959	0.964	0.977	0.978	0.981	0.979	0.976
S.E.	0.930	0.896	0.840	0.664	0.655	0.615	0.641	0.682
N	240	240	240	239	239	239	239	239

t-statistics in parentheses.

‡ significant at the 1 per cent level.

† significant at the 5 per cent level.

* significant at the 10 per cent level.

Column 5 reports on a regression that starts incorporating macroeconomic variables by including the change in inflation, the lagged real interest rate, and current and lagged rates of real output growth. Inclusion of these variables dramatically improves the quality of the regression estimate, as we can see in a jump in the adjusted R^2 statistic and a decline in the standard error of the regression equation. The change in inflation, the lagged real interest rate, and the real GDP growth rate are all statistically significant at the 1 per cent level, and the lagged GDP growth rate, at the 10 per cent level. All have signs consistent with conventional understandings of the effect of macroeconomic policy on unemployment: disinflation raises unemployment, as do higher real interest rates,[6] while faster growth reduces unemployment.

Inclusion of the labour market institution variables causes major changes. First, the union-density coefficient becomes insignificant – an outcome examined in greater detail below. Second, the statistical significance and the magnitude of the tax coefficient fall considerably. Third, the employment-protection and benefit-replacement rate variables take on significance at the 1 per cent level, indicating further coefficient instability surrounding the institutional variables – another issue further discussed below.

Column 6 further augments the model by including the variables for international trade exposure for Europe and Canada. The former is significant at the 1 per cent level; the latter only at the 14 per cent level. Both are negatively signed, suggesting that unemployment declines when stronger economic growth in trading partners spills over into a stimulus for exports. The large magnitude and clear statistical significance of the European trade-penetration coefficient indicates the interdependence of European economies.[7] The signs of the other macro variables remain constant, and all coefficients are statistically significant at the 1 per cent level. The coefficients of these macroeconomic variables are robust and stable with regard to changed model specification, suggesting their value in explaining unemployment. The coefficients on the microeconomic labour market variables, however, remain unstable and inconsistently significant. Unemployment-benefit duration, union density, the aggregate tax rate, and the scale of active labour market programming are all statistically insignificant in this extended regression. The benefit-replacement rate, union coverage, and bargaining co-ordination are statistically significant at the 1 per cent level (the last still with a negative sign, indicating that increased co-ordination reduces unemployment), while the index of employment protection is significant at the 6 per cent level.

Column 7 reports the findings for the full model, which includes all labour market institution variables, all macroeconomic variables, and Ireland and Spain's fixed-effect variables. The coefficients of all the macroeconomic variables remain same-signed, and all except the Canadian openness variable are statistically significant at the 1 per cent level. The Ireland and Spain fixed effects are also both positive and statistically significant at the 1 per cent level. However, most of the labour market institution variables now become statistically insignificant. This holds for the employment-protection index, the wage-replacement rate, benefit duration, and union density. The fully specified model therefore suggests that none of these variables explains unemployment. Spending on active labour market programs is statistically significant at the 1 per cent level, and it reduces unemployment. The overall tax rate is also significant (at only the 10 per cent level), with higher taxes contributing to higher unemployment.

This fully specified model illustrates several features of comparative labour market performance in the OECD countries. First, both union wage coverage and the extent of co-ordination in wage bargaining are significant at the 1 per cent level – and both variables are statistically significant in most of the less complete regressions. These variables have opposite signs – the former, positive, and the latter, negative. The union-coverage index variable takes values ranging from 1 to 3; the bargaining-co-ordination variable, from 2 to 6. The two collective-bargaining variables are strongly positively correlated, with a simple correlation coefficient of 0.49. The two variables therefore co-move strongly and systematically and describe a "system of industrial relations." Co-ordination in wage bargaining lowers unemployment, while union wage coverage raises it. Appropriate pairing of these two features leads to no negative combined impact on unemployment.[8] Problems emerge only with extensive union wage coverage unaccompanied by wage-bargaining co-ordination. This finding is consistent with the work of Calmfors and Driffill (1988).[9]

Second, inclusion of the country-dummy variables for Ireland and Spain renders the employment-protection and wage replacement–rate variables statistically insignificant. The data for Spain in Tables 3.1 and 3.2 indicate extremely high unemployment rates, an extremely high level of employment protection, and a very high replacement rate. The statistical significance of these two institutional variables therefore appears to depend entirely on the Spanish experience; this apparent relationship, in other words, depends on a single outlier data point. When we include only the Spain-dummy variable, both unemployment-benefit coefficients become insignificant. This finding holds for both the full model (compare columns 6 and 7) and the restricted model, which includes only the labour market institution variables (compare columns 3 and 4). Thus existing employment protection and wage replacement rates have not contributed to European unemployment, except perhaps in Spain.

Finally, columns 8 and 9 report estimates of the restricted model including only the macroeconomic variables. These regressions sustain the explanatory power of macroeconomic factors, whose coefficients remain highly statistically significant – same-signed, with little change in magnitude. At the same time, the restricted regressions with just macroeconomic variables perform very well in terms of adjusted R^2 and standard error of the regression, being only marginally inferior to the full model, including the labour market institutional variables.

Further Interpretation of the Results

In summary, the regressions reported in Table 3.4 demonstrate the dominant role of macroeconomic factors in cross-national differences in unemployment. This conclusion is robust to empirical specification. Based on the statistical model reported in column 7 (the most completely specified model), permanently lowering the inflation rate by 1 percentage point increases unemployment by 0.4 percentage points. A rise in real interest rates of 1 percentage point increases unemployment by 0.3 percentage points. Lowering the rate of real output growth by 1 percentage point increases unemployment by 2.1 percentage points.[10] For a European country that exports 20 per cent of its GDP, an increase of 1 percentage point in the growth rate of other European economies reduces that country's unemployment rate by 0.35 points.

There is another way of interpreting the implications of these macroeconomic policy variables. The fully specified regression indicates that an increase of 100 basis points in the real interest rate boosts unemployment by 0.4 percentage points. During the second period of our data sample (1989–94), the U.S. real interest rate averaged just 1.8 per cent; the Canadian, 4.7 per cent, which (according to this regression) raised unemployment relative to the U.S. figure by 1.2 points. In Germany, meanwhile, the real interest rate averaged 4.03 per cent, increasing unemployment there relative to U.S. by 0.9 percentage points. In France, it averaged 6.12 per cent, raising unemployment there by 1.7 percentage points vis-à-vis the U.S. figure. Finally, in the Nordic countries (Denmark, Finland, Norway, and Sweden), the real interest rate averaged 5.87 per cent, increasing unemployment there relative to the U.S. rate by 1.6 percentage points.

For the labour market institution variables, the regressions provide no evidence that weakening employment protection, replacement rates, or benefit duration reduces unemployment. Nor will lowering union density. Cutting taxes, however, would seem to imply less unemployment, but only modestly so. A reduction of 10 percentage points in average labour-income tax rates (which in most countries would require reducing taxes by about one fifth) lowers unemployment by only 0.8 points. Increasing spending on active labour market policies generates a much bigger "bang for the buck". Increasing active labour market spending per unemployed worker by an amount equal to 10 per cent of potential output per worker lowers the unemployment rate by 1.2 percentage points. Spending on job-training and placement programs for the unemployed would therefore seem more cost-effective than tax cuts in fighting unemployment.

Finally, if properly paired, the co-ordination of wage bargaining in conditions of widespread union wage coverage can actually lower unemployment. The maximum implementation of both of these institutions (UNIONCOV = 3, COORD = 6) would reduce unemployment by 0.6 percentage points. Of course if there is widespread union wage coverage without co-ordinated wage bargaining, then unemployment rates will tend to rise.

QUANTIFYING THE CAUSES OF CHANGED UNEMPLOYMENT RATES

The previous section reported several estimates of structural equations determining the causes of unemployment. This section uses these estimates to identify the causes of changes in national unemployment rates between 1983 and 1994. For this purpose, we apply the equation reported in column 7 of Table 3.4 – the one that includes the full set of labour market, macroeconomic, and country-specific dummy variables. According to this equation, one can calculate the contribution of microeconomic institutional factors to unemployment in any time period by summing, across all the microeconomic variables, the product of the value of each with its estimated coefficient.[11] The change in unemployment rates between two periods attributable to changes in labour market institutional factors is then the change in the composite value between the two periods.

Table 3.5 decomposes the actual change in national unemployment rates between 1983 and 1994 into those parts attributable to micro and macro factors. Columns 2 and 3 detail the unemployment rates in 1983 and 1994, respectively, and column 4, the change in rates during that period. Column 5 then reports that portion of the change in unemployment attributable, given our regression results, to changed microeconomic institutional settings. Finally, column 6 details the change in unemployment rates attributable, as a residual, to macroeconomic factors.[12]

Table 3.5 highlights several important findings. First, the effect of the microeconomic variables on unemployment is negative in thirteen of twenty countries, indicating structural policies that have tended to make labour markets more flexible (not less). Second, the impact of macroeconomic factors increased unemployment in fifteen countries, indicating the prevalence of negative macroeconomic outcomes. Third, in Europe's three biggest economies (France, Germany, Italy) these negative macro-shocks

Table 3.5   Decomposition of the causes of changing unemployment rates, 1983–94

1	2	3	4	5	6
	Unemployment rate, 1983 (%)	Unemployment rate, 1994 (%)	Change in unemployment rate, 1983–94 (% points)	Change ascribed to change in micro variables (% points)	Change ascribed to change in macro variables (% points)
Austria	3.8	3.8	0.0	–0.79	0.79
Belgium	11.1	10.0	–1.1	–0.51	–0.59
Denmark	10.3	8.2	–2.1	–0.26	–1.84
Finland	6.1	16.8	10.7	2.29	13.17
France	8.1	12.3	4.2	–0.34	4.54
Germany	6.9	8.4	1.5	–1.61	3.11
Holland	9.7	7.1	–2.6	–0.89	–1.71
Ireland	14.0	14.3	0.3	–0.69	0.99
Italy	7.7	11.4	3.7	–1.68	5.38
Norway	3.5	5.5	2.0	–0.77	2.77
Portugal	7.8	7.0	-0.8	–1.69	0.89
Spain	17.5	24.1	6.6	–0.64	7.24
Sweden	3.7	9.4	5.7	0.23	5.47
Switzerland	0.9	3.8	2.9	1.63	1.27
United Kingdom	11.1	9.6	–1.5	–3.80	2.3
Australia	10.0	9.7	–0.3	–0.38	0.80
Canada	11.9	10.4	–1.5	0.20	–1.70
Japan	2.7	2.9	0.2	0.25	0.05
New Zealand	5.8	8.1	2.3	0.40	1.90
United States	9.6	6.1	–3.5	0.05	–3.45

were large. In all three, microeconomic change should have reduced unemployment, but instead large macroeconomic shocks raised unemployment. Fourth, the U.S. unemployment rate fell by 3.5 percentage points (the biggest decline of any jurisdiction in the table), but entirely because of favourable macroeconomic conditions. American labour market structures did not affect the change in unemployment. Fifth, in Finland, Sweden, and Spain, unemployment rose sharply, almost entirely because of extremely unfavourable macroeconomic forces. Sixth, in Belgium, Denmark, and Holland, unemployment fell, with favourable macroeconomic developments explaining most of the decline in each case.

In sum, in the United States almost all the decline in unemployment is attributable to positive macro-forces; in Europe, most is attributable to negative macro-forces. In those few nations in Europe where unemployment fell, macro-forces were again primarily responsible. The policy implication is clear. Rather than transforming labour market institutions and arrangements, European governments should correct the dysfunctions in macroeconomic policy of the last two decades. The continuation of these dysfunctions is clear, given the starkly different policy responses of the U.S. Federal Reserve and the ECB to the economic slowdown of 2001.

THE POLITICAL ECONOMY OF MONETARY POLICY: HAVE CENTRAL BANKERS WAGED WAR ON UNIONS?

Both Nickell, 1997, and Scarpetta, 1995, report that union density has a statistically significant positive impact on unemployment rates. This stance contrasts sharply with the findings reported here, and this difference is worth exploring.

One clue comes from a comparison of the regressions reported in columns 4 and 5 of Table 3.4, in which the inclusion of macroeconomic variables appears to undo the negative impact of union density on unemployment. In the regressions reported by Nickell (1997), the only macroeconomic variable included was the change in inflation rates. This suggests that the effect may be related to the inclusion of real interest rates in the present regressions.

As a test of this hypothesis, regressions were performed on union density of the average measure of a country's real interest rates. The author performed two pooled least-squares regressions, one of which used a dummy variable to differentiate the two periods, and one of which did not.[13] In both regressions, union density has a positive and statistically significant influence (at the 5 per cent level) on real interest rates. According to these regressions, an absolute increase of 10 percentage points in union density raises real interest rates by roughly 0.3 percentage points.

A simple pooled time-series regression tested the robustness of this union–interest rate hypothesis, with the annual real interest rate in each country regressed on the lagged real interest rate and on the average union density in the period 1983–94.[14] Once again, the union-density coefficient is positive and statistically significant at the 5 per cent level. In this case, a 10-point increase in union density raises real interest rates by 0.35 percentage points, almost exactly matching the results from the earlier regression.

Prima facie, this statistical link suggests that central bankers may have been more aggressive in raising interest rates in economies with high union density. However, it is possible that union density causes inflation and that central banks were really aiming to reduce inflation. To test this hypothesis, the author regressed a country's average inflation rates (as reported in Table 3.1) on its union density, for all twenty jurisdictions in the two periods. Once again, one regression included a dummy variable to distinguish between the two periods, and one did not.[15] Both regressions indicate no statistical relation between inflation and union density. A simple auto-regressive pooled time-series model of country inflation rates (exactly similar to the time-series regression of interest rates on union density above) further verifies this conclusion.[16] In this case, too, union density has no explanatory power regarding inflation. In summary, these results suggest that while union density does not cause inflation, it does seem to be positively associated with higher interest rates. This finding challenges the standard argument that real interest rates are higher in countries with higher union density because unions cause inflation. Instead, it appears that central banks systematically raised interest rates in countries with high union density. This conclusion is fully consistent with the political-economy argument that monetary policy is an instrument of class conflict and that monetary authorities have largely been captured by interests antagonistic to unions (Palley, 1997).

TOWARDS FAIR AND FULL EMPLOYMENT FOR ALL

The conventional wisdom is that rigid and inflexible labour markets cause high European unemployment. These rigidities include excessive employment protection, too-generous replacement rates, too-long benefit durations, and high rates of unionization. The empirical results reported in this chapter challenge this received idea.

These results emerge from empirical investigations of unemployment that consider both microeconomic labour market institution variables and macroeconomic variables. The evidence is clear that macroeconomic factors matter for unemployment, and this evidence is robust to changes in the empirical specification of the empirical model. However, for microeconomic factors, the evidence is much more problematic. The level of wage-bargaining co-ordination and the extent of union coverage matter consistently, but they need not raise unemployment if they are appropriately paired. The level of unemployment-benefit duration and the level of union density are both consistently insignificant. The significance of other microeconomic variables (employment protection, replacement rate, tax burden) is unstable and not robust to changes in specification. Moreover, none of these variables is significant in a fully specified model that takes account of country-specific fixed effects related to Ireland and Spain.

Hence high unemployment in western Europe appears to be the result of self-inflicted macroeconomic policy. Policy-makers adopted a course of disinflation, high real interest rates, and slower growth that raised unemployment. Moreover, since all adopted this course at the same time, they generated a wave of trade-based cross-country multipliers, which further raised unemployment and contributed to continent-wide macroeconomic weakness.

Figure 3.1   The policy menu

Macroeconomic policy	Labour market policy	
	Regulated	*Flexible*
Expansionary	Progressive consensus	United States
Contractionary	Europe	Laissez-faire consensus

The policy implications are clear. Lowering unemployment will require a period of sustained expansionary macroeconomic policy, pursued ideally by all countries. Implementing more flexible labour market institutions will not lower unemployment, as these institutions are not the cause of unemployment. Indeed, if labour market deregulation involves simply reducing the extent of wage-bargaining co-ordination, it could actually raise unemployment. We can summarize these policy conclusions in a two-dimensional macroeconomic–microeconomic policy framework (Palley, 1998), illustrated in Figure 3.1.[17] In this framework, macroeconomic factors cause unemployment. Microeconomic labour market institutions protect workers by giving them voice and bargaining power, which in turn affects distributional outcomes. Weakening these institutions therefore polarizes income distribution but has little effect on unemployment. U.S. macroeconomic policy has been expansionary, but U.S. labour market institutions protecting workers have eroded; the result has been low unemployment and increased income inequality. In Europe, macroeconomic policy has been contractionary, but labour market institutions protecting workers remain largely intact; unemployment has been high but income inequality relatively unchanged.

Restoring the economic prosperity of the post–Second World War era will require expansionary macroeconomic policy combined with labour market institutions that protect workers' voice and bargaining power. Unfortunately, however, the laissez-faire "Washington consensus" that currently dominates policy-making, in both the developed and the developing worlds, recommends exactly the opposite.

APPENDIX

This appendix details the sources and construction of the data used in the regressions reported in Tables 3.4 and 3.5 and in the body of the text. All data for the labour market institution variables came from Nickell, as described in Nickell, 1997. The macroeconomic data came from the *OECD Economic Outlook* (OECD, 1998), the World Bank CD-ROM (World Bank,

2000), and the *IMF International Financial Statistics* CD-ROM (International Monetary Fund, 2000). The series on real GDP growth came from the World Bank series of that name on the CD-ROM, updated from the World Bank's homepage. These series match the figures on real GDP growth reported in the June 1999 *OECD Economic Outlook*, Annex Table 1. Short-term interest rates are from the IMF CD, series 60B, money-market rates. For Ireland, the author used series 60C, Treasury Bills, because money-market series were unavailable. Missing values for New Zealand 1978–82 and Australia 1996–98 were filled in using 60C values. The measures of inflation are the percentage change in consumer prices drawn from the OECD database's purchasing-power-parity figures for private consumption, updated to match the OECD's published 1999 figures. The change in inflation is then computed as the first difference of the annual inflation rates. The real short-term interest rate equals the difference between the short-term nominal interest rate and the CPI inflation rate.

Standardized unemployment rates came from the Statwise database where available and completed manually from the *OECD Economic Outlook* (OECD, 1998), Annex Table 22, with which these figures accord. To extend the series to include values back to 1977, the June 1999 *OECD Economic Outlook* numbers were supplemented by values from the *OECD Economic Outlook* (OECD, June 1994). However, these two series are not always identical because of adjustments made by the OECD. For the sake of compatibility, the 1994 figures were adjusted hard copy from the OECD. The series were adjusted for compatibility according to the following: 1979 Adjusted std.unemp = 1979 std.unemp per OECD June 1994 * (1980 std.unemp per OECD June 1999/1980 std.unemp per OECD June 1994).

Thus earlier measures of the standardized unemployment rate were converted to the new basis by multiplying the old series by an adjustment factor. This adjustment factor was computed as the ratio of the first year of the new series to the old measure of standard unemployment in that year. The first year of the series in Annex Table 22 is 1980. A similar scaling method was used to create standard unemployment-rate values for countries for which they were unavailable. In these instances, values for the commonly used definition of unemployment rates (Annex Table 21) were adjusted according to: Adj. Std.unemp(t) = common unemp(t) * [std.unemp(t+1)/Common unemp(t+1)], where the adjustment factor covered the earliest year for which the standard unemployment series was available. The countries to which this approach was applied are Austria, Denmark, Ireland, and Portugal; New Zealand had a scalar of 1.

The cross-country Keynesian-multiplier openness variable captures the effect of growth in the rest of the European economy on each European country. Canada is especially exposed to growth in the U.S., and a similar variable was therefore also constructed for the Canadian economy. The European country openness variable is defined as:

$$\text{EUROPEN}_{j,t} = \text{SX}_{j,t} \left[\; [\text{EMP}_{i,t} / \text{TOTEMP}_{-j,t}] \; \text{GY}_{i,t} \; \right]$$
$$i = 1$$
$$i = j$$

where sx_j = export share of GDP for country j, EMP_i = employment in country i ($i = j$), TOTEMP_i = total employment in all European countries excluding country j, and GY_i = growth of real output in country i ($i = j$). The logic of this openness variable is as follows. The sx_j component measures the export openness of a country, while the rest of the term measures real growth outside the country. This real-growth component is the employment-weighted average of country growth rates. For all non-European countries, EUROPEN takes on a value of zero. The Canadian openness variable follows a similar logic: $\text{CANUS}_t = \text{sx}_{\text{CAN},t} \, \text{GY}_{\text{US},t}$, where $\text{sx}_{\text{CAN},t}$ = Canadian export share of GDP, and $\text{GY}_{\text{US},t}$ = U.S. real GDP growth rate. For all countries other than Canada it is zero.

NOTES

1 Sawyer's chapter in this volume examines the weak theoretical underpinnings of natural-rate theory in more detail.

2 The OECD continually changes its reported measure of standardized unemployment, and as a result the measures used here do not match earlier measures used by Nickell, 1997. The current measures are from the OECD's *Economic Outlook*, Dec. 1999.

3 The model can be described formally with the following equation, where the variable symbols are defined in Table 3.3:

$$\begin{aligned}
\text{UNEMP}_{j,t} = {} & a_0 + a_1\text{UNEMP}_{j,t-1} + a_2\text{UNEMP}_{j,t-2} + a_3\text{EMPROT}_{j,t} + a_4\text{REPRATE}_{j,t} + \\
& a_5\text{BENDUR}_{j,t} + a_6\text{UNIONDEN}_{j,t} + a_7\text{UNIONCOV}_{j,t} + a_8\text{COORD}_{j,t} + a_9\text{TAXRATE}_{j,t} + \\
& a_{10}\text{ALMPROG}_{j,t} + a_{11}\text{DINFLATE}_{j,t} + a_{12}\text{REALINT}_{j,t-1} + a_{13}\text{GDPGROW}_{j,t} + \\
& a_{14}\text{GDPGROW}_{j,t-1} + a_{15}\text{EUROPEN}_{j,t} + a_{16}\text{CANUS}_{j,t} + a_{17}\text{IREDUM} + a_{18}\text{SPADUM} + u_{j,t}
\end{aligned}$$

4 Over the sample period 1983–94, Spain had average standardized unemployment of 19.2 per cent, and Ireland, 15.3 per cent. The next highest was Belgium, with 11.3 per cent.

5 The regression used a two-stage least-squares method because the active labour market programming variable is defined as the percentage of GDP spent on labour market policies, normalized on the unemployment rate (the dependent variable). The instrument used for this two-stage process was

spending as a percentage of GDP normalized on the average unemployment rate in 1977–79 (see Nickell, 1997: 64).

6 The statistical significance of the real interest rate is at odds with results reported by Scarpetta, 1996, which in turn have influenced much OECD policy analysis. This difference stems probably from differences in the measure of real interest rates. Scarpetta used a measure of world real interest rates based on a GDP-weighted average of domestic long-term rates. The current estimate uses the short-run country interest rate, which is appropriate for assessing the effect of a country's macroeconomic policies on its unemployment rate.

7 Though negatively signed, the Canadian openness variable is only weakly significant. This may be because the variable for domestic GDP growth fully captures the effect of U.S. growth on the Canadian economy.

8 Indeed, given the coefficients in column 4 of Table 3.4, a properly constructed system of co-ordinated wage bargaining and extensive union coverage will actually lower unemployment. The coefficient of COORD is -0.298, while that of UNIONCOV is 0.415. However, the average value of the COORD index is twice that of UNIONCOV, and so the positive effect of co-ordination in reducing unemployment outweighs the negative influence of bargaining coverage.

9 Ireland suffers especially from having high coverage and low co-ordination (UNIONCOV = 3, COORD = 2). Britain, Canada, and New Zealand also suffer, albeit less so (UNIONCOV = 2, COORD = 2).

10 This latter finding implies an Okun coefficient equal to one-half. This is fully in accordance with existing estimates of the Okun coefficient (Palley, 1993), lending additional support to the results presented.

11 More formally, the collective importance of the microeconomic variables can be calculated as:

$$\text{MICRO}_{j,t} = [0.007\text{EMPPROT}_{j,t} + 0.007\text{REPRATE}_{j,t} + 0.007\text{BENDUR}_{j,t} + 0.007\text{UNIONDEN}_{j,t} + 0.541\text{UNIONCOV}_{j,t} - 0.286\text{COORD}_{j,t} + 0.012\text{TAXRATE}_{j,t} - 0.019\text{ALMPROG}]/0.154$$

The change in unemployment due to changes in the microeconomic variables is the differnce in this composite sum between the two periods.

12 This macroeconomic component is computed as: DMACRO = DUNEMP – DMICRO.

13 The regression results are as follows (the second equation includes a time dummy to capture changes in financial-market conditions across the periods 1983–88 and 1989–94):

$$\text{REALINT}_j = 3.505 + 0.032\ \text{UNIONDEN}_j$$
$$\quad\quad\quad (5.33)\quad (2.27)$$
$$\text{Adj.R}^2 = 0.096\quad N = 40$$

$$\text{REALINT}_j = 2.943 + 0.035 \text{ UNIONDEN}_j + 0.923 \text{ TIMEDUMMY}$$
$$(4.12) \quad (2.49) \qquad\qquad (1.77)$$
Adj.R^2 = 0.145   N=40

Figures in parentheses are t-statistics.

14 The resulting regression was:

$$\text{REALINT}_{j,t} = 1.822 + 0.483\text{REALINT}_{j,t-1} + 0.018 \text{ UNIONDEN}_j$$
$$(4.82) \quad (10.11) \qquad\qquad (2.36)$$
Adj.R^2 = 0.333   N = 238

Figures in parentheses are t-statistics.

15 The two regression results are as follows (the second equation includes a dummy variable to control for differences between the two time periods):

$$\text{INFLATION}_j = 3.845 + 0.023 \text{ UNIONDEN}_j$$
$$(3.25) \quad (0.89)$$
Adj.R^2 = −0.005 N = 40

$$\text{INFLATION}_j = 4.839 + 0.019 \text{ UNIONDEN}_j - 1.633\text{TIMEDUMMY}$$
$$(3.76) \quad (0.74) \qquad\qquad (-1.74)$$
Adj.R^2 = 0.045   N = 40

Figures in parentheses are t-statistics.

16 The resulting regression (with t-statistics in parenthesis) was:

$$\text{INFLATION}_{j,t} = 0.514 + 0.776 \text{ INFLATION}_{j,t-1} + 0.001 \text{ UNIONDEN}_j$$
$$(1.59) \quad (26.69) \qquad\qquad (0.14)$$
Adj.R^2 = −0.005   N = 240

17 Stanford (2000), uses a similar framework to compare economic policy in Canada with that in other countries.

REFERENCES

Baker, Dean, and John Schmitt. 1998. *The Macroeconomic Roots of High European Unemployment: The Impact of Foreign Growth.* Washington, DC: Economic Policy Institute.

Bernstein, Jared, and Lawrence Mishel. 1995. "A Comparison of Income, Wages and Employment Trends of the Advanced Industrial Economies," in Lawrence Mishel and John Schmitt, eds., *Beware the U.S. Model: Jobs and Wages in a Deregulated Economy.* Washington, DC: Economic Policy Institute.

Bentolila, Samuel, and Giuseppe Bertola. 1990. "Firing Costs and Labour Demand: How Bad Is Eurosclerosis?" *Review of Economic Studies* 57 (3), 381–402.

Blanchard, Olivier, and Justin Wolfers. 1999. "The Role of Shocks and Institutions in the Rise of European Unemployment: The Aggregate Evidence." NBER Working Paper 7282. Cambridge, Mass.: National Bureau of Economic Research.

Calmfors, Lars, and John Driffill. 1988. "Bargaining Structure, Corporatism, and Macroeconomic Performance," *Economic Policy* 6, 14–61.

International Monetary Fund (IMF). 2000. *International Financial Statistics CD-ROM.* Washington, DC: International Monetary Fund.

Mishel, Lawrence, Jared Bernstein, and John Schmitt. 2000. *The State of Working America, 2000/2001.* Ithaca, NY: Cornell University Press.

Nickell, Stephen. 1997. "Unemployment and Labour Market Rigidities: Europe versus North America," *Journal of Economic Perspectives* 11 (3), 55–74.

Organization for Economic Cooperation and Development (OECD). 1994. *The OECD Jobs Study.* Paris: OECD.

– 1998. *OECD Economic Outlook.* Paris: OECD.

Palley, Thomas I. 1993. "Okun's Law and the Asymmetric and Changing Nature of the U.S. Business Cycle," *International Review of Applied Economics* 7 (2), 144–62.

– 1997. "The Institutionalization of Deflationary Policy Bias," in Harold Hagerman and A. Cohen, eds., *Advances in Monetary Theory.* Dordrecht, Netherlands: Kluwer Academic Publishers.

– 1998. "Restoring Prosperity: Why the U.S. Model Is Not the Answer for the U.S. or Europe," *Journal of Post Keynesian Economics* 20 (3), 337–54.

– 1999. "The Myth of Labour Market Flexibility and the Costs of Bad Macroeconomic Policy: U.S. and European Unemployment Explained," in S. Lang, M. Meyer, and C. Scherrer, eds., *Jobwunder U.S.A. – Modell fur Deutschland.* Munster: Westfalisches Dampfboot.

Scarpetta, Stefano. 1996. "Assessing the Role of Labour Market Policies and Institutional Settings on Unemployment: A Cross-country Study," *OECD Economic Studies* 26, 43–98.

Solow, Robert. 1994. "Europe's Unnecessary Unemployment," *International Economic Insights* 5 (2).

Stanford, Jim. 2000. "Canadian Labour Market Developments in International Context: Flexibility, Regulation, and Demand," *Canadian Public Policy* 26 (supp.), 27–58.

World Bank. 2000. *World Development Indicators CD-ROM.* Washington, DC: World Bank.

4

Institutions and Policies for Labour Market Success in Four Small European Countries

PETER AUER

This chapter discusses the labour market success of four smaller European countries in the late 1990s. It first describes the dimensions of this relative success in terms of their labour market and macroeconomic performance and then outlines the main factors that help to explain this good performance.

During the last 20 years the conventional wisdom has held that the European labour market is sclerotic, in stark contrast to its dynamic U.S. counterpart. The United States experienced higher growth in employment and markedly lower unemployment than Europe. Despite growth rates in gross domestic product (GDP) that have been comparable with U.S. rates over the long term (and at times even higher), economic growth contributed only marginally to an expansion of employment in Europe. Unemployment also continued to rise in the European Union (EU), reaching an average of 11 per cent of the labour force by the mid-1990s. Only recently has European unemployment started to fall below the 10-per cent threshold.

The causes of the U.S. labour market's apparent success were widely identified with its overall free-market approach, flexible wages (resulting in high income differentiation), and low employment protection (resulting in flexibly adjusting employment levels). The prescription of leading economists was to apply the same ingredients to Europe. Deregulation and privatization were to reflect an overall retreat by governments and their social partners from intervention in labour markets. An entrepreneurial spirit, relieved from rules and regulations, and wage determination left to market forces would further improve the economy and the labour market.

Core elements of the traditional European model – such as corporatist and often-centralized collective bargaining, high and downwardly rigid wages, ever-expanding social and employment protection, and a strong state role in the economy – seemed the culprits. Unemployment was supposedly structural and voluntary – rational actors would not work if unemployment benefits were overgenerous. In addition, high levels of public economic activity and public-sector employment allegedly displaced private initiatives, especially in the service sector.

While there was opposition in many European countries to adoption of these market-oriented, supply-side policies, observers agree that this general orientation has dominated policy debate. Discussions about fiscal expansion, regulation, extension of public employment and public ownership, and expansion of the social-security network all took a distant back seat. Policy-makers focused instead on supply-side reforms, deregulation, privatization, and the curbing of public-sector employment.

In recent years a number of smaller European countries have experienced notable declines in unemployment, even labour market recovery. This chapter looks at four countries in particular: Austria, Denmark, Ireland, and the Netherlands – at the nature of and qualifications to their success, at the three pillars of their system, and at the variations and potential applicability of their particular variants.

Unemployment there averaged 3.8 per cent in 2001, compared to the U.S. rate of 4.8 per cent. Consequently, this chapter inquires into whether supply-side policies – in essence, an economic "Americanization" of Europe – have aided the four countries' success. Surprisingly, given the pro-market orientation of so much European policy discourse, these countries have not reduced social spending most, curbed government intervention most drastically, or minimized social partnership. Rather, they have retained, while adapting, their institutions, which today enjoy economic success and strong labour market conditions. Thus it is not the flexibility of the market, but the existence and adaptability of institutions and regulations, that explains their success. Contrary to widespread perceptions, these institutions were not too rigid to survive in a rapidly evolving environment.

RELATIVE LABOUR MARKET SUCCESS

While the European Union as a whole still experiences high unemployment, which has only recently fallen below 10 per cent, some smaller members have a much better record. The four smaller countries selected in this study – Austria, Denmark, Ireland, and the Netherlands – were suitable for several reasons. They have all experienced rates of economic and employment growth above the European average and have considerably reduced unemployment. They either have high ratios of employment to

Table 4.1 Key labour market indicators, selected countries, 1994–99

	European Union			Austria			Denmark			Ireland			Netherlands			United States		
	1994	1999	chg%	1994	1999	chg%	1994	1999	chg%	1994	1999	chg%	1994	1999	chg%	1995	1999	chg%
Employment rates [1]	60.1	62.1	3.3	66.6	68.2	2.4	73.5	76.5	4.0	54.5	62.5	14.6	64.3	70.9	10.2	72.5	73.9	1.9
Male	70.6	71.6	1.4	76.5	76.7	0.3	78.8	81.2	3.0	67.8	73.5	8.4	75.2	80.4	6.3	79.5	80.5	1.2
Female	49.7	54.6	9.8	56.8	59.7	5.1	68.0	71.6	5.3	41.2	51.4	24.7	53.2	61.3	13.3	65.8	67.6	2.7
Part-time share [2]	15.6	17.7	13.4	13.9	16.8	20.8	21.2	20.7	-2.3	11.4	16.7	46.5	36.4	39.4	8.2	14.0[7]	13.3[7]	-5.0[7]
Male	4.9	6.1	24.4	4.0	4.4	0.1	10.0	9.6	-4.0	5.1	7.4	45.0	16.1	17.9	11.2	8.4	8.1	-3.6
Female	30.8	33.5	8.7	26.9	32.6	20.4	34.4	33.9	-1.4	21.8	30.6	40.3	66.0	68.6	3.9	20.2	19.0	-6.0
Temporary job share	11.1	13.2	18.9	6.0	7.5	25.0	12.0	10.2	-15.0	9.5	7.7	-18.9	10.9	12.0	13.9	9.8	9.3	-5.0
Male	10.2	12.4	21.5	5.7	7.3	31.5	11.1	9.2	-8.1	8.0	5.9	-26.2	7.9	9.4	18.9	n.a.	n.a.	n.a.
Female	12.4	14.2	14.5	6.3	7.8	23.8	12.9	11.3	-12.4	11.4	9.9	-13.1	15.0	15.4	2.6	n.a.	n.a.	n.a.
Unemployment rate [3]	11.1	9.2	-17.1	4.0	3.7	-7.5	8.2	5.2	-36.6	14.3	5.7	-60.8	7.1	3.3	-53.5	5.6	4.3	-23.0
Male	10.0	7.9	-21.0	3.1	3.1	0.0	7.3	4.5	-38.3	14.2	5.8	-59.1	6.3	2.3	-63.5	5.6	4.1	-27.0
Female	12.7	10.9	-14.1	5.3	4.5	-15.0	9.3	6.0	-35.4	11.4	9.9	-13.1	8.3	4.7	-43.3	5.7	4.4	-23.0
Youth unemployment rate [4]	10.7	8.4	-21.5	3.5	2.9	-17.1	7.8	7.1	-8.9	10.7	4.2	-60.7	6.9	4.8	-30.4	12.0	9.9	-17.5
Male	11.1	8.4	-24.3	3.4	2.3	-32.3	7.7	7.0	-9.0	12.3	4.5	-63.4	7.5	3.3	-49.3	11.6	10.3	-11.2
Female	10.3	8.4	-18.4	3.7	3.5	-5.4	7.8	7.2	-7.6	9.0	3.9	-65.5	6.4	6.4	0.0	10.7	9.5	-11.2
Long-term unemployment rate [5]	5.3	4.3	-18.8	1.1	1.2	9.0	2.6	1.0	-61.5	9.2	5.7[6]	(-38.0)	3.5	1.4	-60.0	0.5	0.4	(-20.0)
Male	4.5	3.5	-22.2	0.8	0.9	12.5	2.3	0.9	-60.8	9.7	6.2[6]	(-36.1)	3.2	1.1	-65.6	0.6	0.5	(-17.0)
Female	6.0	5.0	-16.6	1.6	1.6	0.0	3.0	1.2	-60.0	8.4	4.7[6]	(-44.0)	4.1	1.9	-53.6	0.5	0.4	(-20.0)

Sources: OECD, EU, KILM national sources.

1 Share of employed population 15–64 in total population 15–64.

2 Percentage of total employment (below 35 hours).

3 ILO definition (out of work, available and actively searching for jobs).

4 Unemployed youths as a share of population 15–64.

5 Unemployed for more than a year as percentage of labour force.

6 Rate for 1997.

7 Share of part-time workers in total in total employment (less than 30 hours) comparable part-time shares in 1999:EU 16.4; Austria, 12.3; Denmark, 15.3; Ireland, 18.3; Netherlands, 30.4.

* For comparison, see text.

population or show strongly increasing labour-force participation. Ireland and the Netherlands have had employment growth similar to, or even greater than, that of the United States.

Table 4.1 accounts for key labour market indicators for the four countries, the EU, and the United States. It shows employment rates in these four countries – a benchmark for the success of employment policy – above the European average. Ireland and the Netherlands, which both reported relatively low employment rates in 1994, have seen a rapid increase during the most recent economic expansion. Denmark has the highest employment rate among all European countries and surpasses the United States (for both males and females).

Part-time employment (working less than 35 hours per week) is higher than the EU average in Denmark and the Netherlands but lower in Austria and Ireland (where part-time employment has also been growing rapidly). Part-time work is less common in the United States than in Europe, although the U.S. data reported in Table 4.1 are not strictly comparable (defining part time as less than 30 hours per week, instead of Europe's 35 hours). However, even adjusted for this definitional difference, the U.S. part-time employment rate is still lower than Europe's (except for Austria), and it declined through the 1990s expansion, while European rates (except in Denmark) generally increased.

Temporary jobs are increasing in the EU, but in our four countries they seem not to be the main area of employment growth: their share has actually declined in both Denmark and Ireland. Austria has the lowest incidence of temporary jobs of the four, and all four countries have lower levels of temporary jobs than the EU average. Once again U.S. statistical data are not strictly comparable (the temporary-worker category for the United States comprises contract workers, temp-agency workers, on-call workers, and independent contractors), but temporary employment is clearly below the European average and declining.

Many observers argue that employment growth in both North America and Europe overstates the true improvement in labour market outcomes, because of growing reliance on part-time, temporary, and contingent-work arrangements. The data above, however, indicate that this argument does not apply universally. Employment success has gone hand in hand with the shifting structure of employment – from permanent, full-time jobs to a more heterogeneous pattern (including part-time and temporary work). On the whole, however, labour markets have not (yet) changed dramatically. In fact, permanent full- and part-time jobs are still dominant in Europe, with flexible positions rather marginal (at least in terms of overall employment). Moreover, job tenure has declined, but only slightly, with increases for women at least partially offsetting losses for men (Auer and Cazes, 2000).

The four countries have been especially successful at reducing unemployment. The decline over the last half of the 1990s was particularly strong in Ireland and the Netherlands, where the unemployment rate fell by more than half. The four countries – together with Luxembourg and Portugal – now have the lowest unemployment in Europe.

The four countries also saw a remarkable decline in youth and long-term unemployment. While long-term unemployment is lower in the United States than in most European countries, youth unemployment is higher for both U.S. women and men. All four success stories have reduced youth unemployment below average European and U.S. levels. In the four countries (except Ireland), as well as in the EU as a whole, long-term unemployment is higher for women than for men.

In summary, these four countries have dramatically improved labour market performance – surpassing other EU countries and the United States along several dimensions. Even if unemployment is very low in these countries, however, none has yet reached full employment, especially if we also consider qualitative aspects of employment. The official unemployment rate, based on ILO definitions,[1] does not indicate the full extent of unemployment and underemployment.[2]

Macroeconomic Performance

A summary overview of the evolution of key macroeconomic indicators shows that our four countries have all experienced GDP growth rates above the EU average (see Table 4.2). Their employment growth rates were also higher than the EU average, especially in the Netherlands and Ireland, which have rates similar (Netherlands) or even higher (Ireland) than the United States. Moreover, employment growth and the employment intensity of growth (which one can measure crudely by the relation between GDP growth and employment growth) have also been higher in Ireland and the Netherlands than in the United States. Austria and Denmark compare less favourably with the United States on these criteria.

In crude measures of productivity (output per worker and output per hour), Austria, Denmark, and Ireland have performed in line with EU averages. The Netherlands lags behind, possibly because of its labour-intensive growth, as well as its particular reliance on part-time work.

Consumer price increases in all four countries have fallen below the EU average (and the U.S. average, as well), indicating that their strong labour market performance did not accelerate inflation. Average real-wage increases are in line with, or higher than, EU averages in Austria, Denmark, and Ireland; they have lagged behind in the Netherlands. Real unit-labour costs have decreased in all four countries, though, except for Ireland, by somewhat less than in the EU as a whole.

Table 4.2 Key macroeconomic indicators, selected countries, Annual percent change, 1985–1999

	European Union		Austria		Denmark		Ireland		Netherlands		United States	
	1985-90	1990-99	1985-90	1990-99	1985-90	1990-99	1985-90	1990-99	1985-90	1990-99	1985-90	1990-99
GDP growth	3.2	1.8	3.2	2.0	1.2	2.2	4.6	6.5	3.1	2.7	3.4	3.0
Employment growth	1.4	0.2	0.8	0.4	0.3	0.4	1.1	3.2	2.3	1.7	2.1	1.3
Average hours worked	-0.4	-0.3	-0.4	-0.3	-0.7	0.1	-0.1	-0.9	-0.8	-0.2	-0.2	0.0
GDP per employed	1.7	1.6	2.4	1.5	0.9	1.8	3.5	3.1	0.8	1.0	1.3	1.7
GDP per hour	2.1	1.9	2.8	1.8	1.6	1.7	3.5	4.1	1.7	1.2	1.5	1.7
Consumer prices	4.4	3.0	2.2	2.3	3.9	2.1	3.3	2.2	0.8	2.5	4.1	3.0
Average earnings	6.4	4.1	4.5	3.4	5.1	3.4	5.6	4.7	1.7	3.0	2.9	3.2
Average real earnings	1.9	1.1	2.3	1.0	1.1	1.3	2.2	2.5	0.8	0.4	-0.9	0.5
Average real labour costs	1.4	1.1	2.0	1.1	0.7	1.2	2.3	1.4	0.8	1.0	0.8	1.3
Real unit labour costs	-0.8	-0.7	-0.4	-0.5	-0.2	-0.6	-1.1	-1.8	-0.3	-0.2	0.1	0.0

Sources: *Employment in Europe*, 2000; *Economic Report of the President*, 2000.

This brief macroeconomic review indicates that while the four countries differ in growth and employment terms from the EU average, in most other dimensions they have performed similarly to other countries in Europe. Of course, many particular country differences are visible. Ireland stands out, with exceptionally high economic and employment growth rates, as well as substantial growth in real wages and productivity. The Netherlands also demonstrates high rates of economic and employment growth, but low growth in productivity and real wages. The other two countries have matched EU averages in macroeconomic performance.

These four countries' general macroeconomic performance has been broadly in line with the EU, but they have translated typical macroeconomic performance into extraordinary labour market outcomes. All four demonstrate higher employment-to-population rates than the EU average. More remarkable, they seem to have largely abolished unemployment, without adopting U.S.-style labour market deregulation. Chronic unemployment seemed to be the Achilles' heel of countries with strong institutional labour market regulation, but this has not been the case for these four countries.

The Gender Dimension

Gender gaps clearly exist in the labour markets of all industrialized countries, and our four case studies are no exception. Equality between the sexes is increasing in some, but changing more slowly in others. There are gender gaps in all labour market dimensions, such as employment, unemployment, and inactivity. One good indicator is the full-time equivalent (FTE) employment rate, which takes into account observed differentials in working time between men and women. While the FTE rate (like the employment rate in general) is on the rise for women in all four countries, differences are still signifcant. By this measure, in the year 2000 Denmark demonstrated the greatest equality, albeit still with a difference of 15 percentage points between male and female FTE employment rates, followed by Austria (27 points), Ireland (30 points), and the Netherlands (35 points). The high incidence of part-time work among Dutch women pulls down their FTE employment rate considerably.

Similarly, male and female unemployment rates have evolved differently in the four countries. In Ireland, unemployment was consistently higher for men until the downturn of the early 1990s, which affected women disproportionally. In contrast, unemployment has been consistently higher for women than for men in Austria, Denmark, and Ireland. The recent employment boom has again seen a diverging pattern. In Ireland, unemployment for women is on a par with that for men and has been declining rapidly (from 12 per cent in 1996 to just 4.2 per cent in 2000). In the

Netherlands and Denmark, women's unemployment has also declined more than mens, thus reducing the gender gap. In 2000, observed gender gaps in unemployment rates were about zero in Ireland, 1 percentage point in Denmark and Austria, and less than 2 percentage points in the Netherlands. Gender gaps in unemployment are much higher in the rest of the EU (averaging about 3 per cent), especially in Italy and France. In general, gender gaps seem to be smallest for younger workers, who tend to possess the most tertiary education.

Closing these gender gaps is a major goal of progressive labour market policy. The four countries have moved considerably towards this goal. Continuation of their efforts will require consideration of the characteristics of households. At present, households participate several ways in the labour market. Single-earner households for both women and men are on the increase. The single breadwinner (including the once-dominant male breadwinner) is generally on the decline, but is still notable in Ireland. In addition, there are varieties of dual-earner households – men and women both working full time, as in Denmark and (to a lesser extent) Austria, or men working full time and women part time (as in the Netherlands). Finally there are households with no one in the labour force. In the Dutch experience, where both one- and two-earner households are common and women continue to perform most unpaid child care, gender gaps in part-time work and hence in overall FTE employment patterns have been more resilient.

These societal trends obviously influence the pattern of labour supply. Education is strongly associated with higher labour market participation, and family structures also strongly influence labour supply. The challenge for employment systems is to offer job opportunities (that is, labour demand) to match labour supply. If we accept the notion of a linear development and convergence in societies, then the Danish model – a dual-earner society, with high employment rates and relatively small gender gaps – might seem the model of the future. But different countries, with their traditions and cultures, offer alternatives for family structures that will influence labour market supply, and Europe may retain a heterogeneity of family structures, with differentiated labour-supply behaviour. This will imply a diversity of working-time patterns, and labour demand will need to be very responsive to these heterogeneous patterns of labour supply.

THE THREE PILLARS

Macroeconomic Policy

The remainder of this chapter considers the contributions of macroeconomic policy, labour market policy, and social dialogue to the labour market success of the four countries. Lack of space prevents detailed consideration of some other important policy dimensions that have enhanced the labour market experience of the four countries. For example, provision of child-care facilities and parental leave have contributed to an expansion of women's employment (see Rubery, 2001). Working-time policies have also helped modernize labour markets, where a diversity of patterns respond to changing labour supply (Bosch, 2001).

The positive global macroeconomic environment in the latter 1990s (with generally strong GDP and trade growth through most of the world) helps explain the four countries' labour market success. These countries are among the most open to trade in the world, with export shares of GDP ranging from 40 to 77 per cent. National and supranational (i.e., EU) macroeconomic policies have also been a major factor. The results of these policies would seem to be quite impressive: macroeconomic conditions in Europe in general are much healthier now than in the 1970s and 1980s, with low inflation, low interest rates, moderate wage growth, and consolidated government budgets. The era of double-digit inflation and interest rates and nominal wage increases is clearly over, as are soaring public deficits. For example, in the EU as a whole consumer prices rose at an annual average rate of only 3 per cent in the 1990s, and nominal wages by just over 4 per cent. Real wages rose by just over 1 per cent annually during the 1990s, almost as fast as during the inflationary 1970s and 1980s (and considerably faster than in the United States).

Of course the EU and the United States experienced a decline in inflation, not just our four case studies, which, however, had somewhat lower inflation than the EU and the United States. The conditions set by the EU helped establish a more stable macroeconomic environment – particularly the macroeconomic stability targets established first in the Maastricht agreement and later in the EU's growth and stability pact. Fewer macroeconomic levers remain at the national level; as Schettkat (2001) notes, for many years the German Bundesbank has mainly determined monetary policies for the four countries (all four pegged their currency to the Deutsche Mark either directly or indirectly through the European Monetary System). Later, with the European common currency, monetary policy shifted to the European Central Bank (Denmark is not a member of the European Monetary Union, but it must maintain its currency within narrow bands relative to the euro). Competitive devaluations are thus now virtually impossible. However, wage-moderation policies gave the Netherlands a de facto devaluation relative to its major trading partner (Germany) and clearly helped to spur the Dutch economy (Hartog, 1999). Claims that beggar-thy-neighbour policies underlie the four countries' superior labour market performance seem exaggerated; despite export gains in manufacturing, employment increased, mostly in services (Schettkat, 2001).

National discretion has also shrunk in fiscal policy, but not disappeared. For example, a targeted and short-term tax cut in Denmark in 1993–94 stimulated demand and helped produce a macroeconomic upswing without creating inflationary pressures. Austria also used fiscal expansion to support its economy – and continuously feels pressure from the European Commission to show more budgetary discipline. State spending, measured as a share of GDP, is significantly higher in Austria and Denmark than for the EU as a whole; in the Netherlands it roughly matches EU averages, while in Ireland it is lower. Despite traditional claims that government expenditures tend to crowd out private demand and investment, more recent evidence suggests that the expenditure elements of GDP are mutually supportive (Schettkat, 2001). Public-sector spending can thus help explain these four countries' success.

Both foreign and domestic demand drives economic growth, and the former tended to increase its role in the 1990s. From 1990 to 1996 alone, exports of goods and services rose by almost 30 per cent in Austria and the Netherlands, by more than 20 per cent in Denmark, and by more than 70 per cent in Ireland. Domestic and foreign investment spending also boosted growth and employment. The Netherlands and Ireland have experienced particularly large per-capita inflows of foreign direct investment.

Tax policies have evolved in each of the four countries, recently reducing social contributions for lower-wage workers as well as (in some of the countries) the highest personal tax rates. Corporate taxes have also fallen, perhaps stimulating investment.[3] Tax revenues have increased in absolute figures but have declined as a share of GDP in Ireland and the Netherlands. In Denmark and Austria, however, increased state revenue created additional public sector jobs; this has obviously not hindered the general improvement of Denmark's economy and labour market. Many cross-national differences remain in tax structures, and these may distort future competition and investment flows in Europe. The formation of the European Monetary Union, and the consequent adoption of a common currency, can only increase pressure to harmonize monetary, fiscal, wage, and tax policies.

While the macroeconomic discretion of individual EU countries has clearly diminished, they still have policy levers to influence their domestic economies, especially in fiscal policy.

Labour Market Policy

Both active and passive labour market policies are valuable tools for regulating employment and unemployment, income distribution, and social cohesion. Despite the increasing role of the European Employment Strat-

Table 4.3   Labour market policy expenditure and participants' contributions, 1999

	Spending			Participants' contributions	
	Total	Active	Passive	Active	Passive
Austria	1.72	0.52	1.20	3.8	23.0
Denmark	4.90	1.77	3.12	25.8	21.9
Ireland*	4.07	1.66	2.42	11.3	19.4
Netherlands	4.61	1.80	2.81	5.2†	7.6†

Source: *OECD Employment Outlook*, 2000
* 1996 data.
†1998 data.

egy, EU members retain much discretion in organizing and implementing labour market policies. This freedom applies particularly to the balance between active and passive measures, as well as to the design of measures. However, this discretion is "path dependent," since the countries have set up their labour markets in specific and sometimes diverging ways, and this context influences and constrains labour market policy.

In overall spending terms, three of our four countries have generously funded labour market programs (see Table 4.3). Denmark, Ireland, and the Netherlands all allocate more than 4 per cent of GDP to labour market policies – about ten times as much as the United States spends. In contrast, Austrias labour market programs are relatively small, with total spending below 2 per cent of GDP (roughly equal to the OECD average).

Although in most countries the largest share of labour market policy expenditure goes to "passive" policies (such as unemployment compensation and early-retirement incentives), "active" policies now account for 30–40 per cent of total spending. Participants' contributions are relatively high for passive measures, especially in the unemployment system. Contrary to the traditional view, unemployment benefits and other passive instruments not only protect workers in adverse circumstances but also facilitate flexible employment adjustment by companies. Unemployment-benefit systems in particular, which can serve as de jure or de facto lay-off systems, provide a useful flexibility buffer, especially for smaller firms. The percentage of the unemployed who return to their previous employer after a short unemployment spell (30–40 per cent of the unemployed in Austria and Denmark) proves that the system is used in this manner. Despite potential cross-subsidization between sectors and employers, such behaviour helps to stabilize small firms (such as those with sharp seasonal patterns) and hence can serve as a flexibility/security device.

Early retirement also provides exit flexibility for firms and permits a better status than unemployment at the end of a working life. In this regard, pension systems have also been used in labour market programming. While this type of supply reduction may help explain our four case studies' successes in reducing unemployment, its continuation might prove problematic. The ageing of the workforce and the high costs of this solution necessitate new solutions. Potential reductions in early-retirement incentives, aimed at reducing costs, might increase unemployment for older workers. In any case, income security at the end of working life, before regular retirement, is a central element of European social protection.

All four countries have used labour market policies – both active and passive – to improve labour market function. Supply-reduction policies have been important, but innovative policies (such as leave schemes and job rotation in Denmark) have addressed labour market problems. And since each of the four countries significantly increased employment-to-population ratios in the latter 1990s, reductions in labour supply cannot entirely or even largely explain their falling unemployment rates.

The European Employment Strategy will increasingly shape national labour market policies, and hence we can expect a marked convergence. This strategy aims to increase employment-to-population ratios. It will reduce the passive part of social protection (unemployment benefits, early-retirement incentives, and social assistance) and increase the active parts. Its activation policy is much in line with the OECD's make-work pay policy. The border between this approach and punitive "workfare" is relatively thin, so it will require a careful weighing of compulsion and choice. It may lead to more effective active labour market policies or reflect a move to compulsion and to sanctions on the unemployed.

Social Dialogue

Each of the four countries considered in this chapter possesses a range of economic and political institutions aimed at facilitating social dialogue among the partners in economic growth (including government, employers, and organized labour). Historically, an insufficiently developed apparatus for this dialogue contributed to the employment crisis in the 1970s and early 1980s, triggered by the two oil crises and resulting financial and macroeconomic shocks. Social dialogue experienced severe stresses; the approach was often adversarial and ideologically charged. However, once it became more pragmatic and oriented towards problem-solving, it eased subsequent employment success. In the 1990s, each country experimented with models of social pacts intended to collectively manage aggregate macroeconomic and labour market variables.

Simply possessing institutions of social dialogue, such as representative union and employer organizations and centralized or coordinated wage bargaining, might not guarantee the sort of social pacts implemented in the 1990s. Success also requires a common understanding that change is necessary, and willingness to act through partnership rather than through adversarial means. Some commentators see these pacts as sophisticated mechanisms simply for accommodating capital and constraining labour (for example, Stanford and Vosko, this volume). Others view them as having been essential for turning around troubled economies. In any event, such pacts have not been entirely peaceful, or devoid of conflict. They involved tough bargains, as well as concessions, and they required strong unions to implement them and affect the economy and society.

In three countries, a concerted effort at social dialogue led to formal social pacts with a national dimension – the Wassenaar Agreement (1982) in the Netherlands, the Declaration of Intent (1987) in Denmark, and the Programme for National Recovery (1987) in Ireland. These pacts expressed the partners' desire to co-operate in order to solve the economy's problems, through a joint approach based on wage moderation to boost competitiveness and on reform of the welfare state. Typical trade-offs for moderate wage increases included tax cuts, reductions in working time, and additional labour market policy measures (such as enhanced cushioning of employment adjustment). Concerted action has been traditional in Austria, and over the last decade it dealt with such issues as the privatization of nationalized industries and the reform of social security.

In general, in each country declining union-density rates reflect sectoral shifts from manufacturing and the public sector to less-unionized sectors such as private services. However, these four countries fared better than others in the OECD: Denmark's already-high union density increased slightly, and, after a decline, Dutch density seems to have recovered. Between 1985 to 1995, Austria registered the biggest decline (almost 20 percentage points) in unionization, while Irish rates fell by 7 percentage points. The Irish unions' more co-operative stance after 1987 seems not to have punished them. Union density has dropped less sharply in the four countries than experienced in some other, more adversarial systems – such as France (37 percentage points) or the United Kingdom (28 percentage points).

There is an ongoing debate about what union members will demand as compensation for earlier wage concessions. In tight labour markets, wage pressures mount, and wage discussions become more difficult. For example, in 1998 in Denmark, after the rejection of a contract settlement by the union's rank and file, the government eventually settled the bargaining round; in the Netherlands, there are growing demands for a new general agreement, in the spirit of Wassenaar; and recently the fifth Irish national social pact (the Programme for Prosperity and Fairness) had to adjust its wage-bargaining settlement because of inflation, surpassing increases initially granted for 2001. In general, both nominal and real wage growth is accelerating in all four countries, to rates well above EU averages.

While the social pacts are not without problems, they have been a pillar of economic and labour market recovery, and they show that bargained solutions based on the mutual agreement of unions and employers are an effective alternative to the unconstrained working of market forces. In some other countries (such as the Britain and New Zealand), the pressures resulting from globalization and technological change led to the dismantling of previous institutions of social dialogue. In the four countries reviewed here, however, the siren song of deregulation (Alan, 1997) reinvigorated social dialogue. A concerted effort by social partners and governments to tackle the problems that afflicted Europe in the 1980s and early 1990s, including weak competitiveness and deteriorating labour markets, permitted these countries to emerge with their welfare state largely intact.

PARTICULARITIES AND APPLICABILITY

Country-Specific Factors

While the three categories of policies considered above (macroeconomic, labour market, and institutions of social dialogue) explain much of the labour market success of these four countries, specific factors have affected each economy.

For example, Ireland has attracted much of its incoming foreign direct investment in one strategic growth sector – information technology – which has produced particularly high GDP growth rates. The inflow of European regional development funds also fuelled expansion, generating an estimated 2 percentage points of annual GDP growth.

The other three countries have demonstrated their own distinctive features. The Dutch have been world champions in the creation of part-time jobs, often in conjunction with an increase in the activities of temporary-work agencies. Austria has benefited from the opening of the former Communist economies, while Denmark's new policy of job rotation and training leaves fits well with its other institutional features (such as a lay-off system and comprehensive adult training). All four countries have also developed specific clusters of production (for example, transport in the Netherlands, information technology in Ireland, and automotive products in Austria), which have proven very growth-intensive.

Combination Effects

More than arising from isolated policy actions, lasting labour market success seems to result from an efficient combination of measures. This review evaluates such interactions. At the macroeconomic level, tight monetary policy, fiscal consolidation, and wage moderation seem to have accommodated each other. Austria is a good example of long-term stability via co-ordination of such policies.

Similarly, relatively weak dismissal protection at the firm level (because regulations are either weak or not strongly enforced – as in Austria) seems to combine well with relatively strong income protection for laid-off workers at the societal level. In these four countries, where small and medium-sized firms prevail, such systems seem to allow scheduling flexibility for employers and income security for workers, making possible low long-term rates of unemployment. Given the abundance of small firms and seasonal employment, this arrangement seems to be a stabilizing force in the four countries.

In general, systemic elements working in the same direction are obviously most efficient. Congruent elements in employment systems generate better performance. The Danish system exemplifies how such elements interact: high labour turnover is supported not only by the lay-off system, but also through labour market training, itself congruent with training-leave schemes. Denmark also provides both parental leave and child care, which make it easier for workers with children to participate in the labour force. In contrast to the United States, which has market-driven flexibility, Denmark has institution-driven flexibility. Danish workers alternate frequently between employment and other status (lay-off, training, or family leave).

A combination of policies that produce both flexibility for firms and security for workers might seem ideal for European labour markets. However, given the complexity of these systems, only further research can determine the precise effect of various policy combinations. Timing is also important: temporary-leave schemes might be efficient bridges to the regular labour market during an upswing, but possibly not in a downturn – since most of the leavers will probably once again be unemployed following their leave. In an unpredictable and complex world, such combinations and appropriate timing also require some luck in order to add up to successful policies.

Table 4.4   The four economies in the European context, 1996

	Austria	Denmark	Ireland	Netherlands
Share in EU's total GDP (%)	2.44	2.00	0.90	4.43
Share in EU's total labour force (%)	2.28	1.67	0.88	4.44

Source: International Labour Organization, CEPR Data Bank.

Do Small Countries Have Specific Advantages?

The four countries under review are all small; only the Netherlands might be considered middle-sized. Together they account for about 10 per cent of the EU's GDP and about 9 per cent of its total labour force (see Table 4.4).

While the three factors analysed above – sound macroeconomic environment and policy, modern labour market policy, and a strong social dialogue – might produce similar, positive effects in larger economies, the size of these countries may also help explain their success. Katzenstein (1985) has outlined some of the factors that distinguish small from larger industrialized countries. First, they must be open – an almost-inevitable feature of small economies. Dependence on imports and exports requires more openness and specialization (Katzenstein, 1985: 87). Second, the four display democratic corporatism based on social partnership – a system of centralized and concentrated interest groups and voluntary and informal co-ordination of conflicting objectives. This social partnership may be easier to attain in a smaller society. For example, a smaller and more defined elite may generate more informality and closer personal relationships, essential conditions for successful bargaining and consensus. Third, other advantages of being small may include a more homogeneous labour force (and thus better co-operation between actors).

But smallness alone cannot be the crucial factor in these countries' success. After all, each experienced a major crisis before its present recovery; smallness did not protect them then and hence cannot fully explain their later successes. And some large countries also have democratic corporatism.

Co-ordination of policies to establish an effective policy mix might also be easier in a small country, with fewer constituents. While smallness may assist governance, economic advantages are less clear. Economic openness can be an advantage or a handicap, depending on the situation in world markets, and large and integrated domestic markets clearly possess economic benefits. In any case, these smaller nations' dependence on larger

EU countries needs further exploration: major shocks in the dominant economies will affect their smaller neighbours and will test the resilience of their policy directions and institutional structures.

What Can Other Countries Learn?

The traditions and cultures that ground policies and institutions in these four countries might make their experience difficult to transfer – particularly democratic corporatism which may not be readily compatible with liberal, pluralist policy formulation.

However, these success stories offer valuable lessons. First, while democratic corporatism per se is not the answer to all labour market problems, genuine dialogue within a framework of corporatism seems to help solve major economic problems. Successful dialogue requires several conditions – recognized and representative partners that can enforce negotiated deals; bargaining trade-offs; a common understanding of the state of the economy; and ongoing interactions between bargaining rounds. Permanent institutions are invaluable – for example, the socioeconomic council and the labour foundation in the Netherlands. Effective dialogue also needs a proactive and credible government to help reach agreements and to represent the general interest.

In the light of these countries' success, corporatism seems to be a form of labour market governance potentially as efficient in economic management as liberal, market-led models. Especially vis-à-vis equity issues, it would seem to offer superior economic and social performance.

These case studies offer other lessons. Economic openness seems to pay off, at least for small, developed countries. It seems to have done little if any harm to the four countries considered. Larger countries could clearly emulate some of the successful policies, such as Danish job-rotation schemes, and Dutch regulations about part-time work. Indeed, Austria, whose institutions resemble Germany's, recently introduced a Dutch-style job-rotation system. A three-pillar financing for retirement (a basic public pension, a contribution-based secondary system, and a subsidized private top-up), as in Denmark or the Netherlands might work in other countries. And the Austrian apprenticeship system (much like the German) could serve as a model for alternative training in other countries.

Despite international diversity in policy experience, however, the European Monetary Union will almost certainly stimulate convergence of policies and regulations and promote more adjustment in various policy fields. The European Employment Strategy's common guidelines and associated monitoring process will similarly lead to more convergence in employment and labour market policies.

CONCLUSION

The relative labour market success of the four countries surveyed in this chapter results partly from country-specific factors and partly from the particular combinations of macroeconomic policy, labour market policy, and social dialogue. The institutions and practices of social dialogue, in particular, helped create a climate of confidence among the major social actors. Wage moderation contributed to competitiveness, and considerable reform to social protection took place, mostly within a climate of negotiation and consensus. Wage moderation was also the corollary of a stabilization-oriented macroeconomic policy that maintained low inflation and low interest rates. Labour market policy (and social protection in general) created the necessary flexibility for adjustment on the labour markets. Labour market policies and social-protection schemes are thus not only means to secure income for those without work but a sort of buffer around regular labour markets. Early-retirement schemes, and proactive lay-off and training systems (such as those in Denmark), are good examples of this general approach.

However, in the face of an ageing workforce, and early signs of labour shortages and rising wage costs, all of the countries have recently reformed their social-protection systems, restricting early retirement and making labour market policy more active. These changes might imply that the welfare state – which I describe here as being integral to these successful efficiency–equity balances – is changing from redistributing wealth through social transfers to maximizing participation in paid work. However, passive policies will still be necessary – for the most disadvantaged, who cannot work, and also because these policies maintain flexibility for firms and protection and security for workers.

The experience of these four countries proves that European labour markets, even with their more extensive regulations and institutional structures, can adjust to a faster-changing environment, with the right policy mix and institutional flexibility. Strong unions and representative employers' organizations, along with fairly interventionist governments, have worked together to solve labour market problems, while changing but not dismantling the welfare state. While these countries have by no means achieved the best of all possible worlds, as inequality and labour market exclusion persist, they have made progress towards full employment and social equity. They have more to do, and it may be difficult to replicate their successes elsewhere. But they have certainly shown that employment success is feasible in a context that maintains a balance between economic and social issues.

NOTES

1 To be classified as unemployed, the respondent has to be without work, available for work, and actively searching for work in the reference period.
2 For a discussion of the concept, see Auer, 2000, 25 ff.
3 The lowest rates occur in Ireland, and its European partners have accused the Irish government of trying to attract foreign direct investment with its low tax rates.

REFERENCES

Auer, P. 2000. *Employment Revival in Europe: Labour Market Success in Austria, Denmark, Ireland and the Netherlands.* Geneva: International Labour Organization.

Auer, P, and S. Cazes. 2000. "The Resilience of the Long-term Employment Relationship: Evidence from the Industrialized Countries," *International Labour Review* 139 (4), 379–409.

Bertola, G., T. Boeri, and S. Cazes. 2000. *Labour Market Regulations in Industrialized Countries: Evolving Institutions and Variable Enforcement.* Geneva: International Labour Organization.

Bosch, G. 2001. "From the Redistribution to the Modernisation of Working Time," in P. Auer, ed., *Changing Labour Markets in Europe.* Geneva: International Labour Organization.

Frühstück, E., P. Gregoritsch, R. Löffler, and M. Wagner-Pinter. 1998. *Die Rückkehr in ein vorübergehend aufgelöstes Beschäftigungsverhältnis.* Vienna: Synthesis.

Graafland, J. 1996. "Unemployment Benefits and Employment: A Review of Empirical Evidence," in W. Van Ginneken, ed., *Finding the Balance: Financing and Coverage of Social Protection in Europe.* Geneva: International Social Security Association.

Hartog, J. 1999. "So, What's So Special about the Dutch Model?" Employment and Training Paper 54. Geneva: International Labour Organization.

Katzenstein, P.J. 1985. *Small States in World Markets: Industrial Policy in Europe.* Ithaca, NY: Cornell University Press.

Madsen, P.K. 1999. "Denmark: Flexibility, Security and Labour Market Success." Employment and Training Paper 53. Geneva: International Labour Organization.

O'Connel, P. 1999. "Astonishing Success: Economic Growth and the Labour Market in Ireland." Employment and Training Paper 44. Geneva: International Labour Organization.

Organization for Economic Cooperation and Development (OECD). 1996. *The OECD Jobs Study, Implementing the Strategy.* Paris: Organization for Economic Cooperation and Development.

– 1998 (Survey in 1997.) *Economic Surveys: Austria, Denmark, Ireland, the Netherlands.* Paris: Organization for Economic Cooperation and Development.

Pichelmann, K., and H. Hofer. 1999. "Austria: Long-term Success through Social Partnership." Employment and Training Paper 52. Geneva: International Labour Organization.

Rubery, J. 2001. "Equal Opportunities and Employment Policy," in P. Auer, ed., *Changing Labour Markets in Europe.* Geneva: International Labour Organization.

Schettkat, R. 2001. "Small Economy Macroeconomics," in P. Auer, ed., *Changing Labour Markets in Europe.* Geneva: International Labour Organization.

Schmid, G. 1995. "Is Full Employment Still Possible? Transitional Labour Markets as a New Strategy of Labour Market Policy," *Economic and Industrial Policy* 11, 429–56.

Visser, J. 2001. "Industrial Relations and the Social Dialogue," in P. Auer, ed., *Changing Labour Markets in Europe.* Geneva: International Labour Organization.

PART TWO

Developments in
Labour Market Structure

5

Challenging Segmentation in South Africa's Labour Market: "Regulated Flexibility" or Flexible Regulation?

MARLEA CLARKE

New legislation must recognize that South Africa's return to the international economy demands that enterprises compete with countries whose employment standards and social costs of production vary considerably. It must therefore avoid the imposition of legal rigidities in the labour market, provide greater flexibility and introduce more responsive mechanisms for variation from statutory standards.
– T. Mboweni, South African Minister of Labour

In response to increased pressure from business, and the growing economic and political crisis of the late 1970s and the 1980s, South Africa's apartheid government began introducing trade liberalization, privatization, and deregulation.[1] It aimed these policies at increasing flexibility in the labour market and promoting the expansion of the small business sector. This move towards labour market deregulation took three forms: legislative change, administrative exemption, and a steady decrease in the monitoring and enforcement of labour legislation. These changes eroded workers' rights by facilitating workplace restructuring intended to create a cheaper and more flexible workforce. One result of deregulation and restructuring was the steady decline of permanent employment and the corresponding rise of non-standard and precarious employment.

Linked to these processes and other factors, the country faced an economic and unemployment crisis when the African National Congress (ANC) took office in 1994. In response, and to fulfil promises made to the trade-union movement, the new government promised a comprehensive labour market policy, with a proactive role for the Ministry of Labour.

Within months the new minister released a five-year program that identified key issues and tasks for restructuring the department, reforming legislation, and developing an active labour market policy (Ministry of Labour, 1994). New legislative reforms aimed to remove the vestiges of the apartheid labour system by increasing workers' rights and extending them, especially to those previously not protected. Other reforms standardised terms and conditions of employment and created institutions and mechanisms to enforce legislation and resolve conflicts. Importantly, the department emphasized elimination of discrimination in the labour market. "The Ministry of Labour is committed to rectifying the racial and gender imbalances in the workplace and promoting equity at all levels in the world of work" (Ministry of Labour, 1994: 8). Further, it proposed consolidation of the tripartite process, seeking to involve organized labour in policy debates, especially in the formulation and implementation of macroeconomic and labour market policies.

To this end the government obtained passage of four key laws to transform and reregulate the labour market: the Labour Relations Act of 1996 (LRA), the Basic Conditions of Employment Act 75 of 1997 (BCEA), the Employment Equity Act 55 of 1998 (EEA), and the Skills Development Act 97 of 1998 (SDA). Of course the development and implementation of this new regulatory framework was no easy task. The government drafted labour laws in the midst of intense debate over its five-year program – specifically over the degree of government intervention in the labour market and the impact of increased regulation on economic growth. Negotiations over legislation, especially the BCEA, sparked heated exchanges with labour and business, pitting increased regulation against greater labour market flexibility for the sake of international competitiveness.

This chapter examines the emergence of this new regulatory framework and its impact on labour market segmentation. It first briefly describes the labour market under apartheid. This overview provides the context for segmentation and the problems confronting the ANC in 1994. Second, turning to the ANC and its BCEA and the resulting debates over regulation and flexibility, the chapter considers the genesis of new labour legislation. The third section discusses the post-apartheid labour market. Tracing employment trends in various sectors, it reveals the loopholes and weaknesses in the new regulatory regime. The proliferation of non-standard and precarious employment has reduced the ability of legislation to protect vulnerable workers. The fourth section analyses recent amendments to the BCEA.

While the new labour market dispensation gestures in the direction of the type of transformation required, laws and policies have not gone far enough in reregulating the labour market. Political shifts within the ANC, domestic and international pressure from business, slow economic growth, and the failure of other policies to create jobs have led the government to retreat from a stronger approach. Loopholes in the legislation, the acceptance of flexibility by way of "regulated flexibility," weak enforcement and monitoring, inadequate regulation of new employment arrangements, and employers' strategies to bypass legislation have contributed to the expansion of non-standard employment. Thus a dual and contradictory process is under way: the labour market is being reregulated and at the same time resegmented. Gender and racial discrimination is continuing, even increasing, for marginalized workers (especially blacks and women) not protected by new legislation.

APARTHEID AND LABOUR MARKET SEGMENTATION

Specific patterns of industrial development and the consolidation of racist social and economic policies under apartheid resulted in a deeply segmented labour market. The government codified and extended a coercive system of control and regulation of the African labour force through the migrant labour system, pass laws, job reservation, and policies aimed at directing and redirecting labour mobility (Southall, 1999: 4). The dualistic system of labour relations created by the pre-apartheid Industrial Conciliation Act of 1924 was further entrenched with the Native Labour Act of 1953 (Settlement of Disputes), and the Industrial Conciliation Act of 1956 (ICA). Aimed at preventing trade unionism among black workers, the ICA excluded them from all its provisions, including collective-bargaining structures. Further, it introduced formal job reservation, with race as the defining criterion for employment in many jobs.

In general, protective legislation evolved to provide safe and secure jobs for white workers, while repressive laws and market regulation determined employment conditions for blacks. An extremely flexible labour market gave employers wide powers to determine wages and working conditions for most black workers. The system was very rigid for most blacks, with employment and job mobility tightly controlled by laws, policies, agreements, and employer discretion.

We can begin to understand women and black workers' positions in the apartheid labour market by exploring the type of employment relationships that surfaced during this period. Scholarship on the changing nature of employment provides useful conceptual tools to understand segmentation in South Africa. Several researchers have analysed employment trends and the changing employment relationship with reference to regulatory developments at national and international levels (Butchtemann and Quack, 1990; Vosko, 2000). They argue that Canada and other advanced capitalist welfare states in Europe and North America in the postwar period developed and consolidated what is commonly called a standard employment relationship (SER), where the worker had one employer and normally worked on his or her premises and under his or her supervision (Vosko, 2000: 24). Typically, the SER included both a standard employment contract (full time and permanent) and a range of social benefits (for example, unemployment insurance and pension schemes).

As Vosko and others have noted, the SER never covered the majority of workers (Pollert, 1988; Vosko, 2000). White males were the main beneficiaries, with most women, immigrants, and non-whites relegated to nonstandard employment relationships (NSERs). Women and non-whites were more likely to work in sectors with less employment security or in jobs that had few of the characteristics of standard employment. NSERs include a range of forms, none of them full time, permanent, or secure or with SER-type social benefits (Vosko, 2000). For example, women and non-whites often obtained part-time, temporary, casual, and/or seasonal jobs, generally non-unionized, with lower wages and few or no social benefits and job security.

Comparable patterns also emerged in apartheid-era South Africa. The state intervened widely in the economy and society to provide welfare and regulate distribution and redistribution even under apartheid capitalism. But apartheid and its policies, programs, and practices shaped standard and non-standard employment. Postwar labour legislation and social security consciously promoted gender and racial discrimination. National programs, such as the Workmen's Compensation Act (WCA) and the Unemployment Insurance Act (UIA) gave benefits and social security to workers defined as employees. Casual labourers, domestic workers, most persons in agriculture or mining, and certain categories of defence workers received no coverage. Given the large percentage of Africans in agriculture and mining, many African workers had no or very limited coverage. Further, as most African women were domestic workers or in agriculture, protective labour and social-security legislation excluded them.

Racially discriminatory policies overlapped with employment practices. With segmentation, organized workers in core sectors obtained high wages and adequate social benefits that completed the social wage, while more peripheral non-"employees" initially lacked these benefits. The self-employed, informally or atypically employed, and non-citizens were ineligible for social insurance and social assistance. Therefore only people in "regular employment" and described by the act as "employees" (or by the UIA as contributors) could receive social-security protection. Thus white male workers in core sectors were the main beneficiaries of the SER. Similar to exclusions elsewhere but even more apparent and deliberate in

South Africa, the government excluded the vast majority of African workers[2] (both male and female) from social security, protective labour laws, and secure, permanent, full-time employment. Therefore non-standard forms of employment emerged alongside the SER, supported by apartheid legislation, social policies, and labour laws that promoted and preserved a dual labour market.

In short, the history of the labour market in South Africa is one of segmentation: a regulated core workforce and a highly flexible, precarious labour force. Employment practices, labour legislation, and social policies overlapped with apartheid policies to create strong racial (and gender) divisions within the labour market. The SER became the normative model of employment, as in other countries, but with different characteristics. South Africa's dualism was uniquely racialized. Further, prohibitions against outwork and other forms of non-standard employment aimed at protecting white workers from downward pressure on wages helped shape the SER. Despite extension of the SER in the 1960s, 1970s, and early 1980s to include more women and blacks, the labour market remained extremely segmented, with many workers excluded from protective legislation.

As a result, the labour market inherited by the ANC in 1994 had four major problems: extreme inequality, high levels of poverty, high and rising levels of unemployment, and particularly intense exploitation. Unions and workers had high expectations that the new government would introduce remedial labour market policies aimed at narrowing the wage gap, reducing inequalities, and increasing minimum wages in order to address poverty and exploitation. Given the exclusion of many African workers from previous legislation, and their frequently poor wages and working conditions, many expected significant improvements. Further, the ANC's election platform – the Reconstruction and Development Plan (the RDP) – set out an ambitious program of institutional change and economic development founded on addressing the needs of poor and working people. It gave special attention to labour and workers' rights, and its implementation promised to realize many of the union movement's long-standing demands. Indeed, the RDP contained a clear commitment to "preserve and extend the gains made by workers through their struggles" (ANC, 1994: 4.8.1).

LABOUR MARKET TRANSFORMATION
UNDER THE ANC GOVERNMENT

It was against this backdrop that the new ANC-led government committed itself to far-reaching labour market reforms. The democratic government, largely through the Ministry of Labour, began modernizing labour laws and introducing new statutes aimed at increasing workers' rights and eliminating discrimination in the workplace. Guided by the framework outlined in the Ministry of Labour's Five-Year Programme, the new government enacted a number of pieces of legislation. The Labour Relations Act (LRA)[3] overhauled collective labour relations, extending organizational and collective bargaining rights to all employees. The Basic Conditions of Employment Act (BCEA)[4] set minimum standards of employment and extended coverage to all employees, including many casuals. The Employment Equity Act (EEA)[5] followed, with the Skills Development Act (SDA)[6] hard on its heels. The EEA aims to eliminate workplace discrimination and accelerate the training and promotion of people from disadvantaged groups, while the SDA sets out a decentralized skills-development strategy through a variety of mechanisms, including a training levy and training programs.

The most important reform of employment standards legislation was the new BCEA, passed in November 1997 and promulgated in full on 31 December 1998. It repealed the BCEA of 1983 and the Wage Act of 1957. Similar to the LRA, it advances equity and workers' rights, while balancing them against the need to create more efficient and competitive workplaces. It extends a floor of minimum employment conditions to all workers except members of the National Defence Force, the National Intelligence Agency, and the Secret Service.

Importantly, it covers many people excluded from the old act, including farm and domestic workers and many casual workers. While previous legislation excluded people who worked less than three days per week, most sections of the new BCEA cover those who work more than 24 hours per month. This marks a significant gain, as many workers previously defined as casual and thus excluded from coverage now receive protection. However, those who do not fit the definition of employee still have no protection. Coverage excludes independent contractors, homeworkers, the self-employed, and casuals or temporaries who work less than 24 hours per month for the same employer. Terms and conditions set out in the act apply to all contracts of employment, unless other laws or agreements provide better terms.

By and large, this act represents a step forward for workers, with better minimum standards and new conditions. It improves working time, maternity-leave provisions, overtime rates, and annual leave; introduces family-responsibility leave; and incorporates the LRA's provisions on severance pay. It reduces maximum working hours to 45 per week[7] (from 48 for farm workers, 60 for security guards, and 46 for other workers) and it provides for an eventual 40–hour week. Overtime pay increases from $1\frac{1}{3}$ times to $1\frac{1}{2}$ times the normal hourly wage. For Sundays, employees who do not usually work that day receive double the normal rate, and those who do,

1.5 times that rate. Annual leave increases from 14 consecutive days in each year worked to 21 days. Women workers may now receive four consecutive months of maternity leave, and most workers are eligible for three days of family-responsibility leave per year.

Despite improved conditions and stronger regulation, standards (apart from core standards) may vary downward. The act outlines four methods: by collective bargaining, sectoral determinations (by the new Employment Standards Commission), individual contracts and ministerial determinations (by the minister of labour).

Employment contracts can vary (with some limitations) the BCEA's provisions on ordinary daily and weekly hours of work, overtime, meal intervals, daily and weekly rest periods, payment for work on Sunday, and sick leave. The act promotes collective bargaining as a method for altering standards, giving bargaining-council agreements significant scope for doing so. Councils can vary any provisions in the BCEA apart from core standards. Subject to certain specified exceptions and apart from core standards, the minister may replace or exclude any basic condition of employment provided for in the act. Sectoral determinations displace the BCEA entirely, except for certain conditions (such as maximum working hours, child labour, and forced labour).

Thus the act sets minimum employment standards and then allows them to vary downward – fostering "regulated flexibility." According to the minister, this system allows the department to balance the setting and protection of minimum standards with the requirements of labour market flexibility (Department of Labour, 1996: 6). Consistent with the promotion of national collective bargaining, bargaining-council agreements have greater scope to vary standards than do other collective agreements. The Green Paper (outlining initial proposals for a new employment-standards document) had introduced these provisions as a response to the challenges facing the country: "New legislation must recognise that South Africa's return to the international economy demands that enterprises compete with countries whose employment standards and social costs of production vary considerably. It must therefore avoid the imposition of legal rigidities in the labour market, provide greater flexibility and introduce more responsive mechanisms for variation from statutory standards" (Department of Labour, 1996: 27).

While allowing increased flexibility through this framework of regulated flexibility, the legislation backs away from stronger regulation in other ways. Despite the lack of research and sector-specific data on changing patterns of employment, general information on labour market trends was available during preparation of new legislation. Background documents and earlier drafts of the legislation directly addressed non-standard work and the need for better protection of those involved. These issues quickly fell aside, and variation became particularly controversial during negotiations. However, the contentious nature of negotiations and wide disagreement on variation and other key areas distracted people from issues of non-standard employment. Indeed, the chapter on the subject in the first draft (the Green Paper) released in February 1996 disappeared completely from the next draft and from the final act. Thus, while the government acknowledged the rise in atypical employment, it did little to regulate it.

Legislation took major steps towards regulation of temporary-employment services (TESS) but only minimally regulated temporary work and protected temp workers. Section 198 of the new LRA makes such workers the employees of the TESS. The new LRA and BCEA make the TES and the client jointly and severally liable for breaches of collective agreements and arbitration awards regulating terms and conditions of employment. This is an improvement over past legislation but it does not ensure that such employment arrangements do not deprive workers of their rights.

First, section 198 retreats from the original proposal in the Labour Relations Bill, which made a TES and its client jointly and severally liable for contraventions of the new LRA. This provision would have made a client responsible for, among other things, the TES's unfair dismissal of an employee.

Second, temporary workers must fit the definition of "employee" to be covered and not be independent contractors (self-employed). The legislation covers those who fit the definition of employee, but not those defined as independent contractors. The traditional reading of "employee" has restricted the ambit of protection that labour legislation offers to people who contracted to provide work under the contract of employment and excludes persons who perform work under the contract of service (i.e., a contract regulating work that is not "employment"). A more generous interpretation of "employee" would include workers who perform personal services for another, whatever the form of the contract. In general, the courts have not read a broader category of worker into the definitions in the new LRA or the new BCEA. Thus, independent contractors, even if they are dependent workers, receive no protection. Thus TESS tend to arrange contractual agreements so as to take advantage of this.

Third, monitoring and enforcement of legislation are key issues affecting workers' protection. Following the LRA, the new BCEA introduced new monitoring and enforcement procedures, which have proven weak and ineffective – processes remain extremely slow, and employers can deliberately delay them or ignore arbitration awards. For temporary employment, monitoring and enforcement are perhaps even weaker than before. For example, the old LRA's requirement that TESS register with the Ministry of Labour is not in the new LRA. TESS must register under the new Skills Development Act – a paper exercise according to the ministry, which has neither the intention nor the ability to monitor agencies vis-à-vis workers' rights and employment conditions. Thus, the lack of monitoring of the TES sector has allowed these practices to flourish.

Overall, instead of strengthening regulation of non-standard employment, including temporary employment, legislation tinkered with definitions (i.e., designating labour brokers as TESS) and clarified rights surrounding this employment relationship. Negotiators missed an opportunity to reverse informalization and casualization and to develop innovative strategies to protect temporary and other non-standard workers. Negotiations were contentious over certain core rights (i.e., maternity leave, hours of work, Sunday work) and variation provisions and over business's concerns about "excessive" regulation and rigidity in the labour market–dominated debate. The labour movement, unprepared for negotiations, made major compromises. Despite not obtaining some of its central demands and its opposition to several sections of the act (specifically on downward variation), labour accepted the legislation as "the best that they could get."

Given the ANC's commitment to labour and workers' rights, what explains the shift towards flexibility and away from stronger regulation? Many forces helped tame the government's more radical impulses, especially on labour market reform. Pressure resulting from globalization and intervention by international capital consolidated a more business-friendly labour regime. Domestic capital had also exerted strong pressure on the government.

From the late 1980s onward, the small-business lobby had become more prominent in policy-making processes. Trade liberalization and deregulation by the apartheid government had exposed firms to highly competitive markets. Many companies were responding by restructuring their workplaces and introducing cheaper and more flexible forms of work. Business strongly opposed introduction of labour regulation that would end these practices. The claim put forward, and one that increasingly gained support from government, was that South Africa's labour market was too rigid. The resulting higher labour costs, it was argued, would make local business uncompetitive, thus undermining job creation, especially by small, medium, and micro- enterprises (SMMEs).

By the time of the BCEA negotiations, the economic and political context had shifted. In a document responding to an earlier draft of the BCEA, the Congress of South African Trade Unions (COSATU) states, "There are a number of challenges we have faced in the negotiations. Most critically has been the overall policy shift in government at a macro level, which is reducing the space for winning new rights for our members, and in fact has forced us to at times, take a defensive position, seeking to protect the rights we have in the current law" (COSATU, 1996). In response to economic stagnation and ongoing unemployment, the government released its draft National Growth and Development Strategy in February 1996, which emphasized macroeconomic stability.

In June 1996, the government released the Growth, Employment and Redistribution Plan (GEAR), a new macroeconomic strategy. GEAR's focus represented a further move away from the RDP and revealed the government's growing preoccupation with macroeconomic policy. Goals such as job creation, reduction in poverty, and equitable economic growth – central to the RDP – gave way to trade liberalization, monetary targets, and reduced social and capital expenditure. In contrast to the ANC's previous commitment to distribute income so as to promote economic growth and build a more equitable society, GEAR saw expanded exports and investment as the only route to economic growth.

Further, the failure of other policies to stimulate growth and create jobs placed more pressure on the labour market. Pressure from national and international business, shifts within the ANC, and the neoliberal policy emphasis of other government ministries helped to undermine the ANC's support for COSATU and for increased regulation of the labour market. COSATU's capacity had weakened as many of the union movement's leaders left for positions in business and government after 1994; thus labour sponsored few research efforts and public interventions in debates over labour market flexibility. By the mid-1990s it was evident that the dominant view in government favoured some regulation and increased flexibility as appropriate responses to the employment crisis and to the demands of an increasingly global economy. The legacies of apartheid-era labour market policies, the failure of the ANC's industrial and economic policies, and the retreat from stronger regulation in new laws have destroyed jobs and allowed non-standard employment to flourish.

CHANGING PATTERNS OF EMPLOYMENT: SECTOR CASE STUDIES

Despite new legislation, the post-apartheid labour market remains extremely segmented along gender and racial lines. Increasingly, the division corresponds to contractual trends: a shrinking group with permanent, full-time jobs in core sectors, protected by legislation and receiving increases in wages and better working conditions, and a growing number in precarious positions at the expanding margins of the economy.

Massive restructuring has led to the proliferation of non-standard employment and growth of the informal economy. "Old" forms of casual and contractual employment have also re-emerged, with some continuing along lines similar to those of the apartheid era, and others reshaped to conform to today's economy.

Although official statistics do not reflect it, recent research has revealed the growth in non-standard forms of employment in all major industries over the last decade, especially in the last five years (Cheadle and Clarke, 2000; Theron and Godfrey, 2000). Sector-specific studies support these claims (Hemson, 1996; Klerck, 1994; Valodia, 1991). Unemployment has increased,[8] as have informal work and employment. Both the quality and the quantity of jobs have changed significantly. Increasingly jobs lack SER-type benefits. Casualization is on the increase in short- or fixed-term contracts and in temporary and seasonal work. Externalization (shifting work from an employment relationship to an unprotected commercial contract) is also casualizing the workforce. Downward pressure on wages and working conditions, and the prevalence of jobs with irregular schedules, further confirm a broad process of casualization.

Non-standard employment is increasing in all sectors (Clarke, Godfrey, and Theron, 2002). As we saw above, such employment is not new, but as the SER was consolidating in the 1960s and 1970s more workers (including women and African workers) became eligible for some or all of the associated benefits. After several decades of consolidation and expansion, the SER is now in decline, with non-standard forms of employment replacing it. Short-term contracts and casual, temporary, and seasonal work are becoming more common in all sectors. For example, labour-intensive sectors such as agriculture have shifted towards seasonal and casual work, the retail industry has seen a similar transformation, and employment patterns have altered in all sub-sectors of transportation. Since national statistics are sketchy and quite unreliable, this section explores sector-specific employment changes in agriculture, transportation, and retail, as well as broad trends in outsourcing, home-working, independent contracting, and temporary work, and it looks at their impact on equality.

Agriculture

Historically agriculture relied heavily on permanent workers who lived[9] on the farms. In contrast, farmers are increasingly hiring seasonal and temporary workers. For example, in the early 1990s Western Cape wine farms were employing tens of thousands of pickers during the late-summer grape harvest (Cameron, 1990: 87). More farmers, especially those unable to acquire new or additional machines, are responding to rising input costs by reorganizing to optimize productivity and reduce labour costs (Hamman, 1996). Typically, permanent workers have continued to form the (shrinking) core, usually receiving skills training and handling tasks (such as pruning) that require great skill. Linked to apartheid policies and to racial, gender, and ethnic stereotypes, core jobs have typically been reserved for coloured[10] male workers, with coloured females taking less-skilled, lower-paid permanent jobs. Seasonal workers are usually African males (and some women), who receive a lower wage and little training.

Recent research shows these trends continuing, with farmers offering less and less permanent employment – "shrugging off the social responsibilities they have traditionally carried" (du Toit and Ally, 2001). As in other sectors, jobs are evaporating at an alarming rate, with employment relationships in flux. Official statistics record a loss of 114,000 regular jobs in commercial agriculture between 1988 and 1996, down 19 per cent in 1994 alone (du Toit and Ally, 2001: 1). TESS are increasingly supplying seasonal and temporary workers.[11] Casual workers (either farm casuals or temps recruited from elsewhere) are more common on many farms. Farmers appear to be increasingly using TESS to recruit and place lower-skilled workers paid exceptionally little for short-term tasks (i.e., picking during harvest season). Although high-skill tasks still tend to go to permanent workers, sub-contracted labour is increasing (Hamman, 1996).

Segmentation by race and gender is apparent in both permanent and casual workforces. As we saw above, coloured males dominated permanent employment in agriculture in the Western Cape. Where African workers have achieved permanent jobs, their status, wages, and benefits are generally lower. Linked to casualization has been the feminization of employment. Hamman suggests that, alongside the shift to temporary labour, more women (often farmworkers' wives) work in the sector. Despite feminization of the shrinking core of permanent workers, men still dominate in permanent work, and women, in temporary. As in other sectors, temporary employees have lower wages, few benefits, and often extremely insecure and precarious employment.

The Retail Industry

Casualization is also apparent in the retail industry. In contrast to other sectors, overall employment has not declined there, but employment is growing through NSERs, and in informal-sector trade (Clarke and Kenny, 2002). Retail stores (especially large grocery retailers) are increasingly replacing full-time permanent workers with casuals and temps. As the old BCEA was in place when employment began to change (i.e., in the 1980s and early 1990s), most stores defined their casual employees (even those on staff for many years) as working less than 24 hours per week. Many stores have two categories of casuals – "regulars" and more temporary casuals (Kenny, 2000). In reality, the majority of the former are part-time workers, employed by the store for many years (some for as long as 10), regularly working weekends, and treated as permanent employees.

Part-timers generally work about two-thirds as many hours as full-timers and receive reduced wages and benefits – one recent survey revealed on average 57 per cent of the permanent wage. For those on a temporary contract, average hourly wages are only 42 per cent of the permanent average wage.[12] Prior to the new BCEA, retail stores generally hired few part-time workers but retained a large pool of casuals for peak hours, holidays, weekends, and late nights (Clarke and Kenny, 2002). Over the last decade employers have increasingly relied on casual labour. Ten years ago, at least 70 per cent of employees were permanent; today the majority of employees in most large retail stores are casual (Clarke, 2000). Such practices flourished, either because of lack of monitoring or because stores had exemptions from the wage determination legislation (WD 478). In one large grocery retailer (Shoprite), the union supported the company's applications for exemptions from WD 478 in exchange for greater job security for permanent workers.

Several grocery stores already rely on TESs for busy peaks for distributing ("pick and pack"), and many use them to recruit temps for warehouses, as shelf-packers, and as stock takers. Management does not worry about the effect of such a process on performance and customer service: "Our cashiers aren't friendly or committed to the company now, but we have to pay them anyway. If we outsource, service can't get any worse and we won't have the hassle and pay problems" (interview, head office of large chain store, March 2000). Many retailers have begun to outsource some activities (such as transport, security, and cleaning) to smaller companies. Subcontracted workers, particularly merchandizers, increasingly work directly for TESs contracted by suppliers. Conditions and wages vary dramatically, although most subcontracted workers receive low wages and no benefits and experience high job insecurity (particularly when contracts change).

The tendency to replace full-timers with casuals or temps recruited by TESs, and the sourcing of products directly from small producers, have both added downward pressure to wages and conditions. These trends, combined with increased competition from convenience and franchise stores, have multiplied insecure and precarious jobs. Women and African workers have been hardest hit, holding disproportionate numbers of non-standard jobs. For example, African workers make up the majority of employees in low-skilled occupational categories, and women (especially Africans)[13] generally have jobs (for example, in services, shops, and market sales) that are increasingly becoming casual or temporary. In addition, the informal economy has grown substantially. By February 2002 almost half (48 per cent) of the retail workforce was in the informal economy.[14] That shift, along with the proliferation of non-standard employment in the formal economy, has left the retail sector increasingly unregulated, with many workers falling outside legislation and the new wage-determination scheme.[15]

Outsourcing in the Public and Private Sector

The shift from large to smaller firms, and the adoption of a core / contingent-worker strategy in both the public and the private sectors, help to explain the growth of non-standard employment in many industries. Increasingly, employers are sub-contracting and outsourcing non-core functions (such as cleaning, maintenance, security, canteen services, and catering) to smaller firms. Workers generally have non-standard or precarious employment and little protection from labour legislation and collective agreements. For example, in response to increased competition and in line with increased flexibility, hotels have outsourced many non-core functions to smaller companies or "insourced" them to workers who have become independent contractors. As one hotel manager stated: "We are in the business of serving our guests, not of doing the laundry or lawn."

Homeworking

Externalization is also occurring through homeworking in the clothing sector. Manufacturers have always relied on homeworkers during peaks in seasonal production. Recently, however, as declining trade barriers have increased competition from legal (and illegal) imports, the informal production and distribution sector has expanded. Gradually more retailers are sourcing directly from the homework and informal sector (Clarke, Godfrey, and Theron, 2002). Most homeworkers are women and, given the lack of regulation and union organizing, are vulnerable, unprotected, and often paid well below rates in the formal sector (Clarke, Godfrey, and Theron, 2002). As we saw above, food retailers are also shifting food packaging and preparation out of house to small, informal producers. One of the large grocery retailers reports buying about 20 per cent of its deli foods from small businesses, many exempt from labour legislation (interview, Woolworth's human resources manager, March 2001).

Transportation

Employment is changing also in transportation (including air, rail, and maritime transport). As in other sectors, permanent full-time jobs have declined over the last decade, and non-standard employment has grown. In 1989, road transportation recorded the most employees in a quarter-century, at 67,326. But by 1995, permanent employment had dropped 15 per cent.[16] Indications of casualization and the rise of other forms of non-standard employment have been the emergence of owner-driver schemes and sub-contracting to smaller companies and an increase in contract labour provided by TESS on the docks (Cheadle and Clarke, 2000: 29).

Owner-driver schemes have become especially prevalent, with drivers encouraged to become the owner-drivers of their trucks. No accurate statistics exist, but initial research suggests about 10 per cent conversion. The drivers are no longer employees but are self-employed and therefore not covered by labour legislation. However, while converted to self-employed business operators, most remain in a de facto bilateral employment relationship, with few rights.

A second trend is outsourcing. Increasingly, firms with ancillary transport services are outsourcing these functions to other companies – often to small transport operations that offer lower wages and fewer benefits. The number of temporary or casual workers has grown significantly in transportation, especially in the maritime sector. Casuals have long been a feature of dockyards in South Africa, often hired on a "needs only basis" in warehouses and ships. As in other sectors, employers more and more use casual, temporary, and seasonal workers. TESS now recruit and place various types of temps. There are perhaps about 600 casuals (seasonal, temporary, and regular) working out of the docks each day in Cape Town, and some 900 in Durban (interview, labour broker, 29 October 2001).

Women remain few in all occupational levels and each sub-sector of the transportation industry – about 15 per cent of the workforce (COSATU, 2000: 18). There is no evidence that casualization has increased their numbers. Instead, employment changes have generally worsened employment conditions for men. Most permanent jobs still belong to men, but fewer men have SER-style wages, benefits, and security. Owner-driver schemes, outsourcing, and the move to temporary workers have hurt men's wages and conditions. The growth of smaller firms and the outsourcing of work to them have put downward pressure on wages and conditions in the sector.

Independent Contractors

In the transport and other sectors, employers have exploited loopholes in labour legislation by externalizing work to non-"employees." Labour consultancies and other organizations such as the Confederation of Employers South Africa[17] (COFESA) have sprung up to "assist employers in the process of restructuring their workforce." This usually occurs through finding "legal" ways to convert employees into "independent contractors." Firms then outsource work and production to these people.

COFESA claims, exaggeratedly, to have so converted over 25,000 clothing workers in Natal alone. This trend has posed a growing problem in clothing and in other sectors. According to the founder and current director of COFESA, about 5 million "independent contractors" are operating in South Africa, with at least 2 million converted with COFESA's assistance (interview, 30 August 2002). As we saw above, transportation has seen many conversions.

Temporary Employment

Temporary-employment agencies and labour brokers have expanded significantly in recent years, now supplying all sectors and for a range of jobs. This industry is one of the fastest growing in the country. Advocates have presented the increase in temporary work as a successful job-creation strategy, offering new opportunities for workers. Despite a lack of any evidence, they often present the rise in temporary work as the result of more people (especially women) seeking more flexible arrangements. The Association of Personnel Service Organizations told hearings on the Basic Conditions of Employment Bill in 1997: "The majority of temporary and casual workers in South Africa take temporary work out of choice. Temporary work provides a wonderful opportunity for people to get training ... This is a fast-growing industry, providing workers in South Africa with access to jobs and employment they might not otherwise have had."

The reality is, of course, very different. Some agencies do little to hide the fact that temporary or contract staff provide a way for employers to bypass employment laws or to solve "staffing problems" by retrenching unionized workers and replacing them with non-unionized temps. Take, for example, this advertisement: "Guest House Temps, Marvellous Maids, Choose-a-char offer WONDERFUL WORKERS available for your selection at a nominal fee: domestics, chars, housekeepers, kitchen hands, restaurant workers, cooks, childminders, nurse aides, clerks, receptionists, drivers, cashiers, labourers. Make one phone call to find staff to fit your requirements, one call can *solve any staffing problem* you might have."[18]

Of course the shift to temporary work, and other changes in the terms and conditions of employment, are neither race- nor gender-neutral. Although the racialized and gendered character of dualism is changing, the labour market remains highly segmented. Women are disproportionately numerous in temporary and other forms of non-standard employment. Although whites no longer have privileged access to jobs with SER-type wages and benefits, blacks dominate the majority of jobs at the bottom end of the labour market. The expansion of these positions and casualization therefore have profound implications for eliminating discrimination in the labour market. Although new legislation has forced some employers to modify their hiring, training, and promotion practices to ensure that workplaces are more representative, other employment trends undermine the regulatory aims of legislation. Thus, while legislation has gone a long way in reregulating the labour market, resegmentation is significantly narrowing the space for generating equality.

LABOUR LAW AMENDMENTS

Despite growing recognition of these trends and the massive rise in employment in unregulated sectors, the government has been slow to respond. In September 2000, Mr. Membathisi Mdladlana, the minister of labour, observed that "there has been a worldwide increase in the use of temporary workers, home workers, subcontractors, and so on." He added, "the increase in atypical workers is a reality which we cannot reverse" (South African Institute of Race Relations, 2000: 1). Whatever the government's reluctance, the labour movement has achieved a set of amendments to labour legislation[19] that tighten existing loopholes. Amendments to the BCEA provide that the minister can deem any category of persons to be employees for the purposes of the BCEA or any other employment law besides the Unemployment Insurance Act of 1966.[20]

Further, a new section inserted into the BCEA provides rebuttable presumptions concerning proof of an employment relationships. This amendment may help close the loophole that employers use to convert employees into independent contractors. The final amendments also adjust the enforcement system, clarifying and simplifying the way in which labour inspectors must secure undertakings from employers, and removing a technical point that could invalidate a compliance order (Godfrey and Clarke, 2002). Amendments to the LRA may also increase employment protection for other groups of vulnerable workers, especially when firms use retrenchment to restructure.

These amendments are a step in the right direction, but they do not go far enough. Overall, regulation has not responded adequately to labour market trends; its definition of "worker" relies on the SER as a normative model. Thus, given the dramatic growth of informal and other NSERs, legislation still excludes the growing group of marginal workers. Further, the department's inability to monitor and enforce legislation has resulted in the rapid proliferation of non-standard employment. Loopholes in the legislation, the narrow and traditional reading of "employed," and weak enforcement have meant that stronger protection in law has not improved standards and conditions for most workers, especially those excluded from protection in the apartheid era. As a result, inequality and segmentation have continued, even increased.

CONCLUSION

Labour legislation introduced since the ANC came to power has gone a long way to reregulate the labour market. Given the challenges facing South Africa at independence and the recent experience of deregulation in other countries highlighted elsewhere in this volume, even the partial transformation of the labour market has been a significant achievement. Recent legislation does begin to address the extreme inequality and discrimination inherited from the apartheid regime. This was not an easy task. Given national and international pressure from business to increase international competitiveness and flexibility, the legislation tried to balance regulation and protection with flexibility. Most explicitly outlined in the BCEA, the key mechanism was "regulated flexibility." Alongside extended and expanded protection for workers, the act provides significant scope for downward variation of standards (apart from core standards).

Overall, this strategy was presented as an appropriate response to the demands of business and the perceived needs of the global economy for flexibility and to workers' need for increased protection and regulation. Thus far, however, the strategy has failed. The legacy of labour market policies under apartheid, rising unemployment, and the massive growth in the informal sector – fuelled by failed or inappropriate macroeconomic and industrial policies – combined with insufficient regulation in the new laws have created an environment in which jobs have been destroyed and non-standard employment has flourished. This result of course undermines the effectiveness of minimum-standards legislation and contributes to the erosion of workers' rights and benefits.

Along with quite extensive provisions in the BCEA for variation, the rapid expansion of the informal economy, legal loopholes, and weak monitoring and enforcement all provide employers with great flexibility. Employers appear to have "won" the flexibility battle, with the labour market remaining very flexible for most of them. "Flexible regulation," rather than "regulated flexibility," would seem better to describe the model. Even with the introduction of new labour statutes, the labour market has not fundamentally changed; new pressures and policies now shape inequality, poverty, and marginalization. Despite labour's apparent legislative victory with the new amendments, these incremental reforms are unlikely to reverse the deeper trends that have dominated the evolution of the labour market in post-apartheid South Africa.

NOTES

1 I am grateful to Shane Godfrey and Leah Vosko for helpful comments on earlier drafts of this chapter and to Janice McMillan for her useful remarks on this chapter.
2 All non-white workers.
3 Act 65 of 1995.
4 Act 75 of 1997.
5 Act 55 of 1998.
6 Act 97 of 1998.
7 Transitional provisions were outlined in the act. For the first 12 months after the commencement of the act, farmworkers' ordinary weekly hours were 48 per week. Security guards' fell to 55 for the first 12 months after commencement and to 50 for an additional 12 months.
8 Statistics South Africa's Labour Force Survey reports an unemployment rate of 29.5 per cent (the official definition) or 41.5 per cent (the expanded definition, which includes discouraged work seekers) as of September 2001.
9 Historically, permanent farmworkers received accommodation on the farms. Although living conditions were very poor, pressure exerted on farmers throughout the 1980s resulted in increased spending on social benefits and housing. More farmers began to contribute to medical care, pension funds, and the upgrading of on-farm housing (Ewert and Hamman, 1996).
10 Apartheid policies divided the population into white, Indian, coloured, and African. Racism continues, and previous classifications still affect the particular patterns of segmentation in the labour market today.
11 Agencies that recruit and place temporary workers.
12 Mesebetsi Labour Force Survey, 1999.
13 According to the Wholesale and Retail Trade SETA, Africans account for 57 per cent (31 per cent women, 26 per cent men) of service, shop, and market sales workers in retail trade. In contrast 45 per cent (29 per cent men, 16 per cent women) of the managerial staff in retail trade. Research shows that employment changes to date have had little impact on employment patterns at the managerial level.

14 Labour Force Survey, Feb. 2002.
15 As of 1 February 2003, wages and working conditions for wholesale and retail employees are set by the new Sectoral Determination 9.
16 Central Statistical Services, South Africa, 1996; South African Labour Statistics 1995, Pretoria, 1996.
17 Established in 1990.
18 Advertisement for temporary workers circulated around various workplaces, including the University of Cape Town campus, June 1999. Emphasis added.
19 After almost two years of negotiations, the final package of amendments – the Basic Conditions of Employment Amendment Act 11 – came into effect on 1 August 2002.
20 The Unemployment Insurance Act of 1966 has been replaced by the Unemployment Insurance Act 63 of 2001.

REFERENCES

African National Congress (ANC). 1994. *The Reconstruction and Development Plan: A Policy Framework.* Johannesburg: Umanyano Publications.
Bezuidenhout, A., and B. Kenny. 1999. "The Language of Flexibility and the Flexibility of Language: Post-Apartheid South African Labour Market Debates." Paper presented at the Industrial Relations Association of South Africa Conference, Cape Town.
Butchtemann, C.F., and S. Quack. 1990. "How Precarious Is Non-standard Employment? Evidence for West Germany." *Cambridge Journal of Economics* 14 (3), 315–30.
Cameron, Edwin. 1990. "Casualties of the Workplace: Casual and Fixed Term Employees," *Employment Law* 6 (4).
Cheadle, H., and M. Clarke. 2000. "'Workers' Protection in South Africa: ILO Country Study." Unpublished research reported prepared for the ILO.
Clarke, M. 2000. "Checking Out and Cashing Up: The Rise of Precarious Employment in the Retail Sector." Unpublished paper presented at the TIPS Annual Conference, Johannesburg.
Clarke, Marlea, Shane Godfrey, and Theron Godfrey. 2002. "Employment Standards in South Africa: A Country Study." Commissioned research report for the International Labour Organization (ILO).
– 2003. "An Overview and Analysis of Homeworking in the Clothing Industry in South Africa." Unpublished research report.
Clarke, Marlea, and Bridget Kenny. 2002. "Falling Out of the Loop: Protection of Casual and Contract Workers in the Commercial, Distributive Sectoral Determination," in *Bargaining Indicators*, Vol. 7. Cape Town: Labour Research Services.
COSATU. 1996. "Supplementary Secretariat Report on the Employment Standards Act Negotiations." Unpublished paper.

– 2000. "Draft COSATU Gender Policy." Report of COSATU National Gender Conference.

Department of Labour. 2001. "Commission for Employment Equity Report 1999–2001." Pretoria: Department of Labour.

Department of Labour, Minimum Standard Directorate. 1996. "Policy Proposals for a New Employment Standards Statute." Green Paper. Pretoria: Department of Labour.

Du Toit, A., and F. Ally. 2001. "The Externalization and Casualization of Farm Labour in Western Cape Horticulture." Unpublished research report commissioned by the Centre for Rural Legal Studies, Cape Town.

Ewert, J., and J. Hamman. 1996. "Labour Organisation in Western Cape Agriculture: An Ethnic Corporatism?" *Journal of Peasant Studies* 23 (2/3), 146–65.

Godfrey, Shane, and Marlea Clarke. 2002. "The Basic Conditions of Employment Act Amendments: More Questions Than Answers," *Law, Democracy and Development* 6 (1).

Hamman, J. 1996. "The Impact of Labour Policy on Rural Livelihoods on Western Cape Wine and Fruit Farms," in De Klerk, Lipton, and Lipton, eds., *Creating Rural Livelihoods in the Western Cape*. Durban: Indicator Press.

Hemson, D. 1996. "Beyond the Frontier of Control: Trade Unionism and the Labour Market in the Durban Docks," *Transformation* 30, 83–114.

Henwood, N. 1998. "The Long Road," *The South African Labour Bulletin* 22 (4).

Kenny, B. 1998. "The Casualisation of the Retail Sector in South Africa," *Indicator South Africa* 15 (4), 25–31.

– 2000. "We Are Nursing These Jobs: The Implications of Labour Market Flexibility on East Rand Retail Sector Workers and Their Households." Unpublished paper presented at the South African Sociological Association meetings, 2–5 July, University of the Western Cape.

Klerck, G. 1994. "Industrial Restructuring and the Casualization of Labour: A Case Study of Subcontracted Labour in the Process Industries." *South African Sociological Review* 7 (1), 32–62.

Ministry of Labour. 1994. "The Five Year Programme 1994–1999." Pretoria: Government of South Africa.

Pollert, A. 1988. "Dismantling Flexibility," *Capital and Class* 43 (34), 42–75.

South African Institute of Race Relations. 2000. "Atypical Workers May Have to Become Typical," in *Fast Facts*. Braamfontein: South African Institute of Race Relations.

Southall, R. 1999. "South Africa in Africa: Foreign Policy Making During the Apartheid Era." Occasional Paper Series, no. 20. Johannesburg: Institute for Global Dialogue.

Theron, J., and S. Godfrey. 2000. *Protecting Workers on the Periphery*. Development and Labour Monograph (Jan. 2000). Cape Town: Institute of Development and Labour Law.

Valodia, I. 1991. "Increase in Casual and Temporary Work: The Case of Shop-workers," *South African Labour Bulletin* 15 (7), 48–50.

Vosko, L. 2000. *Temporary Work: The Gendered Rise of a Precarious Employment Relationship.* Toronto: University of Toronto Press.

Wholesale and Retail Trade Seta. 2000. Wholesale and Retail Trade Sector Skills Plan. Draft 1.1 Pretoria: W&R Seta.

6

The Russian Reforms and Their Impact on Labour: A Transition to What?

MANFRED BIENEFELD, TATYANA CHETVERNINA,
and LIANA LAKUNINA

When the Soviet Union imploded and embarked on its capitalist reforms in 1991, there were high hopes in many quarters. Both internationally and within the Soviet Union, the most widespread view was that the changes would usher in an era that combined democracy and freedom with increased efficiency and growth and that greater prosperity and well-being would soon emerge for most people. The reforms would finally provide some relief for – in the paternalistic language of the international community – the "long-suffering" Soviet people.

Although most observers agreed that there would be some dislocation and short-term pain during the transition, they believed that sufficiently rapid and resolute market reforms would limit these losses. The reforms had to be dramatic and permanent, so as to attract the large amounts of foreign investment expected to provide the capital, management know-how, and technology to unlock the vast productive potential of the sleeping giant.

In practice, the adoption of market-oriented policies throughout Russia's economy, notably including its labour market, has been associated with one of the most sudden peacetime reductions in real living standards of any society in modern history. During the 1990s, real wages for employed workers declined by two-thirds, formal employment shrank drastically, informal and subsistence work became more prevalent, inequality widened substantially, mortality exploded, and life expectancy declined. In the midst of this collapse in living standards (and, indeed, a decline in the country's population), conditions would seem ripe for a forceful rejection of the neoliberal reforms. Sadly, the unwavering commitment of crucial international lenders to the market model, regardless of the evidence, combined with the vested power of that small constituency within Russia that has profited from the economic and human disaster,[2] suggests that the struggle to find a new economic and social approach in Russia will be an uphill one.

This chapter considers the labour market effects, and the human consequences, of Russia's failed experiment with neoliberal shock therapy. The first section considers the inherently ideological nature of neoliberal prescriptions for Russia. This policy recipe adopted the assumptions of leading policy makers about the necessity and the efficiency of free markets. The flow of consistently negative empirical evidence regarding the consequences of their measures only seemed to enhance their determination to carry on with the chosen policy course more quickly and forcefully. The second section summarizes some of the broad indicators of macroeconomic performance during the 1990s. The third reviews the catastrophic impact of the reforms, and of the corresponding economic collapse, on working people in Russia – most notably women, pensioners, and workers outside the main cities. The conclusion considers the need for a fundamental rethinking of the neoliberal assumptions of Russia's experiment. Only a new approach, aimed at preserving and nurturing the country's human and social resources, and enhancing real productive capacity (rather than writing it off in the name of market discipline), could prompt Russia's transition to take a more constructive turn.

NEOLIBERALISM: IDEOLOGY AND POLICY

The recipe for economic change in Russia seemed very simple to the neoliberal reformers. The country had a wealth of natural resources and a highly educated labour force. It needed capital and new technology, which were abundantly available in the global economy, and a new sense of market-driven discipline to increase economic efficiency. The task was to bring all of these factors of production together to produce potentially spectacular rewards. This union would be a marriage made in heaven. But to unlock this golden future, the region's resources, including its human resources, would have to become responsive to market forces. And the new national markets needed for this purpose required close integration with international markets from the outset, if they were to attract foreign capital on a sufficient scale. In short, rapid and radical market reforms, together with an opening of the Russian economy, formed the key to success.[3]

For the neoliberal reformers, the main risks of this strategy related to the fear that it might prove impossible to dismantle the old system rapidly or comprehensively enough. Either the old state or the old bureaucracy might prove too resistant to change; similarly, the old "dependent" mentality of the labour force could block, or impede, the introduction of an efficient market for labour. Unfortunately this fear created a mind-set that tended to respond to every emerging difficulty by demanding ever-more rapid or radical market reforms. There was no time or willingness to consider more moderate and pragmatic policies that might have facilitated a less costly and destructive transition. This blinkered approach eventually transformed the reforms from means into ends, allowing the reformers to claim success simply because many firms had been privatized or many subsidies removed – even if human welfare had declined sharply in the meantime.

Meanwhile the strong focus on eradicating the "old Soviet attitudes of dependence" from the labour force created similar problems. Reformers saw all efforts to protect employment conditions as misguided and unrealistic reflections of this destructive mentality. When combined with the natural tendency of employers – and neoliberals – to reject labour demands on the grounds that they threaten profitability and competitiveness, this helped to diminish labour's ability to protect its working conditions. Once again, it was all but impossible to consider seriously the merits of labour market models other than the neoliberal ones, which are obsessed with "flexibility."

Against this background, Russia's reformers embarked on a program of radical social engineering driven largely by ideology and almost totally immune to unfavourable empirical evidence – since its architects believed so firmly that history and economic science had validated their policies beyond a reasonable doubt. And no amount of contrary evidence from a single country such as Russia could undermine this deeply held, general conclusion. Instead, neoliberals interpreted evidence of the negative economic and social consequences of Russia's shock therapy as proof that the reforms had not gone far enough or had not been implemented sufficiently effectively or rigorously. This explains why the apparent policy failures generally led not to pragmatic re-evaluations, but to policy intensification. This is presumably what Joseph Stiglitz, former chief economist of the World Bank, had in mind when he described the leading reformers, both in Russia and in the main international financial institutions (the World Bank and the International Monetary Fund), as follows: "It is almost as if many of the western advisers just thought the Bolsheviks had the wrong textbooks instead of the whole wrong approach. With the right textbooks in their briefcases, the 'market Bolsheviks' would be able to fly into the post-socialist countries and use a peaceful version of Lenin's methods to make the opposite transition" (Stiglitz, 1999: 22).

After ten years of "reform" associated with virtually unprecedented welfare losses, especially for working people, the Russian government and

Table 6.1   Macroeconomic indicators of the Russian crisis

	1994	1995	1996	1997	1998	1999
Real GDP growth (%)*	−13	−4	−3	1	−5	3
Consumer price inflation (%)	215	131	22	11	84	37
Current account balance (% of GDP)	4	3	3	1	1	10
General government balance (% of GDP)	−10	−6	−9	−7	−5	−4

Source: OECD, 1997, 2000. Data are rounded because of the approximate nature of official Russian economic statistics.
*Published data indicate annual declines in real GDP in Russia of −3 per cent in 1990, −5 per cent in 1991, −15 per cent in 1992, and −9 per cent in 1993, for a cumulative decline in real GDP of over 40 per cent between 1989 and 1997. Consistent data for the other macroeconomic series are unavailable for 1990–99.

the main international agencies continue to promote the same neoliberal policies with which they began. These policies assume that Russia's salvation lies in the further expansion and deepening of free and flexible markets; in its deeper integration into the global economy; and in the creation of a still more flexible labour market. While it is theoretically possible that this approach might soon begin to generate stable growth and large welfare gains, after ten years of spectacular failure and painful human decline, the onus of proof should lie squarely on the shoulders of those who still seek to press on with the same policy direction.

MACROECONOMIC LEGACY OF NEOLIBERALISM

In general, the last ten years have been traumatic for Russia and for most of its people. For most of those who once believed that pro-market reforms would bring prosperity, such dreams are now a distant, bitter memory. And for those who had never shared that initial optimism, the present often surpasses their worst fears. Employment has fallen dramatically, and real wages even more so. Economic insecurity has grown sharply, along with inequality, poverty, alcoholism, and ill health. Even life expectancy – an aggregate statistic that normally changes only very slowly – has fallen significantly in a historically short period.[4] Recently these trends have even begun to undermine the belief in democracy itself – which should have been the greatest and most cherished gift of this latest revolution, but which is now viewed with growing cynicism. More and more Russians have concluded that powerful and self-serving economic and financial interests dominate and manipulate the democratic process. Those elites are virtually the only segment of Russian society to have benefited measurably from the dramatic changes of the past decade.

Table 6.1 summarizes some of the broad macroeconomic evidence regarding Russia's performance under neoliberalism.[5] Real gross domestic product (GDP) declined by over 40 percent between 1989 and 1997 – significantly more than it did in North America in the Depression of the 1930s.[6] It fell further following the foreign bond crisis of 1998. While GDP may have stabilized more recently, with a pattern of slow and unsteady growth emerging, there is no evidence of any significant rebound from the massive economic retrenchment that immediately followed the introduction of neoliberal measures early in the 1990s. The legacy of those policies, then, has not been "short-term pain for long-term gain," but continuing economic hardship, with no clear end in sight. In short, the virtual halving of Russia's economic output now seems to be a long-term, debilitating legacy of the free-market recipe – surely one of the most shocking experiences of sudden and permanent economic contraction in history. Russia has retreated from having the third largest economy in the world during the Communist era to just the tenth-largest today (United Nations Development Programme, 2001: Table 11).[7]

Hyperinflation was one of the most obvious and chaotic consequences of the sudden marketization of the Russian economy. Inflation gradually declined from over 200 per cent per year in 1994 (and probably even higher before that, although reliable data are not available), to under 40 per cent by the end of the decade – albeit with a reprise of hyperinflation in 1998 following the Russian federal government's default on a portion of its foreign debt and the consequent free floating of the Russian currency. The effects of this inflation have been disastrous for wage earners in Russia, as we see in detail below. And the consequences were even worse for pensioners and other people living on fixed money incomes, to say nothing of recipients of social security, typically designed during the era of planned price stability.

Hyperinflation, combined with the organizational paralysis of many newly privatized firms and state agencies, has led to "demonetization" in the Russian economy. Not surprisingly, the country's orthodox financial advisers dictated that Russian central bankers should respond to rapid inflation by clamping down on the growth of the money supply. This standard free-market prescription received added emphasis as part-and-parcel of "hard budget constraints" on newly privatized firms, intended to overcome the Soviet legacy of lax accounting and tolerated losses. This monetary squeeze inevitably and predictably created a crisis in the ability of firms and public agencies to pay their bills. Many agents responded by developing alternative means of paying for needed inputs (including resources, parts, and labour). These methods included barter, informal credit, and unreported monetary transactions. By 2000, non-cash receipts of Russian companies represented over 50 per cent of their total revenues (OECD, 2000: 85).

Demonetization was most notable in more remote regions. While this system is testimony to Russian creativity and resilience, the resulting huge waste and inefficiencies starkly reveal the failure of marketization to allocate resources more efficiently. In fact, with the economy devolving into a pre-monetary system, the opposite has occurred: the economy now dedicates more of its resources to the development of non-monetary means of payment (a problem that should have evaporated centuries ago with the emergence of national monetary systems).

Russia's economy has generated sizeable current-account surpluses from international trade throughout the period of "reform." These surpluses reached 10 per cent of GDP by 2000. Far from indicating "competitive" success in international markets, however, this pattern reveals something more disturbing. Neoliberal reformers had assumed that simultaneous marketization and globalization would attract foreign capital to Russia. This inflow should have generated a mirror-image and offsetting trade *deficit*, corresponding to the expected importation of foreign-made investment goods. But no such inflow has occurred. Foreign corporations remain generally repelled by Russia's instability and corruption. Apart from a few large foreign investments in newly privatized energy and resource companies, foreign investors have stayed away. Meanwhile, the small elite of *nouveau riche* who possess large amounts of liquid financial assets have quietly exported capital, as reflected in the current-account surpluses reported in Table 6.1. Like the destruction of vast quantities of physical capital (through neglect, breakdown, and underinvestment), this flight is only worsening the economy's long-term prospects.[8]

In line with their orthodox and highly ideological worldview, Russia's foreign advisers and lenders have concentrated on reducing the huge fiscal deficits that were incurred at all levels of Russian government through the 1990s. These deficits declined from 10 per cent of GDP in 1994 to less than half that by 2000. Reductions in state expenditure on the whole range of public programs (from social programs, to infrastructure, to the military and space) played the lead role in this retrenchment. The federal government also, with Western encouragement, has been redeveloping its shrunken capacity to collect tax revenues from this new market-based economy. Even market-oriented observers acknowledge that this crisis in the fiscal capacity of the Russian state imposed a huge constraint on the government's ability to provide even a basic network of infrastructure and social services (OECD, 2000) – not to mention its ability to generate funds to repay the government's foreign lenders.

The decline of Russia's physical capital stock, while impossible to describe with accurate empirical data, is another consequence of the country's experiment with market-oriented shock therapy that will take decades to recoup. Capital spending declined by the mid-1990s to approximately one-quarter of its pre-reform level (OECD, 1997: 37). We can see the failure of this premature and sudden exposure to global competition most clearly in multinational firms' largely ignoring this newly opened, resource-rich jurisdiction. Foreign investment has not stepped in to fill the huge void created by the sharp contraction in domestic investment.

Of course, there were many problems with the Soviet regime's pattern of mass, centrally planned investment spending – including the questionable efficiency of much investment and a terrible record of environmental degradation. But the assumption that a free and competitive capital market would automatically make all this better seems incredible, in retrospect. As the priests of laissez-faire have discovered the hard way, both in Russia and in many other developing countries, it takes far more in practice than just openness to world markets and fiscal prudence by governments to attract foreign investors. It takes stability, domestic growth, infrastructure, and a motivated and healthy labour force to make an economy run effectively and productively and hence to make it appealing to foreign investors. None of this, sadly, could be delivered by the Russian reformers, with their simple-minded application of free-market doctrines. The economic collapse, and the consequent social and political instability, produced by neoliberal shock therapy have made Russia considerably *less* attractive to foreign investors than a more cautious and balanced regime might have done.

Even more shocking than the destruction of physical capital, and even more damaging to long-run economic prospects, has been the degradation of the country's once-impressive human resources. The next section thus considers in more detail the labour market implications of the Russian reforms.

LABOUR MARKET CONSEQUENCES OF NEOLIBERAL REFORM

The facts of the decline in human conditions in the wake of Russia's market reforms are frightening and saddening. The past decade has resulted in stunning welfare losses for most Russians. And these losses are all the more painful for a working population long accustomed to high levels of economic and social security; modest but reliable material standards of living; high levels of education and health care; and reasonably high levels of equity.

Women in particular had made much progress under the Soviet regime, by international standards. Their education levels were generally somewhat higher than those of men. Their labour-force participation rates were comparable to those of men – because, like men, they were expected to undertake paid work once they finished school. Thus by the late 1980s women constituted 51 per cent of the Soviet labour force.[9] Moreover, they had moved into many jobs previously deemed inappropriate for women.[10] Finally, women had substantial, if not equal, representation in the main institutions of power, including the Supreme Soviet, where it was common for them to hold one-third of the seats.

At the same time, gender equality was still some way off, even in the Soviet era. The main problem pertained to the so-called double burden, which was especially onerous in the Soviet system, since women were not only engaged in paid work full time but also performing almost all of the housework, child care, and care of elderly relatives. In addition, occupational segregation by gender was widespread, with women tending to be concentrated in sectors with relatively lower wages. And opportunities for promotion within industries and enterprises remained far from equal.[11]

Despite these difficulties, the collapse in labour market opportunities and social security for Russian women during the reform era have dramatically undermined both their relative and their absolute economic positions. In the labour market, women have experienced at least the same deterioration in their opportunities as men (as we see below). Yet, in addition, women have borne the majority of the unpaid costs associated with the breakdown of Soviet-era pension and social welfare programs. Responsibility for most of the financial and physical support of the elderly, children, the sick, and people with disabilities was shifted suddenly and forcefully onto private families in the wake of the economic reforms and the chaotic disintegration of Soviet-era public programs. Needless to say, Russian women have had to respond to these new demands with even more unpaid time and effort. In retrospect, economic and social conditions for women under the Soviet regime – even with its onerous double day – must now seem highly attractive for millions of hard-pressed Russian women.

Many of the labour market implications of the market reforms stem directly and predictably from their stunningly negative impact on real economic activity. The 40 per cent cumulative contraction in GDP went hand in hand with a sharp, though less dramatic, decline in the number of people employed in the economy. Estimates of the size of this reduction vary from one data source to another. Table 6.2 provides a breakdown of employment changes by industry, based on establishment data, and suggests that total employment fell by 14 per cent between 1991 and 1998. Table 6.3 shows changes in employment by age category, based on household surveys, and suggests an even steeper decline in employment – 19

Table 6.2   Changes in Russian employment (000s), by industry, 1991–98

	1991	1998	Change	Change (%)
Industry	22,407	14,132	(8,275)	-37
Agriculture	9,736	8,724	(1,012)	-10
Construction	8,488	5,054	(3,434)	-40
Education	6,138	5,919	(219)	-4
Trade, public catering	5,626	9,257	3,631	+65
Transport	4,876	3,983	(893)	-18
Public health services	4,305	4,453	146	+3
Housing-communal services, non-productive services.	3,159	3,405	246	+8
Science and scientific services	2,769	1,302	(1,467)	-53
Organs of government	1,532	2,777	1,245	+81
Culture and art	1,135	1,114	(21)	-2
Communication	874	837	(37)	-4
Insurance, finance, and credit	439	734	295	+67
Forestry	234	239	5	+2
Economy total	73,848	63,642	(10,206)	-14

Source: *Labour and Employment in Russia*, 1999.

Table 6.3   Changes in Russian employment, by age group, 1992–98

		By age category		
	Employed population	15–24	25–49	50–72
1992				
Thousand people	71,068	9,398	46,643	15,026
% of total employed	100%	13.2%	65.7%	21.1%
1998				
Thousand people	57,860	6,339	42,432	9,089
% of total employed	100%	10.9%	73.3%	15.8%
Decline in employment, 1992–98	18.6%	32.5%	9.0%	39.5%

Source: *Research of the State Statistic Committee of Russian Federation*, various issues.

percent – between 1992 and 1998. In either case, the fact that employment fell less than half as much as output implies a large reduction in average productivity (which was down by as much as 30 per cent over the decade) that relates closely to the collapse in real wages. Moscow's Centre for Strategic Research (2000: 1) estimates that real wages plunged 60 per cent during the decade, reflecting a powerful combination of declining output, falling productivity, widespread non-payment of wages, and hyperinflation. Once again, the miserable performance of Russian labour productivity under the new regime essentially refutes the neoliberal claim that shock therapy would jolt Russians out of their Soviet-style lethargy and usher in a new era of efficiency and productivity.

The Russian economic implosion was accompanied by a dramatic shift in the structure of the economy and hence in patterns of employment. This suggests that the aggregate macroeconomic changes were even more disruptive at the sectoral and regional levels. Consider the industrial dis-aggregation of employment changes summarized in Table 6.2. The four-teen industrial sectors in that table underwent three categories of experi-ence:

- Six sectors, accounting for 21 per cent of all employees in 1991, saw rel-atively minor changes between 1991 and 1998 (with employment rising or falling by less than 10 per cent during that period).
- Five sectors (industry, agriculture, construction, transport, scientific and technical) had large declines – an average of 31 per cent and a maximum (in scientific and technical) of over 50 per cent. This group includes all the major goods-producing sectors; since these five industries together accounted for 65 per cent of employment in 1991, the sharp contraction in their employment pulled down the overall average dramatically.
- Three service sectors (trade, finance, and government) experienced very large increases, averaging almost 70 per cent for the group. This sounds like a "bright side," but this category accounted for only 10 per cent of total employment at the outset of reforms. Their enhanced performance therefore could not offset job losses in other sectors.

The aggregate data therefore mask an unprecedented degree of disrup-tion in the sectoral and regional composition of employment.[12]

And the grim news does not stop with total employment. Even for people who retained jobs, a growing proportion did not receive wages on time. Delays in payments reached a peak in mid-decade. As a proportion of the average computed wage bill, cash wages owing increased from 28 per cent in 1993 to over 80 per cent by 1995. The bond default of 1998 and the consequent inflation crisis worsened delays with wages.

A proliferation of more-or-less desperate "survival responses" frequently saw workers receive payment in kind or through permission to make per-sonal use of company plant and machinery. And so, along Russia's deteri-orating highways, at endless informal roadside stalls, workers tried to sell surplus products from their firms.

For people without work entirely, support was highly unpredictable, and payments were very low when paid. In the early 1990s, when the Russian state's Employment Fund had a positive balance,[13] the wealthier regions paid benefits, but there was no mechanism to allow funds to flow to more remote and crisis-affected regions, where the funds were in deficit. Later in the decade, when formal unemployment started to rise, the Employment Fund's assets quickly ran out, and it eventually stopped functioning. By 2000 it was observed that "the vast majority of the unemployed ... refused to register at employment agencies, since they do not expect to receive material support or any other assistance in the job-hunting process" (Centre for Strategic Research, 2000: 5).

Official unemployment figures, based on the number of registered unemployed, thus became increasingly unreliable and began to diverge more and more sharply from the findings of labour force surveys employing standard definitions of the International Labour Organization. The latter are now the only reliable measures of unemployment. They indicate that formal unemployment reached a peak of 14 per cent in 1996, and remained above 11 per cent in 2000 (Centre for Strategic Research, 2000).

In general, the problem of formal unemployment has been held in check – or, more accurately, obscured – both by the retention of workers in "paper jobs" that pay no wages and require no work and by an exodus out of the labour force by both men and women. Between 1992 and 1998 the labour force participation rate for women of working age fell by 19 percentage points, and that for men, by 18 percentage points (Chetvernina et al., 2001). By any measure, these are dramatic changes over such a short period. The somewhat larger decline in women's participation, combined with their disproportionate concentration in newly created but low-paid positions in private trade and services, shows them bearing more than their share of the costs of adjustment to the new labour market. As we saw above, women are picking up most of the new unpaid domestic tasks resulting from reductions in public services, family fragmentation, and the collapsing real incomes of pensioners.

Meanwhile, as Table 6.3 shows, the exodus from the formal labour force occurred mainly among the youngest and oldest age groups. Whereas the number of employed workers aged 25 to 49 fell by 9 per cent between 1992 and 1998, that between 15 and 24 dropped by 33 per cent, and for those between 50 and 72 it declined by a shocking 40 per cent. Thus, in Russia as elsewhere, a disproportionate share of labour market "flexibility" falls to women, young workers, and older workers. Some observers might see the comparative stability of employment among people in their "core" working years as a positive and rational development (if one assumes that old and young workers are less likely to be household heads). But households in Russia, as in many other places, are fragmented; moreover, the real value of pensions has virtually evaporated in the wake of cumulative inflation. Thus the disproportionate decline in employment prospects for both young and old is adding to the misery of millions of Russian households.

In terms of formal labour legislation, labour standards, and industrial relations, the experience has been equally discouraging.[14] The Russian state's capacity to regulate labour conditions in a privatized, deregulated economy is at least as weak as its noted inability to collect taxes, and its *willingness* is even more in doubt.

In fact, the 1990s saw relatively few changes to the structures of Soviet labour law as the effective deregulation of labour standards and industrial relations took place more through non-enforcement of existing provisions than through explicit policy reform. Later, the federal government began to retool its labour and social policies to address – or, in many cases, to facilitate – practices emerging in the new context of private employment relationships. In the mid-1990s it established a new state labour inspectorate, and in 1998 it implemented its first regulations governing non-state employer pension plans. In February 2002, it implemented a wide-ranging reform of the labour code, which gave employers greater leeway in dismissing workers, allowed for more use of contract labour and other more "flexible" employment contracts, and set initial minimum labour standards in areas such as vacations, minimum wages, and health and safety standards. Employers and international lenders lauded these reforms as allowing greater flexibility, contributing to restoration of the "investment climate," and facilitating construction of an efficient market system (Rutkowski, 1999). On paper, at least, Russian labour legislation is among the more comprehensive in the world. Near-universal lack of meaningful enforcement, however, has permitted deterioration of working conditions and increased the precarious instability of so many workers. Garibaldi and Brixiova (1998) note that effective protection is weak even by eastern European standards, and argue that the resulting insecurity hinders labour market adjustment.

The troubled evolution of Russian trade unions is another feature of the new regime. The unions traversed an unsettled path in the early post-Soviet years, aiming to preserve their institutional and legal standing in the face of pro-market economic and social policy. A package of new laws governing collective bargaining and union activity took effect in early 1996, reflecting a generally tripartite approach that mandated unions to co-operate with newly privatized employers and public agencies for the supposedly mutual benefit of both employers and workers. A hopeful but vague ideology of "social partnership" continues to influence Russian unions' efforts to put a human face on marketization. At the same time, competition and conflict flourish between the dominant trade unions, with their Soviet-era structures (currently affiliated into the Federation of Independent Trade Unions of Russia), and smaller, independent, and generally more militant newer unions in some sectors and regions. The larger unions have attempted to preserve some influence and credibility in federal politics, even as privatization, closures, and non-payment of wages have undermined their influence and capacities at the enterprise level, and unions do continue to represent over one-half of Russian workers (Ashwin and Clarke, 2002: 275), but the gap between their formal rights and their capabilities to act on behalf of their members is as glaring as that between de jure and de facto labour law.

In summary, the experience of Russian workers during the 1990s was shocking. Both employment and real wages plunged as millions of Russians found themselves with jobs that offered no pay – and in many cases no work either. Meanwhile, informal and underground employment has flourished as desperate people seek any opportunity to support themselves and their families and as formal labour law and industrial relations practices inhabit a strange and unstable netherworld, in which workers and their unions continue to possess seemingly strong formal rights, which everyone recognizes as empty. The promises of the market reformers – that deregulation would usher in a hopeful new era of efficiency and prosperity – have brought nothing but declining working and living standards to most of Russia's mistreated but resilient working people.

CONCLUSION: FINDING OTHER WAYS

This pessimistic review of the experience of market-oriented reforms in Russia poses a daunting challenge: how Russia's working people in general, and hard-hit groups (including women, pensioners, and workers in the regions) in particular, might begin to recoup some of their enormous losses and start to build an economic and social model that can improve their well-being. This search for alternative policy regimes may intensify in the wake of the failure of neoliberal therapy. But despite the failures of the market model, and their vast human consequences, its political and ideological dominance – with the Russian government, with the small but powerful segment of Russian society that has benefited from marketization, and importantly with external lenders – remains clear.

As always, the task is both analytical and political. Analytically the challenge is to define and defend an alternative vision that could lead to the creation of a "social market" in Russia and a more balanced approach to managing the transition towards a new economic structure. Politically, the task is to harness and to channel the energies of working people, of pensioners, and of civil organizations so that their voices, and their actions, can become more effective in the policy process. A sense of resistance and opposition to marketization is certainly alive and well in Russia. Large constituencies are explicit in their condemnation of the market model's failure to improve their day-to-day economic and social prospects. To date, however, resistance has surfaced in sporadic, spontaneous, and fleeting ways – as represented, for example, in numerous protests at the enterprise level against privatization and the non-payment of wages. Whether that growing sense of betrayal and opposition can transform itself into a more coherent and potent political and economic force is quite another question – and a very challenging one, at that.

Russia's embattled trade unions must necessarily take a lead in this process, if they want a more balanced socioeconomic model that would combine sustained, stable growth with a wide distribution of benefits and broadly based welfare gains. The union movement finds itself in an uncomfortable and contradictory position, caught between the self-identification of the main unions' leadership as official "partners" in building a new "social partnership" and the deteriorating conditions and misery of most of their members. Despite their recent challenges, Russia's unions still retain a formidable organizational base, popular credibility, and an as-yet-unfulfilled potential to mobilize and inspire their millions of individual members.

The immediate tasks of a more balanced and humane economic and labour market strategy are rather straightforward. A central goal must be to stop the destruction of physical capacity and the exodus of financial capital – both of which will undermine for decades the prospects for recovery in output, growth, and employment. Incentives need to be restored – including through the regulation of financial markets and international financial flows – for Russians to begin investing once again in the recovery and development of their own country, rather than waiting in vain for foreign capital in sufficient quantities to develop their huge economy. And the current disinvestment in human capital must also be reversed. The painful social and labour market consequences of sudden marketization require the quick development of a whole new framework of social and legal protections, and this process is still in its infancy.

One can hope that the emerging frustration of millions of Russians, perhaps together with some critical self-reflection on the part of political leaders, external lenders, and economic advisers, might create the critical mass for a turn towards a more balanced and productive set of economic and social policies. Sadly, however, there is so far little reason to be hopeful. And the more time that passes before rejection and replacement of the naïve and unrealistic dogmas of neoliberal shock therapy, the longer will so many Russians have to endure the catastrophic human costs of this grand, failed experiment.

NOTES

1 See Lipton and Sachs, 1992, for a classic statement of this early optimism.
2 Menshikov (1999) describes the dubious economic and political pedigree of the new Russian "capitalists" who emerged in the wake of the Soviet collapse.
3 Vorobyov and Zhukov, 2000, similarly argue that opening Russia to the forces of globalization was an essential and central feature of the neoliberal reforms.

4 Life expectancy in Russia fell by four years between the 1970s and the end of the 1990s (UNDP, 2001), with almost all the decline occurring since 1990. Another measure of the deterioration of conditions in Russia is the country's free-fall in the UNDP's measurement of human development – from 28th place in the world in 1990 to 55th by 1999 (UNDP, 2001).

5 Understandable difficulties in the accurate and systematic collection of economic statistics in Russia during the 1990s imply that these data are only broadly descriptive.

6 Some estimates put the decline at more than 50 per cent. The shift of much economic activity into the informal economy, or even into the subsistence economy, compounds the usual difficulties with Russian statistical data since 1990.

7 And this ranking uses purchasing-power parity exchange rates; at nominal (or market) exchange rates, Russia possesses just the 15th-largest economy in the world.

8 It is difficult to imagine the indigenous development of a capitalist Russian economy, if there are not genuine Russian "capitalists" who will invest in the private capital accumulation required for capitalism; see Holmstrom and Smith, 2000.

9 In Russia this situation is now frequently described as one of "overemployment," implying that women participated more than they would have had they been free to make a choice. This analysis is especially helpful for advocates who are currently pushing to get women "back into the home" (i.e., to encourage more women to "choose" to withdraw from the formal labour market) in order to make room for men, whom they assume to be the primary breadwinners in families.

10 During the Cold War the West used images of Soviet women driving tractors and operating heavy machinery to highlight the depths to which the godless communists would sink – even forcing women to do such "inappropriate" work.

11 This brief summary of certain aspects of the previous employment situation does not imply that the Soviet model was either preferable or desirable, even though a significant minority of workers, especially older workers, believe that they were better off under that system. These features of that earlier model provide a baseline for discussion of the changes after 1991.

12 Cazes and Nesperova, 2001, indicate that mobility during the transition period has been higher for Russian workers than for workers in any other of the former Communist economies of central and eastern Europe, further undermining the common neoliberal claim that Russia's lack of progress during the reform era results from residual "rigidities" in labour markets and other economic institutions.

13 Two factors helped keep formal unemployment in check: many former workers left the labour force entirely, and many firms retained labour on their formal employment rolls, even though they were unable to pay them – and often had nothing for those workers to do.

14 A recent and thorough review of these developments is Ashwin and Clarke, 2002.

REFERENCES

Ashwin, Sarah, and Simon Clarke. 2002. *Russian Trade Unions and Industrial Relations in Transition*. Basingstoke, England: Palgrave.

Berg, Janine, and Lance Taylor. 2000. "External Liberalization, Economic Performance, and Social Policy." Working Paper No. 12. New York: Center for Economic Policy Analysis, New School University, February.

Cazes, Sandrine, and Alena Nesperova. 2001. "Labour Market Flexibility in the Transition Countries: How Much Is Too Much?" *International Labour Review* 140 (3), 293–326.

Centre for Strategic Research. 2000. *Strategy of Development of the Russian Federation through 2010*. Moscow: Centre for Strategic Research, May.

Chetvernina, Tatyana, Alexandra Moskovskaya, Irina Soboleva, and Natalia Stepantchikova. 2001. "Labour Market Flexibility and Employment Security: Russian Federation." Employment Paper No. 31. Geneva: International Labour Organization.

Garibaldi, Pietro, and Zuzana Brixiova. 1998. "Labor Market Institutions and Unemployment Dynamics in Transition Economies," *International Monetary Fund Staff Papers* 45 (2), 269–308.

Holmstrom, Nancy, and Richard Smith. 2000. "The Necessity of Gangster Capitalism: Primitive Accumulation in Russia and China," *Monthly Review* 51 (9), 1–15.

Lipton, David, and Jeffrey D. Sachs. 1992. "Prospects for Russia's Economic Reforms," *Brookings Papers on Economic Activity* (2), 213–65.

Menshikov, Stanislav. 1999. "Russian Capitalism Today," *Monthly Review* 51 (3), 81–99.

Nesporova, Alena. 1999. *Employment and Labour Market Policies in Transition Economies*. Geneva: International Labour Organization.

Organization for Economic Cooperation and Development (OECD).1997. *OECD Economic Surveys: Russian Federation, 1997–1998*. Paris: OECD.

– 2000. *OECD Economic Surveys: Russian Federation, 2000*. Paris: OECD.

Rutkowski, M. 1999. "Russia's Social Protection Malaise: Key Reform Priorities as a Response to the Present Crisis." Washington, DC: World Bank. Social Protection Discussion Paper No. 9909.

Stiglitz, Joseph E. 1999. "Whither Reform? Ten Years of the Transition," Keynote Address to Annual Bank Conference on Development Economics, World Bank, Washington, DC.

United Nations Development Programme. 2001. *Human Development Report, 2001*. New York: United Nations Development Programme.

Vorobyov, Alexander, and Stanislav Zhukov. 2000. "Russia: Globalization, Structural Shifts and Inequality." Working Paper No. 19. New York: Center for Economic Policy Analysis, New School University, February.

7

Deregulating Industrial Relations in the Apparel Sector: The Decree System in Quebec

Practitioners, academics, and policy makers generally agree that the legal and institutional framework regulating industrial relations in a democracy should ensure reasonable wages and working conditions; allow firms to be efficient, profitable, and competitive; permit unions and managers to perform their respective roles; and finally promote industrial peace (Hébert, 1982). Legislatures rarely leave the labour market completely unregulated, and in most countries employers must at least abide by minimum standards. Thus labour law regulates both the conditions under which the individual contract is determined for the non-unionized worker and the framework under which workers can organize and bargain collectively with an employer, in order to set conditions that extend beyond the legal minimum standards. Québec's Act Respecting Collective Agreement Decrees,[1] extends significant parts of negotiated collective agreements to non-unionized firms within a specific industry and region.

In November 1999, after years of mounting pressure from employers to abolish decrees in the garment sector, the provincial government passed legislation to abolish (effective 1 July 2000) four decrees in the order-apparel industry: in men's wear and jeans, ladies' garments, shirts, and leather gloves.[2] The cabinet adopted an order-in-council[3] determining minimum work conditions in the industry, but that order expired in December 2001. One could only speculate on conditions for non-unionized workers after that date. Many union representatives feared that conditions would ultimately fall to the general minimums monitored by the Labour Standards Board,[4] reducing conditions of work for non-union employees and creating downward pressure on negotiated compensation.

Consistent with the findings of other chapters in this volume (see especially Dave Broad, Della MacNeil, and Sandra Salhani Gamble; and Don Wells), it seems that an anti-labour model of globalization is leading governments towards deregulation of labour markets, with codes establishing minimum standards replacing national regulation through institutional actors.

This chapter seeks to answer the following question: considering that both unions and employers in the clothing industry have lived with a decree system for more than sixty years, were there significant changes in the market, production, or labour conditions to justify abrogation of the decrees? This chapter also tries to anticipate the eventual impact of the decrees' disappearance for the industry as a whole.

In order to convey some background information about the stakeholders, and also to envision tentatively the potential consequences of abolition of the decrees, the chapter first presents an overview of Quebec's garment industry, including its workers, international commercial environment, and system of production and distribution. It then considers the origins, purpose, and nature of the decree system in that industry. The chapter next examines the conditions that led to the employers' challenge of the system in the 1980s and 1990s, then describes the abolition of the decree system in 2000, and briefly anticipates its potential impact. The conclusion relates the decrees' disappearance to overall government strategy to abolish the system in its entirety.

THE GARMENT INDUSTRY

This section first reviews the situation regarding the labour force and working conditions of Quebec's garment industry. It then moves on to the commercial environment and competitive pressures. Finally it describes the production and distribution chain.

Employment and Workers

Canada's clothing industry is concentrated in the province of Quebec. As of December 2002, 55.2 per cent of all jobs in cutting and sewing clothing were in Quebec.[5] That industry represents less than 3.6 per cent of Canada's manufacturing jobs and 2 per cent of Ontario's, but 7 per cent of Quebec's. The last census indicates that the largest occupational group within the Canadian industry consisted of sewing machine operators (accounting for 41.5 per cent of total employment).

Compensation has historically been lowest in manufacturing and remains so (as indicated in Table 7.1). The ratio of average weekly earnings in the garment industry to those in manufacturing as a whole was only

Table 7.1   Estimates of average hourly earnings, manufacturing, Québec, December 2002

Sector	Average weekly earnings ($) (including overtime)
Cutting and sewing clothing	514.65
Fabric mills	691.93
Food	669.16
Wood product	694.98
Metal products	726.56
Furniture and related products	645.72
Computer and electronic products	909.53
Transportation equipment	998.06
Machinery	880.28
Paper	983.58
Manufacturing average	763.91

Source: Statistics Canada, 2002.

67 per cent in Quebec and 63 per cent in Canada. This reflects the impact of the industry's highly competitive market on negotiated settlements and their ensuing extension through decrees to the non-unionized sector. The industry's low wages raise doubts about the argument made by opponents of the decree system that it keeps compensation artificially high.

The labour force is predominantly female, is very heterogeneous ethnically, has less formal training, and tends to be older and more vulnerable. Yanz et al. (1999: 14) report that more than three-quarters of garment workers are women, half are immigrants, and almost 30 per cent are members of a visible minority.

International Commercial Environment

One of the historical and ongoing challenges confronting the apparel sector has been the increasing volume of imports, particularly those from low-wage countries. "Buy Union Made" campaigns initiated by labour organizations in the industry reflected a preoccupation with protecting jobs and collective agreements. Increasing imports from countries whose main competitive advantage rested on low labour costs induced the federal government to design a national policy for textile and clothing in 1970.

In 1973, Ottawa negotiated a Multi-Fibre Arrangement (MFA) within the General Agreement on Tariffs and Trade (GATT). The purpose of this arrangement was to protect domestic companies through the imposition of quotas, while they restructured their operations to become more productive and more competitive. The MFA was renegotiated in 1977, 1981, and 1986. The Uruguay round of GATT undertook to phase out quotas, and the MFA gave way on 1 January 1995 to the Agreement on Textiles and Clothing (ATC) as part of the World Trade Organization agreements (Abernathy et al., 2000: 228–30; Grant, 1992: 225–7). Implementation of the North American Free Trade Agreement (NAFTA) in 1994, following the Free Trade Agreement (FTA) with the United States in 1989, increased pressure on the trade structure of the textile and apparel sectors. The FTA and NAFTA provided for the phasing out of most tariff and non-tariff barriers between the participating countries over ten years, thus increasing competitive pressures on Canadian manufacturers.

Despite these mounting trade pressures, and even though the domestic market has narrowed with the closing of major retailers (such as Eaton's), Canadian producers have been able to increase exports significantly. The Canadian garment industry was essentially domestic in 1989, exporting only 3 per cent of its production. In the wake of the FTA, however, the level of exports with the United States more than tripled from 1992 to 1998. After losing approximately 30,000 jobs between 1988 and 1991, the sector stopped this decline and later regained its position as the principal employer in manufacturing in Quebec.

The weaker Canadian dollar cannot alone account for this surge in exports. Employers were able to find market niches and to increase productivity through innovative work processes and new technology. Successful firms were not those that focused on reducing labour costs, but rather those that invested in upgrading employees' skills and in state-of-the-art equipment (Jodoin, 1999).

Production and Distribution

The garment industry is fragmented: no single firm has a substantial share of the market or can influence the aggregate industry outcome. The industry consists of a large number of small and medium-sized companies (Grant, 1992: 224–5). By definition, a fragmented industry has low overall barriers to potential entrants (Porter, 1980: 191). It also has a very high level of entry and exit movement, particularly in ladies' wear (Grant, 1992: 221). Data compiled by the Ladies' Clothing Joint Commission in the province show that that sector alone had 4,882 entries and 4,821 exits between 1980 and 1998, while the number of firms averaged just over one thousand. Vertical disintegration of the production process separates the assembly of garments into a series of short and simple operations that different locations and contractors can handle. Such decentralization through outsourcing and homeworking can reduce labour costs for employers. Illegal homework has become the main form of non-standard employment. (This situation also holds in South Africa, as Marlea Clarke shows in her chapter in this volume.)

The dominant trend over the last decade has been to keep production in the shop at a minimum and to outsource as much as possible. So the number of larger manufacturers has decreased, and smaller contractors have mushroomed. Manufacturers receive orders from retailers and are responsible for production and delivery of products branded with their trademark; contractors and subcontractors then receive orders from a manufacturer to perform a specific task, such as assembling, located within the longer production process. In 1980, 53 per cent of employers in ladies' apparel were manufacturers (499 of 940), and this proportion dropped to less than 19 per cent by 1998 (192 of 1034). In 1998, even though men's wear is more capital-intensive than ladies' wear and its average plant is larger, almost half of the employers in that subsector (116 of 240) were contractors. Outsourcing production also implies smaller workplaces. In 1998, over three-quarters of firms in the ladies' sector had ten or fewer workers. In men's wear, 43 per cent of firms had ten or fewer workers, and only 10 per cent counted more than one hundred.

Production is also fragmented, with manufacturers, contractors, sub-contractors, and homeworkers integrated through channels that are increasingly controlled and co-ordinated by powerful retailers. In addition to providing retailers with the required combination of sizes, colours, styles, fabrics, and price lines, manufacturers face increasing pressure to deliver finished products in a matter of days from order placement, par-ticularly since computerized code bars allow retailers to know precisely the state of each store's inventory. Each outlet must stock a wide array of prod-ucts, with a small inventory for each item, and this necessitates very quick responses to orders. The intense competition, and the demand-driven market, reinforce this responsiveness. Abernathy et al. (2000: 2) see apparel production as occurring in a channel that gears all firms and rela-tionships to the timely delivery of a product to the market: "A retail-apparel-textile channel typically includes the companies that manufacture synthetic fibres; produce, gather and refine natural fibres; spin fibre into yarn; weave or knit yarn into fabric; manufacture buttons, zippers, and other garment components; and cut and sew fabric into garments. It also includes the retailers ... The retail link often involves services or instruc-tions to suppliers about fabric and garment design, packaging, distribu-tion, order fulfilment, and transportation."

For instance, Benetton concentrates on the strategic operations of dyeing and quality control and outsources more than 80 per cent of its daily production in Europe (Fréry, 1999: 25). The design of the 7,000 boutiques retailing its products follows rigorous specifications, and these theoretically independent franchises sell only its wear and must conform scrupulously to its instructions for computerized restocking and merchan-dizing. Some observers see Benetton as the archetype of the "virtual corporation," comprised of many interdependent businesses sharing information and know-how and adding value through channels of collaboration and transactions (Fréry, 1999).

The division of labour for in-plant garment assembly at the workplace organizes along gender lines. The cutting rooms are a male stronghold, where men lay the cloth and the pattern of fabric and then mark and cut it. Afterwards, women sew the parts together through a still-prevailing progressive bundle system, whereby a worker receives a bundle of unfinished garments, performs a single operation on each garment in it, and then places the completed bundle in a buffer with other bundles waiting for the next assembly step (Abernathy et al., 2000: 27–9).

THE DECREE SYSTEM:
ORIGINS, PURPOSE, AND NATURE

The present profile of the garment industry, its organization of production, and the characteristics of its workers would still seem to suggest that the original purpose of the decree system – namely, to extend to non-unionized workers the benefits of collective bargaining – remains both relevant and justified. The decree system is probably the most original feature of Quebec's legal and institutional framework for industrial relations.

Early experiments with sector-wide collective agreements occurred in the 1920s in the United States, where manufacturers signed collective agreements with the International Ladies' Garment Workers Union (ILGWU) that sought to extend the benefits of collective agreements beyond the unionized workplace. This strategy aimed at "controlling contractors by making the manufacturer responsible in the area-product agreement for its suppliers' behaviour and payment of wages and benefits" (Abernathy et al., 2000: 31). Today, industrial relations systems in some other countries, such as France and Sweden, extend the negotiated conditions of work to an industrial sector or even to non-unionized workers in an industrial branch (Freeman, 1994: 20; Goetschy, 1998: 378–85; Milner, 1990: 73–100).

Quebec's decree system dates back to 1934, ten years prior to introduction of the province's first comprehensive labour relations act. The original decree legislation came in during the Depression, when workers experienced especially unfavourable conditions but unions were too weak to organize or negotiate significant improvements for their members. The period also saw major organizing efforts by, and inter-union rivalry between, established unions and Communist-led organizations, particularly in the ladies' garment sector. The clothing industry in both Montreal and Toronto experienced a turbulent period, as employers scrambled to stay alive by cutting labour costs and workers' conditions deteriorated (Dumas, 1971: 43–75; Steedman, 1997: 142–89).

It was in this climate that the clergy and the Catholic unions affiliated with the Confédération des travailleurs catholiques du Canada (now the CSN) lobbied to import a system used in some European countries (such as the Weimar Republic in Germany), that extended some provisions of collective agreements to workers in non-unionized shops (Beaulieu, 1955). Quebec designed its system (enacted in 1934) to stimulate collective bargaining and labour–management co-operation (Bernier, 1993: 745). Joint committees inspired by the papal encyclicals Rerum Novarum and Quadragesimo Anno would supervise the extended collective agreements (Hébert, cited in Dubé, 1990: 17). The church based its social teaching on labour–management co-operation in an effort to create in the workplace conditions respectful of Christian teachings.

Each decree guarantees to non-unionized workers in a region or an industrial sector certain basic provisions of an umbrella collective agreement negotiated by employers and unions. The goal is to improve conditions of work by keeping wages at least somewhat "out of competition" or by limiting the negative effect of competition on compensation. Decrees exist where many employers, each with a relatively small number of personnel, operate in a highly competitive environment.

Legislators in Quebec were not the only politicians trying sectoral standard-setting to cope with the Depression. Before the U.S. Supreme Court ruled it unconstitutional in 1935, the federal National Recovery Act allowed the U.S. President to ratify private agreements and standardize working conditions in industrial branches (Dubé, 1990: 16). Ontario's Industrial Standards Act of 1935 similarly allowed the minister of labour, on joint request from employers' and employees' representatives, to establish an industry's core conditions, such as minimum wages, hours of work, vacations, and other practices.

In Quebec the decree system represents something between a minimum-wage law and the granting of full collective bargaining rights, and its main features remain unchanged. The Act Respecting Collective Agreement Decrees of 1934 stipulates that government may order that a collective agreement shall bind employers and employees in a given industry, occupation, or region. We thus find regional and province-wide decrees for particular industries and/or occupations (such as garage employees in Montreal and men's wear for the whole province). In September 1999 (prior to abolition of the four decrees in the clothing industry), 27 decrees were in force, covering about 115,000 workers aty 11,500 companies. Abolition of the four apparel decrees, however, has delivered a severe blow to the entire decree system by removing over 22,000 workers

Table 7.2   Number of decrees, employers, and covered workers, 1935–99 (selected years)

Year	Decrees	Employers	Workers
1935	40	n.a.	n.a.
1948	100	18,000	200,000
1959	120	33,000	250,000
1970	75	18,000	140,000
1975	52	12,000	125,000
1985	42	17,250	144,662
1990	34	16,094	142,704
1991	33	16,246	140,347
1992	31	16,137	131,432
1994	29	15,441	126,178
1996	29	13,428	120,420
1999 (September)	27	11,527	113,766
1999 (September, garment decrees excluded)	23	10,298	91,424
2000	20*	10,184	93,717
2001	18†	9,015	71,235
2002 (September)	18	9,069	75,831

*The three decrees abolished in 2000 were in construction material (concrete), corrugated board, and cardboard box.
†The disappearance of the decree in the furniture sector on 1 January ended coverage for 21,374 workers and 683 employers. The decree in bread distribution for the Montréal region ended in March.

and over 1,200 firms from the system – a 20 per cent drop in the number of workers covered by decrees. In 2001 the province eliminated the decree in the furniture sector, producing another loss of 21,000 workers and 700 employers. Table 7.2 summarizes the evolving coverage of the decree system, including both unionized and non-unionized workplaces.

The basic provisions of a decree usually include wages, classification of operations, hours of work, and holidays and vacations. The government may issue a decree ordering the extension of an existing collective agreement with changes that it considers appropriate if, among other reasons, the negotiated conditions of employment to be extended have acquired a "preponderant significance and importance." These conditions of employment must neither seriously hinder competitiveness nor impair job preservation and development. Given recent market and technological developments, and the redundant or overlapping jurisdiction of some decrees, the extended agreement must not (where it classifies operations or employees) unduly burden management.

Supervision of the decree and inspection of workplaces are the task of personnel employed by a joint committee, where employees and employers have equal representation. Funding for the committee comes from all employers and employees covered by the decree; thus unionized workers pay not only their union dues but also for the decree structure. This double burden is the trade-off for taking wages "out of competition," thus reducing pressures from non-unionized workers that could lower unionized wages and eliminate unionized jobs.

EMPLOYERS' CHALLENGES TO THE DECREE SYSTEM: 1980s AND 1990s

The decree system still exists, even though many employers question its legitimacy. Some decrees have disappeared (for example, in 1997 in the flat-glass and woodworking sectors and in garments and furniture). This trend reflects the continuing pressure faced by the decree system since its inception.

The adoption of a minimum wage law in 1937 diminished the status of decrees as a sole source of basic work standards. The Labour Relations Act of 1944 required employers to bargain with a certified union, thus reducing the role and importance of decrees. Coverage peaked in 1959, with 120 decrees (including regional and trade decrees in construction) covering 250,000 people and 33,000 employers (see Table 7.2). "After a dazzling growth period (1934–1944), the decree system was happily forgotten during the Duplessis era: this ensured good working conditions every year for over 200,000 workers. Since the mid-60s, the decree system came under attack by the all-pervasive-State advocates and was simultaneously undermined by severe internal divisions; its coverage fell by half to 125,000" (Hébert, 1990: 412).

Nine the less, the system showed some resilience, because both workers and employers saw its usefulness in balancing the interests of workers with competition in industries dominated by small and medium-size firms. The disappearance of construction decrees in the late 1960s accounted for most of the drop in coverage during that period. Moreover, the state's assumption of the joint committees' jurisdiction over vocational training in 1969 further restricted decrees' role, authority, and importance (Hébert, 1990: 405).

In 1986 the Scowen Report recommended abolition of the decree system (Groupe de travail sur la déréglementation, 1986). It called for privatization and market deregulation – in order to "regulate less, but better." Committee members voiced the objections of many non-unionized employers covered by decrees, who were increasingly resisting the extension of collective agreements. In sectors such as ladies' garments, unionization was continuously decreasing thanks to the outsourcing of production, the growing number of contractors and subcontractors, and the expansion of illegal homework. The government seemed to follow the Scowen Report; delays in extending collective agreements under the decree system became longer as non-unionized employers objected more fiercely.

The report of an inter-ministerial committee in 1994 recommended complete re-examination of the system and tightening of the criteria for passing a decree (Comité interministériel sur les décrets de convention collective, 1994). It reinforced the core arguments of opponents – namely, that decrees inhibit development in sectors exposed to international competition. Its discussion of the disappearance of manufacturing decrees seems to assume an international division of labour in which women garment workers compete for employment on the basis of wages.

Opponents voiced many other criticisms of the decree system. Decrees result in a certain inflexibility, they said, since they extend to smaller units collective agreements negotiated for manufacturers and larger, unionized workplaces. They create too much bureaucratic red tape and control, especially from the joint committees monitoring compliances. Since contracting-out and the fragmentation of production had reduced unionization rates (to below 15 per cent in ladies' garments, for instance), and since only unionized employers had representation on the joint committees, these employers could no longer speak for the majority of the industry's stakeholders. The levies to fund joint committees increased the financial burden for employers already complaining about heavy taxation. The decree system allegedly hindered development of technology and of production by maintaining outdated barriers between products and in some cases imposing double coverage on employers manufacturing products in both men's and ladies' wear. Finally, the decrees specified job classifications considered too rigid and unconducive to the training and efficient use of a much-needed multi-skilled labour force.

Despite this political pressure, the system survived. The desire of unionized employer and employee representatives to maintain it is probably the main reason for its survival in a relatively hostile environment (Hébert, 1990: 406). Nevertheless, the government seemed to aim at creating pre-conditions for its erosion and ultimate abolition. The initial legislation itself has remained almost untouched since its creation in 1934. The government also permitted extremely long delays between the conclusion of a master agreement for union members and its subsequent extension.

The system has historically faced difficult challenges stemming from the lack of co-ordination and harmonization with the province's Labour Code and Act Respecting Labour Standards. Policy makers could have chosen to abolish the decrees act, thus scrapping all decrees at once. But the chosen strategy appears to target specific decrees in each sector separately.

DECREES IN THE APPAREL INDUSTRY, 2000: AN UNJUSTIFIED ABOLITION

The central aim of this chapter is to consider whether changes in the garment industry, in the organization of its production and employers, in its labour force, and/or in the international trade environment might warrant elimination of the four decrees. Quebec manufacturers in some subsectors (such as men's suits) have expanded their U.S. presence, despite the decree system. They did so not through low wages but rather through quality, aggressive and innovative marketing, computer-based technology, better sales and service, and adaptation to the whims of the market[6].

Decrees remain concentrated in low-wage sectors, where small and medium-sized companies operate in highly competitive markets. This is particularly true of the garment industry, which pays the lowest wages in manufacturing, fragments production, and has extremely mobile firms – all this despite an allegedly "restrictive and over-regulated" legal framework, including the decrees. The decree system did not hamper competition while upgrading conditions of work in the least generous manufacturing sector. Furthermore, even though employees benefiting from the agreement's extension might have less motivation to unionize, the system has not discouraged unionization (Bernier, 1993: 757; Boivin and Déom, 1995: 478). Unionization decreased in the ladies' garment industry because of the vertical disintegration of production (which led to closure of larger, unionized workplaces and the multiplication of smaller, non-unionized contractors), not because of the decree system. Finally, the joint committees have facilitated labour–management co-operation, particularly in development of industrial strategies and training.

Decree opponents and most policymakers emphasize lower labour costs as the key ingredient in competitive advantage. Table 7.1 demonstrates that earnings remain low, and hence the system did not prevent competitive pressure from low-wage countries from continuing to limit compensation. But the low-wage approach has obvious limits. Yet even if wages dropped much further, even to the legal minimum level, they would still be much higher than rates overseas.

Other factors have been more important recently. Abernathy et al. conclude that advanced information technologies and changes in planning and production have helped to reduce inventory and thus reduce the surplus of unsold products at season's end: "Yet the distinguishing feature of such high performers is not their success in shaving off labour costs in the assembly room: it is their effort in changing basis aspects of the way they manage their enterprises (Abernathy et al., 2000: 8).

Other experts have also de-emphasized reduction of compensation, focusing instead on innovative management of people and technology: "Modern innovations in work organization can improve apparel jobs, making them more interesting and less boring and tedious by breaking down the autocratic character of employee relations. While labour cost remains important, it is no longer the king of competition. Faster throughput time, greater flexibility, better and more interactive relations with customers and suppliers, and innovations in design and manufacturing processes have all increased in importance. Firms that continue to be primarily preoccupied with reducing labour costs will be at an increasing disadvantage along these dimensions of the competitive process." Adaptation is necessary: "Meeting these new demands will require changes in work design; changes in training; and changes in relationships between supervisors and production workers, among production workers and among firms in the supply chain. Thus apparel makers must begin to take a much broader and more imaginative look at the employment process and search for ways in which they can restructure jobs that will both strengthen their firms' positions and make the jobs more attractive" (Bailey, 1990: 88).

As increasingly sophisticated technologies reach the workplace, the level of skill and training will need to rise. The present, albeit incorrect, image of the garment industry as "declining" often deliberately reflects employers' efforts to recruit a vulnerable workforce that is more likely to accept lower wages and conditions. Training and advancement opportunities appear limited, and this creates additional difficulties in attracting younger people and renewing the workforce.

IMPACT OF ABOLITION

This final section of the chapter examines the potential impact of the abrogation of the decrees on working conditions and union–management relations in the garment industry. The decree system appears to be the only example in Canada of legislation extending multi-employer or broader-based bargaining "that is relevant to contract shop workers and home-workers in the garment industry" (Yanz et al., 1999: 28). After first stressing the greater flexibility and lower costs for employers that will supposedly follow abolition of the four decrees, the minister of labour later acknowledged that abolition, even if unspecified sectoral norms emerge, would worsen conditions of work. Moreover, as employers in Ontario compete with their Quebec counterparts for contracts, wages in Ontario will also experience downward pressures. The gap between union and non-union wage rates is also likely to grow.[7]

This wage differential, of course, will create a competitive advantage for non-unionized employers, thus putting pressure on unionized employers to offer lower pay at the bargaining table in order to get orders and save jobs – or even to avoid or decertify their unions. Considering the industry's relatively peaceful history and generally co-operative labour–management relations, developed through multi-employer bargaining and joint committees, pressure for cheap labour makes conflict at the bargaining table more likely. Worker organizations such as the Union of Needletrades, Industrial and Textiles Employees (UNITE) resist proposals that might imperil members' conditions. As non-union shops become even more competitive, and if many employers seek lower wages rather than innovation, the union movement will have to try to save jobs through accepting lower pay, or keep wages higher while risking plant closures and decreasing membership. Moreover, the jobs that disappear from union shops would not necessarily transfer to non-union shops; the drive to lower labour costs may push work into the underground economy – in homes, sweatshops, or other establishments. Homework in the industry historically developed with the growth of contractors and other forms of vertical disintegration of production (Grant and Rose, 1985). The government has sponsored a provincial campaign, with the slogan "Never under the table," targeting tax evasion in the underground economy. Yet deregulation has facilitated continued expansion of that underground economy.

Abolition of the decrees also ends the joint committees, which the Labour Standards Board replaced as of July 2000. These committees provided forums for labour–management co-operation on a wide range of issues, including the industry's future and development. Therefore the decrees' abolition will probably render industrial relations more confrontational.

The joint committees enforced the decrees, and so abolition of this function will affect working conditions. Their inspection powers enabled them to monitor compliance of employers. In contrast to the provincial Labour Standards Board, which intervenes only when it receives a complaint, the joint committees systematically inspected employers' premises and records.[8] Employers had to file monthly reports on pay, so the joint committee could continuously monitor employers' compliance vis-à-vis working conditions. The joint committee could also sue for joint liabilities from employers in a subcontracting chain for unpaid wages established by a decree. It first attempted to collect from a contractor that had failed to meet its obligation; if this was not successful, it then tried to collect from the manufacturer that was liable for payment.

Article 14 of the act reads as follows: "Every professional employer and every contractor contracting with a sub-entrepreneur or a sub-contractor, directly or through an intermediary, shall be solidarily liable with such sub-entrepreneur or sub-contractor and any intermediary for the pecuniary obligations imposed by this *Act*, a regulation or a decree and for the levies payable to a committee." The act also contains successor-rights provisions that make former and new employers jointly liable for any debt arising from the decree and owed to the joint committee or to workers. The joint committee hired its own personnel, received complaints, initiated inspections, and filed suits in civil court for individuals or groups of workers, paying all costs.

The evolution of sectoral standards, following the end of the transition period in December 2001, is obviously uncertain. Labour market outcomes may at first range between general minimum standards and the superior provisions formerly guaranteed by the decrees. In the long run, however, standards could start to decline towards legal minimums, with market forces alone determining any compensation over the legal minimum. Even though some of the joint committees' powers regarding registration of work have shifted to the board, in all likelihood the board will increasingly limit its role to reacting to workers' complaints.

CONCLUSION

The abolition of decrees in the garment sector appears to be part of a more comprehensive strategy by employers and government to erode the system by abolishing decrees sector by sector. Ultimately the only thing left will be the act itself. This approach may serve as a warning for unions involved in other decrees and for other non-unionized workers covered by the system. In the wake of the decrees' gradual abolition, unions working to protect their members and prevent further deterioration of working conditions will have to try to persuade employers and public officials to improve work conditions voluntarily and to convince both them and the general public that the industry's future lies not in ever-lower compensation but in innovative practices. Successful Canadian firms are those that did not lower wages as the basis of their competitive strategies but invested in innovative workplace practices and state-of-the-art technologies.

NOTES

1 RSQ, c. D-2.
2 SQ 1999, c. 57.
3 OC 678–2000, (2000) 132 GO 2, 3463 (eev 2000–06–14).
4 Author's translation of the official *Commission des normes du travail*.
5 Data for December 2002 estimates total employment in the Canadian clothing industry at 73,300, with 40,500 jobs in Quebec (Statistics Canada, 2002).
6 *Apparel Canada* (fall 1996), 6.

7 See Lemieux, 1999: 10.
8 The Supreme Court confirmed these powers. See (1994) 2 SCR *Comité paritaire de l'industrie de la chemise* v. *Potash*; *Comité paritaire de l'industrie de la chemise* v. *Sélection Milton*.

REFERENCES

Abernathy, Frederick H., John T. Dunlop, Janice H. Hammond, and David Weil. 2000. *A Stitch in Time*. New York: Oxford University Press.

Bailey, Thomas. 1990. "Facing the Labour Shortage Crisis," *Bobbin* (June), 83–8.

Beaulieu, Marie-Louis. 1955. *Les conflits de droit dans les rapports collectifs du travail*. Quebec: Les Presses Universitaires Laval.

Bernier, Jean. 1993. "Juridical Extension in Quebec: A New Challenge Unique in America," *Relations industrielles-Industrial Relations* 48 (4), 745–61.

Boivin, Jean, and Esther Déom. 1995. "Labour–Management Relations in Quebec," in Morley Anderson and Allen Ponak, eds., *Union–Management Relations in Canada*, 3rd ed., 455–93.

Comité interministériel sur les décrets de convention collective. 1994. *Rapport du comité interministériel sur les décrets de convention collective*. Quebec.

Dubé, Jean-Louis. 1990. *Décrets et comités paritaires. L'extension juridique des conventions collectives*. Sherbrooke: Les Editions Revue de Droit.

Dumas, Evelyn. 1971. *Dans le sommeil de nos os*. Montreal: Lemeac.

Freeman, Richard B. 1994. "How Labor Fares in Advanced Economies," in Richard B. Freeman, ed., *Working under Different Rules*. New York: Russell Sage Foundation, 1–28.

Fréry, Frédéric. 1999. *Benetton ou l'entreprise virtuelle*. Paris: Librairie Vuibert.

Goetschy, Janine. 1998. "France: The Limits of Reform," in Anthony Ferner and Richard Hyman, eds., *Changing Industrial Relations in Europe*. Oxford: Blackwell Publishers, 357–94.

Grant, Michel. 1992. "Struggle for Survival: Industrial Relations in the Clothing Industry," in A. Verma and R.P. Chaykowski, eds., *Industrial Relations in Canadian Industry*. Toronto: Holt, Rinehart and Winston, 220–43.

Grant, Michel, and Ruth Rose. 1985. "L'encadrement du travail à domicile au Québec," *Relations industrielles* 40 (3), 473–94.

Groupe de travail sur la déréglementation. 1986. *Réglementer moins et mieux*. Québec: Les Publications du Québec.

Hébert, Gérard. 1990. "Le renouvellement de régime des dècrets de convention collective," *Relations industrielles* 45 (2), 404–13.

Jodoin, Mario. 1999. L'emploi dans le secteur manufacturier au Québec: l'industrie de l'habillement bonne première. Unpublished monograph on file with author.

Lemieux, Diane. 1999. *Mémoire au Conseil des ministres*. Gouvernement du Québec, 25 Feb.

Milner, Henry. 1990. *Sweden: Social Democracy in Practice*. Oxford: Oxford University Press.

Porter, Michael. 1980. *Competitive Strategy*. New York: Free Press.

Statistics Canada. 2000. *Employment, Earnings and Hours*. Catalogue No. 72–002. Dec.

– 2002. *Employment, Earnings and Hours*. Catalogue No. 72–002. Dec.

Steedman, Mercedes. 1997. *Angels of the Workplace*. Don Mills, Ont.: Oxford University Press.

Yanz, Lynda, Bob Jeffcott, Deena Ladd, and Joan Atlin. 1999. *Policy Options to Improve Standards for Women Garments Workers in Canada and Internationally*. Toronto: Maquila Solidarity Network.

8

European Labour Market Regulation: The Case of European Works Councils

MICHAEL JOHN WHITTALL

Recent developments within the European automotive industry, in particular the decision of General Motors (GM) to eliminate jobs in Germany and the United Kingdom, Ford's European restructuring strategy, and BMW's breaking up of the former Rover Group, indicate the inability of Europe's trade unions to control the meanderings of multinational corporations (MNCs).[1] In fact, faced with the threat of even more closures and layoffs, trade unionists may become unwitting accomplices in the internationalization of production. With unions forced at times into concession bargaining (Hancké, 1998, 2000), such agreements further undermine the "embedding"[2] power of nationally oriented industrial relations over capital (Blank, 1998; Hoffmann and Hoffmann, 1997; Keller, 1998; Lecher, 1997; Marginson and Sisson, 1996; Streeck, 1991).

Broader policy trends in the European Union (EU) have enhanced the pressures facing trade unions. European leaders' decision in 1991 to push ahead with the Economic and Monetary Union (EMU) challenged the collective strength of trade unions, adding further pressure for the deregulation of labour markets. By agreeing to the EMU, member states abdicated their right to determine not only levels of national debt but also exchange and inflation rates. Instead, these key economic variables – central pillars of the postwar Keynesian compromise between capital and labour – are now in the hands of market-oriented supranational bodies committed to deflationary policies, such as the European Commission and the European Central Bank (Coen, 1998; Hyman, 2000).

Today Europe's trade union movement is trying to figure out how to counter the march of free-market economics and the unaccountability of

MNCs. Many commentators see the way forward in development of European supranational institutions that promote collective regulation and ultimately lead to a system of European industrial relations (Lecher and Platzer, 1998). However, as this chapter demonstrates, other writers place less faith in European institutions' ability to legislate "positively" on employment.

One supranational institution that came to prominence in the 1990s and has been the focus of much debate and research is the European Works Council (EWC). After twenty years of trade union lobbying, the EWC Directive finally passed in 1994 – its aim "to improve the right to information and to consultation of employees in Community Scale undertakings and Community Scale groups of undertakings" (EWC Directive, Article 1:1). The directive applies to all undertakings with at least 1,000 employees in EU member states and at least 150 employees in at least two member states (EWC Directive, Article 2:1 (a)).

The likes of the European Trade Union Congress (ETUC) and the European Metal Workers Federation (EMF), two leading trade union federations, see the EWC as a bridgehead for building transnational labour solidarity. And although a modest 596 EWCs of an eligible 1,844 had been established in the first five years (ETUI, 1999), Scott (1999) notes that they have become a core part of trade union policy.

However, the EWC Directive deals with a relatively small section of the labour force: direct employees of MNCs. Moreover, its rights include only information and consultation. They are forums for handling broad economic-related issues; while broadly inclusive, they are unlikely to address race, gender, or other issues of inclusion and equality.

Drawing on the results of a four-year case study of BMW's EWC, set up in 1996 after the company took over the British Rover Group in 1994, this chapter explores whether EWCs can serve as a catalyst for international worker solidarity – a pre-condition for collective opposition to deregulation and the negative actions of MNCs. Altogether, of 45 interviewees, 32 respondents had either direct or indirect involvement with the EWC. These included EWC members, full-time officers from all the main unions involved, European trade union federations, and BMW and Rover managers.

The chapter has three sections. The first reviews the foundation of BMW's EWC, looking at the main perceived deficiencies of the EWC Directive and the problem of building cross-national trust in the early stages. The second section describes and analyses the three crises faced by the Rover Group between 1998 and 2000 and looks at the EWC's role in managing and responding to these situations. The third section discusses the perceived strengths and weaknesses, especially bureaucratic, of the EWC model and suggests possible improvements in its internal functioning.

BMW EUROPEAN WORKS COUNCIL (EWC)

Foundation

In the same year that the EWC Directive became legally binding (1996), BMW followed a "pre-emptive," voluntary path to founding such a transnational body. Made possible by Article 13 of the Directive, voluntary EWC agreements allowed firms and employee representatives to shape their own EWC. In the voluntary approach, any structure decided on had to provide "for the transnational information and consultation of employees" (Article 13: 1). These voluntary agreements, however, often reflect a defensive strategy that can hurt relations between EWC members. Employers chose a pre-1996 voluntary agreement principally to limit the EWC's influence (LRD, 1995) and to minimize administrative costs. For employee representatives, the threat of whip-sawing between geographically separate production sites (regime competition) encouraged creation of an EWC (Lecher, 1998; Lecher and Nauman, 1994). The traditions and power structures of their own industrial relations systems also were motivating factors.

In the case of BMW, it was members of its Group Works Council (WC) in Germany who pushed for a voluntary agreement. Two factors were influential here. First, members of the employees' Aufsichtsrat (supervisory board) worried that the allegedly higher productivity, lower wages, and longer hours worked at Rover would strengthen management's bargaining hand in Germany. For example, when BMW bought Rover, its management claimed that productivity was 30 per cent higher in Britain than in Germany – a figure that greatly concerned BMW's WC members. Thus the EWC might be a valuable source for checking the validity of such assertions. Subsequent visits to Rover and meetings with members of its EWC soon helped to alleviate such fears.

Next, the "host factor" came into play, although, as we see below, we should not overemphasize such influence. Schulten (1992) describes this as the "hegemonic" function of host members, often in collusion with central management: to determine such factors as the number of seats, the frequency of meetings and the chair. If BMW was to have an EWC, the German delegates would want to be the dominant party.

Fox's work on trust, particularly on discretion, helps here. Symbolizing power, discretion "enables the few ... to manifest distrust of the many by imposing ... rules which leave little scope for important choices" (Fox, 1974: 14). According to Rover respondents, BMW actors in this crucial phase set out to control the EWC by determining its character. One Rover EWC delegate noted: "In the end they had an in-built majority. In a way we were a similar number of people, but they had the upper hand ... It was also stated in the agreement that whoever the chairman of the Munich WC was, would automatically be the chairman of the EWC. So, in a way they made sure they always had control, if you like."

Consequently, according to Rover delegates, their own inexperience vis-à-vis works councils (WCS), and Munich's perceived dominance, led to a poor EWC agreement (from Rover's perspective) in terms of delegate numbers and frequency of meetings. The BMW's minimalist EWC was to have yearly meetings lasting over one-and-a-half days, with an agenda dominated by plant reports and management presentations and no provision for cross-border coordination of unions. This approach represents what Scott (1999) refers to as "industrial relations tourism": short trips to foreign countries, with all expenses paid. As we see below, this structure suited key protagonists within the BMW's EWC.

In terms of delegate numbers, both BMW management and employee representatives wanted to keep the numbers down, with BMW eventually delegated nine, and Rover, six. However, although both management and BMW's WC members sought an employee-only structure, clashing with British traditions, they did not get everything their own way. Rover's labour representatives compromised such vested interests by insisting on a voice in the negotiations to set up the council – a process that helped to circumvent hegemonic tendencies (Lecher et al., 2001).

Thus, even though the German metal workers' union, the IG Metall, was eventually excluded from the EWC, pressure from British unions forced BMW delegates to concede on trade union officers. As a result, one Rover seat went to Tony Woodley, a full-time officer of the Transport & General Workers Union (T&GWU). However, neither all Rover plants nor all key individuals had representation on the EWC.

The allocation of seats is a critical variable, which illuminates power and cultural differences between national systems of industrial relations. This fact became obvious to European trade unions at an international conference on EWCs in Eastbourne, England, in 1993. Organized by the T&GWU, it brought to the fore policy differences between the IG Metall and the T&GWU. The IG Metall insisted that, in line with German practice, the EWC should have only lay members.[3] The T&GWU delegates bitterly opposed this. They promoted a position, also adhered to by the EMF, the ETUC, and the EWC Directive, that neither full-time officials nor shop stewards should dominate EWC proceedings; rather, representation should replicate collective-bargaining structures in the home country. Rover wanted national officers – the leading negotiators at BMW's British subsidiary – to have guaranteed seats on the EWC.

Building Trust

Paradoxically, the minimalist approach to the EWC at BMW did not improve working relations between BMW and Rover workers. Two early events highlight this point. The first concerned the manufacturing of Mini engines – a joint project between BMW and Chrysler. "It (BMW) dishonestly transferred an engine to Brazil and lied to us on what that engine was and why it was going there. It was done and dusted before we had a chance to put an input in ... The simple truth was, investment and jobs were taken out of Britain, in my view to the benefit of BMW, because at that time there were tariffs by the Brazilian government on the importing of cars and they wanted job swaps and this sort of thing (Tony Woodley)."

The second event concerned BMW's announcement that it would restructure its global production of engines. Again, Rover trade unionists saw this as a threat to jobs in Britain. This time, however, the outcome was to be more favourable to British employees, BMW deciding to produce its three–series engine at a new site in Hams Hall, just outside of Birmingham. BMW based its decision on negotiations with several potential countries for this investment – a strategy that did nothing to alleviate strains between BMW and employee representatives from Rover. The tension came to a head at an EWC meeting in Steyr, Austria, site of one of BMW's engine factories and a plant in contention for future investment. "It became obvious that they (Steyr) were economical with the truth. They put out a letter about the negotiations they were actually doing there. That was a surprise to our Rover management here, because basically we (the unions) and the Rover management were fighting to get the work here (Rover EWC member)."

Rover's EWC members, however, also played the "tendering game." From the beginning, BMW made it very clear to Rover's Joint Negotiation Committee (JNC) that any investment in England would involve a greenfield site. It eventually chose Hams Hall after the JNC agreed to "undercut Steyr" (Rover convenor) by conceding to a six-day working week, Monday to Saturday. By starting at midnight on Sunday, this, according to one Rover EWC member, "went against the grain" of traditional working practices at Rover.

Members of the EWC saw this new body as inadequate for transnational union efforts to hinder management's global whip-sawing strategy. The Hams Hall experience would appear to concur with Wills (2000), Hancké (2000), and Streeck's (1997) argument – that the EWC can actually serve management's aim to promote regime competition rather than undermining it. "The feeling was that we had to fight our own corner and Steyr their corner, and it certainly was not discussed at the EWC as far as I am aware ... I think the feeling was at that time that there was not much faith in the ability of the EWC to deal fairly with us. That was my feeling (Rover EWC member)."

Although EWC delegates did not address engine production, management used such gatherings to highlight its own agenda. Thus, even though BMW and Rover's employee representatives were unable to co-ordinate their approach to proposed changes in working practices and location of production, they were conscious of the concessions that Munich was seeking, which would determine the allocation of investment.

The first two years of BMW's EWC confirms Lecher's (1998) findings of low levels of trust in early exchanges between EWC members. At this stage, interest has more to do with lobbying management on behalf of "local–national" interests than with international solidarity (Lecher et al., 1998). A "communal European way of thinking" (Lecher, 1996a: 711) was not observable in these initial meetings. BMW's German EWC members were anxious first and foremost to protect their superior employment terms and conditions, while their Rover counterparts focused on achieving a representative voice and much-needed future investment.

While these aims were often more complementary than contradictory, solidarity did not come into the equation, which raises the question of whether EWC relations can nurture international unity. Writers such as Streeck and Vitols (1994), Rehfeldt (1998), Hancké (2000) and Wills (2000) find this outcome very unlikely. They base this conclusion mostly on their criticism of the EWC Directive. They argue that not giving employee representatives real rights of co-determination, as well as placing national above supranational law,[4] suggests to EWC members that EWC meetings are little more than a "fashion show," with managers as designers and employee representatives as bidding outletters.

FINANCIAL CRISES AT ROVER, 1998–2000

The Decline of Rover

On acquiring Rover in March 1994, BMW achieved ownership of a mass-market car producer – the final part of its strategy to become a global automobile player. Unfortunately for BMW, it purchased not only production volume, but also a company with a poor management record, reportedly bad labour relations, and little investment for decades (Whisler, 1999).

Between 1998 and 2000 the Rover Car Group went through a number of crises, which at their worst not only threatened 70,000 British jobs, but posed some serious challenges to the EWC. A British trade union officer noted that the events "can only be described as unprecedented, probably the gravest situation which has ever faced the car industry in this country."

In the two-year period 1998–2000, the EWC's role also shifted: contacts between BMW and Rover employee representatives became more intense, distrust slowly abated and the EWC became a vehicle for negotiating change. It featured prominently in negotiations on Rover's future – over the survival plan of 1998, the threat to Rover's Longbridge plant in the West Midlands in 1999, and Rover's break-up in 2000.

Survival Plan, 1998

In 1998, Rover's management (under pressure from Munich to halt daily losses of £2 million) threatened to sack and then re-employ the whole workforce if the JNC rejected far-reaching changes in working practices, especially a new accounting system for flexible working time (FWT). The aim was to lay employees off on full pay in periods of poor sales and model changeover; the company would recoup these hours later in an upturn in production. In addition, management tabled Saturday work, plus lower wage premiums which reduced salaries by 18 per cent.

Conscious of the severity of the situation, the JNC's chief negotiator, Tony Woodley, contacted his BMW counterpart, Manfred Schoch, chair of the EWC and vice-chair of the Aufsichtsrat, for advice. What followed would revolutionize the EWC. Together they came up with a strategy that would see Rover workers agree to FWT in return for the first 35–hour week in British industry. The chair of the EWC, and the rest of BMW's EWC members, would have to use their influence to win such a concession from BMW's board.

Eventually, BMW agreed (against the advice of the Rover board) to a 35–hour week, no Saturday work, and smaller cuts in wage premiums. Moreover, the agreement was "struck behind Rover directors' backs. The final deal was also reached without their agreement (Tony Woodley)." Duncan Simpson, a full-time officer with the Amalgamated Engineering and Electrical Union (AEEU), also present at the negotiations in Munich, stated that, in his twenty years as a convenor at Chrysler and then Peugeot, he had never imagined that British workers might ever have the power and influence to oppose management.

On the day the agreement was finalized, Tony Woodley stated that the EWC's work, particularly that of its chair, Manfred Schoch, represented the best example of Anglo–German trade union solidarity. This European institution, which brought two groups of unionists together for consultation, had made possible this transnational approach. Moreover, the event highlighted what Turner (1993: 13) calls the "tangible benefits" of transcending plant and national levels of organization.

Threat to Longbridge

This new-found trust – based on joint consultation and co-ordination of employees' representation – would soon face a severe test. In February 1999 there was a boardroom battle over Rover's future. Again conscious of a crisis, Rover trade unionists called on their German colleagues to oppose Wolfgang Reitzle (BMW's engineering director and Rover's chairman) and his restructuring policy, which would close Longbridge and cost 14,000 jobs. According to the German press and Rover's trade unionists, BMW's EWC members once again used all their influence on the Aufsichtsrat, this time to save jobs in the West Midlands and to force Reitzle to resign. Duncan Simpson, of the AEEU, sums up the EWC's role in these two crises: "Some of us have been sceptical about European ties with other unions, believing that countries would be parochial. This is tangible evidence that co-operation at European level between unions has worked, did work, will work ... I think that Manfred [Schoch] (chairman of the BMW EWC) was genuinely concerned about the closure of British plants and the disastrous effects it would have had upon the communities."

How do we explain the EWC's sudden transformation from a "low-trust" to a "high-trust" institution? Certainly, altruistic considerations were not the sole motivation for the actions of BMW's EWC members. As co-managers of BMW they had supported the firm's global strategy to become a mass car producer. A change in that course would have entailed a loss of faith among German workers, who from the outset had never fully supported the Rover purchase. In addition, the new 35–hour week at Rover neutral-ized managerial leverage that BMW's EWC members had always feared. But those same people had a strong commitment to basic trade union princi-ples of full employment, justice, and solidarity. When trade unionists commit themselves to fighting the negative consequences of globalization, even if their motives are potentially national, this does not exclude inter-national solidarity. What it reflects historically is the complicated and at times contradictory nature of labour representation under capitalism.

Break-up of Rover

Was the BMW's EWC indeed a "functional and stress resistant network ... which could be turned to when quick or co-operative decisions need be taken" (Altvater and Mahnkopf, 1993: 250)? An additional test occurred in the spring of 2000. With Rover's losses continuing to mount, and its shares falling in price, BMW decided to cut its losses and sell off parts of the Rover Group. To this end it entered negotiations with the venture capital-ist Alchemy and the U.S. automaker Ford Motor Company over the pur-chase of the Longbridge and Land Rover facilities, respectively. BMW remained committed to retaining the Swindon pressing factory and the car assembly plant at Cowley, Oxford. In a desperate attempt to stop the break-up of the Rover Group, British EWC members, together with senior trade union officers, flew to Munich on 15 March, one day before a decisive Aufsichtsrat meeting.

There, BMW's EWC members unconvincingly assured their colleagues from England that they would do all in their power to retain Rover intact. They indicated, however, that BMW's management favoured other options and that the chair of the Aufsichtsrat board (a company representative) would certainly vote for selling Rover.[5] In sum: Rover workers were fighting a losing battle. One member of Rover's EWC noted: "When he (Manfred Schoch) met us it was obvious that he was trying to be careful with the words he uttered. I said to Woodley 'if we depend on them we have no chance' and Woodley replied, 'they are our only hope.'"

At the Aufsichtsrat meeting, German EWC members were unable to deter BMW management from its chosen course. In fact, they supported the strategy, believing it feasible and capable of ensuring the long-term future of both BMW and Rover. Resigned to defeat, Rover's EWC members focused on the sale of Longbridge to Alchemy, a company whose business strategy entailed cutting the workforce from 12,000 employees to 1,500.

In the following weeks a campaign against the Alchemy offer took form, which again harnessed the lobbying powers of BMW's EWC members. The trade unions instigated a rival bid for Longbridge, "Phoenix," headed by Rover's former CEO, John Towers. Although Phoenix wanted to table an offer by 1 April, BMW still had an exclusivity arrangement with Alchemy. BMW could not open its books to a third party until after 28 April. This represented a catch-22 situation for the trade union's campaign. Its inability to get access to crucial data severely hampered its proposal. With BMW committed to a quick deal, Alchemy was clearly in a strong position. This did not deter the Rover activists, however.

April signalled an intensive period of lobbying in Munich on behalf of the "Towers bid." On 26 April, two days before the sale, a trade union delegation travelled to Munich (Atkinson, 2000). At an "extraordinary"[6] EWC meeting, Rover delegates pleaded with their German counterparts to win them extra time to finalize the bid's finances.

These pleas worked. On the 27th, negotiations between BMW and Alchemy collapsed. According to Alchemy, BMW's last-minute demand that it cover franchise dealers' potential compensation costs (about £500 million) jeopardized the deal. As well, claims by suppliers for terminated contracts and redundancy payments added about £100 million to the total price (Maguire, Bannister, and Milner, 2000). BMW blamed Alchemy for failing to reach a settlement, noting that Alchemy CEO John Moulton's original demand that BMW contribute £500 million for restructuring suddenly jumped by £200 million at the last minute (Brady and Lorenz, 2001: 157).

John Moulton has rejected this accusation and threatened legal action against BMW after discovering that its CEO, Joachim Milberg, planned to make this claim at a shareholders' meeting. Milberg left this section out of his presentation.

Why then the sudden collapse in negotiations? And why, after nearly six months of intense discussions, which had left no stone unturned, were there new demands? In particular, why were there not further discussions, especially when the so-called problems were surmountable? According to Brady and Lorenz (2001) – partly corroborated by Schneider (2000) – BMW began to question the deal in late April. One Alchemy employee noted: "This was a polite way of telling us it was off – one of their lawyers was giggling. When we saw the requests it was mission impossible. We did not negotiate. It was a deliberate attempt to scupper the deal" (Maguire, Bannister, and Milman, 2000).

But why would BMW scupper the deal when each extra day Rover remained within the BMW Group not only cost it money but also damaged its image? Brady and Lorenz (2000) argue that several factors combined to "spook" BMW, including the threat of legal action by British dealers. They conclude, however, that the Rover trade union's campaign to save Longbridge was crucial: "More importantly they [BMW] had been taken aback by the strength of union, government and public resistance to the Alchemy bid" (Brady and Lorenz, 2001, 157–8).

How did international links between trade unions, forged between 1994 and 2000, affect events from March to May 2000? Did EWC meetings, especially the final one on 26 April, influence BMW management's decision to jeopardize the deal?

BMW respondents insist that they were instrumental in the negotiations that led to the agreement with Phoenix. Although they initially supported the Alchemy offer, once the Phoenix bid began to take shape – standing on more "stable legs" in the second half of April, according to one BMW respondent – BMW's EWC delegates quickly changed their allegiance, or so they claim. They lobbied BMW's board intensively not only to give the Phoenix group more time but to veer towards the Rover workforce's preferred choice. According to one member of BMW's EWC: "We supported them [Rover workers] in the sense that we influenced the decision to steer toward Phoenix. Schoch played a huge role in Phoenix getting the DM500 million by talking to Milberg. Also various details in the contract have been positively influenced and formed. Okay, the original expectation of the English colleagues, and seen this way they were naturally disappointed with us, was oriented towards a maximum 'we should hinder the sale.' But we are responsible for the whole concern, and one of your questions was how the German workforce viewed events. The German workers put us under pressure to find a solution one way or another, because you could see the results were falling." According to another source: "It seemed that the Alchemy bid would lead to something, but Schoch naturally asked Milberg not to totally disregard the Phoenix bid, but to continue to consider it and that when something should develop and Milberg believed it was workable, then he should follow it through."

Rover respondents have corroborated this position. Once the deal with Towers was signed, Rover informants felt that their colleagues in Munich had made a valuable contribution: "They did what they could to get the Brits the best deal, even though it would have been more costly, potentially more costly to BMW, as long as it did not threaten their survival."

As on the other occasions, BMW respondents claimed that they were conscious of the universal nature of trade union values: "Herr [X] was very clear about this when he drove there [to Munich for the Aufsichtsrat meeting] ... The main concern was to save as many jobs as possible and I think this is what was achieved. We [BMW employee representative] have said we will not close anything and that was the big fundamental influence that the employee representatives had on the supervisory board. (BMW EWC member)."

Manfred Schoch has said: "Plant closure was always the threat faced by the employee representatives of the BMW Group, which includes our English colleagues. In the European works council we were always very clearly opposed to this, despite the DM2.4 billion losses that had piled up. Because we were as one: if we are serious about international solidarity and co-operation, then we have to stand together when it's really important." (Hasel and Ballauf, 2000).

In May 2000 BMW agreed to sell Longbridge to Phoenix for a symbolic £10. The deal involved a package in which the consortium, in return for receiving £500 million (paid in instalments) and Rover's 75, 45, and 25 models, retained the services of 7,000 workers. As for the rest of the Rover group, BMW kept, as planned, the Cowley and Swindon sites and held onto engine production at Longbridge. Ford eventually purchased the Land Rover plant at Solihull, as well as the research and development centre at Gaydon for £1.8 billion. Moreover, the exertions of trade unionists in both Britain and Germany helped minimize job losses – some 2,000 redundancies solely at Longbridge.

STRENGTHS AND WEAKNESSES OF EWCS

The apparent involvement and tacit support of German trade unionists for the break-up of the Rover Group would appear to confirm the arguments of those analysts critical of EWCs. As we saw, these writers suggest that their lack of formal rights of co-determination means that they exacerbate competition between sites in different countries (Hancké, 2000; Keller, 1998; Streeck, 1997; Streeck and Vitols, 1994; Wills, 2000;). Thus, in the words of Altvater and Mahnkopf (1993), it does not qualify as a "functional stress resistant network." German employees' representatives ultimately donned their Aufsichtsrat hats. This danger will always exist in Germany, according to Lecher (1996a), because of its long-standing national system of co-determination. Rover's workforce enjoys no such rights.

When German jobs and bonuses were under threat, transnational trade-union cooperation faltered. Tony Woodley (T&GWU) later stated: "It would be extremely naïve of any trade unionist to think that under these circumstance you would end up with the German workers on the streets for British workers. I only wish international trade union solidarity would stretch to those boundaries. Unfortunately that is not the case. At the end of the day each country will unfortunately look at its own prospects of survival and its own prospects for plants. Human nature and selfishness will always play a part in something like this. "

More hopeful observers argue that, even though the "EWC may be weaker and more flexible than traditional forms of regulation ... they are forming part of a new logic of supranational state regulation and control" (Weston and Martínez Lucio, 1998: 561). To determine whether EWCs are helping to develop a new form of trade union collectivism, we require a more theoretical understanding of "solidarity."

According to Hyman (1999), internationalism is a utopian notion that at best inspires nationalism. Moreover, "solidarity" should not conflate deterministic notions of Marxist class-consciousness: "We are shaped by our direct experiences, immediate milieu, specific patterns of social relations. Broader identities and affiliations are founded on the direct, immediate and specific, through inter-subjectivities which link these to the external and encompassing" (Hyman, 1999: 96).

Thus what Mittelman (1997) calls the "particularistic and localized" conditions trade unionists' concerns. This leads Miller (1999) to conclude that EWC members must transcend the national, parochial basis of working-class unity. Miller believes that it is possible to rise above the "particularistic and localized." In a study of 100 EWC delegates from Germany, Italy, the Netherlands, and the United Kingdom, he located six trade-union values that appear stable and universal: accountability, equity, independence, organizational security, the right to representation, and solidarity. It is these principles that "representatives are able to articulate quite clearly which should prevail in such a body (EWC)" (Miller, 1999: 6); they could ground "organic solidarity" at an international level. The common experience of the labour process under capitalism, given appropriate organizational structures and expressions, could lead to trans-national unity. After all, as Buraway (1985: 18) asserts, "every particularity contains a generality; each particular factory regime is the product of general forces operating at a societal or global level."

Trade unions should look for means to create a common reality that transcends the local setting, highlighting the common nature of the labour process, and ensures "participation, representativeness, debate, transparency, constitutionality and accountability in the supraterritorial realm itself" (Scholte, 1998: 54). Findings from the BMW case study suggest that the EWC Directive partially achieved this goal. It helped open up possibilities for networking and gave British trade unionists influence over management. Further, trust relations between the British and German unionists did improve. Even after the break-up of Rover, both the Britons and the Germans remained committed to the principles of EWCs.

Nevertheless, development of solidarity via EWCs encounters numerous obstacles. This section considers two factors – institutional bureaucracy and bureaucratic determinants – that hindered the growth of organic solidarity and offers recommendations on possible ways to surmount them.

Institutional Bureaucracy

A common theme in all my interviews with BMW and Rover delegates, and confirmed by other EWC studies, relates to the value of informal meetings between EWC members. Such gatherings developed trust and shared information about industrial relations systems and future concerns. Although these events broke down barriers, they also reveal deficiencies – largely bureaucratic – in the formal EWC structure.

BMW's EWC suffers from a "democratic deficit." Rover informants referred to the hegemonic role of the mother country. They noted that all the information flowed through Manfred Schoch's office, resulting in what Miller (1999) calls a lack of transparency/accountability. Lecher, Nagel, and Platzer (1998) claim that relations in such a situation take a hub-and-spoke structure, with the EWC's chair controlling the centre. Like a conductor, chairs "decide which information will be passed on and which will be held back ... and with that secure their own position of power within the EWC" (Lecher, 1998: 232).

However, hegemony was not merely a German problem. For example, the BMW experience also supports the argument of Lecher et al. (1998) that union structures can come to dominate EWCs and so hinder their development. One Rover EWC member observed: "Well, I don't think they (full-time union officers) should be part of the EWC. I think they stifle the development of that committee because they are not employees of BMW. I think that restricts the information they (full-time officers) will be given. It might be conceived as conflicting with other interests" (Rover EWC member).

From the outset, full-time union officers dominated British participation in BMW's EWC. This first became apparent when the EWC was set up: the main discussions involved national union officers in the United Kingdom and members of BMW's Group Works Council in Germany. Rover convenors and shop stewards played a secondary role. Certainly few lay members showed any real interest in setting up an EWC, thus leaving it to the full-time officers. The officers did not make the EWC, during either its initiation phase or its subsequent development, a major topic of discussion at JNC meetings, thus helping to undermine its status even further.

Drawing up the agenda was problematic. Although officers appointed a lay delegate to collect agenda topics, as well as to organize pre-EWC meetings at Rover, they never consulted this individual. Despite support from all Rover lay members, they did not receive official union backing, as they were not a member of the T&GWU, the Rover Group's leading union. Instead, Manfred Schoch, after conferring with his delegation, would usually fax an agenda to Tony Woodley, who would then, often unilaterally, offer amendments. In his study of Nestlé's EWC, Schulten (1996) discovered that full-time union officers controlled proceedings there, too.

Bureaucratic Determinants

Kelly and Heery (1994) rightly criticize simplistic analyses of trade union bureaucracy that acknowledge bureaucratic structures but fail to comprehend or explain their genesis. In the case of the EWCs, one should focus on historical circumstances that made it more difficult for EWC chairs than for lay union members to support transnational unionism. Only by understanding these variables can one devise corrective measures.

First, BMW's EWC chair, Manfred Schoch, faced problems related to "multiple accountability." He was not only chair of the European, Munich, and Group WCs, but also vice-chair of the Aufsichtsrat, as well as a key member on the Bavarian IG Metall collective bargaining commission. Time management must have been an issue, to say nothing of conflicting interests. Irrespective of the state of relations between the BMW and Rover plants, Schoch, in the face of deregulation pressures at home, was doing his best to retain some stability within labour relations at BMW. This effort inevitably influenced and constrained his role in the EWC.

According to Koch (1996), the demise of Rhine-capitalism requires German labour functionaries, such as Schoch, to be ambidextrous, able to conduct themselves politically at many different and conflicting levels. Similar to the decline of sector decrees in Quebec's apparel industry discussed by Michael Grant in this volume, deregulation has affected German industrial relations (Bergmann, Bürckmann, and Dabrowski, 1998; Bispnick, 2001; Ettl and Heikenroth, 1996; Hoffmann, 1997; Koch, 1996; Oppholzer, Wegener, and Zachort, 1986; Whittall, 2001), with a growing predisposition towards plant-level preoccupations and consciousness (Whittall, 2001). For this reason, Schoch was often more of a referee on the EWC rather than an employees' representative. From this perspective, his EWC post became at best a Nebenjob (a side job; Schulten, 1992), at worst an irritant.

For German trade unionists, European economic integration represents a catch-22 situation (Streeck, 1991). Despite great concern about the generally free-market nature of EU policy (Blank, 1998; Keller, 1998; Streeck, 1991), over half of Germany's exports are EU bound. Clearly, German unions have a vested interest in the European project. However, they fear that EU legislation, such as the EWC Directive, may promote an Anglo-Americanization of European industrial relations, ending German industrial-level collective bargaining (Jacobi, 1998).

Weston and Martínez Lucio (1998) note that the EWC Directive complements management's interest in more favourable human-resource arrangements, particularly more flexible working conditions. As we saw above, plant-level trade unionists, in national and international competition for future investment, may bargain over concessions. Therefore BMW's take-over of Rover only added to Schoch's complex and contradictory mix of priorities and responsibilities.

Though functioning in a very different institutional environment, Tony Woodley, the EWC's vice-chair and head of the JNC, had virtually identical problems. His position was even less enviable. The British system of plant-level negotiations, which includes rather than excludes trade unions, looks ideally suited to the challenges posed by the EWC Directive. Given British unions already weakened by a loss of membership (between 1985 and 1999 union density declined from 45 per cent to 30 per cent; European Industrial Relations Observatory, 1999, 2000), as well as by the arrival of new Japanese employment practices (Lecher and Nauman, 1994), the EWC threatens further de-recognition. The EWC might bring back "company unionism." As we saw above, both BMW's EWC members and its management did initially try to exclude all non-employees (union officials) from the EWC.

In addition, British full-time union officers have to contend with multi-unionism and the resulting competition. Though a full-time officer of the T&GWU (Rover's biggest union, with 80 per cent of its union members), Tony Woodley was also answerable to other union constituencies, including the AEEU, the General, Municipal and Boilermakers' Union (GMB), and the Manufacturing Science and Finance Union (MSF).[7] As we saw above, such a constellation did cause difficulties vis-à-vis allocation of EWC seats. On occasion Woodley could not satisfy all parties.

These issues raised the question of legitimacy. Not being a Rover employee, and heading a delegation not composed solely of T&GWU members, Tony Woodley found himself in a precarious situation. Trust was an issue not only with his BMW counterparts, but within his own ranks, too. Therefore he needed to ensure solidarity among the Rover ranks on the EWC and consolidate his own post. However, launching of the EWC changed everything. As a new forum, it represents employees in a way that neither "automatically" falls into the domain of full-time union officers nor has support from all lay members.

The bureaucratic nature of BMW's and other EWCs is the by-product of national-level conflicts and pressures. Furthermore, the EWC's founding, as some writers have noted (Hancké, 2000; Wills, 2000), may intensify the predicaments of leaders such as Schoch and Woodley. The EWC represents not just another meeting to attend. It symbolizes a kaleidoscope of free-market forces that are threatening to burst collective labour's national solidarity. Elevating decentralized factors such as plant egoism to an international level severely challenges nationally tried and tested trade union practices.

Determining what goes on the agenda, restricting the input of EWC members to mere plant reports, and limiting contact between EWC members to yearly meetings appear to be attempts to retain a degree of stability within industrial-relations systems and to hinder the erosion of officers' own positions. However, these same leaders have increasingly to address the problems brought about by globalization, which existing forms of regulation and union activity are unable to curb at the national level.

Getting Beyond Bureaucratic Weaknesses: Recommendations

The dilemmas facing trade union functionaries such as Manfred Schoch and Tony Woodley are not new. The threat of company unionism and fear of union control are as old as organized labour itself. What is new, however, is the challenge of developing a supranational system of dual representation despite the differing industrial relations practices of other countries.

However, with many of the voluntary agreements coming up for renegotiation, and with the European Trade Union Congress (ETUC) and the European Metal Workers Federation (EMF) involved in a complicated review of the EWC Directive of 1994, this is an opportune moment to reconsider EWC relations and practices. For example, if EWCs are to go beyond the "crisis management" approach that hindered evolution of a deeper "common identity," the following internal adjustments might advance lay participation, educate unions about Europe, and bring in full-time union officers.

First and foremost, a greater role for the EWC requires enhancing the status of its lay members. For this reason the profile of lay members needs to be more prominent. At BMW, four reforms might help:

- All plants and trade unions should have representation at EWC meetings.
- Lay members should hold key positions as a means of encouraging more interaction within this stratum.
- Lay members, in conjunction with relevant trade-union officers, should draw up the agenda.
- The chair and organizational responsibilities should rotate among members.

Pushing lay delegates to the fore in setting the agenda and running meetings should develop such occasions beyond the current "plant report" routine. Meetings might facilitate open debate which might produce common positions. To this end, I suggest four recommendations about BMW's EWC meetings.

- Pre-EWC meetings should take place at a national level.
- Meetings should not be rushed.
- Delegates should meet after having gone into conference with management.
- Meetings should occur every quarter.

Second, even these reforms will prove futile if European trade unions do not address the massive educational exercise facing them (Miller, 1999). Except for one EWC member, no respondent had received any training, from trade union or employer, on pan-European issues. Ideally, sabbaticals would allow EWC members to stay for periods in other delegates' countries – a suggestion made by both Rover and BMW's EWC members. This should be a long-term aim of trade unions, around which EWC members could organize. Meanwhile EWC members should seek a better understanding of industrial relations elsewhere. This would lessen the confusion and prejudice that undermine EWC relations.

Third, although the above proposals would enhance the status of lay members, EWCs must include full-time union officers. EWCs pose obvious dangers to unions (Hanké, 1998; Scott, 1999; Wills, 2000). The EWCs can promote internal competition and company unionism, to which lay members are susceptible. Several full-time officers complained that lay members "do not always see the bigger picture" (words of a British full-time officer). Although some people have suggested that lay members are better at making the "transnational step" than union functionaries, remaining in the frontline of company closures, restructuring programs, and flexibility drives can make them vulnerable to deregulatory pressures. Union representatives would help to check this tendency – a function that trade unions have traditionally performed at a national level.

However, such official union attendance must neither undermine the presence of lay members nor be lopsided, as it was at BMW, where the IG Metall failed to send a representative to the EWC. German unions, in particular, should change course. Only their participation in EWC meetings will give this new institution the legitimacy that it needs, in the eyes of both its lay members and management, to function more effectively.

CONCLUSION:
TOWARDS INTERNATIONAL SOLIDARITY

Clearly EWCs have obvious shortcomings. Do these imperfections make this institution a white elephant? On two occasions BMW's EWC unified international labour interests around the crucial problem for working people today – the retention of employment. Although in a third situation international solidarity was less conspicuous, the networking that evolved between 1996 and 2000 did help to produce a more acceptable outcome – in particular for the Longbridge workforce. Reflecting on the eventual break-up of the Rover group, a Rover trade unionist observed: "I don't think in essence that EWCs are valueless, they are valuable mostly because of the links you create, the networks that you create" (Rover convenor). Don Wells writes in this volume about the ineffectiveness of voluntary corporate codes in regulating multinationals. Although EWCs provide only information and consultation rights, and many EWC agreements are voluntary, they do seem able to build meaningful networking that management cannot ignore.

Like any institution, however, the EWC is as good as the individuals who govern it. Given the right commitment to transnational trade unionism, together with the type of changes discussed above, EWCs could evolve into a progressive feature of European industrial relations. Thus evidence presented here suggests that it is inevitable neither that national interests, as some writers argue, will circumscribe international solidarity, nor that the construction of labour unity and a common, supranational identity is an insurmountable goal.

NOTES

1 This case study would not have been possible without the support and interest shown by workers at Rover and BMW. Helpful comments also came from

the editors of this volume, plus Tom Glennon, John Leopold, Alan Tuckman, and Tony Watson. I am also grateful to the Economic and Social Research Council (Award Reference: TO26271321) for helping to fund the dissemination of findings emanating from this research.

2 Hobbes used the term "embedding" in *Leviathan* to describe how the rule of law emerged under bourgeois society to control market forces.

3 Space does not allow for an in-depth review of German industrial relations. For a general overview of the system see Streeck, 1998. For an analysis of relations between works councils and trade unions, see Weber, 1990, and Jacobi, Keller, and Müller-Jentsch, 1992.

4 These writers criticize the subsidiarity character of the EWC Directive, which emphasizes respect for national traditions.

5 Despite notional parity between management and trade unions in seat allocation, the chair, held by management, has the casting vote in a tie.

6 BMW's EWC agreement, in line with the EWC Directive, provides for an "extraordinary" meeting.

7 The AEEU and the MSF have since merged to form Amicus-AEEU.

REFERENCES

Altvater, Elmar, and Birgit Mahnkopf. 1993. *Gewerkschaften vor der europäischen Herausforderung.* Munster: Westfälisches Dampfboot.

Atkinson, Mark. 2000. "Rover Unions Demand More Time as Towers Bid Teeters," *Guardian,* 24 April.

Bergmann, Joachim, Erwin Bürckmann, and Hartmut Dabrowski. 1998. "Reform des Flächentarifvertrags? Betriebliche Realitäten – Verhandlungssyteme – gewerkschaftliche Politik," *Supplement der Zeitschrift Sozialismus.* Hamburg: VSA Verlag.

Bispinck, Reinhard. 2001. "Betriebliche Interesssenvertretung, Entgelt und Tarifpolitik," *WSI Mitteilungen* 54 (2), 124–32.

Blank, Michael. 1998. "Collective Bargaining in the European Union: The Standpoint of the IG Metall," in Wolfgang Lecher and Hans-Wolfgang Platzer, eds., *European Union – European Industrial Relations?* London: Routledge, 157–68.

Brady, Chris, and Andrew Lorenz. 2001. *End of the Road.* London: Prentice Hall.

Coen, Martin. 1998. "The European Dimension to Collective Bargaining Post-Maastricht," in Wolfgang Lecher and Hans-Wolfgang Platzer, eds., *European Union – European Industrial Relations?* London: Routledge, 47–64.

Ettl, Wilfried, and André Heikenroth. 1996. "Strukturwandel, Verbandsabstinenz, Tarifflucht: Zur Lage der Unternehmen und Arbeitgeberverbände im ostdeutschen verarbeitenden Gewerbe," *Industrielle Beziehungen* 3 (2), 134–53.

ETUI. 1999. "European Works Councils in 596 Companies." www.etuc.org/etui

European Industrial Relations Observatory. 1999. "Union Membership Steadies after 18 Years' Decline," *European Industrial Relations Observatory.* www.eiro.eurofound.ie

– 2000. "Comparative Overview," *European Industrial Relations Observatory*. www.eiro.eurofound.ie

Fox, Allan. 1974. *Beyond Contract: Work, Power and Trust Relations*. London: Farber.

Hancké, Bob. 1998. "Industrial Restructuring and Industrial Relations in the European Car Industry," *Discussion Paper* FSI I, 98–305. Berlin: Wissenschaftszentrum für Sozialforschung Berlin.

– 2000. "European Works Councils and Industrial Restructuring in the European Motor Industry," *European Journal of Industrial Relations* 6 (1), 35–84.

Hasel, Margarette, and Hellga Ballauf. 2000. "The Meeting That Saved Rover," *Die Mitbestimmung* 8, 12–15.

Hoffman, Jürgen. 1997. "Geht das Modell Deutschland an seinem Erfolg zugrunde?" *Gewerkschaftliche Monatshefte* 4, 217–23.

Hoffmann, Jürgen, and Reiner Hoffmann. 1997. "Globalization Risks and Opportunities for Labour Policy in Europe." www.etuc.org/etui/publications/DWP

Hyman, Richard. 1999. "Imagined Solidarities: Can Trade Unions Resist Globalization?" in Peter Leisink, ed., *Globalization and Labour Relations*. Cheltenham: Edward Elgar, 94–115.

– 2000. "The Europeanisation – or the Erosion – of Industrial Relations," Plenary Address to the British Universities Industrial Relations Association Annual Conference at Warwick University.

Jacobi, Otto. 1998. "Europäische Kollektivvereinbarungen – Vision oder Illusion?" *Gewerkschaftliche Monatshefte* 6–7, 381–85.

Jacobi, Otto, Berndt Keller, and Walter Müller-Jentsch. 1992. "Germany: Codetermining the Future," in Anthony Ferner and Richard Hyman, eds., *Industrial Relations in the New Europe*. Oxford: Blackwell, 218–69.

Keller, Berndt. 1998. "National Industrial Relations and the Prospects for European Collective Bargaining: The View from a German Standpoint," in Wolfgang Lecher and Hans-Wolfgang Platzer, eds., *European Union – European Industrial Relations?* London: Routledge, 21–46.

Kelly, John, and Ed Heery. 1994. *Working for the Union*. Cambridge: Cambridge University Press.

Koch, Klaus. 1996. "Die Einsamkeit des Funktionärs in der Globalisierungsschlacht," *Gewerkschaftliche Monatshefte* 8, 494–502.

Lecher, Wolfgang. 1996a. "Europäische Betriebsräte – Erfahrungen und Perspektiven," *Industrielle Beziehungen* 3 (3), 262–76.

– 1996b. "Forschungsfeld Europäische Betriebsräte," *WSI Mitteilungen* 48 (11), 710–15.

– 1997. "Europäische Arbeitsbeziehungen – offene Flanke der Gewerkschaften," *Gewerkschaftliche Monatshefte* 48 (6), 360–70.

– 1998. "Auf dem Weg zu Europäischen Arbeitsbeziehungen? Das Beispiel der Euro-Betriebsräte," *WSI Mitteilungen* 50 (4), 258–63.

Lecher, Wolfgang, Bernhard Nagel, and Hans-Wolfgang Platzer. 1998. *Die Konstitu-*

ierung Europäischer Betriebsräte – Vom Informationsforum zum Akteur? Baden-Baden: Nomos Verlagsgesellschaft.

Lecher, Wolfgang, and Reinhard Nauman. 1994. "The Current State of Trade Unions in the EU Member States," in Wolfgang Lecher, ed., *Trade Unions in the European Union – A Handbook.* London: Lawrence and Wishart, 3–126.

Lecher, Wolfgang, and Hans-Wolfgang Platzer. 1998. "Global Trends and the European Context," in Wolfgang Lecher and Hans-Wolfgang Platzer, eds., *European Union – European Industrial Relations?* London: Routledge, 1–7.

Lecher, Wolfgang, Hans-Wolfgang Platzer, Stefan Rüb, and Klaus-Peter Weiner. 2001. *Verhandelte Europäisierung: Die Einrichtung Europäischer Betriebsräte – Zwischen gesetzlichem Rahmen und sozialer Dynamik.* Baden-Baden: Nomos Verlagsgesellschaft.

LRD. 1995. *A Trade Unionist's Guide to European Works Councils.* London: Labour Research Department Booklets.

Maguire, Kevin, Nicholas Bannister, and Mark Milner. 2000. "How the Alchemy Deal Fell Apart," *Guardian.* 29 April.

Marginson, Paul, and Keith Sisson. 1996. "European Works Councils – Opening the Door to European Bargaining," *Industrielle Beziehungen* 3 (3), 229–36.

Miller, Doug. 1999. "Towards a 'European' Works Council," *Transfer* 5 (3), www.etuc.org/ETUI/Publications

Mittelman, James H. 1997. "Restructuring the Global Division of Labour: Old Theories and New Realities," in Stephen Gill, ed., *Globalization, Democratization and Multilateralism.* London: MacMillan, 77–103.

Oppolzer, Alfred, Hartmut Wegener, and Ulrich Zachert. 1986. "Flexibilisierung und Beschäftigungsföderungsgesetz – eine Zwischenbilanz," in Alfred Oppolzer, Hartmut Wegener, and Ulrich Zachert, eds., *Flexibilisierung – Deregulierung – Arbeitspolitik in der Wende.* Hamburg: VSA-Verlag, 7–19.

Rehfeldt, Udo. 1998. "Der Renault–Vilvoored Konflikt und seine Bedeutung für die europäische Gewerkschaftspolitik," *WSI Mitteilungen* 50 (7), 450–59.

Schneider, Michael. 2000. "Stoppte Blair Rover – Deal?" *Die Welt am Sonntag,* 30 April.

Scholte, Jan. 1998. "Beyond the Buzzword: Towards a Critical Theory of Globalisation," in Eleonore Koffman, ed., *Globalisation Theory and Practice.* London: Pinter, 41–57.

Schulten, Thortsen. 1992. *Internationalismus von unten – Europäische Betriebsräte in Transnationalen Konzernen.* Marburg: Verlag Arbeit & Gesellschaft.

– 1996. "Der Europäische Betriebsrat bei Nestlé," *Informationen über multinationale Konzerne* 6, 42–52.

Scott, Regan. 1999. "EWC Development and Strategy," Bremen Conference, *Europäische Betriebsräte: Entwicklung und Strategie,* Universität Arbeiterkammer, Dec.

Streeck, Wolfgang. 1991. "More Uncertainties: German Unions Facing 1992," *Industrial Relations* 30 (3), 317–49.

– 1997. "Neither European nor Works Council: A Reply to Paul Knutsen," *Economic and Industrial Democracy* 18 (2), 325–37.

– 1998. *The German Model of Co-determination and Cooperative Government.* Gütersloh: Bertelsmann Foundation/Hans-Böckler Foundation.

Streeck, Wolfgang, and Sigurt Vitols. 1994. *European Works Councils: Between Statutory Enactment and Voluntary Adoption.* Berlin: Wissenschaftszentrum Berlin.

Turner, Lowell. 1993. "Beyond National Unionism? Cross-National Labour Collaboration in the European Community." Discussion Paper, Wissenschaftszentrum Berlin für Sozialforschung. June.

Weber, Herman. 1990. *100 Jahre Industriegewerkschaft Chemie-Papier-Keramik.* Cologne: Bund Verlag.

Weston, Syd, and Miguel Martínez Lucio. 1998. "In and Beyond Works Councils: Limits and Possibilities for Trade Union Influence," *Employee Relations* 20 (6), 551–64.

Whisler, R. Timothy. 1999. *The British Motor Industry, 1945–94.* Oxford: Oxford University Press.

Whittall, Michael. 2001. "Modell Deutschland: Regulating the Future?" in Steve Jefferys, Fredrick Mispelblom, and Christer Törnqvist, eds., *European Working Lives: Continuities and Change in Management and Industrial Relations in Scandinavia, France and the UK.* Cheltenham: Edward Elgar, 115–29.

Wills, Jane. 2000. "Great Expectations: Three Years in the Life of a European Works Council," *European Journal of Industrial Relations* 6 (1), 85–108.

PART THREE

The Differential Effects of Labour Market Deregulation

9

Racializing the Division of Labour: Neoliberal Restructuring and the Economic Segregation of Canada's Racialized Groups

GRACE-EDWARD GALABUZI

Canada's economy and its labour market are increasingly stratifying along racial lines, as indicated by disproportionate representation of racialized group members in low-income sectors and low-end occupations, under-representation in high-income sectors and occupations, and persistent racial inequality in unemployment rates, employment income, and the incidence of low income. This stratification has numerous adverse social effects, leading to differential life chances for racialized group members. Racial segregation in the labour market occurs within the context of the restructuring of the global economy, the shift towards neoliberal forms of governance, labour market deregulation aimed at flexible labour deployment, and the persistence of historical forms of systemic discrimination in employment. The growing dominance of flexible work arrangements, facilitated by the state's deregulation and reregulation of the labour market and the reversal of state anti-discriminatory policies and programs, has disproportionately affected racialized groups. Despite higher levels of educational attainment, disproportionate numbers of racialized workers are confined to casualized forms of work in certain sectors of the economy, amplifying racial segmentation in the labour market and racialized income inequality and poverty.[1]

The process of racial segmentation of the labour market represents an intensification of the racialization of class formation under the neoliberal order, as suggested by key structural patterns of wage discrimination and occupational segregation in the Canadian labour market (Creese, 1999; Das Gupta, 1996; Galabuzi, 2001; Hiebert, 1997; Li, 1998). Racial segmentation in the labour market determines such social outcomes as differential access to housing, neighbourhood selection, contact with the criminal justice system, health risks, and political participation. The result is a deepening of the racialization of poverty and of the racial segregation of low-income neighbourhoods and the intensification of social exclusion for Canada's urban-based racialized group communities. But while the racialization of class formation represents an intensification of oppression for racialized groups, it also suggests the possibility of racially conscious but class-based struggle and a shift towards a workplace-based politics of resistance to the neoliberal agenda.

This chapter reviews three dimensions of racialized segmentation in the Canadian labour market. The first section describes the dimensions of racialization along several axes, including its historical evolution in Canada, recent changes in the composition of Canada's population and labour force, the links between these trends and the twin processes of globalization and domestic deregulation, and the growing gap in labour market outcomes between racialized and non-racialized labour market segments. The second section analyzes the ways in which the Canadian labour market defines and enforces racialization, including employment practices, professional and trade regulations, and sectoral and occupational patterns. The last section discusses some political and organizational responses that could help challenge and overcome patterns of labour market racialization.

RACIALIZATION AND THE DIVISION OF LABOUR

Current processes of economic restructuring and demographic change have helped create a more multicultural, multi-racial society in Canada. Parallel labour market developments include the neoliberal restructuring of Canada's economy, the massive deregulation and reregulation of the labour market, the dismantling of the welfare state and the privatization of public services, and increased immigration from the South as a key source of new labour. These interrelated processes have occurred within the context of a broader restructuring of the global economy, which has imposed a flexible mode of accumulation, a global division of labour, escalating South–North immigration flows, and greater domestic inequality. Canada, as a resource-rich and labour-poor country that is highly integrated into the global economy, has historically met its labour shortages through immigration. In the 1960s, the demands of an expanding economy and diminished migration from Europe led to the removal of legal restrictions against non-European immigration. The outcome has been a dramatic shift in immigration, with over 75 per cent of Canada's immigrants coming from the South in the 1990s.

The complex dynamics of Canadian immigration policies have historically aimed both to maintain a viable capitalist economy and the "white
character" of the nation. Racial hierarchies became more prominent in
the organization of the Canadian economy in the 1970s, as the numbers
of racialized immigrants grew. Along with the historical social-class,
gender, and race hierarchies in Canada's economy, the sheer numbers of
"new" immigrants from the South represented a qualitative departure for
Canada's labour force. Race as a social construct, based principally on
superficial differences in physical appearance, has always been an important part of Canada's population–economy complex. From early European
attempts to take control of the land, resources, and trade from the First
Nations, which involved restricting their economic participation, to the
selective importation of African-American, Asian, and Caribbean labour
for specific sectoral and occupational deployment, race has substantially
determined access to economic opportunity in Canada.[2]

Historical structures of racial discrimination have influenced the incorporation of racialized immigrants into the labour market, leading to patterns of racial and gender stratification. Many potential immigrants from
the South could work only as domestics and labourers in earlier periods,
despite professional and other qualifications. Similarly, today's racialized
immigrants, most selected on the basis of their skills, often end up with
similar labour market participation patterns – in sectors with largely casualized employment and low-end jobs. Examples of labour market displacement and exclusion, especially during tough economic times, are widely
documented (Anderson and Lynam, 1987; Brand, 1987; Das Gupta, 1996;
Reitz, Calzavana, and Dasko, 1981). Whether as enslaved Blacks or
"freemen," as Chinese railway workers, South Asian farm and forest
workers, or Japanese apprentices in the nineteenth and early twentieth
centuries, or more recently as Caribbean migrant farm workers and Filipino domestic workers, they all fit into a hierarchy of labour that imposed
differential levels of exploitation to ensure capitalist accumulation and a
form of "racial dividend" from labour market differentiation.

There is a continuity of racial segregation in the labour market whose
roots trace back to Canada's inception as a "white settler colony." Within
that context, the late-twentieth and early-twenty-first-century congruence
of the emergence of contingent or non-standard forms of work as a dominant phenomenon of the neoliberal restructuring of the economy, the
shift towards flexible accumulation, and the growth of the size of racialized
communities in urban areas highlight racial stratification. This segmentation has become a prominent feature of the economy, leading some
observers to refer to a "colour-coded" vertical mosaic.

The demand for labour in the urban industrial heartland has made
waves of racialized immigrants destined for urban centres sizeable minori-

ties, while in Canada's biggest metropolis (Toronto) they will soon constitute a majority. These developments have occurred in the context of the
continued focus of Canadian immigration policy on three labour market
goals: "managed" labour-force growth: setting modest immigration targets
to prevent hardship to the existing workforce; selectivity: maintaining
administrative categories of desirable and undesirable newcomers; and
assimilation: heightened demands for certain skills emphasize such criteria as professional occupations in determining immigration eligibility, at
the expense of family reunification.

Yet a growing literature has pointed to a contradictory reality – miscon-
ceptions of the "diminishing value" of immigrant human capital are
undermining the occupational and earning potential of racialized immigrants and partly explain their unequal access to employment, which in
turn intensifies racial segregation. These studies represent part of a debate
in which the "structural barriers" analysis counterposes the differential
economic performance of racialized group members, particularly of
recent immigrants, against the "diminishing value of human capital"
school. This latter approach features prominently in the Economic
Council of Canada's 1991 report, "Economic and Social Impacts of Immigration," which argues that immigrants (and refugees), increasingly from
the South, have lower human-capital quality and so they have trouble integrating into the labour market. This school became prominent in the late
1980s and early 1990s and had a noticeable impact on immigration policy,
leading to limits in refugee approvals and emphasis on the selection of
independent-class immigrants over family reunification.

Despite its influence, the school has not effectively addressed documented inequality in returns to investment in human capital – both educational attainment and experience – between racialized and non-racialized workers; the gap exists as much among those with Canadian
post-secondary education as between Canadian- and foreign-educated
workers. This chapter suggests that, on balance, the structural-barriers
analysis better explains the inability of racialized group members to obtain
returns from their investment in human capital commensurate to non-
racialized Canadians. Non-racialized Canadians realize higher earnings
and occupational status, despite being outstripped in educational attainment by Canadian-born and immigrant racialized group members,
because many employers use race (and immigrant status) to determine
employability – a practice that neoclassical thinkers refer to as "statistical
discrimination," but that structuralists identify as systemic discrimination.[3]

Racialization and Canada's Changing Population

Canada's population has become more ethnically and racially diverse over
the last thirty years. Population growth now depends disproportionately on

Table 9.1 Racialized group population as percentage of total Canadian population, 2001

	Total population	Racialized population	Racialized group share of total population (%)	Regional racialized population as share of Canada total (%)
Canada	30,007,094	3,983,845	13.4	100
Newfoundland	512,930	3,850	0.8	0.1
Prince Edward Island	135,294	1,180	0.9	0.0
Nova Scotia	908,007	34,525	3.8	0.9
New Brunswick	729,498	9,425	1.3	0.3
Quebec	7,237,479	497,975	7.0	12.5
Ontario	11,410,046	2,153,045	19.1	54.0
Manitoba	1,119,583	87,110	7.9	2.1
Saskatchewan	978,933	27,580	2.9	0.7
Alberta	2,974,807	329,925	11.1	8.2
British Columbia	3,907,738	836,440	21.6	20.9
Yukon	28,674	1,025	3.6	0.0
N.W.T.	37,360	1,545	4.2	0.1

Source: Statistics Canada (2003)

immigration from source countries dominated by people of colour. The percentage of racialized minorities – under 4 per cent in 1971 – grew to 9.4 per cent by 1991 and reached 13.4 per cent by 2001. It may rise to 20 per cent by 2016 (see Table 9.1). Given Canada's continued reliance on immigration for population growth, and with globalization escalating, these trends are likely to continue (Statistics Canada, 1998a). Canada's racialized population concentrates mainly in urban centres (see Table 9.2), with nearly three-quarters (73 per cent) in the three largest cities in 2001. Racialized groups account for 43 per cent of the population in Toronto; 49 per cent in Vancouver; and 23 per cent in Montreal. Other cities with sizeable racialized populations include Edmonton (15 per cent), Calgary (18 per cent), Markham, Ont. (56 per cent), and Richmond, BC (59 per cent) (Statistics Canada, 2003a). According to the 2001 census, racialized group members made up 19 per cent of the population in Ontario, Canada's largest province. That share may rise to 25 per cent by 2015. British Columbia had the highest proportion of racialized group members, at 22 per cent. While 68 per cent of Canada's racialized group members are immigrants, 32 per cent are Canadian born (Statistics Canada, 1998a).

The heightened conditions of globalization are rapidly changing the ethnic and racial composition of the labour force in many countries in the North (Mittelman, 1994; Richmond, 1994). The political, economic, and social destabilization brought about by economic restructuring, together

Table 9.2   Racialized group population as a percentage of census metropolitan areas (CMAS), 2001

CMA	Racialized Groups as Share of CMA Population (%)
Canada total	13.4
Vancouver	36.9
Toronto	36.8
Calgary	17.5
Edmonton	14.6
Ottawa-Hull	14.1
Montreal	13.6
Windsor	12.9
Winnipeg	12.5
Kitchener	10.7
Hamilton	9.8
London	9.0
Victoria	8.9
Halifax	7.0
Oshawa	7.0
Saskatoon	5.6
Regina	5.2
Kingston	4.7
St. Catharines–Niagara	4.5
Saint John	2.6
Sherbrooke	2.6
Thunder Bay	2.2
Greater Sudbury	2.0
Quebec	1.6
St. John's	1.4
Trois-Rivières	0.9

Source: Statistics Canada (2003)

with growing inequality between the North and the South, have transformed population flows around the world. A combination of these new movements and the unequal articulations of capitalist development have created what is now called "South in the North": mostly communities and neighbourhoods in the North where conditions increasingly resemble those in the South. That process racializes neighbourhoods, cities, and regions (Fong and Gulla, 1999). In 1961, over 95 per cent of Canada's population had a European heritage, reflecting the history of racist immigration policies. Since the 1970s, increasing numbers of immigrants have come from Africa, Asia, the Caribbean, Latin America, and the Middle East, with Asian born accounting for more than half (58 per cent) of the 1.8 million arrivals in the 1990s and now making up 6.2 per cent of the total population (Statistics Canada, 2003a).

By 2001, Canada was home to 5.4 million immigrants, or 18.4 per cent of the total population – the highest proportion in 70 years. The figure should rise to 25 per cent by 2015. Immigrants increased by more than three times the growth rate of Canadian-born (Statistics Canada, 2003a). Immigration accounted for 70 per cent of the net growth in the labour force between 1991 and 1996 and should be the source of all net labour-force growth by 2011 (Human Resources Development Canada, 1999). The increase in immigration from non-traditional areas has led to some tension in the integration process and an upswing of anti-immigration sentiment and discourses. These have changed public debates and policy options (Ekos Research, 2000; Stoffman, 1993).

Some observers have used the concept of neo-racism to explain anti-immigrant discourses and policy actions in the North in response to the new migration. Neo-racism represents a social construction of race during current globalization and applies racial categories to differentiate values of groups of labour. Consistent with the "South in the North" phenomenon, this race-based labour stratification gives the capitalist class cheap labour, but also fuels working-class resistance to increased immigration. Capital wants the discounted human resources, while the working classes see cultural difference as a basis for resisting non-white labour inflows. The ideological tension reflects the divergence of class interests between workers and capitalists, both of whom embrace difference to justify the (un)desirability of immigrant racialized labour. These ideologies are culturally pervasive and devalue the human quality of racialized immigrant labour and further segregate the labour market. In North America, the term "immigrant" has come to refer to racialized group members, especially Africans, East Asians, South Asians, West Asians, Caribbeans, and Latin Americans. It is an identifier for a certain quality of human capital based on stereotypical assumptions about the abilities of racialized group members. Its popular usage represents a slippage in categories between immigrants and racialized group members (including Canadian born), imposing common assumptions about the lower quality of human capital on the two groups.[4] This characterization is similar to Bonacich's (1972) theory of split labour markets, which seeks to explain tensions between capital (employers), workers from the dominant culture, and minority workers in industrial workplaces. Bonacich argues that racially defined competition leads to four possible outcomes: displacement, exclusion of racialized workers, a submerged system with barriers to mobility for racialized workers, or a radical coalition between majority and minority labour. There are observable signs of exclusion in Canada, but also the potential for a class-based response to intensified exploitation (Galabuzi, 2001). Balibar (1991), writing about Europe, has suggested that neo-racism is a phenomenon of late-twentieth-century globalization, representing a response to the reversal of historic population movements southward and to Northern workers' heightened vulnerability under neoliberal globalization.

Globalization, the Changing Nature of Work, and the Racialization of the Labour Market

"Globalization" refers here to current processes of socioeconomic and political transformation. It involves the neoliberal restructuring of the global and national economies through processes of flexible accumulation (such as flexible production and labour processes, the expansion of information technologies, and the globalization of financial markets) and the dismantling or retrenchment of the regulatory state. Its effects are identifiable in all dimensions of everyday life – social, cultural, economic, and political. The shift from the predominance of Fordist modes of production and accumulation to flexible accumulation (Harvey, 1989; Lipietz, 1987) reinforces the racial segmentation of work. The overriding pressure of "global" competition has imposed distinctive conditions for a new global capitalist accumulation order, with demands for flexibility of labour processes, production, innovation, and investment. Flexibility is both an enabling and a defining feature of the transformation of national and global economies (Harvey, 1989; Lipietz, 1987). The "competitiveness and flexibility model" is restructuring the relations of production in ways that reinforce flexible work arrangements, deregulation, and the privatization of public assets and that also limit state legislative and policy responses to inequality in employment, protection of workers in their workplaces, and the crisis of social reproduction (Castells, 1998; Gill, 1995).

The state's diminished economic role intensifies exploitation of the most vulnerable workers and weakens the position of labour as a whole. Neoliberal restructuring serves to undermine the power of labour in a number of ways. First, it introduces labour back into competition through the transnationalization of the division of labour, since wages in the South are pitifully low. Second, it creates conditions of political and socioeconomic crisis that send massive immigration flows northward, thereby adding to the pool of those likely to accept relatively poor working conditions and low wages. Third, it creates the conditions for the expansion of non-standard and precarious work.

The aggressive introduction of new technologies and the shift towards flexible labour management arrangements signal major changes in work and in power relations within the workplace and the labour market. Hence flexibility – in the form of casualization of work – is central to the present-day racialization of class formation, especially in Canada's urban areas. By reproducing pre-existing, racially discriminatory structures in the labour market and by devaluing the labour of racialized group members, it subsidizes global capital. This was evident during a period of relative prosperity in Canada, such as 1995–98, when the gap between rich and poor became wider and increasingly racialized (Galabuzi, 2001; Jackson, 2002).

Racialization and Labour Market Deregulation

In Canada, global restructuring and the deregulation of the labour market have exacerbated previous fissures of racial and gender inequality based on systemic discrimination. A growing body of Canadian studies suggests that the creation of flexible work arrangements has particularly disadvantaged racialized groups, especially racialized women (Barker and Christensen, 1998; de Wolff, 2000; Fox and Sugiman, 1999; Hughes, 1999; Ornstein, 2000; Vosko, 2000; Zeytinoglu and Muteshi, 2000). Racialized groups experience disproportionate access to sectors and occupations where non-standard forms of work are dominant. Given as well the impact of persistent discriminatory labour market structures, what emerges is a deepening of racial segmentation of the labour market, racialization of poverty, racialization and segregation of low-income neighbourhoods, and intensification of social exclusion. Racialized groups' disproportionate participation in precarious work is central to the growing racialization of the division of labour.

These developments bring with them increased intra–working class tensions and competition for decent employment, which, from time to time, unleash expressions of overt, "competitive" racism (Bolaria and Li, 1988; Satzewich, 1998). Competition arising out of the deregulation of work arrangements drives down wages and increases exploitation and vulnerability for all workers. While historically, the majority of immigrants have achieved some economic success, recent trends suggest different trajectories. Since the early 1980s, when most immigrants began arriving from the South, immigrants' earnings have stalled, and they are no longer converging with those of comparable Canadian-born workers. Both Toronto and national data find racialized workers disproportionately at the bottom of the economic ladder, in terms of income, employment, and access to high-paying sectors and jobs (DeVoretz, 1995; Galabuzi, 2001; Jackson, 2002; Ley and Smith, 1997; Lian and Matthews, 1998; Mata, 1994; Ornstein, 2000).

Racialized groups predominate in low-income sectors (such as commercial and retail, domestic work, hospitality and other service industries, light manufacturing, and textile and garment), as well as in low-status occupations (clerical, domestic work, food service, harvesting, janitorial, low-end health-care work, manual, and sales). The focus of the political response to intensified exploitation may be shifting towards workplace-based efforts to strengthen workers' ability to bargain better wages and working conditions. New forms of organization, such as the Asian Canadian Labour Alliance and the Ontario Coalition of Black Trade Unionists, are articulating community opposition to what they term "economic apartheid." Toronto Organizing for Fair Employment (TOFFE) focuses on racialized workers involved in temporary, casual, part-time, and contract work. So while oppression is intensifying in the short term, material conditions suggest the emergence of a class-based (yet racially conscious) form of struggle against the inequalities generated by global capitalism.

THE INCOME, UNEMPLOYMENT, AND POVERTY GAPS

The impact of racialized segregation on income distribution is clearly observable in the statistical data. For example, Galabuzi (2001) reports that during 1996–98, a period of relative prosperity in Canada, a sustained double-digit gap persisted between the incomes of racialized group members and other Canadians. In 1996 racialized Canadians received average pre-tax earnings of $19,227, while non-racialized Canadians made $25,069, or 23 per cent more. Based on median incomes, the gap was even larger and actually widened during the late 1990s' economic expansion.[5]

The gap in employment income between racialized groups and other Canadians partly reflects their unequal access to work opportunities suggested above. In 1996, 75 per cent of non-racialized adults were employed, compared to 66 per cent of racialized adults. The data show that unemployment was much higher among specific racialized groups, including women, youth, people without postsecondary education, and those living in Quebec (Kunz, Milan, and Schetagne, 2001). In Toronto, in 1996, the unemployment rate among racialized group members was 13 per cent, compared to 7 per cent for non-racialized individuals; as high as 25 per cent among select racialized immigrant groups, and even higher among some women and youth (Ornstein, 2000). In 1995 the national unemployment rate for racialized women was 15.3 per cent, compared to 13.2 per cent for racialized men, 9.4 per cent for other women, and 9.9 per cent for other men (Chard, 2000). In 1999, 54 per cent of racialized group employees worked all year, compared to 59 per cent in the non-racialized group. In 1998, 58 per cent of recent immigrants (arriving 1991–96) had work all year, compared to 70 per cent of adult Canadians. The incidence of full- and part-year unemployment was also significantly higher for recent immigrants (Smith and Jackson, 2002). Nevertheless, the proportion of their income consisting of government transfer payments fell from 19 per cent in 1995 to 11 per cent in 1998, reflecting the significant drop in state-funded social protection.

For many racialized group members, educational attainment has not translated into comparable compensation, labour market access, or workplace mobility. Racialized immigrants (who now constitute 68 per cent of the total racialized group) with university education experienced a 10.4 per cent unemployment rate, compared to 6.6 per cent for comparable non-racialized immigrants and 4.2 per cent for non-racialized Canadian born. The unemployment rate for university-educated racialized Canadian-born was 6.3 per cent (Kunz, Milan, and Schetagne, 2001; Smith and Jackson, 2002). Racialized immigrants also face structural barriers to accreditation of their imported skills and job experience and also denial of access to trades and professions by provincially regulated licensing bodies.[6] For the most recent immigrants, higher documented levels of unemployment also reflect their relatively short time in the country. Recent studies show that racialized group members also suffer higher levels of poverty, with some groups of racialized women sustaining poverty rates as high as 60 per cent (Galabuzi, 2001; Jackson, 2002; Ornstein, 2000).

According to data from Statistics Canada, the incidence of low income was significantly higher among racialized group members than the national average over the period 1993–96. In 1996 36.8 per cent of women and 35 per cent of men in racialized communities earned low incomes, compared to 19.2 per cent of other women and 16 per cent of other men (Statistics Canada, 1998b). The low-income rate for racialized children under the age of six was an astounding 45 percent, compared to the overall average of 26 percent. The poverty gap among those in the over-65 age group is also substantial. The elderly low-income rate is 32 per cent among racialized groups, compared to the national average of 19 per cent (Statistics Canada, 1998b). In 1996, in urban areas, poverty rates were 52 per cent for immigrants arriving in 1991, and 38 per cent for all racialized groups, compared to 20 per cent for the rest of the population. Racialized group members accounted for 21.6 per cent of the population in Canada's urban centres in 1996, but 33 per cent of the urban poor. In some cities such as Richmond and Vancouver, BC, and Markham, Mississauga, Richmond Hill, and Toronto, Ontario, more than half of the people living in poverty were racialized group members (Lee, 2000). This "racialization of poverty" relates to the deepening social exclusion of racialized groups not just in the labour market but also in other areas of society, as economic, political, and social power continues to concentrate in the hands of fewer and fewer people.

To sum up, racialized group members experience inequality in Canada's labour market in the form of a double-digit income gap, higher unemployment rates, underrepresentation in high-income sectors and occupations, and overrepresentation in low-income sectors and occupations, and they are twice as likely to be poor. A number of structural causes, policies, and practices contribute to this racial inequality. The neoliberal restructuring of the economy, and the attendant deregulation of the labour market and casualization of labour, along with expanding immigration from the South, have made racialized group members more vulnerable to historical forms of wilful and unintended (systemic) racial discrimination. This results in differential access to the labour market and the increasingly well-documented phenomenon of a racially segmented labour market – complete with the segregation of racialized groups into low-income sectors and low-end occupations.

MECHANICS OF RACIALIZATION

Explaining Racial Discrimination in Employment

Various theories seek to explain racial inequality and lower returns to racialized human capital in the Canadian labour market. Mainstream economists apply the neoclassical concept of marginal productivity. In a competitive labour market, employment and earnings for factors of production depend on marginal productivity. Thus, given equal levels of productivity, racialized and non-racialized labour should have equal earnings opportunities, since employers seek to maximize their profits from labour. Racial inequality in economic life derives from racial differences in productivity, which in turn reflect the varying quality and quantity of human and non-human factors that racialized and non-racialized workers contribute to production. Racial differences in outcomes flow from differences in the ownership and deployment of qualitative and quantitative human and non-human resources, not from "discriminatory" structures or conduct in the market (Arrow, 1972; Becker, 1971; DeVoretz, 1995).

This framework poses a number of problems. First, it assumes perfectly competitive conditions in the labour market as a basis for efficient allocations of labour and compensation. That is clearly not the case, given differential access to information and the existence of "networks" that make employment information and decision-making subjective, or at least less transparent than would be optimal for a competitive market. Most jobs are filled through word of mouth, not through regional or national postings, which confers an advantage on those in the workplace and a disadvantage to those who are socially excluded.

Second, the neoclassical approach explains the income gap on the basis of human-quality differentials between racialized and non-racialized workers. Yet the purportedly lower levels of educational attainment, experience, and perhaps communication skill attributed to racialized workers are not so. Relevant data show that not only is their educational attainment higher than many cohorts that outperform them in the labour market, but the income gap is still evident even among groups with equal education (that is, among university graduates and among those with only high school education). Moreover, data consistently indicate an advantage in educational attainment for both foreign-born (immigrant) and Canadian-born racialized group members, intra-group variation not withstanding (Akbari, 1999; Kunz, Milan, and Schetagne, 2001; Reitz, 2001; Wanner, 1998).

Third, employment patterns do not conform to the optimal allocation of labour that underlies the competitive model; many highly qualified racialized workers have low-wage jobs in low-income sectors or have higher unemployment rates (Galabuzi, 2001; Kunz, Milan, and Schetagne, 2000; Reitz, 2001). While racialized group members may be subject to economic discrimination because some are recent immigrants going through a process of adjustment, they are also subject to exclusionary discrimination as employers impose prejudicial assumptions about their abilities on the hiring and promotion processes (Abella, 1985; Henry and Ginsberg, 1984; House of Commons, 1984).[7]

Numerous studies point instead to structural causes of inequality, with racial and gender discrimination a key factor in unequal access to the workplace and differential outcomes for racialized groups. Among the most prominent Canadian studies are two federal reports – the *Report of the Royal Commission on Equality in Employment* (Abella, 1985) and *Equality Now* (House of Commons, 1984), a parliamentary report on racialized groups and employment discrimination. Both suggest differences in access to employment, in unemployment rates, and in incomes that are "social indicators" of job discrimination and find such discrimination to be systemic. Racial discrimination in employment is also the subject of a substantial body of continuing scholarly work.[8]

Some of the studies draw from theories of social closure to explain the historical marginalization of racialized group members in the labour market. Social-closure theory emphasizes the role of privilege and power and the protection of such privilege by dominant groups. Members of dominant groups maintain privilege by constructing racial categories and by assigning negative value to immutable attributes such as skin colour and cultural background, using these to evaluate the suitability of minority candidates for employment, compensation and workplace mobility.

Critical anti-racism seeks to explain racialization in institutions such as labour markets. While acknowledging the cultural role of racist ideologies, it proposes a more structural understanding of how class, gender, and other forms of oppression intersect with race to create the exclusion experienced by racialized group members in capitalist society. As Winant (1994) has remarked, this approach views race as a "fundamental organizing principle of contemporary life" organizing work. Race acts as a determinant of access to the labour market without negating the overarching logic of capital (Calliste, 2000a). And it is here that the segmented-labour theory intersects with critical anti-racism. Henry and Ginsberg (1984), using actors with comparable qualifications, found that for the same jobs on offer, white candidates got three offers for every one for a black candidate. This and other studies conclude that employment processes, policies, and practices in the Canadian labour market betray racial biases that help create structural differential access to employment, compensation, and mobility. Some recent writers present the immigrant status of the racialized group (signifying a shorter period of stay in Canada) and a lack of language skills as major explanations for income and occupational inequalities (Chiswick and Miller, 1988; Devoretz, 1995; Stoffman, 1993). Others have identified a combination of factors, including diminished immigrant quality, racial discrimination, and restructuring in the labour market, as key to this phenomenon (Bloom et al., 1994; Wanner, 1998). While immigrant status is an important consideration, Canadian data show that racialized immigrants have more in common with Canadian-born racialized group members than with immigrants from Europe arriving in the same period, in terms of their experience of unemployment and underemployment and the incidence of low income. In fact, there is a racialized gap in immigration experiences, with the income gap between European immigrants and other immigrants significant and growing.[9]

EDUCATION AND ECONOMIC ATTAINMENT
OF NEW IMMIGRANTS

The shift towards more newcomers from the South has led to a noticeable lag in economic attainment among members of the immigrant groups. This has occurred despite Canada's 1990s' emphasis on bringing in skilled immigrants. Ironically, the selection process has become more stringent in response to charges that immigrant quality has declined, leading to a shift towards a majority of people arriving through the independent (skilled) class – over 60 per cent in recent years (Citizenship and Immigration Canada, 2003). About 34 per cent of recent immigrants (1991–96) aged 25–44 had completed university, compared to 19 per cent in the rest of the Canadian population. In 1996, 43 per cent of all recent immigrants aged 25–44 were postsecondary graduates (Statistics Canada, 1998c). Among even more recent immigrants (1996–2000), 62 per cent had postsecondary education, compared to 23 per cent among Canadian-born. A 1999 study on the "quality" of immigrants who arrived from 1956 to 1994 shows that the percentage of those without a high school education has been declining and is lower than that in the Canadian population throughout the period, while the proportion of university graduates has been growing and outpacing the level in the Canadian population (Akbari, 1999). These findings would seem to contradict the popular assumption that quality of human capital is diminishing among immigrants.

Differential Access to Regulated Professions and Trades

Immigrant's higher educational attainment has not led to better labour market performance partly because of barriers to accreditation of trade and professional qualifications. A number of studies have dealt with foreign-trained professionals and tradespeople in the Canadian labour market. Many immigrants face barriers in obtaining recognition for such credentials, in becoming licensed to practice in their fields, and in converting their skills into economic compensation (Cummings et al., 1989; Fernando and Prasad, 1986; Mata, 1994; McDade, 1988).

Government immigration and labour market policies, provincial inaction and a lack of federal-provincial co-ordination help perpetuate this inequality. As part of the immigration process, the government's "Occupations List" assigns points by required occupation to newcomers. The number of points assigned to an occupation reflects demand in the Canadian labour market. Of the skilled workers selected in 1998 (accounting for a majority of all immigrants that year), fully 72 per cent had university degrees (Brouwer, 1999). While labour shortages persist, this has not translated into jobs for this highly educated group. Nor have governments made serious commitments to training and upgrading for immigrants, except in language training, which often is not occupation-specific. In 1991, Ottawa established the Canadian Information Centre for International Credentials (CICIC) to act as a clearing-house for information about regulated trades and professions. However, most of the regulation of trades and professions falls under provincial jurisdiction, with many self-regulating, putting a premium both on federal–provincial co-ordination and on ensuring that self-regulating bodies open up to newcomers. Some provinces have set up independent credential-assessment agencies, but their results are not necessarily accepted by the regulating bodies, and many foreign-trained immigrants charge that such gatekeeping bodies often further inhibit access since few even allow for an appeal process.[10] Recently, the growing shortage of skills, especially in health and education, has renewed interest in credential recognition, as have international and internal trade agreements for labour mobility.[11]

The absence of an infrastructure for assessing foreign educational, training, experience, and professional standards, and lack of familiarity with regulatory bodies, employers, and academic institutions, mean that many immigrants face major and sometimes-insurmountable barriers to obtaining occupational licences. Some observers have attributed the resulting mismatch to personal factors such unfamiliarity with the Canadian labour market and occupational requirements, low official-language skills, and the quality gap in higher education between countries of the South and industrialized Northern countries (Basavarajappa and Verma, 1985; DeVoretz, 1995; Stoffman, 1993). However, a recent Ontario study of foreign-trained professionals arriving after 1994 found that almost three-quarters of those who had their academic qualifications assessed after immigrating had academic qualifications equivalent to those granted by Ontario universities. Some 76.8 per cent had good or excellent official-language abilities (OLAs), and 88.7 per cent had good or excellent occupation-specific language abilities (with some variation by gender and year of immigration). Moreover, 63.8 per cent of these immigrants came from Africa, Guyana and the Caribbean, the Middle East, and Latin America; one-third from Asia and the Pacific Rim; and just 3.1 per cent from Europe (Ministry of Training, Colleges and Universities, 2002). Thus employers' and governments' emphasis on individuals' language skills or on the non-convertibility of occupational skills and academic credentials is inappropriate; the focus should be on more systemic barriers.[12]

The racialized experience of barriers to access to professions and trades creates substantial costs – both to individual immigrants and their families and to Canadian governments, businesses, and the economy. The result is a highly educated and experienced underclass of unemployed or under-employed immigrant professionals and tradespeople, with many finding only low-end, low-skill, contract, temporary or part-time, casualized employment. Many highly trained immigrants end up as newspaper carriers, janitors, or taxi drivers, deliver fast foods, or work as security officers in urban areas (de Wolf, 2000; Galabuzi, 2001; Jackson, 2002). Employers' standard demands for "Canadian experience" often push professionals and tradespeople out of their field of training, and their skills degrade over time (Vosko, 2000). Over 90 per cent of those who fail to find work in their field in the first three years of immigration tend to end up permanently in other sectors. Table 9.3 illustrates a select group of tradespeople and professionals experiencing this mismatch.

Given these conditions, immigrant professionals and skilled tradespeople, especially those arriving after 1986 (a disproportionate majority of them racialized), have not been able to convert their educational advantage into higher occupational status or income. Advocates for immigrants have termed this situation a "brain waste." For example, the systematic failure to recognize foreign credentials increases costs to Ontario's welfare system, imposes losses on employers who are unable to find employees

Table 9.3   Refugees in professional/management occupations in country of origin, and occupations in Canada when interviewed

Occupation in country of Origin	Occupations in Canada
Accommodation services manager	Machine operator
Banking manager	Accounting clerk, Taxi driver
Computer systems analyst	Property administrator
Dentist	Welder
Economist	Truck driver
Editor	Sales assistant
Engineers	Labourer, Cleaner, Drafting technician, Dispatcher, Delivery driver, Gas worker, Drywaller
Financial accountants	Foodservice , Cleaner, Hairdresser, Courier, Accounting clerk, Nursing aide, Mechanical assembler, Machine operator
Graphic artist	Sales clerk
Journalists	Labourers
Judge	Secretary
Land surveyor	Survey technician
Lawyer	Paralegal, Labourer
Librarian	Labourer, Landscaping
Manufacturing manager	Labourer
Musician	Retail supervisor
Officer, armed forces	Meat cutter, Mechanical assembly
Pharmacist	Health services aide
Registered nurses	Nursing assistants, Social service workers, Cleaner, Sales clerk, Decorator, Food service
Retail, Sales manager	Labourer, Flight attendant, Early childhood educator, Tailor, Metal contractor, Purchasing agent
Scientist	Service station attendant
Social worker	Food server
Specialist physicians	Nursing aides, Cleaner, Medical lab
School teachers	Cleaner, Social service workers, Early childhood educator, Kitchen helper, Accounting clerk, Labourer
College lecturers	Customer service clerk, Electrical mechanic, Meat cutter, Welder
Veterinarian ·	Nursing aide

Source: 1998 Survey of Settlement Experiences of Refugees by Abu-Laban et al. (1999).

with the skills and abilities that they desperately require, and necessitates redundant retraining for foreign-trained individuals.[13]

Neoliberal Deregulation
and the Intensification of Racial Segmentation

Racial discrimination in employment, the casualization of work, and sectoral segregation are complementary processes that facilitate the racial segmentation of the labour market. Flexible labour deployment thrives on the existence of a pool of vulnerable workers whose weak bargaining position inclines them to accept less pay as well as less than optimal working arrangements. These unequal articulations of capitalist development stratify labour markets, reinforcing historical forms of segregation (Bonacich, 1972; Gordon, Edwards and Reich, 1982; Krahn and Lowe, 1988; Reitz, Calzavana, and Dasko, 1981).

Contingent work has become a major feature of the Canadian labour market. While this type of work is not new, its prevalence departs from previous experience. Broad (2000) posits five interrelated structural transformations that have combined to make casual work so prominent: the globalization of capitalist production; the emergence of the neoliberal state; flexible production; the rise of the service economy; and the increased re-entry of women into the workforce.[5] For our purposes, these factors combine with increased flows of immigrants from the South to Canada's urban areas and with persistent forms of discrimination in employment to intensy racial segmentation of the labour market.

The author uses a variation of the concept of segmented labour to explain the segregated experience of racialized workers, women, and immigrants in the Canadian labour market. Segmentation is observable through the structural nature of gender-, ethnic-, and racially-defined concentrations in the labour market. The analysis divides jobs and industries into primary and secondary (or peripheral) sectors and occupations, on the basis of differential wages, employment stability, potential for promotion, working conditions, unionization, job rights, and barriers to mobility (both within and between sectors). The primary sector has higher wages and employment stability, while secondary-sector work is "marginal," non-standard, and low-paying. People in the secondary sector have little or no bargaining power and expereince intensified exploitation.

While the categories of primary and secondary sectors imply a permanence and rigidity that is not sustainable, the approach can help draw out the racialized and gendered structural patterns of labour market participation that reflect the historical incorporation of racialized groups into the labour force through low-skill, low-paying jobs and sectors. Because they are socially (and politically) disconnected from the rest of the labour force, and because assumptions about the quality of racialized, gendered, and immigrant labour devalue their labour, they will often take any work available at the lowest wages and with the poorest conditions. As the last hired and first fired, many find themselves revolving in and out of contract, temporary, and part-time work. In essence, they act as a reserve pool of labour for an economic system that intensifies their exploitation, using their discounted labour as a subsidy.

Gendered Racism and the Division of Labour

The particular experience of racialized women is instructive because of their vulnerability to both racial and gender segmentation. Racialized immigrant women are predominantly relegated to four sectors in the labour market: processing and light manufacturing, low-end service-sector jobs in health and hospitality, clerical work, and homework – including domestic work and piece work (Anderson and Lynam, 1987; Bakan and Stasiulis, 1995; Beach and Worswick, 1993; Boyd, 1985; Brand, 1987; Preston and Giles, 1997; Vosko, 2000). According to Das Gupta (1996), in 1996 as many as one-third of Toronto's employed racialized women worked as nursing attendants in homes for the aged.

Gendered racism is embedded in the Canadian labour markets and makes itself manifest in various ways. Racialized women are often portrayed as less competent, less skilled, and less disciplined and as secondary wage earners. However, evidence suggests that racialized women actually have more education than other women, work longer hours than men, often have greater responsibilities, and are largely primary wage earners (Chard, 2000). Yet racialized women experience greater marginalization and ghettoization in the labour market. In predominantly female occupations such as nursing, studies indicate persistent discrimination as racialized nurses face barriers to management positions and over-concentrate in nurse's-aide, orderly-work, and other low-end positions. Racism and sexism interact with class to define the place of racialized women workers in the labour market, even in relation to other women workers. They account for the disproportionate participation of racialized women workers in the helping and nurturing occupations, where they experience marked pay inequity (Calliste, 2000a). This is evident in such occupations as nursing, garment working, domestic work, community service, health care, human services, and commercial service; while these sectors are female-dominated, access to management is racialized, and racialized women disproportionately fill low-skill, low-end jobs.

Sectoral and Occupational Segmentation

Segmented-labour theory can augment anti-racism analysis in explaining racial inequalities in the labour market. We draw from the two theories here for a sectoral analysis of the Canadian labour market. Racial segmentation is clearest in occupational and sectoral segregation. An analysis of unpublished 1996 data on census workplace equity from Human Resources Development Canada finds racialized group members under-represented in many high-paid occupations, over-represented in low-paying sectors, and under-represented even in the higher-paying jobs within those low-

Table 9.4   Racialized group employment numbers by select underrepresented occupations

Occupation	Racialized group members	Total employment	Racialized group proportion (%)
Lawyers and Quebec Notaries	2,885	56,625	5
Secondary School Teachers	8,385	155,825	5
Elementary/Kindergarten School Teachers	9,465	229,990	4
Air Pilots	310	11,145	3
Air Traffic Controllers	95	4,345	2
Police Officers	1,850	54,785	3
Fire Fighters	335	22,095	2
Carpenters	4,620	111,975	4
Electricians	2,330	45,850	7

Source: Human Resources Development Canada (1999).

paid sectors (Human Resources Development Canada, 1999). The sectoral segregation is observable across a cross-section of industries. Industries such as clothing (where 36.2 per cent of employees are members of racialized groups), banking services (15 percent), and textiles (24.5 percent) typify the over-representation of racialized groups; racialized group workers are under-represented in the motor-vehicle industry (7 per cent of the workforce), primary steel (4.2 percent), and even the federal government (5.6 percent).

Table 9.4 provides a list of some well-paying occupations in which racialized group members are under-represented. While racialized groups accounted for 13 per cent of Canada's total population in 2001, they are substantially under-represented in key high-income professional and blue-collar occupations, such as law, education, building trades, and fire-fighting. In contrast, Table 9.5 lists those mostly low-income occupations in which racialized groups are over-represented, including janitorial services, food preparation, harvesting, and nursing attendants.

An analysis of job categories and classifications in selected industries further indicates the effect of differential access to the labour market. Data from the automobile, steel, and federal-government sectors confirms the under-representation of racialized group members, especially at the managerial and supervisory levels. Conversely, a review of data from the retail, textile, and clothing industries shows the reverse over-representation of racialized group members in low-paid occupations (Human Resources Development Canada, 1999). Given its socio-political position, the public sector, specifically the federal public service, is particularly noteworthy. The recent report of a federal task force characterized the 5.3 per cent participation rate of racialized groups in the federal public service as inde-

Table 9.5   Racialized group employment numbers by select overrepresented occupations

Occupation	Racialized group members	Total employment	Racialized group proportion (%)
Light Duty Cleaners	26,505	142,770	19
Food Service Counter Attendants and Food Preparers	22,995	132,415	17
Kitchen and Food Service Helpers	26,945	111,235	24
Harvesting Labourers	4,410	11,035	40
University Professors	6,500	48,000	14
Post-secondary Teaching and Research Assistants	8,385	27,060	31
Registered Nurses	25,095	216,335	12

Source: Human Resources Development Canada (1999).

fensible, 15 years after the introduction of a voluntary federal program of employment equity for women, racialized groups, aboriginal people, and persons with disabilities (Federal Taskforce, 2000).

In sum, using a combination of anti-racist and segmented theoretical analysis, we identify significant, documented patterns of racialized groups' vulnerability to racial discrimination in employment, of gendered racism, and of differential access to professions and trades, which explain the racial inequality in income, employment, and life chances described in the first section of the chapter. Neoliberal restructuring has intensified these factors, through the market regulation and flexible deployment of labour, the prevalence of causalization, and the resulting racial segregation in the Canadian labour market; through the racialization of class formation as racialized labour market segmentation becomes more entrenched; and through racially defined sectoral and occupational structures that intersect with other dimensions of exclusion (such as the spatial concentration of poverty, especially in urban areas).

ORGANIZATIONAL RESPONSES TO THE RACIALIZATION OF THE DIVISION OF LABOUR

Racialized groups have identified segregation in the labour market as fundamental to their Canadian experience and a major impediment to full citizenship. In the past, the most emphatic responses to this situation have employed the racialization framework and been organized around demands for key legislated anti-discriminatory policies and programs (inspired by section 15 of the Canadian Charter of Rights and Freedoms). The most prominent of these initiatives have included employment-equity and pay-equity policies. Employment equity addresses differential treatment in common workplaces and, to some degree, issues of income, access, and mobility within sectors. According to Abella (1985), it is a policy "designed to obliterate the present residual effects of discrimination and to open equitably the competition for employment opportunities to those arbitrarily excluded." Legislated programs of employment equity at the federal and provincial level have lacked the enforcement powers necessary to succeed yet have still provoked a backlash in discourse and legislative action (the most drastic being the complete 1995 repeal of the Ontario Employment Equity Act by the incoming Conservative government). This backlash has been attributed to the contradictory objectives embodied in these policies (Bakan and Kobayashi, 2000; Ferrel et al., 1998). Moreover, the policies represent a limited approach to dealing with policies and practices imbued with unequal power relations. Bakan and Kobayashi's (2000) review of provincial programs suggests that they have been ineffective at or inappropriate for eliminating discriminatory structures in the labour market, partly because of the persistence or re-emergence of public discourses inspired by racist, sexist ideologies, but also because they do not address the many intersecting oppressions that ground the racialized experience of social exclusion in Canada and their specific forms in different regions. Moreover, neoliberal market reforms have imposed new competitive tensions among workers, as opposed to expanding employment opportunities for all segments of society.

An alternative approach would be to take a workplace-based approach to improving employment and income opportunities and protection. There is no doubt that coalition-building across race and gender lines, building a political movement, and strengthening collective bargaining rights would help racialized workers to resist the capitalist push towards more flexibility and casualization of labour, address issues of privilege and unequal power relations, increase access to all sectors and occupations, and improve wages and working conditions in the sectors in which racialized groups are predominant.

Table 9.6 indicates that a key category in comparing incomes of racialized and non-racialized employees is unionized employment. Within unionized workplaces the income gap between racialized and non-racialized workers is in the single-digit range (8 per cent), and average wages for racialized group members are comparable to those of employees with university degrees. This suggests that unionization is a promising, short-run, non-legislative option for dealing with racial inequality in the labour market. Of 2.9 million unionized workers in Canada in 1998, 200,000 were racialized group members, representing 7 per cent of the union population. Reitz and Verma (2000) confirm that racialized men have much lower levels of unionization than other men, while the levels for women

Table 9.6   Employment income of full-year/full-time racialized persons in unionized workplaces before taxes, 1998

	Income, total population ($)	Income, racialized groups ($)	Income, non-racialized groups ($)	Income gap ($)	Income gap (%)
Average	44,451	41,253	44,919	3,666	8
Median	41,450	38,755	42,000	3,245	7

Source: Centre for Social Justice special run of data from the Statistics Canada, Survey of Labour and Income Dynamics, 1999-2000, as reported in Galabuzi (2001).

were only marginally lower than for other women. Their study suggests that employment discrimination affects access to union jobs, especially in certain occupations and industries.

The documented over-representation of racialized groups in certain sectors, industries, and occupations would suggest that unionization there would increase wages. Similarly, greater access for racialized group members to unionized sectors, industries, and occupations would also increase their employment income and improve their working conditions. Unionization could also benefit racialized workers in non-standard work environments such as garment-making, harvesting, kitchen and food service, and retailing. Workplace organizing as the focus of the response to discrimination and employment segregation thus seems to have significant potential. The emergence of the Asian Canadian Labour Alliance, the Ontario Coalition of Black Trade Unionists, Toronto Organizing for Fair Employment (TOFFE), and other related initiatives presents an innovative approach to an integrated class–race analysis of oppression. In 2001, a much-publicized union drive involving the mostly racialized newspaper carriers at the *Toronto Star* collapsed, but it was a sign of things to come, as racialized workers begin to assert themselves in the workplace. The material conditions of capitalism make a class-based, racially conscious organizational response a new source of potential resistance against the inequalities of global capitalism.

CONCLUSION

The neoliberal restructuring of the Canadian economy and the retreat of the Canadian state from its regulatory role have intensified racial stratification of the labour market. The emergence of non-standard forms of work and the increased numbers of racialized members in the labour market through Canada's reliance on immigrants from the South have deepened sectoral segregation and helped racialize poverty. Key social and economic indicators such as income, the incidence of low income, unemployment, and patterns of sectoral participation reveal how neoliberal restructuring and deregulation have combined with persistent racial discrimination to intensify racial inequality in the economy. In material terms, the sectoral segregation exemplified by the disproportionate concentration of racialized populations in part-time work, temporary work, and homework leads to their over-representation in substandard and increasingly segregated housing, to higher health risks, and to growing tensions between racialized communities and the criminal justice system. In major Canadian urban centres such as Calgary, Montreal, Toronto, and Vancouver, where racialized group populations are statistically significant, the cumulative impact of racially segmented labour markets and other dimensions of racial inequality have heightened social exclusion for whole segments of racialized groups. Increased immigration, persistent devaluation of racialized human capital, social marginalization, and racial polarization in the labour market have made racialized groups into a reserve army of labour that bears a racial dividend for capital. Yet, rather than intensifying competitive racism and weakening the working class, the struggles of racialized groups are increasingly becoming class-based in the sectors in which they are disproportionately represented.

NOTES

1 "Racialized groups" refers to persons other than Aboriginal peoples, who are non-Caucasian in race or not white in colour. Racialized categories include Chinese, South Asian, black, Arab/West Asian, Southeast Asian, Filipino, Latin American, Japanese, Korean, and Pacific Islanders (based on the U.S. Federal Employment Equity Act definition of visible minorities).

2 There is a substantial body of literature dealing with the experience of racialized minorities and their incorporation in Canadian society and the Canadian labour market. Most of the research demonstrates the persistence of structural inequalities in access to and mobility in the labour market, along with historic restrictions on owning commercial properties leading to labour market segregation defined by concentrations in certain sectors and occupations or "enclaves". Historically, from enslaved blacks, or largely segregated "free" blacks in Nova Scotia, New Brunswick, Quebec, and Ontario, to Chinese railway workers in British Columbia, South Asian businessmen seeking government contracts, Japanese professionals (denied accreditation in medicine, and law), Caribbean and Filipino domestics, Caribbean farm workers, and more recently immigrants from Africa, the Caribbean, China, Latin America, the Middle East, the Philippines, and South Asia, the incorporation of these groups in the Canadian economy has been subject to their racialized status in Canada. The phenomenon speaks to the organization of

the labour deployment under Canadian capitalism in ways that assure cheap sources of labour and produce a "racial" dividend for capital.

3 The "structural factors" argument, suggesting the impact of racial discrimination in the labour market, is the subject of a number of recent studies. See Akbari, 1999; Galabuzi, 2001; Kunz, Milan, and Schetagne, 2001; Lian and Matthews, 1998; Ornstein, 2000. A number of these studies reject the assertion that occupational and earnings differentials pertain to differences in education quality, language skills, or cultural differences, as the "diminishing value" school claims, finding – other factors notwithstanding – occupational and earnings inequality even between Canadian-born racialized and non-racialized groups. Employment discrimination and barriers to access to professions and trades are two often-cited causes of the inability of racialized members to translate educational attainment into commensurate income and occupational status. A number of these studies control for a range of factors, such as variation in sex, length of employment, age, level of education, field of study, occupation, period of stay in country, province of residence, census metropolitan area, place of birth (Canada or abroad), mother tongue, yet still conclude that racial discrimination is a significant factor in income and occupational inequality. Other studies looking at recent immigrants include Reitz, 2001.

4 As we saw above, while the two categories overlap, there is still a significant difference. Immigrants make up two-thirds of the racialized group, the other third being Canadian born. Significantly, however, they share many of the patterns associated with racialized participation in the labour market.

5 Galabuzi, 2001, uses data from Statistics Canada's Survey of Labour and Income Dynamics (SLID) for 1996–98; Two recent studies by the Canadian Council on Social Development – Kunz, Milan, and Schetagne, 2001, on racialized groups (analysing 1996 census data) and Smith and Jackson, 2002, looking at labour market performance by recent immigrants (a disproportionately racialized group) – present similar findings, although Smith identifies a small narrowing of the gap over the 1995–98 period. The income gap continues even among high-end earners as well as the university educated. See also Jackson, 2002, on racial-minority workers' income inequality, and Reitz, 2001, whose analysis of census data from 1981 to 1996 shows progressively lower levels of income and high rates of inequality between immigrants and Canadian born.

6 Employers have pointed to limited period of stay in country and lack of Canadian qualifications and of language abilities as making immigrants less attractive for hire or promotion. Immigrants and their advocates, in contrast, suggest that the institutional failure of prior-learning assessment and accreditation of international qualifications, gatekeeping by professional organizations and lack of transparent application processes, and closed union trade shops have devalued and degraded their qualifications and contributed to occupational and wage inequality. See Brouwer, 1999; Cummings et al., 1989; Reitz, 2001.

7 Economic discrimination occurs when employers, unable to assess the ability of members of a group, make generalized assumptions about the worth of

their human capital, as may be the case when the value of qualifications from a certain country or region is unclear. Exclusionary discrimination occurs when members of a group do not receieve work or commensurate wages or, once hired, promotion regardless of their skills and experience. Both forms have been documented among racialized group members, and that may explain the congruence between foreign- and Canadian-trained racialized members in the labour market.

 8 These include Agocs and Burr, 1996; Alliance for Employment Equity, 1998; Bakan and Kobayashi, 2000; "Employment Equity, Affirmative Action and Managing Diversity: Assessing the Differences," in *International Journal of Manpower* 17 (4–5); and Henry and Ginsberg, 1985.

 9 The income gap between racialized and non-racialized immigrants was largest among those who immigrated between 1991 and 1995 (27 per cent) but was still large (19 per cent) for the 1986–90 group and for the 1976–85 group (Statistics Canada, 1998a).

10 Along with the Canadian Centre for International Credentials, provinces have used a variety of services for credential assessment.

11 The Framework for the Social Union, signed in 1999, requires provincial governments to comply with the mobility provisions of the Agreement on Internal Trade, and the Red Seal Program was established to facilitate the mobility of skilled workers across provincial borders. Canada is also a signatory to the North American Free Trade Agreement (NAFTA) and the World Trade Organization (WTO), both of which contain provisions relating to skilled-labour mobility.

12 A study performed for Citizenship and Immigration Canada and the Canadian Chamber of Commerce surveyed the opinions of employers regarding foreign-trained accreditation, and while some thought the licensing processes too restrictive, many believed that immigrants' lack of information about the fields in which they wanted to practice and poor language skills led to their failure to win accreditation or that their qualifications did not meet Canadian standards. However, some employers were not aware of the government-mandated prior-learning assessment services, and others were wary of the government's forcing them to accept their outcomes as a basis for certification.

13 Other studies quantifying the economic loss of unrecognized credentials include one by Bloom and Grant (2001) for the Conference Board of Canada, which suggests that close to 540,000 Canadian workers, 47 per cent of whom are racialized group members, lose $8,000 to $12,000 of potential income per year, or a total of between $4.1 billion and $5.9 billion annually. A study by Reitz, 2001, put the figure at a much higher $55 billion.

<h3 style="text-align:center">REFERENCES</h3>

Abella, R. 1985. *Commission Report on Equality in Employment*. Ottawa: Supply and Services Canada.

Agocs, C. and C. Burr. 1996. "Employment Equity, Affirmative Action and Managing Diversity: Assessing the Differences," *International Journal of Manpower* 17 (4–5), 30–45.

Akbari, A.H. 1999. "Immigrant 'Quality' in Canada: More Direct Eevidence of Human Capital Content, 1956–1994," *International Migration Review* 33 (1), 156–75.

Alliance for Employment Equity. 1998. *Charter Challenge: The Case for Equity.* Toronto: Alliance for Employment Equity, spring.

Anderson, J., and J. Lynam. 1987. "The Meaning of Work for Immigrant Women in the Lower Echelons of the Canadian Labour Force," *Canadian Ethnic Studies* 19 (2), 67–90.

Arrow, Kenneth. 1972. "Some Models of Racial Discrimination in the Labour Market," in A.H. Paschal, ed., *Racial Discrimination in Economic Life.* Lexington, Mass.: D.C. Heath.

Badets, J., and D. Howatson-Lee. 1999. "Recent Immigrants in the Workplace," *Canadian Social Trends* (spring), 16–22.

Bakan, A., and A. Kobayashi. 2000. *Employment Equity Policy in Canada: An Interprovincial Comparison.* Ottawa: Status of Women Canada.

Bakan, A., and D. Stasiulis. 1995. "Making the Match: Domestic Placement Agencies and the Racialization of Women's Household Work," *Signs: Journal of Women in Culture and Society* 20 (2), 303–35.

Balibar, E. 1991. "Is There a Neo-racism?" in E. Balibar & E. Wallerste, *Race, Nation, Class: Ambiguous Identities.* London: Verso.

Barker, K., and K. Christensen, eds. 1998. *Contingent Work: American Employment Relations in Transition.* Ithaca, NY: Cornell University Press.

Basavarajappa K., and R. Verma. 1985. "Asian Immigrants in Canada: Some Findings from the 1981 Census," *International Migration* 23 (1), 97–121.

Beach, C., and C. Worswick. 1993. "Is There a Double Negative Effect on the Earnings of Immigrant Women?" *Canadian Public Policy* 19 (1), 36–53.

Becker, G. 1971. *Economics of Discrimination.* Chicago: University of Chicago Press.

Bolaria, B.S., and P. Li, eds. 1988. *Racial Oppression in Canada.* Toronto: Garamond Press.

Bonacich, E. 1972. "Theory of Ethnic Antagonism: The Split Labour Market," *American Sociological Review* 37 (Oct.), 547–59.

Boyd, M. 1985. "At a Disadvantage: The Occupational Attainment of Foreign Born Women in Canada," *International Migration Review* 18 (4), 1091–1119.

Brand, D. 1987. "Black Women and Work: The Impact of Racially Constructed Gender Roles on the Sexual Division of Labour," *Fireweed* 25, 28–37.

Broad, D. 2000. *Hollow Work, Hollow Society: Globalization and the Casual Labour Problem in Canada.* Halifax, NS: Fernwood Publishing.

Brouwer, A. 1999. *Immigrants Need Not Apply.* Ottawa: Caledon Institute of Social policy.

Calliste, A. 2000. "Nurses and Porters: Racism, Sexism and Resistance in Segmented Labour Markets," in A. Calliste and G. Sefa Dei, eds., *Anti-Racist Feminism*. Halifax, NS: Fernwood Publishing, 143–68.

Castells, M. 1998. *The Information Age: Economy, Society and Culture, Vol. III*. Oxford: Blackwell Publishers.

Chard, J. 2000. "Women in Visible Minorities," in *Women in Canada*. Ottawa: Statistics Canada.

Citizenship and Immigration Canada. 2000. *The Economic Performance of Immigrants: Education Perspective*. Ottawa: Citizenship and Immigration Canada, Strategic Policy, Planning and Research.

– 2003. *Facts and Figures*. Ottawa: Citizenship and Immigration Canada.

Creese, G. 1999. *Contracting Masculinity: Gender, Class, and Race in a White Collar Union, 1944–1994*. Toronto: Oxford University Press.

Cummings, P., et al. 1989. *Access! Report of the Taskforce on Access to Trades and Professions*. Toronto: Ontario Ministry of Citizenship.

Das Gupta, T. 1996. *Racism and Paid Work*. Toronto: Garamond Press.

DeVoretz, D.J. 1995. "New Issues, New Evidence, and New Immigration Policies for the Twenty-first Century," in D.J.

de Wolff, A. 2000. *Breaking The Myth of Flexible Work: Contingent Work in Toronto*. Toronto: Contingent Worker's Project.

Ekos Research/Toronto Star Survey, June 2000.

Federal Taskforce on the Participation of Visible Minorities in the Federal Public Service. 2000. *Report of the Federal Taskforce on the Participation of Visible Minorities in the Federal Public Service*. Ottawa: Supply and Services Canada.

Fernando, T., and K. Prasad. 1986. *Multiculturalism and Employment Equity: Problems Facing Foreign-Trained Professionals and Trades People in British Columbia*. Vancouver: Affiliation of Multicultural Societies and Services of British Columbia.

Ferrel, V., et al. 1998. Attorney General of Ontario, Respondent on Appeal, Court of Appeal for Ontario, 1998, Factum of Eboe-Osjui C. and the Alliance for Employment Equity.

Fong, E., and M. Gulia. 1999. "Differences in Neighbourhood Qualities among Racial and Ethnic Groups in Canada," *Sociology Inquiry* 69 (4), 575–98.

Fox, B., and P. Sugiman. 1999. "Flexible Work, Flexible Workers: The Restructuring of Clerical Work in a Large Telecommunications Company," *Studies in Political Economy* 60 (autumn), 59–84.

Galabuzi, G. 2001. *Canada's Creeping Economic Apartheid: The Economic Segregation and Social Marginalization of Racialized Groups*. Toronto: Centre for Social Justice.

Gill, S. 1995. "Globalization, Market Civilization and Disciplinary Neoliberalism," *Millennium* 24 (3), 399–422.

Gordon, D., R. Edwards, and M. Reich. 1982. *Segmented Work, Divided Workers: The Historical Transformation of Labour in the United States*. Cambridge: Cambridge University Press.

Harvey, D. 1989. *The Condition of Postmodernity*. Cambridge, Mass: Blackwell.

Henry, F., and E. Ginsburg. 1985. *Who Gets the Job? A Test of Racial Discrimination in*

Employment. Toronto: Urban Alliance on Race Relations and Social Planning Council of Metro Toronto.

Hiebert, D. 1997. "The Colour of Work: Labour Market Segregation in Montreal, Toronto and Vancouver, 1991," Working Paper No. 97–02. Burnaby, BC: Simon Fraser University, Centre of Excellence, Research on Immigration and Integration in the Metropolis.

House of Commons. 1984. Parliamentary Taskforce on the Participation of Visible Minorities in Canada. *Equality Now: Report of the Parliamentary Taskforce on the Participation of Visible Minorities in Canada.* Ottawa: Queen's Printer.

Hughes, K. 1999. *Gender and Self Employment: Assessing Trends and Policy Implications.* Ottawa: Canadian Policy Research Network.

Human Resources Development Canada. 1999. A Review of the 1996 Census Data. Ottawa: HRDC, Data Development, Labour Standards and Workplace Equity. Unpublished.

Jackson, A. 2002. "Is Work Working for Workers of Colour?" Research Report No. 8. Ottawa: Canadian Labour Congress.

Krahn, H., and G. Lowe. 1988. *Work, Industry and Canadian Society.* Toronto: Nelson Canada Publishing.

Kunz, J.L., A. Milan, and S. Schetagne. 2001. *Unequal Access: A Canadian Profile of Racial Differences in Education, Employment and Income.* Toronto: Canadian Race Relations Foundation/Canadian Council on Social Development.

Lee, K. 2000. *Urban Poverty in Canada: A Statistical Profile.* Ottawa: Canadian Council on Social Development.

Ley, D., and H. Smith. 1997. "Immigration and Poverty in Canadian Cities, 1971–1991," *Canadian Journal of Regional Science* 20 (1/2), 29–48.

Li, P. 1998. "The Market Value and Social Value of Race," in V. Satzewich, ed., *Racism and Social Inequality in Canada.* Toronto: Thompson Educational Publishing.

Lian, J.Z., and D.R. Matthews. 1998. "Does the Vertical Mosaic Still Exist? Ethnicity and Income in Canada," *Canadian Review of Sociology and Anthropology* 35 (4), 461–81.

Lipietz, A. 1987. *Mirages and Miracles: The Crisis of Global Fordism.* London: Verso.

Mata, F. 1994. "The Non-Accreditation of Immigrant Professionals in Canada: Societal Impacts, Barriers and Present Policy Initiatives," paper presented at Sociology and Anthropology Meetings, University of Calgary, 3 June.

McDade, K. 1988. *Barriers to Recognition of Credentials of Immigrants in Canada.* Ottawa: Institute of Policy Research.

Ministry of Training, Colleges and Universities. 2002. *The Facts Are In: A Study of the Characteristics and Experiences of Immigrants Seeking Employment in Regulated Professions in Ontario.* Toronto: Ontario Ministry of Training, Colleges and Universities.

Mittelman, J. 1994. "The Global Restructuring of Production and Migration," in Y. Sakamoto, ed., *Global Transformation: Challenges to The State System.* New York: United Nations University Press.

Ornstein, M. 2000. *Ethno-racial Inequality in Toronto: Analysis of the 1996 Census.* Toronto: Access and Equity Centre of Metro Toronto.

Pellerin, H. 1997. "New Global Migration Dynamics," in S. Gill, ed., *Globalization, Democratization and Multilateralism.* New York: MacMillan/United Nations University Press.

Preston, V., and W. Giles. 1997. "Ethnicity, Gender and Labour Markets in Canada: A Case Study of Immigrant Women in Toronto," *Canadian Journal of Urban Research* 6 (2), 135–59.

Reitz, Jeffery. 2001. *Immigrant Skill Utilization in the Canadian Labour Market: Implications of Human Capital Research.* Toronto: University of Toronto, Centre for Industrial Relations and Department of Sociology.

Reitz, J., L. Calzavara, and D. Dasko. 1981. *Ethnic Inequality and Segregation in Jobs.* Toronto: Centre for Urban and Community Studies, University of Toronto.

Reitz, J., and A. Verma. 2000. *Immigration, Ethnicity and Unionization: Recent Evidence for Canada.* Toronto: Toronto Centre of Excellence for Research in Immigration and Settlement.

Richmond, A. 1994. *Global Apartheid: Refugees, Racism, and the New World Order.* Toronto: University of Oxford Press.

Satzewich, V., ed. 1998. *Racism and Social Inequality in Canada: Concepts, Controversies and Strategies of Resistance.* Toronto: Thompson Publishing.

Smith, E., and A. Jackson. 2002. *Does a Rising Tide Lift All Boats? The Labour Market Experiences and Incomes of Recent Immigrants, 1995–1998.* Ottawa: Canadian Council on Social Development.

Statistics Canada. 1998a. 1996 Census: Sources of Income and Earnings. *Daily,* 12 May.

– 1998b. *Daily,* 14 April.

– 1998c. *Daily,* 17 Feb.

– 2003a. Census of Population. *The 25 Municipalities with 5000+ Population Having the Highest Proportion of Visible Minorities, 2001.*

– 2003b. *The Daily,* Thursday 21 Jan. Census of Population. *Canadian Ethnocultural Portrait: The Changing Mosaic.*

Stoffman, D. 1993. *Towards a More Realistic Immigration Policy in Canada.* Toronto: C.D. Howe institute.

Vosko, L. 2000. *Temporary Work: The Gendered Rise of a Precarious Employment Relationship.* Toronto: University of Toronto Press.

Wanner, R. 1998. "Prejudice, Profit or Production: Exploring Returns to Human Capital among Male Immigrants to Canada," *Canadian Ethnic Studies* 30 (3), 4–55.

Winant, H. 1994. "Racial Formation and Hegemony: Local and Global Developments," in A. Rattansi and S. Westwood, eds., *Racism, Modernity and Identity.* London: Polity Press.

Zeytinoglu, I., and J. Muteshi. 2000. "Gender, Race and Class Dimensions of Non-Standard Work," *Industrial Relations* 55 (1), 133–66.

10

Towards Perfect Flexibility:
Youth as an Industrial Reserve Army
for the New Economy

STEPHEN McBRIDE

Labour market conditions for young people have deteriorated over the past twenty years both in Canada and in other OECD countries. The experience of Canadian youth is not unique. The precise percentages may vary between countries, but the systematic deterioration of labour market conditions for young people is fairly widespread within the OECD area. Where possible, this chapter provides comparative data to contextualize the Canadian situation. Given a widely shared experience, the explanations for the labour market situation of young people are likely to be general rather than country-specific.

This is true even if, as this chapter argues, public policy choices have helped create the difficult labour market terrain that young people encounter. Specifically, this chapter first describes the labour market characterized by inequality and insecurity that has emerged from the interplay of globalization and neoliberalism; in this deregulated market, it shows, youth serve as a highly flexible reserve army of labour. It then considers the roles of globalization and neoliberalism. Finally, it looks at policies in terms of international pressure and Canadian practice.

YOUTH LABOUR MARKETS:
INEQUALITY AND INSECURITY

Summarizing the general conditions that young people face, we can say that youth employment rates are lower than formerly; the employment gap between the youth and adult cohorts has widened; young people are more likely to be unemployed; and youth incomes are in decline when

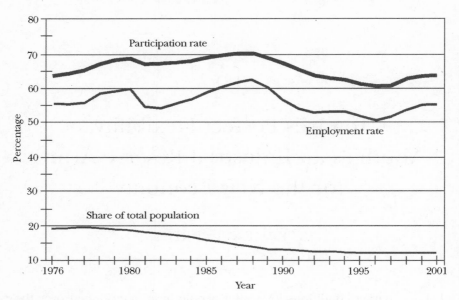

Figure 10.1   Trends in youth labour market indicators, Canada, 1976-2001
Source: *Statistics Canada, CANSIM, 15-24-year cohort.*

compared to those of adults. Dependence on parents, as indicated by living at home, has increased. Moreover, there is evidence of growing inequality within the youth cohort.

This package of negative labour market features looks surprising. Other things being equal, young people's labour market conditions should have improved in the 1980s and 1990s (Blanchflower and Freeman, 2000). As a result, a number of explanations, reviewed here, have emerged to explain this unexpected situation.

One reason for surprise about the poor labour market conditions encountered by young people is that youths' share of the population declined during the same period. There was a relative scarcity of young people at the age when they might expect to enter the labour market. Normally this should enhance their scarcity value and bargaining power.

Figure 10.1 summarizes the Canadian situation. It shows that youth as a percentage of the total population have been shrinking. Whatever the reasons for the decline in labour-force participation of young people after 1989, or for their declining employment rate, which also appear in Figure 10.1, an over-supply of youth is not one of them. A lower percentage of young people were working in 1997 than at any time in the previous 20 years, despite their declining share of the population. Intuitively, a shortage of jobs, or increased competition for those jobs that did exist,[1] rather

Table 10.1   Explanations for deterioration in youth's economic position

Explanation	Evidence
Aggregate economic conditions: high unemployment especially harmful for youths	Considerable
Influx of women: substitute for youth workers	Not much
Increased LDC trade: substitute for youths	Not much
Baby boomers are substitutes for younger cohort	Not much
Youths are less skilled	Not much
Composition of industrial demand	None

than an excess of young people, would seem to be the reason (see also Cheal, 2000).

Other factors that ought to have improved labour market conditions for youth included changes in the composition of employment, which moved in the direction of services such as retail and hospitality establishments. These industries are heavy users of youth labour. The increased use of computer technology ought to have benefited the age group most comfortable with the technology. Finally, education levels, as measured by years of education, which are often linked to labour market success, increased (Freeman, 1999: 90–1).

Why have these favourable conditions been associated with a deterioration in the youth labour market? Freeman (1999: 90–1), reviewing evidence from the OECD, sought to test six possible explanations – overall economic conditions including high unemployment, more women entering the labour market and replacing young people, imports from less developed countries eliminating jobs for youth, baby boomers substituting for youth, lower skill levels among the young, and the composition of industrial demand. His results are presented in Table 10.1 (Freeman, 1999).

Only the first factor turned out to be significant. Adverse overall labour market conditions are likely to hurt people just starting in the job market. Openings will be fewer, and to the extent that employers prefer experienced personnel, those lacking experience will find it difficult to break in. Even if youth experience particular difficulties in poor labour market conditions, the question of why labour market conditions have been so poor remains open.

There are other explanations advanced. Some blame youth for their inability to find work – allegedly unskilled, unmotivated, and lazy. Work-to-welfare programs, whatever the soothing rhetoric, flow from this perception.

Notwithstanding the policy influence of this stereotype, it has little scientific basis. Many formerly entry-level jobs taken by youth are now becoming permanent for them. Even worse, should they move from such positions, it is typically from low-wage work to unemployment (Bowers, Sonnet, and Bardone, 1999: 16; Krahn, 1991; Organization for Economic Cooperation and Development, 1997: 11). This is not typically a result of lack of skill, motivation, or effort. Youth in general face insecure jobs, low pay, and often not very satisfying work.

Despite the often harsh and alienating experience of entering the working world, there is evidence that young people do want to work. Several studies that examined unemployed youth and those on training schemes found that, contrary to some beliefs, the majority of youth want to work. This is true, even if the message that they are receiving about the labour force is "Enter at your own risk" (see Hutchens, 1994; Mizen, 1995: 199; Lee et al., 1990).

Many young people respond by furthering their education in hopes of situating themselves better in the labour market. They do so even though public policies have off-loaded some of the costs of education onto youth themselves. Statistics indicate that the more education one has the better off one is in the labour market (Statistics Canada, 1999a: 19). Economic theorists often liken education to an investment – in this case not in physical but in human capital.

Neoliberal versions of human-capital theory hold that the beneficiaries of investments in human capital should bear the costs of the investment. Extreme versions consider that all benefits flow to individuals, who should therefore pay the full costs of education (Friedman, 1962). Others concede that society also benefits but rationalize increased tuition – for example, on the grounds that it has traditionally represented too small a share of education costs and that individuals gain more from their education than they are currently contributing in fees.

Such analysts would take satisfaction from the fact that since 1990 tuition fees for postsecondary education in Canada have increased on average by 125 per cent.[2] One indicator of students' increased share of the costs is student debt and default rates. Statistics Canada reported that postsecondary students borrowed more money than ever to pay for their education and found it increasingly difficult to pay it back (Statistics Canada, 1999b). Studies by Human Resources Development Canada reveal the size of the extra borrowing: "At the time of graduation, the average 1995 university graduate who borrowed from a government student loan program owed $12,200 in student loans compared to $8800 for the average 1990 graduate and $7600 for the average 1986 graduate (in 1995 constant dollars)" (Human Resources Development Canada, 1999: 13). Over the period 1986–95, therefore, an increase of some 60 per cent occurred. However, the study concluded that, despite rising tuition and increased debt, the "economic returns to postsecondary education remain high" (13).

Table 10.2   Labour force participation, employment, unemployment rates, by gender and age (years), Canada and OECD averages

	1979			1997		
	15–19	20–24	25–54	15–19	20–24	25–54
Labour-force participation (%)						
Canada men	57.3	86.5	94.9	47.6	79.2	91.1
Canada women	51.1	72.4	58.5	45.9	71.8	76.6
OECD men	48.4	81.4	94.7	34.8	73.3	92.2
OECD women	42.1	67.9	55.8	29.7	62.1	69.2
Employment–population ratio (%)						
Canada men	48.0	77.0	90.4	36.8	67.8	83.9
Canada women	43.0	64.9	54.2	36.4	62.8	70.5
OECD men	41.6	74.6	91.6	29.1	63.8	86.8
OECD women	34.5	60.9	53.3	24.1	53.2	63.9
Unemployment (%)						
Canada men	16.3	10.9	4.7	22.8	14.4	7.9
Canada women	15.8	10.3	7.3	20.7	12.6	7.9
OECD men	13.8	8.3	3.2	18.5	13.4	5.9
OECD women	18.5	10.6	4.6	23.0	15.4	7.6

Source: OECD, 1999.

It is undeniable that higher education provides advantages. It is a classical "positional good" – possessing more of it than others do confers an advantage. However, it is not necessarily a route to work that is commensurate with the level of education and skill achieved. Many highly educated, skilled, and trained individuals have jobs that do not use their skills, education, and training (Borghans and De Grip, 2000; Lowe, 1998; Shields, 1996: 64). In Ontario in 1990, 62 per cent of employees were not using the full range of their skills (Livingstone, 1998: 85).

Another explanation attributes youths' deteriorating labour market conditions to their lack of effective organizations that can represent their plight and argue for alleviation. But is this enough to explain the severity of the conditions, described below, that youth experience?

Table 10.2 summarizes data on labour-force participation, employment, and unemployment, by age group and gender, and includes OECD average figures for comparison.

Qualifications are in order; conditions are actually worse than Table 10.2 indicates The unemployment rates may understate unemployment. In Canada, the labour-force participation of young people was generally above the national average until, in the recession of the 1990s, it

Table 10.3   Change in ratio of earnings of 20–24 year olds to 35–44 year olds, OECD countries, 1980s compared to 1990s (change in percentage points)

	Male	Female
Australia	–10	–10
Canada	–20	–10
Denmark	little change	little change
Italy	–10	–10
Japan	–5	–10
Norway	–5	–5
Sweden	little change	little change
United Kingdom	–10	–10
United States	–20	–10

Source: Freeman, 1999: 98.

plummeted by about 10 percentage points, before recovering somewhat later in the 1990s. If we assume that the 1989 youth (15–24 years) labour-force participation rate (70.6 per cent) represents the high point of how many young people would like to work if conditions permitted, it follows that 6–10 per cent of the youth population dropped out of the labour market entirely in the 1990s. This group is not "unemployed," since it is no longer part of the "official" labour market. Nor do the figures include young people who are working part time because they cannot find full-time work. About 26 per cent of young part-time workers work part time "involuntarily" – up from 17.6 per cent in 1989 (Loughlin and Barling, 1999). That number represents about 10 per cent of the youth labour force. And this statistic understates the extent of underemployment. It includes neither those voluntary part-time workers who would like more hours, even though they prefer to work part time, nor those who might be termed "discouraged, involuntary part-time workers" – part-timers who no longer identify themselves as wanting full-time work because they believe it unattainable (Burke and Shields, 1999). In 1970, 29 per cent of young earners worked full year, full time. By 1995, this group had declined to only 16 per cent (Statistics Canada, 1998b).

Youth unemployment is consistently above the national average rate. While the size of the gap fluctuates, it was about as large in the late-1990s "recovery" as it was in the early-1980s recession. Unlike the recovery after the early-1980s recession, the labour market for youth 15–24 did not immediately improve following the recession of the early 1990s. On the contrary, youth employment rates and participation rates continued to decline steeply through most of the 1990s, particularly for teenagers. While the adult population enjoyed several years of job growth, employers started hiring more youth only in 1998. At the end of 1997, 51.2 per cent

Table 10.4   Young people living with their parents, by age and gender, Canada and OECD, 1985 and 1996/7

| | 15-19 | | | | 20-24 | | | |
| | Men | | Women | | Men | | Women | |
	1985	1996/7	1985	1996/7	1985	1996/7	1985	1996/7
Canada	88.9	90.8	82.2	84.7	49.8	53.4	30.4	39.1
OECD	93.7	93.1	89.8	90.1	67.5	68.4	48.6	54.2

Source: OECD, 1999: 62.

of youths were employed; at the end of 1998, 54.4 per cent; and in October 1999, 54.9 per cent. Through much of the 1990s the unemployment rate for youth was about 1.8 times higher than that for adults. During late 1996 and 1997, the adult unemployment rate dropped, while the youth rate continued to increase, and the youth-to-adult unemployment-rate ratio increased above 2. Since then this ratio has remained at about 2.2, as youth and adult unemployment rates have fallen at a similar pace (Statistics Canada, 1999a: 8).

In most OECD countries, difficult labour market conditions have predictably reduced earnings. Table 10.3 provides a rough comparative description of the decline in incomes that young people have experienced relative to adults. It is based on the ratio of earnings of 20–24 year olds to those aged 34–44 in the 1980s and 1990s; in most countries the ratio became more adverse for the younger group by the percentages indicated (Freeman 1999: 98).

Young people are finding it increasingly difficult to leave the family home and establish independent lives. Table 10.4 provides one indicator of this trend. Survey data from the European Union (EU) reveal the most common reason for staying longer in the parental home: "Can't afford to move out."

Table 10.5. summarizes another worrying trend – the proportion of young people who have never worked. Perhaps reflecting this prolonged dependence, "youth" has become a flexible category. The age group covered by public policies targeted at "youth" is essentially arbitrary. In Canada, for example, the definition has evolved in keeping with cultural norms and understandings of the policy challenge, shifting from an upper limit of 17 in the mid-1960s to 30 by the end of the 1980s.

Decreased youth earnings do not appear to be entirely a function of a lower incidence of work or of a decline in hours worked resulting from the shift from full- to part-time employment. Picot (1998) blames a downward

Table 10.5   Percentage of youth who have never worked, Canada, 1989 and 1998

Age (years)	1989	1998
15–24	9.7	23.9
15–16	32.0	59.7
17–19	9.2	26.3
20–24	2.4	8.0

Source: Statistics Canada, 1999a: 13.

shift in real hourly wages: "Much of the decline in the real annual earnings of the young (men in particular) occurred in and around the 1981–82 recession. Their earnings did not recover during the economic expansion and fell again during the 1990s, however. But unlike the story for the population as a whole, this decline is related largely to declining hourly wages, rather than a relative change in hours worked. There has been a downward shift in the real hourly wages of young people" (2).

Hourly wages for those under 35, relative to those over 35, fell by just over 20 per cent in the period 1981–93 (Picot, 1998: 21). Vosko (2000) interprets the convergence of earnings between young men and women with caution. First, convergence, which is attributable to declining wages among the male cohort, affects only those under 25. Higher-age groups continue to exhibit gender-based differentials. It remains an open question whether the trend among the under-25 group will persist as that cohort ages.

Taken as a package, these aspects of the youth labour market are probably not the result of young people's lack of political power. And the notion that they are a function of generally bad economic conditions probably hides as much as it reveals. We turn, then, to the more promising explanation that structural pressures and employers' preferences associated with the new global economy, together with changes in public policy, have led to an unequal and insecure labour market, with youth constituting a highly flexible reserve army.

GLOBALIZATION AND NEOLIBERALISM

There is widespread agreement that the labour market has undergone dramatic changes over the past two decades and that employment expectations now reflect chronic insecurity and variability in work patterns. Technology has allegedly transformed the very structure of economies, leading to a shift from manufacturing and resource extraction to services. In both services and manufacturing, technology has altered the nature of work and provided management with a wider range of options. The exercise of managerial choice respecting work arrangements has radically changed the structure of work. Work now occurs in less concentrated establishments, which employ advanced technologies that require increased flexibility in work organization, use more skilled labour, and have "flatter" managerial hierarchies (Chaykowski and Giles, 1998: 5–6).

Globalization

Production is increasingly international. This is facilitated both by political factors, such as liberalization of trade and capital movements, and by technological developments, which permit smaller-scale and dispersed production sites that allow firms to purchase an optimum blend of more expensive high-skilled and cheaper low-skilled labour (Chaykowski and Giles, 1998: 6). In this situation of increased flexibility, labour rights have been "increasingly perceived as costs of production to be avoided in the interest of enhancing or maintaining 'national competitiveness'" (Standing, 1999: 584).

Strategies of workplace flexibility – part-time, temporary, casual, and contract work – have been described as a response to the economic crises of the 1970s, the recessions in the 1980s and 1990s, and increased international competition (Zehtinoglu and Muteshi, 2000). The International Labour Organization (ILO) has summarized the costs and benefits. Benefits include rising productivity and reduced wage costs for employers. Greater job instability, increased part-time work, reduced overtime pay, and greater assignment of work in "unsocial" hours are among the costs borne by workers (International Labour Organization, 190: 10–11). For employers, the ability to respond quickly to changes in the business environment, to adapt to technological change, and to increase efficiency by linking work more closely to fluctuations in demand is clearly beneficial (Ainger, 1995). Employers off-load the adjustment costs of such advantages onto the workforce. However, some observers claim that part-time and other forms of flexible work are the result of workers' choice. We have seen, however, that about one-quarter of young part-time workers are involuntary part-time workers, and there are reasons to believe that this is an underestimation.

There seem to be at least two models of workplace flexibility. The first is flexibility within a high-skill, high-wage, and advanced-technology economy, where well-trained individuals with in-demand skills see change as a source of opportunity. In this flexible workforce, employment forms may have changed, but skill confers its own security, pay and conditions are good, and workers may accept the rhetoric of a new economy displacing older, more traditional economic forms with little cost and possibly with advantages to the workforce. The second flexible labour market involves the unemployed, low-waged workers generally, and all those people who have insecure jobs in the low-wage, low-skill sector (see Broad, MacNeil, and Gamble in this volume). These are people "who are neither born flexible nor achieve flexibility but have flexibility thrust upon them" (Uden, 1995: 269; see also Good and McFarland in this volume).

The question remains, however, whether this situation is primarily structurally induced or whether policy choices have helped in its construction. The policy environment is both domestic, driven by neoliberal ideology, and international, whereby neoliberal international organizations advocate and promote flexibility in the labour market.

Neoliberalism

Several aspects of the policy environment have contributed to an insecure, deregulated job market and to the emergence of a reserve of low-wage, readily available labour power. First, the triumph of neoliberal ideology in the 1970s and 1980s in major countries such as the United States and Britain had an effect on policies in other countries and on major international organizations. The rise of neoliberalism is associated with the end of full employment and the restoration of labour discipline through unemployment (McBride, 1992). Full employment is not an objective of neoliberal framework policies. Indeed, neoliberal economists prefer to think of a natural rate of unemployment, which is consistent with low and stable inflation (Setterfield, 1996). The most that policy can do is facilitate achievement of an actual unemployment rate that is at or close to the natural level, or perhaps even lowering of the natural rate itself (Derek Robinson, 1986: 383–98).

Any role for labour market policy lies in encouraging the labour market to function more "efficiently." Such efforts might include providing information, assisting workers' geographical mobility, providing assistance to specific groups that find it difficult to participate in the labour market, and, possibly, training and retraining workers affected by structural economic changes. Information, mobility, and providing work experience are all hallmarks of the current approach to youth employment programming. There is considerable evidence that this view of the causes and cure for unemployment is entirely mistaken. Palley (in this volume) shows that the bulk of European unemployment is attributable to errors in macroeconomic policy rather than to labour market rigidities.

None the less, action at the micro level is central to the neoliberal approach, which favours deregulation of the labour market to achieve greater flexibility. It aims to remove or diminish measures, such as unemployment benefits,[3] that hinder flexibility and change. Its advocates have designed policies to eliminate or restrict such programs, while similarly constraining institutions such as trade unions through which collective power can modify market outcomes. The aim is to increase individuals' attachment to the labour market, partly by denying them alternatives to it. Measures based on this principle have served to redefine the concept of "active labour market policy." In the past, this often referred to adjunct policies designed to complement full-employment, macroeconomic management. Today, the term describes the integration of social policy with labour market policy, including training, workfare, and work-experience programs. The stated aim is to decrease individuals' dependence on the state by minimizing benefits, increasing the stringency of conditions attached to them, and promoting attachment to the labour force. In practice, this means requiring individuals to enter and participate in whatever labour market exists.

POLICIES

International Pressure

Domestic policy preferences of this type have been reinforced by strong international political pressures directed to producing neoliberal policy responses at the national level and also to limiting the future capacity to deviate from these responses. These include efforts at moral persuasion exercised by international organizations through reports and other activities.

Some commentators have argued that international trade and investment agreements between economically advanced countries are the equivalent of the conditionality imposed by the International Monetary Fund (IMF) and the World Bank in their dealings with developing countries (Grinspun and Kreklewich, 1994). In economically advanced countries, the conditions are self-imposed, at least as far as the governing elite is concerned. This would also be true of decisions to follow "advice" received from international organizations. Bowing to such pressures entrenches a minimalist view of the state and alters "the conditions under which economic and social decision-making is conducted domestically" (Grinspun and Kreklewich, 1994: 34). From this perspective, any "straitjacket" constraining nation-states is political, rather than structural (see also Clarkson, 1993; Ian Robinson, 1993).

Evidence has begun to emerge of the IMF's role as a source of policy advice that prefigured fundamental changes to Canada's social programs in the mid-1990s. Under Article IV of the IMF's articles of agreement, the fund sends a delegation of economists to member countries to evaluate economic performance and proffer policy advice each year. The *Economic Justice Report* (Ecumenical Coalition for Economic Justice, 1999) reveals a close correlation between IMF advice and federal budget decisions involving reform to transfer payments for health, education, and – crucially in the current context – social assistance.

Reports and pressure from other international organizations such as the OECD, though by no means a strait-jacket on domestic policy-makers, may seem to validate their policy choices. The OECD's *Jobs Study* (Organization for Economic Co-operation and Development, 1994) represents a major effort at moral persuasion on the part of an international organization. The OECD secretariat received instructions in the early 1990s to study unemployment and make substantive policy recommendations for member states. The recommendations would form the basis of the eventual OECD Jobs Strategy. Grounded in neoclassical economic theory, the *Jobs Study* represented a sustained plea for greater flexibility and removal of political and policy obstacles to the unfettered operation of market forces:

Structural unemployment grows from the gap between the pressures on economies to adapt to change and their ability to do so. Adaptation is fundamental to progress in a world of new technologies, globalization and intense national and international competition ... Policies and systems have made economies rigid, and stalled the ability and even willingness to adapt. To realize the potential gains, societies and economies must respond rapidly to new imperatives and move towards the future opportunities ... [Governments'] challenge will be to embrace change rather than succumb to pressure to resist it through protectionism or other measures to restrict competition. Governments are faced with designing and redesigning a range of policies across the economy and society in order to help foster – or in some cases, stop hindering – adaptation to evolving ways of production and trade. (OECD, 1994: 7)

The OECD identified social policies as a key area for change if adequate flexibility was to be achieved. It called for an examination of "the full range of policies that have been put in place over the last 30 years to see where, and to what extent, each may have contributed to ossifying the capacity of economies and the will of societies to adapt; and then to consider how to remove those disincentives without harming the degree of social protection that it is each society's wish to provide" (OECD, 1994: 30). From this base the OECD outlined a broad, ten-point program, or "Jobs Strategy," which, it argued, member states should implement in a "co-ordinated manner" (OECD, 1994: 43–9).

The OECD subsequently operationalized these principles in the form of over fifty specific recommendations, which promoted a broadly deregulated labour market. The OECD believed that rigidities, like union strength, social benefits, and legislation and regulations on employment conditions, were responsible for increased unemployment in the OECD.[4] Its policy, urged repeatedly on member governments, was to remove the rigidities and rely on unfettered market forces to produce, if not full employment, then at least employment at its "natural" level.

The OECD has been a leading advocate of neoliberal labour market policies and has sought to track member states' implementation of the *Jobs Study* recommendations.[5] Canada has received few recommendations for improvement, indicating that it already adheres broadly to the neoliberal paradigm favoured by the OECD.

The OECD's *Jobs Study* identified two particular methods for dealing with youth unemployment. The first focused on skills development and investment in human capital as a route to high-wage, high-value-added production. The second encouraged low-waged employment.[6] Far from being competing strategies, they were complementary (Marquardt, 1998: chap. 7). An ideal type of policies associated with human-capital development included educational reforms designed to make the system more responsive to the needs of a competitive economy; to increase access to education, including postsecondary education; and to improve school-to-work transitions through co-op education, internships and youth apprenticeships, more effective counselling, and provision of information.

Encouragement of low-wage employment might be achievable through policies such as reducing payroll taxes, the minimum wage (either in nominal or in real terms), and/or unemployment insurance coverage and benefits, all in order to increase incentives to find work; creating welfare-to-work schemes involving low-end training and work experience; encouraging self-employment and entrepreneurship among young people; and setting up work-experience programs for those not continuing on to postsecondary education. Such a package clearly accepts, and may magnify, existing differentials in life chances.

Canada

Canada's labour market policies directed at young people reflect this bifurcated approach of the OECD. At the low end, two federal measures heightened insecurity in the low-waged labour market. The first was the replacement of Established Program Financing (EPF) and the Canada Assistance Plan (CAP) by the Canada Health and Social Transfer (CHST) in 1995. The CHST exposed social-assistance recipients to work-for-welfare programs in a way not previously possible (except for pilot projects) because of federal conditions on CAP funding. Work-for-welfare programs have now become standard in many provinces.

The second measure involved restructuring of training and unemployment insurance. Previously, the active components of labour market policy built on relatively generous unemployment insurance.[7] The federal government has now largely withdrawn from training, restructured employment insurance, and shifted responsibility for active employment measures to the provinces.

In 1996 Ottawa began to transfer to the provinces responsibility for active employment measures funded through the Employment Insurance account. These measures included targeted wage subsidies to aid employers in hiring and thus providing on-the-job experience; self-employment assistance to help individuals start their own businesses; and job creation partnerships with provinces, the private sector, and communities. Other programs were announced: wage top-ups to encourage the unemployed to accept low-paid jobs, and skills loans and grants. The latter program makes funds available so that individuals can choose the form of training best suited to them. It rests on the belief that better outcomes, defined as end-of-program employment, result when people take responsibility for improving their human capital by sharing in the costs of training (Human Resources Development Canada, 1996: 17–18).

The agreements devolving active measures to the provinces embody neoliberal principles. For example, they typically commit governments to reducing dependence on public assistance and elicit a commitment from recipients of employment benefits and support measures to identify their own employment needs and locate services to meet them – including, if appropriate, sharing the cost of such assistance (as provided for in, for example, the Canada–British Columbia Agreement on Labour Market Development of 1997).

Public expenditures immediately fell. By 1998 income benefits declined by 8.4 per cent, the number of initial claimants dropped by 14.5 per cent, more clients were receiving short-term interventions such as information and counselling, and fewer were receiving longer-term interventions such as training. As a result, "average costs per participant in Employment Benefits and Support measures declined from $7300 to $3900," or by 46.6 per cent (Human Resources Development Canada, 1998: ii–iii).

Changes to unemployment insurance (see Human Resources Development Canada, 1996) included calculating qualification periods in terms of hours worked rather than of weeks worked. The government claimed that this would be more equitable for part-time and women workers in particular and that it reflected increasing part-time work. Other changes reduced the benefit replacement rate for repeat claimants and introduced a supplement for low-income family claimants, increased the claw-back of benefits from high-income earners, and reduced premiums and maximum insurable earnings.

Coverage declined sharply. A Canadian Labour Congress (1999) study showed that the percentage of unemployed workers covered by unemployment insurance in 1997 was less that half of what it had been in 1989 – 36 per cent, as compared to 74 per cent. Young people, whose coverage rate fell from 55 per cent to 15 per cent, and women, whose coverage declined from 70 per cent in 1987 to 31 per cent in 1997, were particularly hard hit.

The primary reason for declining coverage was that the number of hours of work required to qualify for benefits increased dramatically. Under a new "hours system," workers must accumulate at least a minimum number of hours of work (ranging from 420 to 910) to qualify for benefits, regardless of how many hours they may work per week. The impact on part-time workers was immediate and dramatic, since they had to maintain employment much longer in order to meet the new hours requirements. Women and young people are over-represented among the part-time workforce. In youths' case, total hours required to qualify for benefits tripled – from 300 to 910 for new labour-force entrants.

The effect of these reforms was consistent with developments elsewhere in the developed world. Referring to the EU, Standing noted: "Income security for the unemployed has been declining, due in part to the chronic character of mass unemployment and in part to the explicit and implicit disentitlement to benefits" (1999: 599).

Most Canadian provinces have attempted to integrate labour market, education, and social-welfare policy, generally in neoliberal ways. Job readiness has become an articulated priority in education policy. This approach emphasizes applied studies and training, scientific and technological fields, and, at the primary and secondary levels, core skills. Whether these fields do, in fact, provide such advantages is unclear. Many managers state that they prefer workers with sophisticated problem-solving abilities, creativity, and social well-roundedness. These are attributes that one normally associates with a more comprehensive approach to education.

Likewise, social-welfare policy has shifted towards a "welfare-to-work" approach for people deemed unduly dependent on government transfers and social services. Participation is increasingly mandatory and involves a mixture of incentives and sanctions. Incentives represent increased access to supply-side active labour market measures (the so-called integration of passive and active labour market measures). The sanctions consist of reduced benefits and tighter restrictions on access to them.

Enlarging the pool of low-skilled labour to encourage low-waged employment seems to accept growing inequality in Canadian society (Marquardt, 1998: 133–4). Public policies recognize that young people and graduating students are not homogeneous groups but may be divisible into more finely grained target groups so that policymakers can better tailor policies to specific labour market needs.[8] The emphasis therefore is not on transforming the prospects of particular groups of young people, but on making sure that they enter the labour market at levels appropriate to their existing skill level:

- "Disadvantaged" or "marginalized" youth face systematic labour market and workplace barriers and include members of aboriginal communities and the physically and mentally disabled.
- "At-risk" or "vulnerable" youth have less favourable employment and career prospects or are susceptible to long spells of unemployment because of low skill levels and include high-school dropouts and truant teenagers.
- "Young achievers" or "advanced" youth have demonstrated high levels of aptitude and have above-average career prospects.

Differences exist in the segments of the youth cohort. As Table 10.6 indicates, provincial expenditures tend to emphasize unemployed and at-risk youth, and federal expenditures emphasize already well-qualified young people.

Existing policies lean towards short-term and low-cost interventions that rely on the proliferation of information and the promotion of occupations widely expected to be the most lucrative in the future. The focus is on adjusting the individual to whatever market conditions prevail.

There is evidence that this approach compounds existing differences in the youth cohort based on class, race, and gender. The Canadian Federation of Students (2000: 2) noted a growing gap between poor and wealthy youth in participation rates in postsecondary education. This class difference has widened significantly since the mid-1980s and can reasonably be depicted as a product of neoliberal policies. A study by the University Institute for Social Research found that "graduates from low income and visible minority families had a tougher time finding full-time work than those from affluent families of European backgrounds, even when there were similarities in the program of study, ... generic skills, marks, part-time work, and job networks" (quoted in Rehnby and McBride, 1997: 14). And gender differentials continue in graduates' earnings (14).

The same pattern occurs at the provincial level. A study of youth labour market programs in British Columbia noted that they tended to reinforce existing inequalities within the labour market – preparing youth on welfare, for example, for low-waged, low-skilled employment (Wong and McBride, 2000). Participants in the largest such program, Youth Works, which seeks primarily to remove young people from the welfare rolls, are likely to find themselves in low-paid and unstable jobs subject to high turnover rates.

Meanwhile the overall message is one of individual responsibility. The BC Ministry of Education's web site aptly advises that career self-manage-

Table 10.6   Spending on youth employment programs by target, 1998

	Students	PSE grads	All youth	Unemployed youth	At risk: low income, SAR	Other
Provincial ($million)	85.2	8.5	79.3	95.8	234.9	20.5
Provincial (%)	16.25	1.6	15	18.3	44.8	3.9
Federal ($million)	114	35	118	108	17	25
Federal (%)	27.3	8.4	28.3	25.9	4	6
Total ($million)	199.25	43.5	197.3	203.8	251.9	45.5
Total (%)	21.2	4.6	21	21.6	26.7	4.8

Source: Adapted from McBride and Stoyko (2000).

ment means "[n]ot relying on any business, organization, government or union to look after your interests ... You are in charge of your career all the time, every day, in every situation."[9] Individuals should chart their own future. In particular, they are to take responsibility for developing their own human capital. Provision of information is increasingly the primary form of assistance. Individuals are held to be able to make appropriate choices about their participation in the labour market, if only they have the proper information. By implication, the problem facing youth in the labour market results from inadequate information rather than from inadequate opportunities.

CONCLUSION

In fact, the labour market that youth find so difficult to navigate is a politically constructed one. Possession of adequate information and the right kind of human capital may advantage one individual over another. However, the deterioration of youth labour market conditions has occurred as the overall educational levels of young workers have increased. The overall problem, therefore, does not seem solvable by neoliberal orthodoxy.

Today's labour market is a result of the interplay of globalization and neoliberalism. Youth's role is becoming that of a highly flexible reserve army of labour. Youth can play this role well because the period of transition between dependence on parents and independence in the labour market is flexible. Many young people can stay longer in the parental home if the labour market does not demand their services. They are susceptible to ideological arguments that their skill levels are insufficient to generate job offers. As a result they are willing to spend time investing in their human capital by withdrawing from the labour market and going back to school, college, or university for further training or education. Increasingly they, or their parents, are willing to accept a greater share of the costs of such investments through higher tuition fees and by financing further education through loans.

For those who might formerly have left home and used state assistance to help with subsistence, the terms of engagement have changed. Large numbers are now ineligible for social assistance, and, for those who remain qualified, devices such as work-for-welfare schemes apply coercion. The effect is that the state increases the pool of available low-wage labour, with a depressing effect on wages.[10] It is this context that enables employers to realize their preferences for a flexible labour market.

Why, then, have youth labour market conditions deteriorated? Technology altered the possibilities open to capital. Capital's interests lay in creating a flexible labour market. This required deregulation of the active labour market. State policy was responsive to capital's needs. It has structured policy so as to withdraw social responsibility for labour market transitions and transfer it onto individuals. Policy is tolerant of high unemployment and of labour market conditions such as contingent work that accentuate insecurity. In this deregulated context, youth constitute a new, highly flexible, and relatively docile reserve army.

NOTES

1 Standing, 1999, points to growing labour-force participation, especially by women, over the last decade. Some countries, including Canada, saw a net gain despite declining participation by men.

2 *Catholic New Times* 24 (3) (fall 2000), 5.

3 Neoliberals base their opposition to unemployment benefits and minimum-wage legislation on the ability that such measures give workers to refuse jobs at wage rates that the market might determine, thus keeping unemployment levels higher than they might otherwise be. In addition, unemployment benefits encourage participation in the labour force because some individuals allegedly seek work to make themselves eligible for unemployment benefits.

4 One weakness of the theory is that the economy was highly regulated (and thus "inflexible") in previous periods of full employment. See Britton, 1997.

5 For a detailed account, see McBride and Williams, 2001.

6 As Marquardt (1998: 133) observes, these designations are equivalent to Albo's (1995) distinction between "progressive competitiveness" and "competitive austerity.".

7 For a review and rebuttal of literature suggesting that the unemployment insurance system acted as a disincentive to work and hence raised the unemployment rate, see Jackson (1995: 3–9); see also McBride (1992: chap. 6).

8   This section is based on McBride and Stoyko (2000).
9   Government of British Columbia Web page, "The World of Work," available at www.bced.gov.bc.ca/careers/planning/work/world.htm
10 On the state's role in managing the supply of labour, see Peck (1996: 26–9).

REFERENCES

Ainger, Jon. 1995. "Flexible Labour Markets and the Resourcing of Training," *Adults Learning* 6 (9), May.

Albo, Greg. 1995. "'Competitive Austerity' and the Impasse of Capitalist Employment Policy," in R. Miliband and L. Panitch, eds., *The Socialist Register 1994: Between Globalism and Nationalism.* London: Merlin Press.

Barling, J., and E.K. Kelloway, eds. 1999. *Young Workers: Varieties of Experience.* Washington, DC: American Psychological Association.

Blanchflower, David G., and Richard B. Freeman. 2000. "The Declining Economic Status of Young Workers in OECD Countries," in Blanchflower and Freeman, eds., *Youth Employment and Joblessness in Advanced Countries.* Chicago: University of Chicago Press.

Borghans, L., and A. De Grip. 2000. *The Overeducated Worker.* Northhampton, Mass.: Edward Elgar Publishing, Inc.

Bowers, N. 1998. *OECD Data on Skills: Employment by Industry and Occupation.* OECD, Directorate for Science, Technology and Industry, STI Working Papers 4. Paris: OECD.

Bowers, N., A. Sonnet, and L. Bardone, 1999. "Background Report: Giving Young People a Good Start: The Experience of OECD Countries," in *Preparing Youth for the 21st Century: The Transition from Education to the Labour Market Proceedings of the Washington D.C. Conference, 23–24 February 1999.* Paris: OECD.

Britton, Andrew. 1997. "Full Employment in a Market Economy," in J. Philpott, ed., *Working for Full Employment.* London: Routledge.

Burke, Mike, and John Shields. 1999. *The Job-Poor Recovery: Social Cohesion and the Canadian Labour Market.* Toronto: Ryerson Social Reporting Network.

Cameron, Duncan, and Mel Watkins, eds. 1993. *Canada under Free Trade.* Toronto: Lorimer.

Canadian Federation of Students (CFS). 2000. Submission to the House of Commons Standing Committee on Finance, Ottawa, Sept.

Canadian Labour Congress (CLC). 1999. *Left Out in the Cold: The End of UI for Canadian Workers.* Ottawa: CLC.

Chaykowski, Richard P., and Anthony Giles. 1998. "Globalization, Work and Industrial Relations," *Relations industrielles* 53 (1), 3–12.

Cheal, David. 2003. "Age Related Differentiations within the Working Age Population," in Danielle Juteau, ed., *Social Differentiation: Patterns and Processes.* Toronto: University of Toronto Press.

Clarkson, Stephen. 1993. "Disjunctions: Free Trade and the Paradox of Canadian

Development," in Duncan Cameron and Mel Watkins, eds., *Canada under Free Trade*. Toronto: Lorimer.

Dunk, T., Stephen McBride, and Randle Nelsen, eds. 1996. *The Training Trap: Ideology, Training and the Labour Market*. Winnipeg and Halifax: Society for Socialist Studies/Fernwood Publishing.

Ecumenical Coalition for Economic Justice. 1999. *Economic Justice Report*. Toronto: Ecumenical Coalition for Economic Justice.

Freeman, Richard. 1999. "The Youth Job Market Problem at Y2K," in *Preparing Youth for the 21st Century: The Transition from Education to the Job Market*. Paris: OECD.

Friedman, Milton. 1962. *Capitalism and Freedom*. Chicago: University of Chicago Press.

Grinspun, Ricardo, and R. Kreklewich. 1994. "Consolidating Neoliberal Reforms: 'Free Trade' as a Conditioning Framework," *Studies in Political Economy* 43 (Spring), 33–61.

Human Resources Development Canada (HRDC). 1995. News Release, 1 Dec. Ottawa: HRDC.

– 1996. *Employment Insurance: A Guide to Employment Insurance*. Ottawa: HRDC.

– 1998. *1997 Employment Insurance: Monitoring and Assessment Report*. Ottawa: HRDC.

– 1999. *Applied Research Bulletin*, summer.

Hutchens, S. 1994. *Living a Predicament: Young People Surviving Unemployment*. Brookfield: Aldershot.

International Labour Organization (ILO). 1998. "Flexibility Boosts Productivity, Poses Challenges," *Worklife Report* 11, 10–11.

Jackson, A. 1995. "The NAIRU and Macro-economic Policy in Canada." Research Paper No. 12. Ottawa: Canadian Labour Congress.

Juteau, Danielle, ed. 2000. *Social Differentiation: Patterns and Processes*. Toronto: University of Toronto Press.

Krahn, H. 1991. "Non-standard Work Arrangements," *Perspectives on Labour and Income* (3/4), 35–45.

Lee, D., D. Marsden, P. Rickman, and J. Duncombe. 1990. *Scheming for Youth: A Study of YTS in the Enterprise Culture*. Research paper presented to the Learning and Skills Development Agency conference "Making an Impact on Policy and Practice." Cambridge, 5–7 Dec. 2001

Livingstone, D.W. 1998. *The Educational Jobs Gap: Underemployment or Economic Democracy?* Aurora, Ont.: Garamond.

Loughlin, C., and J. Barling. 1999. "The Nature of Youth Employment," in J. Barling and E.K. Kelloway, eds., *Young Workers: Varieties of Experience*. Washington, DC: American Psychological Association.

Lowe, G.S. 1998. "The Future of Work: Implications for Unions," *Industrial Relations* 53 (2), 235–57.

MacLean, Brian K., and Lars Osberg, eds. 1996. *The Unemployment Crisis: All for Nought?* Montreal: McGill-Queen's University Press.

Marquardt, Richard. 1998. *Enter at Your Own Risk: Canadian Youth and the Labour Market*. Toronto: Between the Lines.

McBride, Stephen. 1992. *Not Working: State, Unemployment, and Neoconservatism in Canada*. Toronto: University of Toronto Press.

McBride, Stephen, and Peter Stoyko. 2000. "Youth and the Social Union: Intergovernmental Relations, Youth Unemployment and School-to-Work Transitions," in Tom McIntosh, ed., *Federalism, Democracy and Labour Market Policy in Canada*. Montreal: McGill-Queen's University Press.

McBride, Stephen, and Russell A. Williams. 2001. "Globalization, the Restructuring of Labour Markets and Policy Convergence: The OECD 'Jobs Strategy,'" *Global Social Policy* 1 (3), 281–309.

McIntosh, Tom, ed. 2000. *Federalism, Democracy and Labour Market Policy in Canada*. Montreal: McGill-Queen's University Press.

Miliband, Ralph, and Leo Panitch, eds. 1995. *The Socialist Register 1994: Between Globalism and Nationalism*. London: Merlin Press.

Mizen, P. 1995. *The State, Young People and Youth Training: In and against the Training State*. London: Mansell Publishing Limited.

Organization for Economic Cooperation and Development (OECD). 1994. *The Jobs Study*. Paris: Organization for Economic Cooperation and Development.

– 1997. "Labour Market Policies: New Challenges. Theme 1: Policies for Low-paid Workers and Unskilled Job Seekers," *OECD Working Papers* 5 (no. 86). Paris: Organization for Economic Cooperation and Development.

– 1999. *Preparing Youth for the 21st Century: The Transition from Education to the Job Market*. Paris: Organization for Economic Cooperation and Development.

Peck, Jamie. 1996. *Work-Place: The Social Regulation of Labour Markets*. New York: Guilford.

Philpott, J., ed. 1997. *Working for Full Employment*. London: Routledge.

Picot, Garnett. 1998. "What Is Happening to Earnings Inequality and Youth Wages in the 1990s?" Statistics Canada, Business and Labour Market Analysis Division Working Paper No. 116, July.

Rehnby, Nadene, and Stephen McBride. 1997. *Help Wanted: Economic Security for Youth*. Ottawa: Canadian Centre for Policy Alternatives.

Robinson, Derek. 1986. *Monetarism and the Labour Market*. Oxford: Clarendon Press.

Robinson, Ian. 1993. *North American Free Trade as if Democracy Mattered*. Ottawa: Canadian Centre for Policy Alternatives.

Setterfield, Mark. 1996. "Using NAIRU as a Basis for Economic Policy: An Evaluation," in Brian K. MacLean and Lars Osberg, eds., *The Unemployment Crisis: All for Nought?* Montreal: McGill-Queen's University Press.

Shields, John. 1996. "Flexible Work, Labour Market Polarization, and the Politics of Skills, Training and Enhancement," in T. Dunk, Stephen McBride, and R.W. Nelsen, eds., *The Training Trap: Ideology Training and the Training, and the Labour Market*. Winnipeg and Halifax: Society for Socialist Studies/Fernwood Publishing.

Standing, Guy. 1999. "Global Feminization through Flexible Labour: A Theme Revisited," *World Development* 27 (3), 583–602.

Statistics Canada. 1998a. *Labour and Income Dynamics* 7 (2), June. Cat. No. 75–002–XIB.

– 1998b. 1998 *Labour Force Update.* Catalogue 71–005–XPB, summer.

– 1999a. *Daily,* 30 July.

– 1999b. *Labour Force Update: Youth and the Labour Market,* Autumn, Catalogue No. 71–005–XPB.

Uden, Tony. 1995. "Flexible Labour Markets and the Adult Learner," *Adults Learning* 6 (9), 267–69.

Vosko, Leah F. 2003. "Gender Differentiation and the Standard Non-standard Employment Distinction: A Genealogy of Policy Interventions in Canada," in Danielle Juteau, ed., *Social Differentiation: Patterns and Processes.* Toronto: University of Toronto Press.

Wheelock, J., and J. Vail, eds. 1998. *Work and Idleness: The Political Economy of Full Employment.* Boston: Kluwer Academic Publishers.

Wong, Linda, and Stephen McBride. 2000. "Real Training Versus Employability Training: Youth Programmes in British Columbia." Paper presented at the Annual Conference of the Labour Education and Training Research Network, Vancouver, Oct.

Zehtinoglu, Isik, and Jacinta Muteshi. 2000. "A Critical Review of Flexible Labour: Gender, Race and Class Dimensions of Economic Restructuring," *Resources for Feminist Research* 27 (3/4), 97–120.

11

The Crisis in Rural Labour Markets:
Failures and Challenges for Regulation

MARTHA MacDONALD

This chapter examines the spatial dimension of labour market restructuring and the failure of policy to meet the needs of non-urban workers. How are labour market deregulation and reregulation affecting employment relationships and the well-being of rural workers, families, and communities? This chapter explores these questions, drawing on insights from economic geography and feminist political economy into the spatial and gendered contours of restructuring. Evidence for Canada as a whole, as well as examples from ongoing research on Atlantic Canada, provide preliminary answers.

The geographical analysis of restructuring has tended to concentrate on the national level and on issues within and between nation-states. The focus has been on the international mobility of capital, facilitated by the neoliberal state and by bilateral, regional, and international trade agreements, and on their implications for workers in particular countries. Studies emphasize overall trends such as the increase in non-standard forms of employment and deregulation of labour markets. In the new political economy, "regional" more often describes national groupings, such as North America or Europe, than sub-national areas. While Canadian politics is still intensely regional, elements of national economic policy such as trade agreements and Bank of Canada policy take a "one size fits all" approach.

The rural–urban dimension of globalization and restructuring has received little attention, and only in the context of specific resource sectors. The collapse of the Atlantic groundfishery demonstrates the impact of global competition on natural resources and the failure of government to regulate the industry in a way that maintains stocks, livelihoods, and rural communities. World Trade Organization (WTO) negotiations on agriculture, and Canada's own farm crisis, are drawing attention to the effect of global competition on that sector (Barlow and Clarke, 2000; Winson, 1990). How do rural areas fare in the competition for new jobs, as the traditional resource base erodes? Some writers point to the success of small industrial districts and to the role of new communication and transportation technology in lessening the traditional location disadvantages of remote areas (Piore and Sabel, 1984). Others, however, see new economies of scope and agglomeration that put rural areas at a disadvantage – at least without massive government support for infrastructure and training (Flora, 1990; Harrison, 1994; Storper, 1997; Winson and Leach, 2002). This support has not been forthcoming. There has been an erosion of infrastructure support to rural communities – whether for roads or for wharves – and a failure to address the retraining needs of rural workers.

Policies that traditionally supported rural economies and communities – for example, unemployment insurance (UI) – have been gutted. Cutbacks in essential transportation services and the centralization of other services, such as health and education, have undermined rural communities and industries. Programs of regional economic development have given way to community economic development, which challenges struggling communities to find their own solutions.

Policies implemented to address specific rural crises, such as the collapse of the Atlantic groundfish stock, have failed. Their failure reflects both the current lack of will to regulate the market seriously in the interests of workers and a profound lack of understanding and/or tolerance of rural reality. A clear example of the latter was the attack on seasonal workers that drove employment insurance (EI) reform.

A rural focus can help us understand the distributional outcomes of labour market regulation and deregulation. Researchers typically disaggregate outcomes by factors such as industry, occupation, age, and gender, showing the impact on different workers. Do current trends and policies disproportionately disadvantage rural workers and their communities? Do rural–urban differences reflect compositional effects (for example, more rural workers have low levels of education, so they are less able to get high-tech jobs) or structural differences in rural labour markets?

Furthermore, a rural focus may further the overall political economy analysis. Just as feminist political economy goes beyond gendered effects to look at gendered processes (Bakker, 1994, 1996; Beneria, 1999), so a rural analysis may offer insights into economic processes that are inherently spatial. The early political economy tradition associated with staples theory in Canada recognized this. While work by economic geographers on post-Fordism (Harrison, 1994; Harvey, 1989; Storper and Walker, 1988) highlights the spatial dimension, there has been little examination of the rural–urban dimension. Processes of economic restructuring may be particularly transparent in a rural setting. For example, a rural perspective draws attention to sustainability and to the erosion of non-market economic relations, with implications that extend far beyond the rural settings in which they are most obvious.

In considering these issues, this chapter draws on the authors' ongoing research on restructuring in Atlantic resource-based communities, the failure of adjustment policies such as the Atlantic Groundfish Strategy (TAGS), and the impact of EI reform. This work pays attention to the gendered effects of regulation/deregulation and the need to look at families and communities, not just at individual workers, in analysis of labour market policies. A feminist political economy lens reveals the role of gender in labour market deregulation. Key concerns from the literature include the gendered increase in non-standard employment, intensification of unpaid work (for example, privatization increases women's responsibilities for "care"), and gender differences in labour-adjustment options, given gender divisions in the household and in the workplace. The interaction of spatial and gender issues is important in the rural context as families and communities grapple with restructuring.

The first section of this chapter outlines the reality of rural life in Canada in terms of population, employment, and income. The second examines the effects of deregulation and reregulation on resource entitlements, welfare entitlements, and access to new jobs.

RURAL REALITY IN CANADA:
TRENDS IN POPULATION, EMPLOYMENT, AND INCOME

Rural Canada is not homogeneous. There is tremendous diversity in rural Canada, some of it regional and related to differences in the resource base (farming, fishing, forestry, mining), some of it related to proximity to urban settings. Recent empirical work demonstrates this diversity and provides key indicators of the influence of restructuring on rural Canada.[1]

The diversity in rural areas becomes evident when one examines population characteristics and migration trends. Rural depopulation has occurred in Canada for over a century, as past rounds of economic restructuring led to urbanization. At present, from one-fifth to one-third of Canadians live in rural regions, depending on the definition used (du Plessis, Beshiri, and Bollman, 2001). The 2001 census showed that the rural population declined for the first time since 1981, although it continued to grow in areas close to metropolitan centres; but the rural population has declined steadily as a *share* of total population. Rural and small-town (RST) divisions (towns with < 10,000 inhabitants, plus rural areas) that lost population from 1991 to 2001 were concentrated in the Atlantic provinces, on the south shore of the St Lawrence, and in Manitoba and Saskatchewan (Bollman, 2002; Fellegi, 1996; Statistics Canada, 2002a).

Negative net migration characterized much of Canada outside the largest urban centres in the 1990s (Fellegi, 1996; Statistics Canada, 2002b). The age distribution of the population in rural areas, fuelled by migration of young people, is of particular concern (Rothwell et al., 2002). Between 1991 and 1996 about 30 per cent of rural teenagers left their communities (twice the rate of urban teenagers), and rural communities were net losers of teenagers, with the highest rates in Newfoundland and Saskatchewan (Dupuy, Mayer, and Morissette, 2000). We can see the variation in rural areas in youth migration statistics, with rural British Columbia, and to a lesser extent Alberta, gaining 15–29 year olds while Manitoba, the Maritimes, Newfoundland, and Saskatchewan had losses. Net migration is positive, however, for 30–64 year olds (again, except in rural Newfoundland and Saskatchewan). The migration pattern means that the rural population is ageing faster than its urban counterpart. There is also evidence that the rural leavers tend to be the best and brightest (Fellegi, 1996).[2]

The migration figures reflect the different economic opportunities in rural and urban areas. Rural unemployment rates are generally higher than urban ones in all provinces except the prairies (where farmers, by virtue of their self-employed status, cannot be unemployed), and employment rates are lower. The rural economy is more diversified in the east than in the west, even though most rural communities depend on a few key employers.

When we compare the industry distribution of employment between rural and urban labour markets, we find that both show a similar increase in the scale of service-sector employment; however, a noticeable difference is the under-representation of the higher-paid, dynamic producer (business) services in rural areas (Beshiri and Bollman, 2001; Tigges and Tootle, 1990). A recent study finds that rural areas have a disproportionate share of traditional manufacturing jobs – a sector in which job loss is occurring – and a low share of jobs in complex manufacturing, despite some recent gains (Beshiri and Bollman, 2001).

The prevalence of non-standard work is of particular interest in the context of labour market restructuring and deregulation (Vosko, 2000,

2002). A key difference between rural and urban work is the higher proportion of seasonal jobs in rural labour markets, especially in the east. Of the four industries characterized by Marshall (1999) as "highly seasonal," three are associated with rural areas (agriculture, fishing and trapping, logging and forestry). Furthermore, Rothwell (2002) finds higher rates of seasonal employment in rural areas even *within* highly seasonal industries. Seasonality contributes to higher rural unemployment rates. The incidence of non-permanent jobs is higher outside census metropolitan areas (CMAS), including temporary and casual as well as seasonal jobs (Perusse, 1997). Rural areas also have higher rates of part-time employment (Curto and Rothwell, 2002).

The standard employment relationship (SER) was never as firmly established in rural areas, so non-standard work is not necessarily new. However, in many rural areas old forms of non-standard work have given way to new, and the gains made in standardizing employment (for example, through fisheries unions) have eroded as resources collapse. Recent evidence from over 200 resource-dependent communities in Canada shows a decrease in the share of full-time work (Randall and Ironside, 1996). Other research in both Canada and the United States demonstrates the higher – and increasing – rates of underemployment for both male and female rural workers (Lichter, 1989; Tigges and Tootle, 1990; Vera-Toscano, Phimister, and Weersink, 2000). Leach and Winson (1995, 2002) find that rural women displaced by plant closures are more likely than their male counterparts to experience occupational "skidding" or to choose more precarious work close to home, given their care responsibilities. Neis, Grzetic, and Pidgeon (2001) report an increase in seasonal, insecure jobs in fish processing for both men and women in rural Newfoundland – an example of the "feminization of labour," where all jobs become more like traditional women's jobs. Rural areas also have almost twice the share of employees in small businesses as urban areas, and they have higher rates of self-employment.

Employment instability, as well as non-standard work, characterizes the rural labour market. Hours and earnings tend to fluctuate. Seasonal workers often work long hours during a short season, and hours can also be irregular and fluctuate over the course of the season. Rural workers may have more or longer gaps in work, either with one employer or between jobs.

While occupational pluralism has been associated with rural areas, this seems to have decreased in recent years. Rural workers are now more tied to one job, using UI/EI or the work of other family members to make up an adequate income (Flora, 1990; MacDonald, 1994). This is partly a response to regulations, ranging from fishing-licence requirements to UI rules, that reward attachment to one job.

Rural family incomes are lower than urban, and they have been equally flat throughout the 1980s and 1990s (Singh, 2002). Federal transfers make up a larger share of rural residents' income, especially UI/EI, pensions, and child benefits. Sub-provincial income disparities increased in the 1990s, and the rural–urban income divide is now more important than the provincial divide (Alasia and Rothwell, 2003). Statistics Canada (Fellegi, 1996) characterized 104 census divisions as having family incomes above average and growing, of which the only rural areas are those with key mining, oil, or hydro construction projects. The 17 divisions characterized as behind but gaining include some cottage-country areas and some rural areas that have attracted manufacturing (such as King's County, NS) or producer services (such as call centres). However, the 122 divisions that are behind and falling back include agricultural Manitoba and Saskatchewan, most of rural Atlantic Canada and Quebec, and many northern areas. The final group of 23 divisions that are ahead but lagging on family incomes have lost high-paying jobs in the primary sector, especially in mining and forestry. Thus, despite diversity, rural areas are disproportionately "behind" and/or "lagging" in terms of family income trends.

This same Statistics Canada report developed a summary typology to measure economic outcomes across census divisions, using a mixture of the variables discussed above, including income levels, education levels, employment rates, and migration rates (Fellegi, 1996). It found that census divisions in large cities have outcomes superior to the rest of the country, with the "urban frontier" divisions not far behind. The "rural nirvana" group of rural divisions, which represent migration of city dwellers to the country, are also doing well. The "agro-rural" group, however, is experiencing rapid population decline, out-migration of youth, and high dependence on government employment and social transfers. The "rural enclave" group has declining employment opportunities in manufacturing, forestry, and fishing, with low education, low incomes, and high dependence on government transfers. The final group of "rural resource" areas is benefiting from mining and oil – however, such boom-towns tend to come and go.

DEREGULATION AND REREGULATION IN RURAL CANADA

This review of the data suggests some of the ways in which restructuring is playing out in rural Canada. The farming and fishing resource sectors are in crisis. High-paying SER jobs in mining and forestry are disappearing. Opportunities are not opening up to keep young people in the communities. Non-standard employment, while not new in rural areas, is growing.

There has been a loss of "good" jobs in the public sector (education, health care), in finance (rural bank closures), and in resource industries. Deregulation and reregulation have been part and parcel of this restructuring – affecting, as we see in this section, resource entitlements, welfare-state entitlements, and access to new economic opportunities. The effects are different by gender, age, and place.

Resource Entitlements and Access

In the farming sector there has been a decrease in the number of farms, an increase in the average size of farms, and an increase in off-farm work, to support the family farm (Bokemeier, 1997; Flora, 1990; Reimer and Apedaile, 2000; Winson, 1990). The fisheries sector has been in crisis on both west and east coasts, with over-fishing resulting in a collapse of stocks. Resource sectors have experienced the pressure of increased concentration and industrialization, supported by state policy.

In the Atlantic fishery, it was the mass-production industrial sector, supported by state subsidies, bailouts, and favourable fisheries regulations, that was responsible for over-fishing. Regulatory changes in the 1970s and 1980s continually supported the growth of this sector. While companies diversified and globalized, workers and communities became increasingly specialized and were ill-equipped to handle the collapse of the ground-fishery (MacDonald, 1994). Flora (1990) makes the same point in relation to farm families, noting that while vertically integrated enterprises diversified, family farms became more specialized, achieving what flexibility they could through off-farm activities, such as the wage labour of family members, often women.

The story is similar in each resource sector – an increase in scale, concentration, and environmental stress. While Canadian resource policies have long supported these developments and favoured big capital, strong voices for the family farm and the inshore fishery resulted in some policies that enabled these sectors to survive, if not prosper. UI, farm subsidies, boat loans, public wharves, extension services, and licensing policies all helped to support smaller operators. The deregulation experienced is not so much a change in the overall thrust of policy – which has always supported the capitalist development of resource industries – as the erosion or loss of those gestures that ensured smaller-scale operators a place in the industry.

Around the world privatization is played out in fisheries management policies such as individual tradable quotas (ITQs) that privatize and control access to the resource. Evidence suggests that this leads to concentration of ownership, squeezing out smaller operators. Local fishers may lose their traditional access to the resource to the corporate sector and absentee owners (McCay, 2000). Also, women find access further restricted (Munk-Madsen, 1998). Formulas to assign quotas or licences ignore their traditional contributions to fishing. Export-oriented policies mean that countries focus on industrialized production in one fishery, displacing traditional fisheries and the communities dependent on them. Similar patterns have been documented for agriculture. Small producers experience diminished access to dwindling resources, processors, and markets.

The pressures of free trade reinforce these trends (MacDonald, 2002). WTO negotiations over agriculture concerning market access, domestic support, and export subsidies will establish whether there is anything more to agriculture than just producing food for profit – that is, whether food safety, food security, and environmental sustainability have any legitimacy (Barlow and Clarke, 2000). The precedents that are set will readily apply to fisheries. Another important trade issue concerns intellectual property (Trade in Intellectual Property, or TRIPS) – for example, the ability of corporations to patent life forms and indigenous knowledge, both of which have valuable fisheries applications. Negotiations on trade in services are also crucial, as they affect the outlook for health, education, income support, and other services in rural communities. If these are privatized, or government policy is further restricted in these areas, rural communities will be especially at risk.

Welfare-state Entitlements

Deregulation in Canada has been particularly notable in the gradual erosion of social security protection and the implementation of EI and the Canada Health and Social Transfer (CHST) (MacDonald, 1999). The reform of unemployment insurance in particular, involving the introduction of a renamed "Employment Insurance" benefit, constitutes a key aspect of labour market reregulation. Various analysts have written about this reform as part of a low-wage economic strategy (Canadian Labour Congress, 1996; Myles, 1995), meeting the competitive needs of employers (decreasing premiums and increasing the flexibility of the labour market). The changes are also consistent with the neoliberal agenda of less government (particularly the attack on "dependency"). Where does this leave rural workers?

The Social Security Review of 1994 identified primary industries, the Atlantic region, and seasonal workers as "heavy users" of UI. While the analysis did not particularly focus on rural versus urban patterns of UI use, seasonal workers and primary industries are associated with rural areas. The review paid particular attention to the issue of frequent claimants, for whom UI was argued to constitute a program of income supplementation rather than insurance (Human Resources Development Canada, 1994: 19). The new EI system was designed to discourage frequent use and create incentives for longer job tenure and increased work time. The reform met with considerable opposition from rural representatives and groups, who clearly felt that they were being unfairly targeted and penalized for labour market conditions over which they had little control.

The key program elements that potentially have had differential rural–urban effects include the hours criteria for eligibility, the way in which gaps in employment affect the calculation of benefit levels, the intensity rule, and the claw-back of benefits from high-income earners. The switch to hours-based eligibility makes it harder for some people and easier for others to qualify. The number of required hours prevents those with very few hours from qualifying. However, those with more than 35 hours per week can qualify more easily under EI. Those with fluctuating hours or 15–35 hours per week might have enough insured weeks under the former UI system, but not enough hours for EI. Overall, the EI reforms have reduced eligibility (Human Resources Development Canada, 2000a). Whether rural workers are harder hit in this regard depends on the mix of work situations. While rural workers more probably work more than 35 hours per week, they are also more likely to have irregular work. These factors may offset each other in terms of EI eligibility.

A recent paper attempts to document rural–urban differences in the probability of receiving UI/EI and the impact of the reform (MacDonald, Phipps, and MacPhail, 2000). Using data from 1995–97, the research found greater reliance of rural workers on UI/EI that is only partially explained by differences in individual and job characteristics, such as education, seasonality, hours worked, industry, and regional unemployment rates. This difference probably reflects the relative lack of job opportunities in rural areas. Qualifying for benefits was less likely under EI, compared to UI, for *both* urban and rural unemployed workers, other things being equal. However, there does not appear to be a statistically significant *difference* between rural and urban workers in the reform's effect on access to EI; it has hurt both groups.

The attempts to reduce UI dependence of frequent claimants such as seasonal rural workers focused on benefit levels, duration, and claw-backs, rather than on eligibility. The change in the basic formula for calculating average insured earnings and thus benefit levels (using the last 26 weeks, with minimum divisor) implies that the new rules hurt those with gaps in employment or with weeks with small earnings. For seasonal workers who just meet the minimum hours for eligibility, the minimum-divisor rule lowers their average earnings. Given the work patterns noted above, the benefits of rural workers have probably dropped more than those of urban workers under the reform. The intensity rule, which reduces benefit rates based on previous EI claims, has also probably affected rural workers more, given their greater reliance on UI/EI. Similarly, claw-backs are also based on past EI use.

In terms of the duration of benefits, the use of hours to determine weeks of benefit entitlement decreased the length of entitlement for anyone who works less than 35 hours a week. The incentive structure of the program assumes that workers are able to increase their work effort, punishing them for low hours or irregular or seasonal work. Yet rural workers have few options to respond to these incentives.

Empirical work on the rural impact of EI is limited. Focus-group research in rural areas and small towns in Nova Scotia and British Columbia (Phipps, MacDonald, and MacPhail, 2000) indicated that the new EI regulations were making it difficult for the many workers who do not have steady, full-time jobs, regular seasonal jobs (for example, full time for four months), or steady part-time jobs (for example, 20 hours every week). The actual employment patterns of many workers are far more complex, particularly in the rural context. The focus-group participants gave many examples of how EI was harder to get than UI and provided lower benefit levels for a shorter duration, and the rural groups seemed to have been hit the hardest, as their work patterns did not fit the implicit norms supported by the new program. Interviews with women in fishing communities in Nova Scotia also documented decreased EI support (CRIAW – Nova Scotia and Nova Scotia Women's Fishnet, 2000).

The government has acknowledged the hardship that the intensity rule and the claw-back have caused and the inability of the vast majority of rural residents to change their work patterns (Human Resources Development Canada, 2000b). Recent legislation introduced to eliminate the intensity rule and modify the claw-back particularly targets Atlantic voters. The proposed changes, however, do not address the effect of gaps in employment and irregular earnings on benefit levels, which is of particular concern to rural workers. The program retains an incentive for workers to take any and all bits of work that they can find, facilitating the growth of non-standard employment relationships.

Other aspects of welfare-state reform have also affected rural areas. Cuts to health care have resulted in a loss of services, as many provinces have consolidated health-care delivery into larger centres. In many rural communities, health-care services are less available than a generation ago (Rodgers, 2000). Similarly, education takes place in larger, consolidated schools. The loss of these services and other government supports makes it difficult for rural communities to organize and pursue the development strategies urged on them (Reimer and Apedaile, 2000).

Access to New Economic Opportunities

As jobs evaporate in the resource sector, rural workers cannot easily take advantage of new opportunities. While new technologies facilitate more decentralized production, urban areas are disproportionately gaining. Theorists of the territorial dimensions of restructuring argue that new economies of scope and agglomeration lead to new spatial concentrations of economic activity (Harrison, 1994; Storper, 1997; Storper and Walker, 1989). At the same time, government is getting out of the "development business." It has abandoned the old interventionist, handout approach to local development, and the new mantra is community economic development and self-organization, in keeping with a liberal self-help ideology. The tools with which to conduct this endeavour are often sorely lacking. The lower educational levels of the existing workforce also hamper these efforts. And, as we saw above, deregulation has reduced the service role of the state, and, with it, the supports needed for rural areas to harness new opportunities (Osberg, Wien, and Grude, 1995).

Furthermore, few new programs address the serious challenges of labour market adjustment faced by individual employees, their families, and their communities. Shifts in the employment structure include changes in the conditions of work and in the skills required for, and the location of, jobs (Human Resources Development Canada, 1997; Osberg, Wien and Grude, 1995). In general, Canada has not pursued an active labour-adjustment policy in response to these changes. There is the ever-present threat that international trading partners will challenge adjustment programs as illegal industry subsidies. Furthermore, pressures for decreased intervention in the market and a reduction in the scale of government have led to cutbacks in existing programs aimed at labour adjustment (MacDonald, 1998).

However, during the process of economic restructuring the state has intervened to deal with crises in specific industries or communities. Resource-based communities in particular have faced dramatic employment losses in which the resulting structural unemployment has location as well as skill dimensions. The Atlantic Groundfish Strategy (TAGS) provides an interesting example of rural labour market adjustment policy. Introduced in 1994 in the wake of a 1992 moratorium on groundfish harvesting, TAGS was a major intervention for this non-interventionist era. Based on my research in fishing communities before the moratorium and my participation in the evaluation of the TAGS program, I suggest that the program's failings arose from a misunderstanding of the process of adjustment, especially in a rural context. The lessons learned from this rural situation, however, have broad implications for labour-adjustment policy in general.

TAGS was an ambitious mixture of income support, active labour market adjustment measures, industry restructuring, and community economic development. The overall TAGS budget was $1.9 billion over five years, of which Human Resources Development Canada (HRDC) distributed $1.7 billion.[3] The HRDC component consisted of income support and labour market adjustment measures to assist TAGS clients to move out of the groundfishery.[4] At the outset, every client was expected to be "active" while on TAGS. Each would receive counselling and would develop an action plan identifying goals for adjustment and/or active participation and measures to achieve them. Available program elements included professionalization training for those designated for the future fishery, training to leave the fishery, community volunteer work (COP) and employment projects (Green Projects), self-employment assistance, early-retirement programs, mobility assistance to relocate, wage subsidies, and an employment bonus for people who found permanent work outside the fishery (Human Resources Development Canada, 1998).

The TAGS program illustrates three problems with labour-adjustment policy (above and beyond its emphasis on adjusting workers, rather than labour demand), each of which is particularly transparent in the rural context. First, this program, like most, focused on "adjusting" the individual displaced worker. However, labour adjustment is a household and community process. An individual experiences a complex web of economic relationships with household members, extended family, and community. Thus the restructuring of work affects more than just the individual, and decisions made in response take place in a household and community context. While eligibility for TAGS was individual, people's responses to the program's opportunities were affected by their family or household's overall situation, including other members' paid and unpaid work.

Second, adjustment involves a reconfiguration of work done in the market and outside the market to earn, or make, a livelihood. Concomitantly, assessment of the costs and benefits of adjustment must take account of the use of all resources, including unpaid labour in the household and community and the value of monetary and non-monetary assets such as houses and social networks. Too often it ignores the value of non-monetary exchanges, assets, and networks. Labour market adjustment programs tend to focus on replacing earnings, not assets, but household adjustment involves both. The informal economy is especially important in close-knit, rural communities and includes exchanges of services (child care, repairs, transportation) as well as goods. Both formal (volunteer groups) and informal support networks have an economic value to the household. The non-monetary economy is central to the process of, and barriers to, adjustment. TAGS participants felt that the program ignored these considerations, and TAGS counsellors found the seeming recalcitrance of recipients frustrating.

Third, the TAGS program failed to take account of gender differences in adjustment. Too often the lone individual whom policy measures address is implicitly male – a primary provider who can uproot his family to find a new job or can commute to a nearby town to attend a training program. Yet differences in the gender division of labour in the home may result in different options and needs for support for male and female job seekers. The gender division of labour and decision-making in the home creates different constraints on women and men's labour-force activity and mobility. Women are the traditional emotional managers and absorb more stress in a time of crisis. Most accounts of the impact of the moratoriums have emphasized this fact. Some women may be less able to make independent decisions about their work futures than men. They may face barriers in accessing both training and employment, especially in rural areas, where commuting is often necessary. Yet counsellors may wrongly assume their economic dependence and do less to facilitate their adjustment. Finally, the design of training and employment programs may incorporate gender biases.

A household study that was part of the evaluation of TAGS found these three problems present during the first two years of TAGS, when the "active" adjustment measures were still in place (Human Resources Development Canada, 1998). The report noted gender biases in determining eligibility for TAGS, given the different roles and experiences of men and women in the fishery. It also found gender stereotyping in training, job-creation, and mobility-assistance programs.[5] There were also issues related to age, as the average participant was over 40.

The study suggested taking better account of household processes, gender differences, and community characteristics and, in general, recommended programming that was more flexible and gender sensitive. These changes would facilitate women's adjustment:

- more flexible child-care supports and training allowances to fit various family situations
- co-ordination of adjustment options when both spouses are eligible for a program
- greater family involvement in counselling/career planning processes
- more local provision of training, correspondence courses, and community projects that are compatible with family responsibilities and other members' work

Other suggestions included allowing families to choose which member could best benefit from access to TAGS programs and lump-sum payments for families to use as they see fit. Another factor raised was the importance of home ownership and other tangible and intangible assets that families have in communities. In many cases these assets have low market value but are irreplaceable to the family.

By the time these recommendations appeared, TAGS had become mostly an income-maintenance program, with active adjustment measures essentially abandoned, as across Canada (McBride, 1998). Displaced workers are increasingly on their own, in keeping with deregulation. Despite some gestures towards community economic development, TAGS also demonstrated the government's lack of will to work with communities on the demand side of the labour market. In fact, TAGS was widely perceived as another resettlement program. This, coupled with the government's refusal to acknowledge its responsibility for the collapse of the ground-fishery, caused great anger and frustration, undermining the capacity of people and communities to rebuild their lives.

CONCLUSION

This chapter has examined the spatial dimension of labour market restructuring and the failure of policy to meet the needs of non-urban workers. While rural Canada is diverse, and some areas are prospering, most current restructuring has favoured urban areas and their rural satellites. This is the result of both economic forces and the regulatory regime that supports and shapes them. This chapter has provided a brief overview of changing conditions in rural areas. Work opportunities in traditional resource sectors have declined, rural communities are unable to compete for the new "high-end" economic opportunities, and the "low-end" jobs in tourism and call centres do not make up for what they have lost. On a trip to Elliot Lake (a former mining town in northern Ontario) a few years ago I visited the old United Steelworkers union hall – now a senior's centre – where an afternoon bingo game was in progress. That image symbolizes for me the transformation of many rural communities.

Policies of deregulation have resulted in the loss of infrastructure and services in rural communities. Resource policies have favoured intensification and concentration of farming, fishing, and forestry production. Trade policies have further encouraged export production and specialization. Social security reform has targeted rural workers. Labour-adjustment policies, where implemented, have failed to reflect the economic and social reality of rural families and communities. Each of these policies has gender as well as spatial effects.

A rural lens provides some insight into economic processes that are inherently spatial. It draws attention to sustainability and the erosion of non-market economic relations, with implications that extend far beyond the rural settings in which they are most obvious. The fishery, for example, reveals the destructive nature of globalization. Competitive pressures and the application of increasingly sophisticated technology result in stocks being exploited to near-extinction. When this happens in a particular area, workers and communities suffer, but capital can move on – to exploit new species and new communities. Companies have diversified and achieved flexibility, while workers and communities have lost flexibility. The undermining of non-market economic activities and social supports is also strikingly clear in rural communities. As the market becomes pervasive, the health and well-being of families and communities often suffer. Women manage the crises, make ends meet, and intensify their care-giving.

Like the canary in the coal mine, the fate of rural Canada can tell us a lot about our collective prospects.

NOTES

1 Statistical analysis must first define "rural" and "urban." Statistics Canada data distinguishes between census metropolitan areas (CMAS, or urban areas with population greater than 100,000), census agglomerates (CAS, or towns and cities of between 10,000 and 100,000 people), smaller towns, and rural and small towns (RSTS, with fewer than 10,000 inhabitants). Researchers use different definitions of "rural" and "urban," depending on the level of detail in the data available to them. Usually "rural" includes towns with fewer than 10,000 people and rural areas (RSTS), while urban includes CMAS and CAS. Some researchers are able to take account of commuting patterns in defining RSTS as either urban or rural. Recent Statistics Canada work classifies CMAS, CAS, and their commuting areas (defined as an urban fringe where more than 50 per cent of the population commutes) as urban (Bollman et al., 2000). Given the definitional differences, there is considerable variation in statistical summaries of rural–urban characteristics.

2 Education levels also differ systematically between rural and urban Canada. The rural population has lower educational attainment (higher percentage with less than grade 9, lower percentage with university) at all ages.

3 Three federal departments were involved: Human Resources Development Canada (labour adjustment and income support), the Department of Fisheries and Oceans (industry capacity reduction, including licence buybacks) and the Atlantic Canada Opportunities Agency (community development).

4 While projections were based on 30,000 participants, 40,025 displaced groundfish fishers and trawler and processing workers qualified for

income support of $211–$382 per week (based on average UI claims in 1990–92 minus 6 per cent) for up to five years (later reduced to four years), depending on attachment to the industry (Human Resources Development Canada, 1998a).

5 A Newfoundland study of TAGS training found women over-represented in ABE courses (despite higher levels of education than men) and under-represented in trades training (other than service-related) and in fisheries-related training programs (Neis, Grzetic, and Pidgeon, 2001).

REFERENCES

Alasia, Alessandro, and Neil Rothwell. 2003. "The Rural/Urban Divide Is Not Changing," *Rural and Small Town Analysis Bulletin* 4 (4), Statistics Canada. Cat. No. 21–006–XIE.

Bakker, Isabella, 1994. *The Strategic Silence: Gender and Economic Policy.* London: Zed Books and the North–South Institute.

– ed. 1996. *Rethinking Restructuring: Gender and Change in Canada.* Toronto: University of Toronto Press.

Barlow, Maude, and Tony Clarke. 2000. "The Battle after Seattle: A Working Paper for Strategic Planning and Action on the WTO." www.cid.harvard.edu/cidtrade.

Beneria, Lourdes. 1999. "Globalization, Gender and the Davos Man," *Feminist Economics* 5 (1), 61–84.

Beshiri, Roland, and Ray Bollman. 2001. "Rural and Small Town Employment: Structure by Industry." Statistics Canada, Agriculture and Rural Working Paper No. 50, Cat. No. 21–601–MIE.

Bokemeier, Janet. 1997. "Rediscovering Families and Households: Restructuring Rural Society and Rural Sociology," *Rural Sociology* 62 (1), 1–20.

Bollman, Ray. 2002. "Rural Canada: From Strength to Strength." Agriculture Divison, Statistics Canada. Presentation to Voluntary Planning, Halifax, Nov.

Canadian Labour Congress (CLC). 1996. "Proposed Changes to the Unemployment Insurance Program." Submission to the Standing Committee on Human Resources Development.

CRIAW – Nova Scotia and Nova Scotia Women's Fishnet. 2000. "Women's Health in Six Nova Scotia Fishing Communities." Final Report.

Curto, Justin, and Neil Rothwell. 2002. "Part-time Employment in Rural Canada," *Rural and Small Town Analysis Bulletin* 4 (1), Statistics Canada, Cat. No. 21–006–XIE.

du Plessis, Valerie, Roland Beshiri, and Ray Bollman. 2001. "Definitions of Rural," *Rural and Small Town Analysis Bulletin* 3 (3), Statistics Canada, Cat. No. 21–006–XIE.

Dupuy, Richard, Francine Mayer, and René Morissette. 2000. "Rural Roots," *Per-*

spectives on Labour and Income 12 (3), 60–68, Statistics Canada, Cat. No. 75–001–XPE.

Fellegi, Ivan. 1996. "Understanding Rural Canada: Structures and Trends." Statistics Canada, Cat. No. 21F0016XIE.

Flora, Cornelia Butler. 1990. "Rural Peoples in a Global Economy," *Rural Sociology* 55 (2), 157–77.

Fulton, John, Glenn Fuguitt, and Richard Gibson. 1997. "Recent Changes in Metropolitan–Non-Metropolitan Migration Streams," *Rural Sociology* 62 (3), 363–84.

Harrison, Bennett. 1994. *Lean and Mean: The Resurrection of Corporate Power in an Age of Flexibility*. New York: Basic Books.

Harvey, David. 1989. *The Condition of Post-Modernity*. Oxford: Basil Blackwell.

Human Resources Development Canada (HRDC). 1994. "From Employment Insurance to Unemployment Insurance: A Supplementary Paper." Improving Social Security in Canada. Ottawa: Minister of Supply and Services.

– 1996. "The Atlantic Groundfish Strategy: Background Paper, TAGS Household Study". SP-AH007E-BP1–01–96, Ottawa: Human Resources Development Canada.

– 1997. "Report of the Advisory Committee on the Changing Workplace." LT-060–05–97E. Ottawa: Human Resources Development Canada.

– 1998. "The Evaluation of the Atlantic Groundfish Strategy: Final Report." SP-AH046–03–98, Ottawa: Human Resources Development Canada.

– 2000a. "Employment Insurance: 1999 Monitoring and Assessment Report." Ottawa: Human Resources Development Canada.

– 2000b. "Proposed Changes to Employment Insurance Legislation." Press release. 28 Sept. Ottawa: Human Resources Development Canada.

Leach, Belinda. 1999. "Transforming Rural Livelihoods: Gender, Work and Restructuring in Three Ontario Communities," in Sheila Nesmith, ed., *Restructuring Caring Labour: Discourse, State Practice and Everyday Life*. Toronto: Oxford University Press.

Leach, Belinda, and Anthony Winson. 1995. "Bringing Globalization Down to Earth: Restructuring and Labour in Rural Communities," *Canadian Review of Sociology and Anthropology* 32 (3), 341–64.

Leborgne, D., and A. Lipietz. 1988. "New Technologies and New Modes of Regulation: Some Spatial Implications," *Environment and Planning: Society and Space* 6 (3), 263–80.

Lichter, Daniel. 1989. "The Underemployment of American Rural Women: Prevalence, Trends and Spatial Inequality," *Journal of Rural Studies* 5 (2), 198–208.

MacDonald, Martha. 1994. "Restructuring in the Fishing Industry in Atlantic Canada," in Isabella Bakker, ed., *The Strategic Silence: Gender and Economic Policy*. London: Zed Books and the North-South Institute.

– 1998. "Gender and Social Security Reform: Pitfalls and Possibilities," *Feminist Economics* 4 (1), 1–27.

– 1999. "Restructuring, Gender and Social Security Reform in Canada," *Journal of Canadian Studies* 34 (2), 57–88.
– 2002. "Lessons and Linkages: Building an Analysis of Gender, Globalization and the Fisheries," *Women and Environments International* 54/55 (Spring), Special Issue on Women, Ecology and Economic Change.
MacDonald, Martha, Shelley Phipps, and Fiona MacPhail. 2000. "Rural–Urban Differences in the Impact of EI." Paper presented at the conference on Rural/Urban Differences in Economic Development, Canadian Research and Employment Forum, Laurentian University. Sept.
Marshall, Katherine. 1999. "Seasonality in Employment," *Perspectives on Labour and Income* 11 (1), 16–22.
McBride, Stephen. 1998. "The Political Economy of Training in Canada." Paper prepared for the Working Group on Labour Market Flexibility, Centre for Work and Society, York University.
McCay, Bonnie. 2000. "Globalization and the Transfer of 'Rights-based' Fisheries Management Approaches, Particularly Individual Transferable Quota (ITQ) Management Regimes: Lessons from Canada and the U.S.," presented at the Gender and Globalization of the Fisheries Workshop, St John's, Newfoundland.
Munk-Madsen, Eva. 1998. "The Norwegian Fishing Quota System: Another Patriarchal Construction?" *Society and Natural Resources* 11 (3), 229–40.
Myles, John. 1995. "When Markets Fail: Social Welfare in Canada and the United States." Discussion Paper 68. Geneva: United Nations Research Institute for Social Development.
Neis, Barbara, Brenda Grzetic, and Michelle Pidgeon. 2001. "From Fishplant to Nickel Smelter: Health Determinants and the Health of Newfoundland's Women Fish and Shellfish Processors in an Environment of Restructuring." Research Report. Sociology Department, Memorial University, St John's.
Osberg, Lars, Fred Wien, and Jan Grude. 1995. *Vanishing Jobs: Canada's Changing Workplace.* Toronto: James Lorimer.
Perusse, Dominique. 1997. "Regional Disparities and Non-permanent Employment," *Perspectives on Labour and Income* 9 (4), 25–31.
Phipps, Shelley, Martha MacDonald, and Fiona MacPhail. 2000. "Impact of the Family Income Supplement." Final Report. Strategic Evaluation and Monitoring Directorate. SP-AH133–03–00E. Ottawa: Human Resources Development Canada.
Piore, Michael, and Charles Sabel. 1984. *The Second Industrial Divide: Possibilities for Prosperity.* New York: Basic Books.
Randall, James, and Geoff Ironside. 1996. "Communities on the Edge: An Economic Geography of Resource Dependent Communities in Canada," *Canadian Geographer* 40 (1), 17–35.
Reimer, Bill, and Peter Apedaile. 2000. "The New Rural Economy in Canada." Paper presented at the conference on Rural/Urban Differences in Economic

Development, Canadian Research and Employment Forum, Laurentian University. Sept.

Rodgers, Theresa Heath. 2000. "Work, Household Economy and Social Welfare: The Transition from Traditional to Modern Lifestyles in Bonavista, 1930–1960." Master's thesis, Memorial University.

Rothwell, Neil. 2002. "Seasonal Variation in Rural Employment," *Rural and Small Town Analysis Bulletin* 3(8), Statistics Canada, Cat. No. 21–006–XIE.

Rothwell, Neil, Ray Bollman, Juno Tremblay, and Jeff Marshall. 2002. "Migration to and from Rural and Small Town Canada," *Rural and Small Town Analysis Bulletin* 3(6), Statistics Canada, Cat. No. 21–006–XIE.

Singh, Vik. 2002. "Rural Income Disparities in Canada: A Comparison across the Provinces," *Rural and Small Town Analysis Bulletin* 3 (7), Statistics Canada, Cat. No. 21–006–XIE.

Statistics Canada. 2002a. "Profile of the Canadian Population by Mobility Status: A Nation on the Move, 2001 Census." 2001 Census Analysis Series. Cat. No. 96–F0030XIE2002006.

– 2002b. "A Profile of the Canadian Population: Where We Live." 2001 Census Analysis Series. Cat. No. 96F0030XIE010012001.

Storper, Michael. 1997. *The Regional World: Territorial Development in a Global Economy.* New York: Guildford Press.

Storper, Michael, and Richard Walker. 1988. *The Capitalist Imperative: Territory, Technology, and Industrial Growth.* New York: Basil Blackwell.

Tigges, Leann, and Deborah Tootle. 1990. "Labor Supply, Labor Demand and Men's Underemployment in Rural and Urban Labor Markets," *Rural Sociology* 55 (3), 328–56.

Vera-Toscano, Euan Phimister, and Alfons Weersink. 2000. "The Dynamics of Employment: Labour Force Instability in Rural Canada." Paper presented at the conference on Rural/Urban Differences in Economic Development, Canadian Research and Employment Forum, Laurentian University. Sept.

Vosko, Leah. 2000. *Temporary Work: The Gendered Rise of a Precarious Employment Relationship.* Toronto: University of Toronto Press.

– 2002. "Rethinking Feminization: Gendered Precariousness in the Canadian Labour Market and the Crisis of Social Reproduction." Monograph, Annual Robart's Chair Lecture Series, John P. Robarts Centre for Canadian Studies, York University, Toronto.

Winson, Anthony. 1990. "Capitalist Coordination of Agriculture: Food Processing Firms and Farming in Central Canada," *Rural Sociology* 55 (3), 376–94.

Winson, Anthony, and Belinda Leach. 2002. *Contingent Work, Disrupted Lives: Labour and Community in the New Rural Economy.* Toronto: University of Toronto Press.

12

Technology, Gender, and Regulation: Call Centres in New Brunswick

TOM GOOD and JOAN McFARLAND

"New Brunswick is the call centre capital of North America," declares a glossy government brochure. Boosterism aside, the claim highlights the rapid emergence of a new industry in the province, which started a decade ago and now employs about 20,000 people in more than 100 call centre locations.[1] Currently, one worker in every 20 in New Brunswick works in a call centre; most are young, and they are predominantly women. Call centres – or "customer contact centres," the industry's preferred designation – have been a major source of employment growth in recent years across Canada and internationally. According to a study by Price Waterhouse Coopers (cited in Buchanan and Koch-Schulte, 2000: 4), by mid-1998 the industry employed 330,000 people in Canada in 219,000 agent positions and was growing at a rate of 20–25 per cent per year.

New telecommunications technology has given the industry a global reach – from Jacksonville, Florida, where AT&T pioneered a 1–800 centre in 1983, to Ireland, where call centres have contributed to the republic's "economic miracle," to Bangalore, India, where women who pretend to be U.S.-based receive about a dollar an hour to answer calls from U.S. customers on behalf of U.S. companies (Landler, 2001: A1). As the industry evolves, it assumes more and more of the characteristics of the new international division of labour, in which marginalized workers in relatively low-wage areas provide corporate services for businesses based in economically advanced regions.

This chapter explores the rise of the call-centre industry in the 1990s, focusing on New Brunswick. The first section examines how changes in telecommunications technology have facilitated reorganization of work in a call-centre format and why these arrangements have spread so widely.

Most call-centre work requires a combination of clerical and interpersonal skills usually identified as "feminized" labour processes. Moreover, the organization of work – the heavy reliance on part-time workers, non-standard conditions of employment, and tight workplace discipline – also has a gender dimension. The second section seeks to explain the reasons for this gendered labour process and the increasing mobility of call centres as they pursue a marginalized labour force composed primarily of women and young people.

The New Brunswick government's role in promoting the industry goes far beyond glossy brochures; it has undertaken an aggressive effort to market the province's labour to these highly mobile businesses. Significantly, this is its first economic development strategy not directed at the core labour market of male "breadwinners." The third section of the chapter details the package of provincial neoliberal policies to restructure labour markets to create a low-cost "Workready Workforce" – available, flexible, and capable – for the industry.

Although we ground our analysis in the specifics of one industry and a single jurisdiction, restructuring usually involves collaboration between corporate interests and state power and has similar consequences everywhere for the workers involved. The final section chronicles typical experiences of the women – and men – working in call centres in New Brunswick: wages, working conditions, on-the-job supervision, and pervasive insecurity. We conclude by pointing out that what the future holds for workers there – indeed for the industry itself – depends on new technologies, labour market developments, and political choices.

NEW TECHNOLOGY
AND THE EMERGENCE OF CALL CENTRES

As businesses scan the economic horizon in search of new profitable opportunities, they typically look to exploit new technologies and changing market conditions. From a Schumpeterian perspective, the economy is never in stasis. Instead, it constitutes a dynamic world in which firms struggle with firms for competitive advantage, and businesses struggle with labour to reduce the wage share (Palley, 1998: 17).

Call centres, which combine innovations in telecommunications technology and growing consumer interest in on-demand services, illustrate how this fundamental dynamic of capitalism works. As "firms struggle with firms for competitive advantage," call-centre jobs are created to handle reservations, sales, and banking transactions and to dispense customized information and technical support. In the course of this process, other jobs disappear – from travel agencies, bank branches, retail sales and service departments, even the post office. What drives these changes is the pursuit of profits; what results is an ongoing reorganization of work. Air Canada, for example, by operating a large 1–800 service based in New Brunswick, makes ticket sales directly and avoids sharing revenues with independent travel agents. Moreover, by reducing its dependence on travel agencies, Air Canada strengthens its bargaining power, enabling it to drive down the commissions paid on tickets still handled by these agencies. Another example is bank-by-phone services, which reduce banks' operating costs, strip local branches of some business, and facilitate branch closings and layoffs.

As the number of new ways to apply the call-centre model of business organization has proliferated, the industry has undergone rapid expansion and increasing differentiation. Perhaps the most familiar segments of the industry are the "outbound" call centres, where the call centre initiates contact, usually on the basis of randomly generated telephone numbers. Companies involved in outbound calling – telemarketing, public opinion surveys, fund-raising – are typically stand-alone businesses, which rely on short-term, fee-for-service contracts and commissions for their revenues. These firms are generally considered the low end of the industry and offer low wages, little job security, and a high-pressure work environment.

The fastest-growing and most dynamic segments of the industry are "inbound" call centres, where customers initiate contact through 1–800 numbers. The most common type are in-house call centres, in which major corporations employ call-centre workers directly as part of a strategy of vertical integration. This arrangement is most likely where the accurate handling of proprietary data is vital to the company (as with airline reservations or financial transactions) or where firm-specific knowledge is necessary (as with help desks and technical-support call centres). Data-processing jobs in these large in-house call centres represent the broad middle of the industry in terms of wages and working conditions, and the small number of technical-support positions, the high-end.

A second – and increasingly common – form of inbound call centre is the 1–800 specialist firm, which offers services to client corporations wishing to outsource specific customer-relations activities such as dispensing product information or receiving complaints. Typically, these specialist firms operate in many locations, achieving the benefits of economies of scale and innovation. A leading-edge example is Canadian-based Minacs Worldwide, a company with 20 call centres on two continents, which offers "customer relations management" for businesses such as General Motors and employs not only telephone technology, but also e-mail and web-based systems. The outsourcing model may become more prevalent as these service providers become more established and more reliable – a pattern familiar in other areas of production.

Key to the emergence of the call-centre industry in its various forms has been the development of new telecommunications technology, which has driven down long distance charges and generated new types of capital equipment – fibre-optic networks, digital switching systems, and integrated connections to networked computers and firm-specific software (telephony computer integration, or TCI).

At the core of call-centre operations is the switching system, which organizes work by queuing incoming calls, distributing them to workers (often through caller "menu" options), arranging recorded messages ("Your call is important to us ..."), and even rerouting calls to other cities or countries in multi-site call-centre operations. Nortel's Meridian MAX and similar devices also provide valuable electronic monitoring functions (Delottinville, 1994: 33), including the capacity to:

- track the amount of time that agents spend on routine calls
- determine daily traffic patterns and schedule agents appropriately for fluctuations in call activity
- monitor individual agents' call-handling activities, allowing supervisors to assess their performance

As a result, many of the management functions associated with operating call centres are embedded directly in the hardware and software systems; so too are most of the workers' functions.

A GENDERED LABOUR PROCESS

In most call centres 60–80 per cent of the workers are female, reflecting the gendered content of the labour process – routine clerical tasks, telephone skills, and the "emotional labour" of personal interactions. The organization of work also assumes gendered characteristics, with a high proportion of part-time and shift work, non-permanent status, strict workplace discipline, and working conditions involving stress and soft-tissue injuries – the so-called women's workplace diseases (Fenety, Putnam, and Loppie, 1999; Messing, 1998). The presence of a substantial number of males – particularly young males – has had little impact on the nature of work; rather, as in other sectors, "jobs for both sexes increasingly take on the characteristics of women's work" (Fox and Sugiman, 1999: 61).

The job of a typical worker, or telephone service representative (TSR), follows Taylorist principles, with a minimum number of carefully defined, highly specific tasks linked together mechanically through specialized computer software systems to achieve an integrated work flow. The Taylorized workplace also eliminates most of the employee–employee and employee–customer socializing which is characteristic of many retail services. The machine-controlled pace of work creates significant opportunities for speed-up. And close electronic monitoring increases the intensity of work effort. All these factors reduce per-unit labour time and increase potential profits.

Although much of the work is standard and routine, TSRs require a substantial and flexible set of skills. Each is a primary contact point between a company and its customers, and the ability to project a positive corporate image – competent, friendly, and helpful – is crucial. As the connecting link between customer and computer, a TSR converts the customer's desires into data for the computer. This requires not only the skill-base to work with the computer but also the communication skills and versatility to perceive and respond effectively to each caller. Moreover, workers deal with stressful situations. Few jobs that are machine-ordered and machine-paced require workers to engage with others in any kind of direct, personal communication, let alone engage strangers in often-contentious circumstances – especially for outbound TSRs, who must regularly deal with annoyed people, and inbound TSRs on the "complaints desk."

Organizing the labour process in most call centres requires the use of a "just-in-time" workforce. Typically, the volume of telephone traffic ebbs and flows, with peak hours of the day, peak days of the week, and peak seasons of the year. To minimize costs, the number of TSRs scheduled at any particular time must correspond closely to the expected volume of calls. If more than enough people are on duty, unit costs rise; if insufficient, calls back up and customers become irritated. Management uses standardized performance indicators (such as calls per agent per hour) generated by the electronic monitoring system to determine the minimum number of workers needed for each shift. For this reason, most call centres rely heavily on shift work, irregular schedules, and part-time employment.

Flexible scheduling is one aspect of management's efforts to maximize profits by minimizing unit labour costs (i.e., the cost of the labour required to perform each discrete activity – each sale made, each complaint handled, each service rendered). For employers, minimizing unit labour costs is crucial, because call centres are labour-intensive, with wages and fringe benefits by far the largest cost: approximately 60 per cent of total costs, followed by long-distance charges of 20–25 per cent (Boyd Company, 1999: 12). Following the formulation of Bowles and Edwards (1993: 186), unit labour costs (ulc) depend on the average wage rate (w), the efficiency of the workplace (e), and the average work effort of employees (d):

$$ulc = \frac{w}{ed}$$

Unit labour costs fall when the average wage rate declines, efficiency improves, or the work effort extracted from employees increases. Minimizing unit labour costs is not a straightforward exercise for management, since the variables are interdependent, generating more than one possible strategy. Many comparative studies discuss two distinct management strategies. David Gordon (1996: 144) contrasts them: "The 'high road' seeks to build economic growth and prosperity through cooperation and strong worker rewards, including rapid real wage growth. The 'low road' relies on conflict and insecurity, control and harsh worker punishments, and often features stagnant or even declining real wage growth. Both are coherent strategies, both can conceivably work."

Most call centres are "low road" employers, depending on low and stagnant wages and tight management control over workers in order to minimize unit labour costs. For this approach to succeed, call centres need a labour force in which individual workers face a high cost of job loss. Bowles and Edwards (1993: 193–5) define the "cost of job loss" as follows:

The loss of income inflicted on the worker by the loss of a job is termed the *cost of job loss*. The higher the cost of job loss, the more power the employer has over the worker ... How much is it worth to the worker to avoid the income loss associated with losing the job? ... If the current job pays $10 an hour, the worker might respond that keeping the job and only getting $6 an hour would be as big a loss as losing the job. The lower wage – $6 an hour – is called the *worker's fallback wage*, defined as the worker's prospects in the absence of the current job ... The fallback wage is defined as the wage low enough so the worker doesn't care about getting fired ... (hence) the worker will be as lax or as diligent as he or she pleases ... The higher the wage, the more the worker has to lose and the more the worker is likely to accept the employer and the work.

Where the fallback wage is low, employers can obtain the advantages of a high "cost of job loss" without paying correspondingly high wages. This is the ideal situation for the "low road" employer: minimal unit labour costs, and maximum profits, and a low wage rate (w), while using management's dominant position to achieve efficiency gains (e) and to intensify work effort (d) through techniques such as flexible work schedules and electronic monitoring.

Workers with the lowest fallback wages are typically marginal: living in locations outside the economic mainstream and belonging to marginalized labour segments, such as women, youth, and racialized groups. Call-centre executives leave no doubt that their choice of site depends on the "availability of labour" – a ready supply of clerically competent and co-operative but marginalized workers.

When the call-centre industry began to expand in North America in the early 1990s, technology rather than labour supply was management's chief concern. While some technology was generic, much of it needed customization for particular businesses. Design and development fell to fairly senior personnel in a central location with access to a matrix of support services. However, once they had standardized systems, they could spin off most call centres as free-standing operations, with very little loss of control. At this stage, call centres become "footloose." This characteristic became highly significant by the late 1990s, when better economic times and the growth of the business made the lower end of the labour market much tighter in many areas of the United States and some parts of Canada. This, in turn, triggered an intense search for new call-centre locations.

In an era of globalization, corporations have become not only increasingly adept at segmenting highly mobile bits of the production process, but much more aggressive in seeking out low-cost locations and much more willing to relocate. Recently, for example, Convergys (direct descendant of the original AT&T call centre in Jacksonville, Florida) decided not to expand in Jacksonville (Uchitelle, 2000: 7): "The pay for call center operators has risen by about $2 an hour in the last 18 months, to between $10 and $12 an hour. Turnover is also rising, and Jacksonville is losing its luster as a suitable site for low wage call centers. So Convergys opened its newest center in Brownsville, Texas. [In the words of a company executive,] 'the unemployment rate reached 14% and we were able to hire very good people. They consider our job to be a white collar job.'"

With current telecommunications technology, relocation or expansion of this type is as likely to occur abroad as between regions – with call centres becoming major employers in the north of England, India, Ireland, New Zealand, and a host of other locations, including New Brunswick.

NEW BRUNSWICK'S CALL-CENTRE INITIATIVE

Labour-intensive, fast-growing, and footloose, the call-centre industry inevitably caught the attention of governments in high-unemployment areas such as New Brunswick. The province has a long history of double-digit unemployment and low labour-force participation. Out-migration has been the traditional adjustment mechanism as surplus labour moved to other parts of Canada during boom periods, but this process normally slows or even reverses during economic downturns (Veltmeyer, 1979: 26ff). Given the lacklustre performance of the Canadian economy in the 1990s, and the corresponding erosion of jobs in New Brunswick's traditional base of forestry, mining, and fishing, the province had 40,000 officially unemployed, 20,000 part-time workers seeking full-time jobs, about 15,000 self-employed on the margins, and some 30,000 discouraged workers outside the official labour market altogether (New Brunswick Department of Economic Development and Tourism, 1999; Statistics Canada, 2000). Overall, the estimated labour surplus totalled almost 100,000 – about 25 per cent of the labour force.

Motivated by the political imperative of "job creation," Frank McKenna's Liberal government launched a campaign in the early 1990s to promote "the knowledge-based service sector, of which call centers represent a significant part" (New Brunswick/NBTel, 1999: 6). Old-style development strategies had focused on expanding male jobs in resource extraction and manufacturing; the new approach aimed at non-core segments of the labour market.

The early years saw false starts and unmet expectations, as the government groped towards a workable strategy. Initially it hoped that call centres would employ many of the 3,000, mostly female, participants in its much-heralded "New Brunswick Works" training program, designed to move welfare recipients into paid labour. But employers took advantage of other options – for example, the province's first call centre, Camco (a subsidiary of General Electric), hired only bilingual university graduates (New Brunswick Department of Economic Development and Tourism, 1996). Provincial planners initially anticipated a competitive advantage in call-centre recruitment because of the province's many bilingual workers. But new switching technology enabled customers to reach unilingual agents in separate locations ("for service in English, press 1"). Another failed possibility was for call centres to pick up the slack as manufacturing and the resource industries dumped older workers.

The government's major challenge was to interest large corporations that were developing call centres to consider New Brunswick. The premier became chief salesman, with his own toll-free line: 1–800–McKenna. The results were slow at first, but by the latter 1990s he and his colleagues had recruited a number of call centres operated by Canadian companies and by Canadian-based subsidiaries of American multinationals, including Air Canada, Camco, Canada Post, Royal Bank, and UPS. In the past four years, growth has accelerated dramatically, tripling call-centre employment. The pattern of growth has been changing too, with more recent arrivals direct from the United States, including inbound call centres operated by Speigel, Unilever, and Xerox (which simultaneously closed its Rochester location) and outbound centres operated by large, multi-site companies such as ICT and RMH. In 2001, Qualiflier, an alliance of eleven airlines led by Swissair, became the first European entry.

From its conception, New Brunswick's call-centre project has featured state sponsorship, in collaboration with the local, private-sector telephone company, NBTel. The extensive, almost organic, partnership is not new to New Brunswick, but the continuation of a long-standing corporatism in the province's resource-extraction and manufacturing sectors (dominated by companies such as Irving, McCain, and Noranda). The NBTel/government "team" provides a single point of contact for prospective call centres (referred to as "customers": NBTel promises competitively priced, up-to-date technology, and the government, a low-cost "workready workforce." In the words of one of their joint publications (New Brunswick/NBTel, 1999: 7): "The partnership works! ... Both the Province of New Brunswick and NBTel believe in a lifetime commitment to their customers – customers truly are their business ... They work hard every step of the way to ensure the success of their customers."

NBTel (now part of Aliant) was the first telephone company in Canada to construct a full fibre-optic network, and it prides itself on its innovative capacity. It currently employs over 250 people in call-centre support, offering assistance to new centres: "Design and set-up of the centre, telephone design, partnership strategies, full installation and testing of telecommunications infrastructure, real estate acquisition ... as well as recruiting and training. This 'turnkey' solution is provided at no charge!" (New Brunswick/NBTel, 1999: 7).

In addition, NBTel provides 24-hour support services and the use of telecommunications equipment with no capital outlay: "NBTel's Business Communications Service (BCS) is a unique business approach to providing telecommunications service, where call centres are charged on a per-agent, per-month basis. NBTel will purchase most telecommunications hardware and software ... This protects call centres from financial risk, since they are not required to outlay any capital to establish their telecommunications platform. NBTel maintains and upgrades the platform, which reduces the call centres' business risk" (New Brunswick/NBTel,1999: 7).

By increasing the volume of calls on its system, NBTel increases profitability, because of the industry's declining marginal costs. While it receives no direct subsidy, in 1994 the government removed the 11 per cent provincial sales tax on telephone bills for 1–800 numbers.

The government has focused direct subsidies on labour costs – the crucial budget item for most call centres. From the outset, it has offered cash incentives to businesses to locate call centres in the province. Payments normally take the form of three-year, "forgivable" loans, which the firm need not repay if it meets specified employment targets. Ostensibly, the government offers money for training, recruiting, and set-up costs, not as an operating subsidy. However, until recently it has provided assistance based on 10 per cent of the estimated overall wage bill for a call centre's first three years of operation (Hrabluk and Tutton, 1999: B1). The 10 per cent share is equal to approximately the amount of income and other taxes that it would expect to collect from the employees during this initial period. Since 1991, call centres have received close to $50 million in forgivable loans and grants – an average of about $6,000 per full-time job equivalent – and some early centres (including Camco and UPS), over $10,000 per job (Buchanan and Koch-Schulte, 2000: 93). In the 1990s only a handful of centres (including Canada Post and the Royal Bank) did not obtain forgivable loans; however, more recently, the province has scaled back this program.

The cash-for-jobs payments are subject to bilateral negotiation with each firm. In the words of a heavily involved government representative, "we bid the job."[2] The province can adjust each bid in the light of competing offers. Not surprisingly, other provinces have attacked these deals as "job poaching" and a "race to the bottom," particularly the $11 million paid to UPS – the world's largest private-sector courier – for 1,030 jobs that it relocated from British Columbia and Ontario (Buchanan and Koch-Schulte, 2000: 93). However, neither the size of the subsidies nor the use of beggar-thy-neighbour policies has yet been contentious in New Brunswick.

Call centres on the "low road," of course, consider not only initial wage costs in determining site location, but also the prospect of ongoing, low, and stable wage rates. This explains in large part their migration towards "pockets of unemployment," such as New Brunswick. Chronic high unemployment tends to lower the whole wage structure, since workers lack good alternative employment opportunities. For women, whose average wages are considerably less than men's, and for young people, whose wage rates actually fell in the 1990s (as McBride documents elsewhere in this volume), their wages are especially low in depressed regions. Moreover, these areas have low rates of labour-force participation. These low rates imply an untapped supply of labour that can be mobilized to offset any upward pressure on wages. In 1991, the participation rate for women over 25 in New Brunswick was seven percentage points below the Canadian average (49.7 per cent versus 56.7 per cent), and for youth 15 to 24, ten percentage points (58.5 per cent versus 68.0 per cent) below the national average (Statistics Canada, 2000). For call-centre operators, therefore, these economic conditions suggest the availability of many capable workers at low and stable wages.

The government developed its initiative as part of a set of neoliberal policies designed to accentuate the advantages to employers by lowering non-wage payroll expenses, increasing the available labour supply, and keeping out unions.

Non-wage payroll costs are always a concern for employers in labour-intensive industries, and government policy can influence many of these costs. In the early 1990s the government changed workers' compensation, restricting claims and reducing benefits (New Brunswick Workers Compensation Board, 1992). As a result, employer premiums fell to near the lowest in Canada, and coverage for injured workers was substantially reduced. Especially significant for the call-centre industry, the reform disallowed claims based on workplace stress except as the result of a traumatic event and severely curtailed claims based on soft-tissue injuries. As well, it created a special reduced-premium classification for call centres.

The federal government also reduced employers' payroll costs when it transformed unemployment insurance in the mid-1990s, restricting eligibility and curtailing benefits. Once again, the burden fell on workers, as program changes reduced weekly benefits and cut the maximum number of weeks of entitlement. Ottawa curtailed eligibility by increasing the hours of work required to qualify for benefits and denied benefits to anyone leaving a job "without just cause." As a result, a program that had provided benefits for 83 per cent of unemployed Canadians in the late 1980s benefited only 32 per cent by 1997 (Little, 1998: 2). The new rules were particularly onerous for people entering the workforce for the first time, for those re-entering after a significant absence, and for those working part-time hours – precisely the people most likely to have jobs in call centres.

The government based its effort to increase the labour supply, particularly of female and young workers, on a strategy of making the alternatives to paid work increasingly unattractive, rather than making paid work more attractive through better wages and labour standards. In fact, for most of the 1990s the minimum wage remained at $5.25 to $5.50 an hour, one of the lowest rates in Canada, and labour standards actually worsened. Federal and provincial cutbacks to social programs and restrictive fiscal policies produced stagnating or falling real incomes, especially for families with middle and lower-end incomes (Jackson et al., 2000: 115ff). This in turn increased the pressure on families to provide additional wage earners. In New Brunswick between 1991 and 2000, the participation rate for women over 25 rose by five percentage points (from 49.7 per cent to 54.6 per cent) compared with a two-percentage-point increase (from 56.7 per cent to 58.8 per cent) for Canada as a whole (Statistics Canada, 2000).

For students, too, the cost of non-participation in the labour force was also rising. Cuts in government operating grants for postsecondary education, higher tuition fees, and the conversion of student aid almost exclusively into student loans generated a financial crunch for many. Between the late 1980s and the mid-1990s the average loan for a graduating university student in New Brunswick doubled to about $15,000, and it has continued to rise since then (Maritime Provinces Higher Education Commission, 1998: 41). To avoid this heavy debt load, more and more students have been seeking part-time work; by the mid-1990s more than half of the province's university students were working both during the school year and in the summer (41). Call centres clearly stand to benefit: Cendant, for example, made a deal with a local university, designating certain part-time positions for students, while the university provided the workers.[3]

Most of the increase in working women and students has occurred in and around urban areas, where most call centres have located. Despite the severely depressed rural economy, which MacDonald discusses elsewhere in this volume, only a few small call centres – mainly outbound – are located in rural communities, even though the province has been offering firms about \$7,500 per job to locate there. But this pattern may change: recent innovations in switching technology allow a call centre to link with individual workstations in private homes. Virtual Agent Systems currently operates six small call centres in rural areas of the province, and the government hopes to bring more rural women into paid labour through home-based call-centre networks (*Daily Gleaner,* 2003: A3).

These policies helped maintain excess labour supply during the 1990s. While unemployment fell across the country as the economy improved late in the decade, New Brunswick's unemployment rate dropped less than the Canadian average (Statistics Canada, 2000), and stable wages prevailed. However, in 2000, call centres – through their trade association – and other low-wage employers began voicing concerns about wage pressures flowing from a perceived tightening of the labour market. Even though unemployment in 2000 still hovered around 10 per cent, an anxious government moved quickly to slow expansion of the industry by reducing cash incentives and through administrative measures (Richardson, 2000: A1; Stewart, 2000: A1). Thus management of labour demand, as well as of supply, became part of the government's low-wage employment strategy.

The government's strategy also confronted unions as a way to provide employers with a weak and divided workforce. It set the tone in 1991 when it provoked a bitter confrontation with its own public-sector workers by breaking signed collective agreements to impose a wage freeze. Later in the decade, it sat by idly as three large private-sector strikes and lockouts dragged on for years. It used this anti-union environment as a selling point in its call-centre initiative. Its 1996 web site (New Brunswick Department of Economic Development and Tourism, 1996) was surprisingly candid:

- The telecommunications industry in New Brunswick has the lowest rate of unionization in Canada.
- Some call centres that were unionized elsewhere have consolidated as non-union operations in New Brunswick.
- NBTel is Canada's only telephone company with non-unionized clerical staff.

Air Canada has New Brunswick's only unionized private-sector call centre, organized before it moved to the province.[4] There have been several unionization efforts, including a bitter – and unsuccessful – fight in 1997 at UPS in Fredericton. In 1999, workers successfully unionized the

Saint John site of ICT Group, a large, U.S.-based call-centre business with over 30 locations; however, the company soon closed the operation. The government took no action to protect the workers' rights or their jobs, despite the funds that it had given to the company (Malik and Tutton, 1999: A1). "You unionize, your job is gone," said Cindy Caissie, a 24-year-old telemarketer who had been at the centre for two years. "That's the message here."

JOBS ON THE LINE

The general weakness of New Brunswick's labour market, reinforced by government policies, has produced the kind of "availability of labour" that enables employers to pick and choose their workers. The first wave of call centres had 10 to 20 applicants for each job opening (McFarland, 1996: 12), although the recent rapid expansion has considerably tightened the market. Our own studies of the industry,[5] including surveys and interviews with both workers and managers over several years, indicate that most call-centre workers in the province are under 30, with the average age declining as the industry expands. Most employees are female, although managers tend to be male. Two out of three workers have at least some post-secondary education, and a growing number, a college or university degree. This is the "workready workforce" that the government promotes and that employers pursue. For example, a representative of Hospitality Franchise Systems, an American hotel-reservation service that set up in the province, told us (quoted in McFarland, 1996: 12): "We had new employees that set records for every training class ... They grasped the information we were trying to communicate better than any of the classes that we had ever put through, in any of our programs, in any centre." And a manager at UPS commented on the "innate customer service skills and positive attitudes of the local labour force" (quoted in New Brunswick/NBTel, 1999: 8).

For recruitment and retention, call centres typically pay well above minimum wage. Actual pay rates[6] in the industry are subject to much confusion, since individual companies, and the trade association, frequently publicize inflated figures for public-relations purposes. Our own data from employees and employers suggest that top-end call centres pay about $15 per hour (slightly above the average service-sector wage in New Brunswick). The majority, including most of the large inbound call centres, pay in the range of $9 to $12 per hour. An estimate by private consultants in 1999, for example, set an average weekly wage of $366 a week – about $10 per hour – for a new financial-services call centre in New Brunswick (Boyd Company, 1999). Call centres at the low end – often outbound – pay $7 to $9 per hour, usually with some sort of incentive bonus for above-quota performance. They offer fringe benefits, including supplementary health and pension plans, but typically only for "full-time" employees – a policy that excludes most workers in most centres. In fact, it is common to designate employees as part time even if they work essentially full-time hours, in order to avoid paying fringe benefits and to maintain scheduling flexibility.

Part-time hours and irregular shifts are two of the major workplace problem areas identified by employees. For example, in two of the largest centres – one with 700 workers and the other with 550 – the only full timers are managers – everyone else is "part time." Shift work affects the quality of jobs, as a recent Nova Scotia study shows (Fenety, Putnam, and Loppie, 1999: 221): "Although a number of women worked fixed daytime, evening or night shifts, the majority of participants' hours were based on a variable and rotating weekly schedule that entailed a variety of start times as well as weekend hours ... The majority of workers reported little control of their weekly schedule, days off, or holiday shifts ... For some, work schedules often interfered with other job obligations and family responsibilities."

Part-time shift workers depend completely on management to "get a good schedule" to avoid disruption of non-work life and to "get enough hours" for an adequate income. In Saskatchewan, as Broad, MacNeil, and Gamble recount elsewhere in this volume, these same concerns led the NDP government to try to improve labour standards for contingent workers, in the face of employers' intense opposition. However, New Brunswick promotes vulnerable workers as a selling point with employers, not as an issue for the legislative agenda.

Call-centre work typically takes place in large, open areas (located in shopping malls, warehouses, and office buildings) arranged into rows of cubicles, each about a metre wide, containing a computer terminal, keyboard, telephone and tape recorder. While the pace seems to energize a few employees, most find the work "boring," "monotonous," and "mundane" – predictable responses on a Taylorized assembly line, where workers control neither the content nor the pace. They usually describe the workload as "heavy" and "stressful"; "they expect too much." One noted with an air of resignation: "260 calls a day from rude and angry people ... it's hard to deal with at times." Several centres have stress rooms where workers can go to "cool down" after an especially stressful call.

Adding to the stress is regimentation of work. From the time employees enter the workplace and the front door locks behind them, they are under close supervision and tight control. The normal management structure includes an overall supervisor, or shift manager, and "team leaders" (paid the same as workers on the line), who micro-manage small groups of workers – motivating individual TSRs, and troubleshooting. A gender division is evident within management: most supervisors are male, and most team leaders, female. Management activities revolve around electronic surveillance and monitoring. Performance indicators are pervasive, with team scores sometimes posted on electronic screens in the workroom for all to see. Supervisors can, and do, listen in on calls at any time – heightening the sense of perpetual surveillance.

The modern call centre is an electronic Panopticon beyond even Jeremy Bentham's fertile imagination. The original Panopticon was an architectural design for a prison – although Bentham thought that it also had industrial applications – in which the inmates could be observed at any time but could not see their overseers. Zuboff writes (1988: 319–21): "Struggling to establish their legitimate authority, employers invented techniques to control the labouring body. The French historian Michel Foucault has argued that these new techniques of industrial management laid the groundwork for a new kind of society, a 'disciplinary society,' one in which bodily discipline, regulation, and surveillance are taken for granted ... The Panopticon represents a form of power that displays itself automatically and continuously ... The psychological effects of visibility alone are enough to ensure appropriate conduct."

Employers have reason to believe that workers are most likely to accept this "discipline, regulation, and surveillance" in places such as New Brunswick, where employment options are few and the "cost of job loss" is relatively high. The province's promotional materials note that "New Brunswick's turnover rate of 5 percent per annum is 70 percent lower than the North American average" (New Brunswick/NBTel, 1999: 2). Call-centre employees are quite aware of the situation; in the words of one worker: "The company feels that New Brunswick is a cheaper place in wages and benefits. They see New Brunswick as desperate, whose workers will settle for anything as long as it is a job" (McFarland, 1996: 15).

Managers can confidently deal with any resistance by workers on an individual basis, so that their systems of control are effectively beyond challenge. As another worker told us: "The potential is there to abuse people, when people don't know their rights or their recourse – and are afraid to talk to each other" (McFarland, 1999: 15).

Typically, workers interact little, and many managers warn employees not to discuss their work off the premises ("gag orders"). Consistent with our own findings, the Nova Scotia study (Fenety, Putnam, and Loppie, 1999: 220) found: "Either (workers) couldn't voice their opinions, their suggestions were not taken seriously, or they were simply not addressed. In some cases, workers believed that if they voiced their opinion, it could result in negative repercussions ranging from humiliation to job loss ... Several workers reported call centre managements' use of fear, punishment, verbal abuse (e.g. yelling) and unnecessary restrictions (e.g. not being able to have a sweater on the back of a chair) to motivate and/or control staff."

In our interviews, workers described sanctions ranging from verbal and written reprimands, through the assignment of undesirable shifts and demands for unpaid hours of work "to meet quota," to outright dismissal.

Because of their dominant position, employers are able to organize the labour process as they see fit. Faced with this reality, workers have few choices. Internal promotions are rare; most of those people who talk about "getting ahead" think of switching to another call centre, in the hope of better wages and working conditions. Few expect a career in call centres. Most of interviewees treat the work as "just a job" that they are willing to do "for a while longer" – ranging typically from "a few months" to two or three years. Deciding when to quit is one of the only workplace decisions that a call-centre worker directly controls. Paradoxically, the idea that they can quit allows many of them to "put up with the job." Nevertheless, many do leave, and many former call-centre workers say that they are "never going back." A high quit rate may well force employers to adjust their practices, but, as long as the participation rates of women and young people continue to increase, replacements will be easy to find and present work arrangements easy to maintain.

However, in the longer term, the status quo is unlikely to continue, despite the current powerful alliance of corporate interests and neoliberal government policies, which together have created a seemingly insurmountable position for capital. The ongoing transformation of communications technology, the continued upsurge in demand for 1–800 services, the emergence of a tighter low-wage labour market, and the potential for government policy alternatives all foreshadow a rather different future for the industry.

NOTES

1 List of call centres with the number of jobs in each supplied by Valerie Adams of the New Brunswick Department of Economic Development and Tourism; total provided by Norm Betts, minister of business, New Brunswick, CBC Radio New Brunswick interview, 14 March 2003.
2 Interview with Brian Freeman, New Brunswick Department of Economic Development and Tourism, 16 May, 1997.
3 St Thomas University memo dated 16 March, 2000.
4 The administrative office of Purolator Courier in Moncton was organized by the Teamsters and certified in March 1995. However, attempts to organise Purolator's call centre in Moncton have failed.

5 Because Statistics Canada does not consider call centres a separate industry, but rather a component of many industries, comprehensive data are not available.
6 Our empirical data come from studies conducted by and/or under the supervision of Joan McFarland in the period 1994–2001:

- interviews and surveys of call centres and call-centre workers in Moncton in the summer of 1995; research assistant Cathy Goodfellow
- in Saint John in the summer of 1996; research assistant Andrew Rioux
- in New Brunswick in the summer of 1996; co-researcher Ruth Buchanan
- survey and interviews of selected call centres in New Brunswick and a survey of workers in a specific call centre in academic year 1999–2000; Katie Durling, an honours-economics student researcher at St Thomas University

Some of the data have been presented and analysed previously in different contexts in McFarland, 1996, and Buchanan and McFarland, 1997.

REFERENCES

Bowles, S., and R. Edwards. 1993. *Understanding Capitalism*, 2nd ed. New York: Harper and Row.
Boyd Company Inc. 1999. *A Comparative Cost Analysis for Financial Services Call Center Operations*. Princeton, NJ.
Buchanan, R., and S. Koch-Schulte. 2000. *Gender on the Line: Technology, Restructuring and the Reorganization of Work in the Call Centre Industry*. Ottawa: Status of Women Canada.
Buchanan, R., and J. McFarland. 1997. "The Political Economy of New Brunswick's Call Centre Industry: Old Wine in New Bottles?" *Socialist Studies Bulletin* 50, 17–40.
Canada and New Brunswick Department of Economic Development and Tourism. 1996. *Advantage New Brunswick Canada*. Fredericton: Harley-Mallory Strategic Communications.
Delottinville, P. 1994. *Shifting to the New Economy: Call Centres and Beyond*. Toronto: Copp Clark Longman.
Fenety A., C. Putnam, and C. Loppie. 1999. "Self-Reported Health Determinants in Female Call Centre Tele-operators: A Quantitive Analysis," in G.C.H. Lee, ed., *Advances in Ergonomics and Safety*. Amsterdam: IOS Press.
Fox, B., and P. Sugiman. 1999. "Flexible Work, Flexible Workers: The Restructuring of Clerical Work in a Large Telecommunications Company," *Studies in Political Economy* 60 (autumn), 59–84.
Gordon, D.M. 1996. *Fat and Mean*. New York: Martin Kessler Books.
Hrabluk, L., and M. Tutton. 1999. "Ten Years Into the Call Centre Era, Critics Are Questioning the Payback." *New Brunswick Telegraph Journal*. Saint John. 20 March.

Jackson, A., and D. Robinson, with B. Baldwin and C. Wiggins. 2000. *Falling Behind: The State of Working Canada, 2000.* Ottawa: Canadian Centre for Policy Alternatives.

Landler, M. 2001. "Hi, I'm in Bangalore (But I Dare Not Tell)," *New York Times,* New York, 21 March.

Larner, W. 2000. "Governing Globalization: The New Zealand Call Centre Attraction Initiative." Manuscript.

Little, B. 1998. "Why So Many Jobless Don't Get UI." *Globe and Mail,* Toronto, 26 Oct.

Llewellyn, S. 2000. "CIBC Job Fair Attracts Hundreds." *Daily Gleaner,* Fredericton, 15 Sept.

Malik, K., and M. Tutton. 1999. "Call Centre Closure Plans Anger Saint John Workers." *New Brunswick Telegraph Journal,* Saint John, 13 Nov.

Maritime Provinces Higher Education Commission. 1998. *Survey of 1996 University Graduates.* Fredericton: Baseline Market Research.

McFarland, J. 1996. "Many Are Called, But What Are the Choices?" *New Maritimes.* 14 (6), 10–19.

McLaughlin, H. 2001. "CIBC to get $1m more." *Daily Gleaner,* Fredericton, 8 May.

Messing, K. 1998. *One Eyed Science: Occupational Health and Women's Work.* Philadelphia: Temple University Press.

New Brunswick Department of Economic Development and Tourism. 1996. www.cybersmith.newbrunswick

– 1999. gnb.ca/nb/first/

New Brunswick/NBTel. 1999. *From Start to State of the Art.* Saint John: New Brunswick Call Center Team.

New Brunswick Workers' Compensation Board. 1992. 74th Annual Report. Fredericton.

Palley, T.I. 1998. *Plenty of Nothing.* Princeton, NJ: Princeton University Press.

Richardson, D. 2000. "Call Centre Flip-Flop." *Daily Gleaner,* Fredericton, 3 Nov.

Ross, D.P., E.R. Shillington and C. Lochhead. 1994. *The Canadian Fact Book on Poverty.* Ottawa: Canadian Council on Social Development.

Stanford, J. 1996. "Discipline, Insecurity and Productivity: The Economics Behind Labour Market 'Flexibility,'" in Jane Pullingham and Gordon Ternowetsky, eds., *Remaking Canadian Social Policy: Social Security in the Late 1990s.* Halifax: Fernwood.

– 1999. "Paper Boom." Ottawa: Canadian Centre for Policy Alternatives and James Lorimer and Company.

Statistics Canada. 71–001–XPB, various issues. *The Labour Force.* Ottawa.

– 71–201–XPB, 2000. *Historical Labour Force Statistics.* Ottawa.

Stewart, L. 2000. "Tough Time Keeping Staff." *Daily Gleaner,* Fredericton, 4 Nov.

Daily Gleaner. 2003. "N.B. Backs Call Centre: Firm to get $625,000 in Aid," Fredericton, 28 Feb.

Turner, C. 2001. "High 5: Postcards from Canada's New Tech Boomtowns," *Report on Business Magazine,* April, 75–86.

Uchitelle, L. 2000. "A New Corporate Wanderlust Puts a Quiet Brake on Salaries." *New York Times on the Web*, 24 July.

Veltmeyer, H. 1979. "The Capitalist Underdevelopment of Atlantic Canada," in R.J. Brym and J.R. Sacouman, eds., *Underdevelopment and Social Movements in Atlantic Canada*. Toronto: New Hogtown Press.

Walker, R. 1989. "Machinery, Labour and Location," in S. Wood, ed., *The Transformation of Work?* London: Unwin Hyman Ltd.

Zuboff, S. 1988. *In the Age of the Smart Machine: The Future of Work and Power*. Oxford: Heinemann.

13

Neoliberalism, Social Democracy, and the Struggle to Improve Labour Standards for Part-time Workers in Saskatchewan

DAVE BROAD, DELLA MacNEIL,
and SANDRA SALHANI GAMBLE

Western working classes have waged a long struggle to improve working conditions and social welfare through labour market regulation.[1] In the nineteenth century workers and social reformers in Western countries fought for legislation prohibiting child labour, producing such victories as the Factory Acts in the United Kingdom. There were struggles for 12-, 10-, and 8-hour workdays. In the 1930s labour in Europe and North America even campaigned for a 30-hour workweek. This never came to pass, but by the 1960s and early 1970s sociologists and others devoted considerable attention to the shifting balance between work and leisure. For example, the Canadian Television (CTV) network broadcast a weekly program entitled "Here Come the Seventies," which described the pursuit of new ways to fill leisure time as the main challenge of the future.

Then came the 1980s, and the trend to increasing leisure became a thing of the past. The global crisis of capital accumulation, which began in the late 1960s, led business and governments to focus more on increased productivity and economic growth, even though new technologies had phenomenally increased output per worker (Schenk and Anderson, 1995). Too many workers have little leisure time because they find themselves pushed to work more overtime hours (Schor, 1992; White, 1999). Meanwhile, another group has more "leisure time" than ever – but many of these people have few resources with which to enjoy their leisure, because they are unemployed or underemployed. More than one in five people in Western countries works at a low-wage part-time job – many

The Differential Effects of Labour Market Deregulation

because of a lack of full-time employment, and some because of the absence of child care and other supports (Duffy, Mandell, and Pupo, 1989; O'Reilly and Fagan, 1998).

This chapter first looks at neoliberal deregulation of the labour market. It then considers the structural changes that have given rise to the "contingent economy," based on part-time and other forms of casual labour, and examines proposals for legislation that might improve the working and living conditions of these casual labourers.

Within this broader context, we next analyse the politics and reactions surrounding attempts in 1993–94 to revise the Saskatchewan Labour Standards Act and Regulations to enhance workers' rights and benefits, for part-time workers in particular. The result was one of the most advanced pieces of labour standards legislation in North America, but the government's failure to proclaim some key provisions (its concession to a very hostile business lobby) drastically watered down the initiative's real-world effectiveness.

Next – and similar to the situation in South Africa discussed by Clarke elsewhere in this volume – part-timers interviewed for our study speak favourably of the legislative changes in Saskatchewan, but are very disappointed with their enforcement. Their stories and recommendations reveal much still to do to improve the lot of part-timers.

The conclusion offers some recommendations for improving the working and social-welfare conditions of part- and full-time workers in the contingent economy.

NEOLIBERAL DEREGULATION

One of the central concerns of our study is whether labour standards legislation can benefit part-time workers in a context of "neoliberal"[2] globalization. There is, of course, great debate over state capacity in the face of globalization (Burke, Moores, and Shields, 2000; Midgley, 2000). Some analysts forget that states have actively promoted neoliberal globalization, usually while repeating Margaret Thatcher's claim that "there is no alternative" (TINA). Perhaps the biggest struggle for those interested in improving working conditions and social welfare is to challenge the notion of TINA; there are always alternatives. But what is most frustrating for the labour leaders whom we interviewed is that governments seem to be following the most reactionary rather than the more progressive businesses in setting social policy. It is an anti-labour model of globalization that · appears to inform deregulation of labour markets, as we see in the discussion below of Saskatchewan's backtracking.

McBride (2000) argues that Canada has recently experienced two phases of labour market policy in response to globalization. From the early

1980s to the early 1990s there was some attempt by government to implement a corporatist "progressive competitiveness" strategy, promoting economic growth through active policies of labour market preparation and training (for example, through the Canadian Labour Force Development Board). But after the early 1990s governments shifted more aggressively to neoliberal deregulation, incorporating only residual notions of social welfare. This approach sees government's economic intervention and income support programs as impeding the "free" workings of the capitalist market (Albo, 1997). The shift that McBride describes helps account for Saskatchewan's promises to workers in the early 1990s and its backtracking and deregulation strategies after 1994.

Albo (1997) discusses how social-democratic governments have promoted "shaped advantage" at the regional or national level through three competing but complementary strategies – "progressive competitiveness," "shared austerity," and "international Keynesianism." The first, "most closely allied to the views of shaped advantage, emphasizes the demand-side *external* constraint produced by internationalization" (16). Employment policy should emphasize productive capacity and productivity growth. Closer to the low-wage strategy of neoliberalism is the second, "shared austerity," which "stresses that the *internal* constraint of distribution relations is critical" (17). It advocates incomes policy to spread work through wage restraint. The third, "international Keynesianism," suggests exercising the *political will* to relax the demand constraint on output by re-establishing expansionary policies at the global level.

Albo critiques each of these strategies, showing how governments trying them tend to run up against the "capitalist reformers dilemma" of having to bow to market-led processes and concurrently succumbing to capital's push for more "flexible" labour markets. He refers to the experience in Sweden; "although developing the foremost social market and raising its relative competitive position, Sweden has had an 'employer offensive' for over a decade to lower real wages, cut taxes and allow unemployment to rise" (13).

Social policy in Saskatchewan following the re-election of the New Democratic Party (NDP) in 1991 reflects Albo's three strategies. Many scholars have argued that Saskatchewan's economic policy is not typical of Canada, because of its heritage of social democracy. Despite differences between NDP policies in Saskatchewan and policies in Conservative Alberta, however, Saskatchewan may be simply "a kinder road to hell," as Wiseman (1996) describes Australian social democracy.

Saskatchewan perhaps continued with its strategy of progressive competitiveness somewhat after the national shift to neoliberalism. Its government has certainly paid more attention to labour-force development and to welfare programs such as low-income supplements and child benefits.

Crown corporations have also promoted technological development and overseas investment. And despite more progressive labour market policy, the government has nevertheless responded to neoliberal globalization with the more Anglo–American approach – "adopt a strategy of devaluing labour and (promoting economic) informalization" (Albo, 1997: 23). The situation is comparable to that in Ontario under the former NDP government of Bob Rae, which attempted to improve labour and social policy and faced a threatened capital strike. Consequently, Rae sought the middle ground, perhaps confirming former Liberal Prime Minister Louis St Laurent's contention that social democrats are simply "liberals in a hurry" (Teeple, 1972).

Recent attempts by social-democratic governments to develop market-based alternatives to neoliberal globalization reveal, among other things, the danger of relying on government initiatives to ensure labour standards. Tabb (1999: 6) reminds us that "we cannot expect the needs of working people to be uppermost in the minds of governments that serve capital, and will continue to permit and encourage systematic violation of worker rights in the name of competitiveness." "Progressive globalism" should emphasize "labour rights" rather than labour standards. "Labor *rights* are about the responsibilities of employers and governments to respect workers and their organizations, and above all, about the power of the working class to organize itself" (4). Tabb continues: "It is also important that the working class has the power to redefine the rules governing the relations between capital and labor. Labor standards are granted. Labor rights are won." (4) Tabb agrees that the struggle for labour standards can help limit capital and raise consciousness, but, he emphasizes, the ultimate struggle must be for working-class power.

Given Saskatchewan's experience, where most part-time workers are not unionized, we might conclude that labour standards will be granted only when labour rights are fought for and won. Perhaps trade unions in Saskatchewan relied too much on the good will of government and must now reassert the struggle for labour rights in the face of a capitalist globalization that has insisted on neoliberal social policy (cf. Teeple, 2000). We resume this discussion below, after looking at the "contingent economy" and presenting our findings from Saskatchewan.

THE CONTINGENT ECONOMY
AND LABOUR STANDARDS LEGISLATION

Since the 1970s, labour market scholars have noted a steady growth of "contingent" or "non-standard" labour, which includes part-time, temporary, and contract work and self-employment. Some refer to these forms of work as "precarious employment," because they generally lack job security or benefits. Historically, this sort of work has been called "casual labour" (Jones, 1984). The contemporary growth of the casual labour force derives from a restructuring of the international division of labour, which, as we noted, neoliberal free-market policies are aiding and abetting. Transnational corporations have tried to cut costs by "downsizing" – laying off workers. This is one part of the shift towards flexible production. The flexible labour market shifts more and more components of production from the individual firm to a series of suppliers. This is occurring in the production of both goods and services. In the drive to lower overhead costs, many companies, especially large ones, are now contracting out much of the work previously done "in-house" (Broad, 2000).

The basis for these changes is a "new international division of labour" (NIDL), which came to the fore about 1970 (Frobel, Heinrichs, and Kreye, 1980). The classical international division of labour inherited from European colonial expansion and the Industrial Revolution relegated peripheral areas to producing primary products, with the imperial centres monopolizing manufacturing. But this old arrangement began to change in the 1960s as capital sought to increase profits, undercut organized labour in more developed countries, and escape social and environmental regulation by government. Advances in production, shipping, and transportation made the NIDL possible. New technologies in production, such as computers and robotics, allowed the breaking up of production processes to facilitate manufacture of components for commodities (such as automobiles) at dispersed sites. Improvements in shipping, such as containerization and airfreight, made possible easy and cheap transport of commodities throughout the world. And advances in communications meant that large corporations could manage dispersed operations from a head office anywhere (Sassen, 1991).

These changes increased the global reserve army of labour. One author says that capital has emancipated itself from labour (Sivanandan, 1997). While we might debate this conclusion, workers in the old industrial countries now compete more directly against those in industrializing countries such as Mexico and South Korea. And capital often uses simply the *threat* to relocate production to exact concessions from workers and governments in the centre. Labour thus has to be "flexible" regarding pay, benefits, and hours of work. So capital uses involuntary overtime and casualization of labour to assert control over labour markets and processes.[3]

Casual work has been the fastest-growing form of employment across Canada in recent years. A decade ago the Economic Council of Canada (ECC, 1990, 1991) estimated that two in five Canadian workers were non-standard workers, and data from Statistics Canada (2003) indicate that 20 per cent of Canadian jobs are part time. Various authors have documented the increase and impact of the growth of other forms of casual labour (for example, Duffy, Glenday, and Pupo, 1997; Peck, 1996; Schellenberg and Clark, 1996; Shalla, 2003; Vosko, 2000). And a federal body (Advisory Group on Working Time, 1994) corroborates the Economic Council's conclusion that most workers face further deskilling and declining standards of living.[4]

Part-time workers tend to earn less than full-timers and have fewer benefits and less job security (Broad, 2000; Duffy and Pupo, 1992; International Labour Organization, 1997; Schellenberg, 1997). Many part-timers have on-call relationships with their employers, and, given their low wages and few benefits, more and more of them hold several jobs. Over the last 20 years the number of multiple jobholders in Canada has more than tripled (Sussman, 1998). One in ten employed Canadians holds two or more jobs at some time during the year (Marshall, 2002). Saskatchewan's rate is almost twice the national rate for employed workers, and about 30 per cent of part-timers are multiple jobholders (Elliot, 2000: 24). Three-quarters of part-timers are women. Some observers blame part-timers' lower pay and lack of benefits on the fact that fewer part-timers than full-timers are union members. In 2001, 23 per cent of part-timers were unionized, compared to 32 per cent of full-timers (Akyeampong, 2001, 2002). Clearly, part-timers have less control over their working lives, are continuously trying to balance paid work and family responsibilities, and worry constantly about their economic security. The resulting emotional and physical stress takes its toll on individual and family well-being.

A major problem for workers, of course, is how to counter the resulting degradation of their working and welfare conditions. Trade unionists are concerned that the growth of contingent labour both runs counter to their historical struggles for full and better employment and contributes to the current social and labour market polarization in Canada – to the particular disadvantage of women and youths.[5]

Some social-democratic labour economists argue for a "share economy" as a more humane way to increase human-resource flexibility. The share economy "is represented by long-term employer–employee relationships that can be adjusted based on norms, standards or various formulas. Some of the key institutions of the share economy include profit sharing, gain sharing, performance bargaining, leaner job ladders, retraining, and redeployment" (Belous, 1989: xi). Belous describes this as the "new deal model" of human-resource management. This model emphasizes partnerships between labour, business, and government and long-term economic planning. It sounds positive, but, given the problems with progressive competitiveness and Saskatchewan's experience, we need to be wary.

According to labour and women's groups, flexible work schemes have too often helped advantage the employer and harmed the employee – it is the worker who must be flexible. However, some flexible arrangements are more "worker-friendly." "Flex-time" arrangements allow a better balance of work and family responsibilities. Some types of "job-sharing" permit two employees working part time to share one full-time job. Especially in Europe, advances in "work-sharing," through reduced hours for full-time workers, help incorporate the unemployed and underemployed into the active labour force (see the chapters by Auer and Jefferys in this volume, as well as Hayden, 1999; International Labour Organization, 1999). This option has been advocated for Canada as well (Advisory Group, 1994; O'Hara, 1993) but is not far advanced.

Part-time work in particular may facilitate phased retirement of older workers or phasing in of younger or disadvantaged workers by giving them workplace experience. And in Sweden, for example, workers may work part time while they have young children, without losing seniority or benefits (Sundstrom, 1987, 1992). But this example illustrates the crux of the problem: part-time work is most attractive and beneficial to employees if they are guaranteed their rights and benefits, at least pro-rated, in terms of hours worked and seniority.

As to improving conditions for part-timers, labour activists see two obvious possibilities. The first is to expand collective bargaining to incorporate part-timers, many of whom remain unorganized. The second is to improve labour legislation to give part-timers broader rights and benefits. Such reforms would raise the minimum standards in the labour market overall. Many contingent and women workers fall outside the provisions of labour standards. Fudge (1991: 16) argues: "Existing labour standards legislation have failed to protect workers from employers' attempts to exploit flexible labour." The length of employment with a particular employer often helps determine entitlement to benefits. This system, Fudge says, encourages employers to use labour flexibly through on-call labour (the employment counterpart to just-in-time inventory), temporary and part-time work, contracting out, and lay-offs. Yet employers take on few burdens for the social costs of this model (21).

Fudge (1991, 1996, 2001) explains how labour standards could apply to various sorts of leaves, hours of work, employment income, job security, and promotion of labour market equity. Moreover, the majority of non-unionized workers would benefit from higher minimum standards, which would create a sort of "level playing field" for all employees. Of course, many employers would object to such strengthening of legislation, as happened in Saskatchewan (Broad and Foster, 1995). Workers need to struggle for labour rights, not just for labour standards. We return to this discussion below.

REFORMING LABOUR STANDARDS
IN SASKATCHEWAN, 1993–94

Saskatchewan's trade unionists have been struggling for years for reforms to the provincial Labour Standards Act. After a lengthy process of public consultation, which pitted the trade union movement and progressive social activists against a determined business lobby, on 2 June, 1994 the legislature passed Bill 32, the Labour Standards Amendment Act, 1994. This bill would give more protection to contingent workers, though less than the labour movement would have liked. But the government stated that it wanted to consult before enacting the new provisions through regulations (see below).

Bill 32 raises minimum labour standards to give part-time workers better conditions of work and more control over their working and family lives. One provision stipulates a one-week notice of work schedules to employees. It ends "on-call" working arrangements, which leave employees waiting by the phone for a call to work. A second provision grants an unpaid meal break of at least 30 minutes within every six or more consecutive hours of work. A third provision, "Additional hours of work," reads as follows: "(1) Where required to do so by the regulations, an employer shall offer to part-time employees in accordance with their length of service and qualifications any additional hours of work that become available, except in the case of emergency circumstances within the meaning of subsection 12(4). (2) No employer shall take disciplinary action against an employee who refuses to work or to be at the disposal of the employer for the additional hours of work offered in accordance with this section of the regulations." This provision would prevent employers from replacing full-time workers with lower-waged part-timers who lack benefits and job security.

Unions have long argued for more worker control over availability of hours. Allowing workers with seniority to take the most available hours, up to a full-time shift, makes it harder for employers to use part-time work as a way to prevent or undermine unionization, wages, and benefits. At the same time, individuals obtain more control over their hours of work, so that they can work full time or remain part time. This is especially important to women who are balancing paid work and child care. Other provisions in Bill 32 deal with pro-rating of benefits for part-timers, statutory holidays, and notice of termination.

A business lobby, led by the regional office of the Canadian Federation of Independent Business and some members of the Saskatchewan Chamber of Commerce, mounted an aggressive campaign to gut the most progressive elements of the bill. The lobby succeeded in having important details removed. The government decided to enact the provisions through regulations, not through legislation, meaning that cabinet would decide their extent and content. Labour leaders told us that they would have felt more secure if a formula for accepting additional hours or for pro-rating benefits were in the act itself, not just in the regulations.

To translate the amended Labour Standards Act into a set of regulations, the government sought recommendations from business and labour. It established a joint business–labour commission and 14 sectoral committees to undertake consultations on implementing the act's new provisions. Differences were obvious in the deliberations of the joint commission and in its inability to agree on most available hours and pro-rating of benefits for part-timers. For example, it recommended: "Where full-time employees in a job category receive benefits, part-time employees in the same job category shall receive like benefits to the minimum as outlined in the above scope of benefits" (Joint Commission on Part-time Work, 1994: 52). The commission further recommended that part-timers, to qualify, must have worked at least six months for the employer, except where existing plans provide for earlier access; at least 780 hours in the previous fiscal year to maintain eligibility; and at least 15 hours per week. Ostensibly, meeting these conditions shows an employee's commitment to the workplace. But, as labour leaders ask, what is to stop employers from lowering part-timers' weekly hours to less than 15, or laying them off before they reach the 780-hour annual minimum, just to avoid benefit costs, and then rehiring them? As well, the joint commission agreed to exclude from benefits employees entitled to benefits under treaty rights and full-time students. It assumed that Treaty Indians have all the benefits that they need and that students are working only for cash and have no long-term attachment to their job. The commission noted that its recommendations on benefits would cover only seven per cent of part-time employees in the province (69).

Cabinet passed the new labour standards regulations effective 3 February, 1995. And officials with the Saskatchewan Federation of Labour (SFL) found them very disappointing – being watered down even more than expected. Provisions for posting work schedules a week in advance were maintained, and part-timers gained rights to pro-rated dental, group-life, accidental-death and -dismemberment insurance and to prescription-drug plans. But this applies only if such benefits are already available; if a firm's total of employee hours reaches the equivalent of 10 full-timers working 40 hours per week; if part-timers work 390 hours in the first six months of employment to become eligible; and if they work 15 or more hours per week and maintain employment of at least 780 hours per year, based on an annual review – otherwise they are not eligible for benefits until the next yearly review. And full-time students are not eligible for benefits. Employers were to extend the new benefits provision to workers by August 1995, with collective agreements revised to reflect the new regulations by February 1996.

The important "most available hours" provision of the act remained unproclaimed. In reference to Bill 32, the commission commented: "The Government of Saskatchewan has introduced part-time work provisions respecting the distribution of additional hours and the provision of benefits which are ground breaking" (Joint Commission, 1994: 71). But the business lobby's opposition grounded the provision.

According to the SFL's "Labour Column," Roy Romanow's NDP government "made it a habit to introduce good, progressive changes to our labour laws, then spend the next several weeks backing away from the changes and ultimately watering them down." SFL officials argue that this is what occurred with Bill 32, Bill 54 (amending the provincial Trade Union Act), and amendments to other labour acts. The SFL complained that "the government did not stick with the original language in the Bills. Instead, government officials and cabinet ministers decided there was some political mileage in being seen responding to the objections of a small, but loud group of employers who opposed the legislation."

In discussions with us, some SFL officials accused the government of duplicity. They say that the government went so far as to *encourage* business opposition to the labour bills. In the close to 300 non-labour bills that went through the legislature after Romanow's NDP replaced the Conservatives in 1991, revisions were few and minor. But with the six labour bills introduced after 1991, five had substantial revisions made during second reading to satisfy business lobbyists. Labour saw the joint business–labour commission, and 14 sectoral committees of 1994 as yet another way for business to express its opposition. Gary Whelan, a leader of the Hotel Employees and Restaurant Employees Union (HERE) who sat on one of the sectoral committees, thought it all a "waste of time and money," although "if something had come of it, it would have been okay."

According to Barb Byers, former president of the SFL, the labour movement worries that, without good labour standards legislation, employers will continue to use part-time work to keep unions out and workers unorganized. But both Byers and Chris Banting, Saskatchewan secretary-treasurer of the Retail, Wholesale, and Department Store Union (RWDSU), many of whose members are part-timers, stress that the movement wants to better conditions for all workers, not just for unionized full-time workers. This is why labour pushed so hard for the labour standards amendments. Labour leaders such as Byers and Banting do not oppose part-time work as such, because they know that many people depend on part-time jobs. They are also aware that part-time jobs are unlikely to be replaced by full-time ones overnight, so labour must work to improve conditions for part-timers.

The 1994 amendments promised people such as those whom we interviewed a little more control over their lives. Glenn Stewart of the United Food and Commercial Workers Union says: "What needs to be done is to educate people about minimum standards. There should be more discussion about raising the minimum wage and putting more money in the worker's pocket. Having more money means you're going to spend more, and that helps the economy. But the corporate agenda is lower wages, higher profits. We need to focus on creating well-paid employment rather than cutting good jobs and replacing them with part-time work."

Ironically, the debate over part-time work recalls the historical struggle over minimum wage. Many businesses opposed the creation of a minimum wage in the nineteenth century, while some argued in favour, on the grounds that it would create some stability in the marketplace. Similarly, members of the Saskatchewan Chamber of Commerce split over the labour revisions of 1994, with some supporting them. In fact, given the cost analysis done by the Department of Labour, business's opposition seems exaggerated. Both the costs of providing benefits and those of allowing for advance scheduling and additional hours are minimal. An official with the Saskatchewan Department of Labour, who was privy to the hearings and consultations of the 1994 review, suggested to us that business opposition was really about control more than cost.

As we saw above, the emergence of the contingent economy is part of a corporate drive to regain control over labour markets and production processes to increase profits. This all comes under the heading of restructuring to improve corporations' global competitiveness, which neoliberal policies often facilitate. Saskatchewan's legislation, in contrast, gives workers more control over their lives; it does not fit the neoliberal trend. This sparked a powerful, though not unanimous, backlash from employers. The government, apparently not wanting to upset business or to subvert the dominant paradigm, left the most important parts of Bill 32 unproclaimed.

Why would an ostensibly pro-labour NDP government introduce progressive labour legislation and then backtrack? Prior to its election in 1991, the NDP had promised its labour supporters reforms. But in hindsight we can see that the new NDP government faced severe structural impediments to promoting social-democratic policy.

Politics had changed dramatically since the NDP was last in office in the early 1980s, and especially since Allan Blakeney's interventionist government of the early 1970s. After a decade of neoliberal government under the Conservative Party of Grant Devine in the 1980s, labour and social activists had mounted a strong movement to return to a social-democratic path and campaigned hard for the NDP. Through the Saskatchewan Coalition for Social Justice, trade unionists, social activists, and NDP members articulated a progressive vision in response to the privatization, deregulation, and cutbacks of the Devine government. The NDP *did* promise the movement to adhere to this vision if returned to office. The fact that the party, once elected, began to pay more heed to business and New York bond-rating agencies than to a strong social justice agenda seemed a betrayal to some social activists and trade unionists and to some NDP members. But the NDP government's apparently business-friendly agenda derives from the global dominance of the neoliberal paradigm. The post-1980 neoliberal era is a difficult one in which to promote new labour policy to assist those on the lowest rungs of the ladder. Some people would go further and say that social democracy itself is unviable in this context (Albo, 1997; Teeple, 2000).

In November 2000 we conducted follow-up interviews with SFL President Barb Byers and RWDSU Secretary-Treasurer Chris Banting, along with Larry Kowalchuk, a labour lawyer who works with RWDSU, about part-time work and labour standards in Saskatchewan. All agree that part-timers' conditions in the province have not noticeably improved and that significant problems with labour standards remain. Their experience accords with that of the part-timers whom we interviewed.

Byers admits that the SFL probably compromised too much over the Labour Standards Regulations but says that it understood that the "most available hours" provision would be proclaimed and the act would be enforced. She has heard countless stories similar to those told by our participants about employers' ignoring provisions of the act and about the Labour Standards Branch turning a blind eye to abuse of workers.

Byers says that labour's compromises helped make the regulations more convoluted and difficult to understand and that they need cleaning up and simplifying. But this is no impediment to enforcing the regulations or to declaring unproclaimed provisions. Byers argues that the government should proclaim the "most available hours" provision and the layoff provisions that would benefit both part- and full-time workers. She says that at least once per year since 1994 a senior government official – a minister of labour, a deputy premier or a premier – has assured her that the "most available hours" provision will be proclaimed, but part-timers in the province still wait.

At RWDSU, Banting and Kowalchuk deal with issues of part-timers and labour standards every day. Their experience is that the practices and demands of the most backward employers seem to set standards in the labour market. When we asked him whether problems of part-time work and labour standards are related to economic globalization, Kowalchuk replied that there is generally a difference between the way in which local and international companies treat their employees. In its day-to-day experience, RWDSU, finds that many Saskatchewan employers have some concern for their employees and communities. But companies such as

Wal-Mart focus on imposing conditions set by a distant head office with sights set only on the bottom line. Kowalchuk concedes that such companies set the terms for the so-called labour market flexibility that accompanies globalization, but he argues that even some of the larger international companies are starting to recognize the value of workers' loyalty and participation in improving productivity and competitiveness.

However, given the generally poor experience of social-democratic progressive competitiveness and attempts to construct a "share economy," including the legislative reforms in Saskatchewan, we must ask if a few progressive companies will counter the trend of neoliberal globalization. We return to this question after considering the experience of Saskatchewan part-time workers themselves.

WORKING PART TIME IN SASKATCHEWAN

A central purpose of our study was to ask Saskatchewan part-timers themselves how the provisions of the revised Saskatchewan Labour Standards Act, as enacted through the new regulations, might affect their living and working conditions. We also asked those interviewed what further improvements they would like to see in labour-standards legislation. The provisions identified as important by part-timers were those dealing with scheduling, breaks, benefits, and additional hours.

The following summary, based on interviews conducted with Saskatchewan part-time workers, seems fairly typical of the situations that part-timers everywhere confront. The overwhelming majority of our participants were women. In addition to revisions to the act, issues related to child care and maternity leave often surfaced.[6] Most participants were classified as permanent part time, although some were seasonal employees, and some casual. Most were not currently in school, but nearly all had at least high school education. If participants were not in school, they were not usually part time by choice. As one woman put it, "The growth of part-time work is scary. It means that many people have to take more than one job to stay afloat, and then scheduling your life gets to be difficult, and days off are rare."

Many unionized workplaces do offer extra hours based on seniority and availability. But if employees have little seniority, this provision is not beneficial to them. And if employees restrict their hours, then they lose their seniority. Moreover, some participants claim that employers work their way around seniority-based scheduling rules by asking to extend shifts, using restricted availability and work performance, and not following job classifications. Most of the part-timers with whom we spoke felt that they would benefit from proclamation of the act's provision on most available hours.

Student participants usually took several jobs in the summer to earn enough money for tuition, since they were unable to get full-time hours through one job. Multiple jobholders who were not students and sought full-time hours usually worked seven days per week and sometimes had less than eight hours of rest between jobs. Employers sometimes posted schedules with a week's notice, but often with less – in the range of three or four days – and sometimes changed schedules during the week, so that workers had to go in to check every day. Again it is clear that the burden of "flexibility" tends to fall on the workers, with the benefits accruing to employers. Breaks were available in theory, but often employees had to work through them, particularly in the service industry. Restaurant and retail employees rarely had uninterrupted lunches (although they were not paid for their lunch hours), and they very often skipped their breaks, usually because there was no one to "cover" for them if customers arrived. Participants usually classified this decision as "voluntary" but explained that, while they would have liked a break, it simply was not an option – they would have been in trouble with managers had they just sat down when there were customers.

Few retail and restaurant employees enjoyed benefits, with generally only unionized part-time workers receiving them. Most service employees counted on additional shifts to supplement their income; often they were scheduled for a base number of hours and then hoped to get more. One participant observed, "It would be better to have more steady shifts, and once you've been there a certain length of time, they should have to offer you full-time, by law." The current system was both good and bad for participants: good if they were able to get the hours and needed the money, but bad because they could not count on the hours from week to week and because they sometimes had to accept more work than they could handle or risk removal from the "call-in" list. Answers varied about public holidays – usually compulsory if one's name was on the schedule – but sometimes workers could ask for the holiday off in advance.

As for the corporate drive for labour "flexibility," vacation holidays were rare among the part-timers interviewed, unless they were unionized. But many would not take holidays because they needed the money; instead, they just take time off when necessary. One commented, "If there was truly a social safety net people wouldn't have to take such terrible jobs; if they could make it so that people weren't so desperate. The growth of part-time work is indicative of a marginalizing of our population – most workers don't have any rights or security anymore – the trend just serves to feed corporate profits." Some of the women interviewed had taken maternity leave, usually with no complaints or difficulties, although for some the benefit cheques were negligible because they were part time prior to taking leave. And typical of the kind of sexual discrimination that we found, one woman recounted how her "friend, every time she has a child, is back at work one week after the birth, but she got fired from one job after telling them she was pregnant." Many participants noted that when they were terminated from jobs it was usually with very little notice and with no pay in lieu of notice.

Overall, the best part-time working conditions seem to exist for professionals who work part time by choice. Next come people in unionized retail positions, those in large non-unionized retail organizations, and finally workers in smaller, non-unionized retail or restaurant establishments. This last group suffers the majority of labour standards violations and consists mostly of younger women.

An important issue that makes women a sort of reserve army of part-timers is the lack of affordable, quality child care. One woman told us: "There should be limits on how many part-timers you can hire. The fact that it's all women working these jobs is indicative of prejudice. People don't believe that we're smart enough to hold full-time jobs and they use pregnancy as an excuse against you, to not give you full-time work. Plus, women often work just to pay the babysitter. They should have more child-care facilities at the workplace. This would benefit the employer too, because women wouldn't have to call in sick to stay home if their child is sick."

Another participant recommended that "government initiatives should include a national child-care system – this is necessary, and should be fully government-funded." Yet another suggested: "[Government] should raise the minimum wage so we don't have to work two or three jobs. Also, they should make it so that older single women don't have to work to supplement their income. The politicians should look at how low-income women live and work to make legislation."

Many participants stated that the labour standards provisions would be adequate if they all were proclaimed but could also be improved through extending or broadening their scope (for instance, increasing advance notice for work schedules or giving all employees benefits). However, complaints about widespread violation of the regulations reveal the extent to which part-timers are regarded as disposable labour. We received this complaint from both part-timers and trade unionists. According to one participant, "Lots of places violate the Labour Standards Regulations and people don't do anything about it because they're afraid." Those part-timers who had phoned the Labour Standards Branch with complaints said that they were casually shrugged off with suggestions to talk to their employers or unions. The Branch has too little staff, and one participant recommended: "There should be more staff to enforce labour standards [there are currently 20 for the whole province] and it should be easier to make a complaint." Another urged: "They should get tough on employers – enforce the legislation better. It's fine to write it down, but you should actually do something about it – give fines, etc."

The feedback that we received from both part-time workers and trade unionists about conditions for part-timers and about the government's lack of will to improve conditions by even proclaiming and enforcing its own labour standards legislation suggests the extent to which the NDP government has fallen prey to neoliberal pressures to deregulate labour markets. The evidence also supports Tabb's (1999) recommendation that it is essential for workers and trade unions to fight for labour rights, which would give the working class more power to push governments to enact and enforce progressive labour legislation. It is apparent that workers cannot expect government to defend their interests automatically.

Our conclusion is that legislating improved standards for workers is only one step towards improving working conditions and social welfare. It is unlikely to succeed in a general context of global labour market deregulation without constant pressure from labour and other social movements. The fact that the Saskatchewan government did not proclaim parts of its own legislation, and has been lax in enforcing what is in effect, bears this out.

CONCLUSION:
PART-TIME WORK FOR ALL?

Harry Braverman (1975) forecast the growth of "second jobs" – the sort of positions that people used to take in addition to their primary jobs for extra income. Increasingly, according to Braverman, these second jobs, which the Economic Council of Canada (1990) labelled "bad jobs," would be the only "choice" for many people. A quarter-century later, Braverman's prediction seems validated. Our participants' constant "search for hours" supports the view that many people now face an unending struggle to piece together a living from a range of insecure "second jobs."

One possible solution, advocated by the labour movement in Canada and elsewhere, and reflected in the revised Saskatchewan Labour Standards Act, is to let part-time workers have more hours, with better pay and benefits, so as to turn "bad" part-time jobs into better full-time positions. This certainly seems to be the preference of many of those interviewed for our study.

A second theme that surfaces from our interviews is that people face a parallel struggle to balance their work and their personal lives. This balancing act is more difficult under neoliberal policies, which privatize social reproduction and emphasize individualized responsibility and discipline. An alternative program that supported shorter working hours, in the context of higher-quality jobs and enhanced flexibility for *workers* (not just for employers), would assist workers and their families with this work–family juggling act.

In response to the insecurity and hardship typical of contingent and part-time work in the neoliberal vision, therefore, is it possible to imagine an alternative vision in which people work shorter hours, on average, but in a labour market that enhances their broader economic and social security rather than undermining it? In other words, why don't we *all* work less? This direction might seem far-fetched within the current political-economic climate. But in the long run, it is an essential element of progressive strategies to restructure labour market relationships. We must redefine notions of "standard labour"; the idea that part-time and other sorts of casual labour are "non-standard" is an artificial, historical construct. An alternative vision could promote the notion of "part-time work," with good wages, benefits, and employment security, as the new "standard."

Back when it was still flirting with "progressive competitiveness" (McBride, 2000), the Canadian government also picked up the idea of reduced work time as one solution to a range of labour market issues, including unemployment. In establishing his Advisory Group on Working Time and the Distribution of Work, Human Resources Minister Lloyd Axworthy stated: "It is clear that there are too few jobs. However, the challenge lies not only in the number of jobs but also in their distribution. Redistribution of work could help Canadians to better balance work and family life, provide greater access to employment for those in need, and enhance opportunities for people to pursue education and skills upgrading. It could also offer an option for people who would, under certain circumstances, prefer to work fewer hours" (Advisory Group, 1994: 1). While the minister tended here to view people as "human resources," he admitted that they may have interests other than paid work. Later, however, came a more explicit shift to neoliberal deregulation, and the Advisory Group's recommendations had little influence.

For effective redistribution of work, it is not sufficient to redistribute low-paying, alienating jobs or hours. A stronger approach would counter labour market and social polarization in all of its dimensions – social, economic, and political. This requires a focus on social rights, in contrast to the current neoliberal free-market agenda (Broad and Antony, 1999).

We could conclude with proposals for improving working conditions – those of part-timers in particular. We need only refer, however, to the largely-ignored report from the previous federal Commission of Inquiry into Part-time Work (Labour Canada, 1983); the more recent Advisory Group on Working Time, also largely ignored (Advisory Group, 1994); Saskatchewan's 1994 amendments to its Labour Standards Act, left unproclaimed; and other recommendations for improving working conditions and hours of work (Hayden, 1999; O'Hara, 1993, 1994).

The real challenge is to break the blockage preventing reforms from being enacted and enforced. In Saskatchewan it is common to hear the lament that if only the NDP had a stronger, social-democratic leader (like Tommy Douglas), then more progressive policies would follow. However, Teeple (2000) asks whether it is simply a question of leadership. The deeper problem in promoting social change is one of dealing with structural challenges such as the new international division of labour. The historical record reveals that social-democratic notions of market reform, including more recent strategies such as progressive competitiveness, tend to devolve into more aggressively market-oriented approaches such as neoliberalism. Hence we have concluded that only a *socialist* economic program can implement the sorts of labour market changes discussed above.[7] We close by reiterating another lesson of history that the evidence presented in this chapter reinforces: fundamental social change does not descend from on high, but comes only from struggles for social rights (Broad, 1998). Ultimately, improvements in living and working conditions will result only from the efforts of progressive social movements fighting for social rights.

NOTES

1 Research for this study was partially funded through a grant from the Social Sciences and Humanities Research Council of Canada. We wish to thank Fern Hagin and Michelle Moar for their assistance with the research.

2 We use the term "neoliberal" here to refer to current political-economic practices based on notions of free-market capitalism à *la* Adam Smith's "invisible hand" of the market. These "neoconservative" practices received their biggest push under conservative governments in Britain, Canada, and the United States and hold an element of social conservatism. But the affinity with classical liberalism and emphasis on free-market capitalist economics above all else makes "neoliberal" the more apt term (Broad and Antony, 1999).

3 For a more complete discussion of the relationship between the NIDL and the casualization of labour, see Broad, 2000.

4 On Saskatchewan, see Ternowetsky and Thorn, 1991.

5 Not only is this a waste of human potential, the trend appears to be generating high rates of youth crime and attraction to fascistic political movements, which prey on alienation by offering simplistic explanations for problems (for example, that non-white immigrants are taking all the good jobs). But there is also increased activism by young workers and people protesting global trade agreements.

6 See also Broad and Hagin, 2002.

7 See, for example, Albo, 1997 and Miliband, 1994.

REFERENCES

Advisory Group on Working Time. 1994. *Report of the Advisory Group on Working Time and the Distribution of Work.* Ottawa: Human Resources Development Canada.

Akyeampong, Ernest B. 2001. "Fact Sheet on Unionization," *Perspectives on Labour and Income* 13 (3), 46–54.

– 2002. "Unionization and Fringe Benefits," *Perspectives on Labour and Income* 14 (3), 42–46.

Albo, Gregory. 1997. "A World Market of Opportunities? Capitalist Obstacles and Left Economic Policy," in Leo Panitch, ed., *Socialist Register 1997.* London: Merlin Press.

Beechey, Veronica, and Tessa Perkins. 1987. *A Matter of Hours: Women, Part-time Work and the Labour Market.* Minneapolis: University of Minnesota Press.

Belous, Richard S. 1989. *The Contingent Economy: The Growth of the Temporary, Part-Time and Subcontracted Workforce.* Washington, DC: National Planning Association.

Braverman, Harry. 1975. "The Degradation of Work in the Twentieth Century," *Monthly Review* 34 (1), 1–13.

Broad, Dave. 1997. "The Casualization of the Labour Force," in Ann Duffy et al., eds., *Good Jobs, Bad Jobs, No Jobs: The Transformation of Work in the 21st Century.* Toronto: Harcourt Brace Canada, 53–73.

– 1998. "New World Order versus Just World Order," *Social Justice* 25 (2), 6–15.

– 2000. *Hollow Work, Hollow Society? Globalization and the Casual Labour Problem in Canada.* Halifax: Fernwood Publishing.

Broad, Dave, and Wayne Antony. 1999. *Citizens or Consumers? Social Policy in a Market Society.* Halifax: Fernwood Publishing.

Broad, Dave, and Lori Foster. 1995. "Saskatchewan Standards Struggle: Taking the Part of Part-timers," *Our Times* 14 (1), 30–3.

Broad, Dave, and Fern Hagin. 2002. *Women, Part-time Work and Labour Standards: The Case of Saskatchewan.* Regina: University of Regina, Social Policy Research Unit.

Burke, Mike, Colin Moores, and John Shields, eds. 2000. *Restructuring and Resistance: Canadian Public Policy in an Age of Global Capitalism.* Halifax: Fernwood Publishing.

Card, David, and Alan B. Krueger. 1995. *Myth and Measurement: The New Economics of the Minimum Wage.* Princeton, NJ: Princeton University Press.

Darier, Eric. 1996. "Paul Lafargue's *The Right to Be Lazy:* Laziness as a Green Project?" *Socialist Studies Bulletin* 46, 23–46.

Duffy, Ann, Daniel Glenday, and Norene Pupo, eds. 1997. *Good Jobs, Bad Jobs, No Jobs: The Transformation of Work in the 21st Century.* Toronto: Harcourt Brace Canada.

Duffy, Ann, Nancy Mandell, and Norene Pupo. 1989. *Few Choices: Women, Work and Family.* Toronto: Garamond Press.

Duffy, Ann, and Norene Pupo. 1992. *Part-time Paradox: Connecting Gender, Work and Family.* Toronto: McClelland & Stewart.

Economic Council of Canada (ECC). 1990. *Good Jobs, Bad Jobs: Employment in the Service Economy*. Catalogue EC22–164/1990E. Ottawa: Economic Council of Canada

– 1991. *Employment in the Service Economy*. Catalogue EC22–1172/1991E. Ottawa: Economic Council of Canada.

Elliot, Doug. 2000. *Saskatchewan Labour Market Trends Report*. Regina: Saskatchewan Post-Secondary Education and Skills Training.

Frobel, Folker, Jurgen Heinrichs, and Otto Kreye. 1980. *The New International Division of Labour*. Cambridge: Cambridge University Press.

Fudge, Judy. 1991. *Labour Law's Little Sister: The Employment Standards Act and the Feminization of Labour*. Ottawa: Canadian Centre for Policy Alternatives.

– 1996. "Fragmentation and Feminization: The Challenge of Equity for Labour-Relations Policy," in Janine Brodie, ed., *Women and Canadian Public Policy*. Toronto: Harcourt Brace, 57–87.

– 2001. "Flexibility and Feminization: The New Ontario Employment Standards Act," *Journal of Law and Social Policy* 16, 1–22.

Hayden, Anders. 1999. *Sharing the Work, Sparing the Planet: Work Time, Consumption and Ecology*. Toronto: Between the Lines.

International Labour Organization (ILO). 1997. "Part-time Work: Solution or Trap?" *International Labour Review* 136 (4), 557–79. www.ilo.org/public/english/support/publ/revue/persp/97–4.htm

– 1999. "Europe's Employment Revival: How Smaller Countries Create Jobs," *World of Work* 29 (April/May).

Joint Commission on Part-time Work. 1994. *Final Report of the Joint Commission on Part-time Work*. Regina: Saskatchewan Labour.

Jones, Gareth Stedman. 1984. *Outcast London*. Harmondsworth: Penguin.

Labour Canada. 1983. *Part-time Work in Canada: Report of the Commission of Inquiry into Part-time Work*. Ottawa: Labour Canada.

Lafargue, Paul. 1983. *The Right to Be Lazy*. New York: Charles H. Kerr Publishing.

Levin-Waldman, Oren M. 1999. *Do Institutions Affect the Wage Structure? Right-to-Work Laws, Unionization and the Minimum Wage*. Annandale-on-Hudson, NY: Jerome Levy Economics Institute, Bard College.

Marshall, Katherine. 2002. "Duration of Multiple Jobholding," *Perspectives on Labour and Income* 14 (2), 17–23.

McBride, Stephen. 2000. "Policy from What? Neoliberal and Human Capital Theoretical Foundations of Recent Canadian Labour Market Policy," in Mike Burke et al., eds., *Restructuring and Resistance: Canadian Public Policy in an Age of Global Capitalism*. Halifax: Fernwood Publishing, 159–77.

Midgley, James. 2000. "Globalization, Capitalism and Social Welfare: A Social Development Perspective," *Canadian Social Work* 2 (1), 13–28.

Miliband, Ralph. 1994. *Socialism for a Sceptical Age*. London: Verso.

Mitter, Swasti. 1986. *Common Fate, Common Bond: Women in the Global Economy*. London: Pluto Press.

Morissette, René and Deborah Sunter. 1994. *What Is Happening to Weekly Hours Worked in Canada?* Analytical Studies Branch, Research Paper Series No. 65. Ottawa: Statistics Canada.

Noble, David F. 1995. *Progress without People: New Technology, Unemployment and the Message of Resistance.* Toronto: Between the Lines.

O'Hara, Bruce. 1993. *Working Harder Isn't Working: A Detailed Plan for Implementing a Four-day Workweek in Canada.* Vancouver: New Star Books.

– 1994. *Put Work in Its Place: How to Redesign Your Job to Fit Your Life.* Vancouver: New Star Books.

O'Reilly, Jacqueline, and Colette Fagan, eds. 1998. *Part-time Prospects: An International Comparison of Part-time Work in Europe, North America and the Pacific Rim.* London: Routledge.

Peck, Jamie. 1996. *Work-Place: The Social Regulation of Labour Markets.* New York: Guilford Press.

Rifkin, Jeremy. 1995. *The End of Work: The Decline of the Global Labor Force and the Dawn of the Post-Market Era.* New York: G.P. Putnam's Sons.

Sassen, Saskia. 1991. *The Global City: New York, London, Tokyo.* Princeton, NJ: Princeton University Press.

Schellenberg, Grant. 1997. *The Changing Nature of Part-time Work.* Ottawa: Canadian Council on Social Development.

Schellenberg, Grant, and Christopher Clark. 1996. *Temporary Employment in Canada: Profiles, Patterns and Policy Considerations.* Ottawa: Canadian Council on Social Development.

Schenk, Christopher, and John Anderson, eds. 1995. *Re-Shaping Work: Union Responses to Technological Change.* Toronto: Ontario Federation of Labour.

Schor, Juliet B. 1992. *The Overworked American: The Unexpected Decline of Leisure.* New York: Basic Books.

Shalla, Vivian. 2003. "Part-time Shift: The Struggle over Casualization of Airline Customer Sales and Service Agent Work," *Canadian Review of Sociology and Anthropology* 40 (1), 93–109.

Sivanadan, A. 1997. "Heresies and Prophecies: The Social and Political Fallout of the Technological Revolution," in Jim Davis et al., eds., *Cutting Edge: Technology, Information, Capitalism and Social Revolution.* London: Verso Books, 287–96.

Statistics Canada. 2003. "Full-time and Part-time Employment," www.statcan.ca/english/Pgdb/labor12.htm

Sundstrom, Marianne. 1987. *A Study in the Growth of Part-time Work in Sweden.* Stockholm: Arbetslivscentrum.

– 1992. "Part-time Work in Sweden and Its Implications for Gender Equality," in Nancy Folbre et al., eds., *Women's Work in the World Economy.* New York: New York University Press, 213–23.

Sussman, Deborah. 1998. "Moonlighting: A Growing Way of Life," *Perspectives on Labour and Income* 10 (2), 24–31.

Tabb, William. 1999. "Progressive Globalism: Challenging the Audacity of Capital," *Monthly Review* 50 (9), 1–10.

Teeple, Gary. 2000. *Globalization and the Decline of Social Reform.* Toronto: Garamond Press.

Teeple, Gary, ed. 1972. *Capitalism and the National Question in Canada.* Toronto: University of Toronto Press.

Ternowetsky, Gordon, and Jill Thorne. 1991. *The Decline in Middle Incomes: Unemployment, Underemployment and Falling Living Standards in Saskatchewan.* Regina: University of Regina, Social Policy Research Unit.

Vosko, Leah F. 2000. *Temporary Work: The Gendered Rise of a Precarious Employment Relationship.* Toronto: University of Toronto Press.

White, Julie. 1999. "Workers' Attitudes to Shorter Hours of Work," in Christopher Schenk and John Anderson, eds., *Reshaping Work 2: Labour, the Workplace and Technological Change.* Toronto: Garamond Press, 157–72.

Wiseman, John. 1996. "A Kinder Road to Hell? Labour and the Politics of Progressive Competitiveness in Australia," in Leo Panitch, ed., *Socialist Register 1996.* London: Merlin Press.

PART FOUR

Alternative Visions

14

Labour Market Deregulation and the U.S. Living-Wage Movement

STEPHANIE LUCE

Among industrialized nations, the United States has conducted perhaps the premier experiment in labour market deregulation. Over the past few decades, federal, state, and local governments have pursued strategies designed to weaken labour market institutions and to increase the power of capital relative to labour, all in the name of economic growth. This broad trend has included failure to increase the federal minimum wage in line with consumer prices, elimination or reduction of social safety nets such as Aid to Families with Dependent Children (AFDC), further privatization or contracting out of public services, and failure by courts to recognize and punish labour-law violations committed by employers.

Despite resistance to this general policy direction, efforts that counter this trend are few in number and generally won only with costly struggle. Labour struggles such as the Justice for Janitors Campaign (see the chapter by Cranford in this volume) have won higher wages and better conditions for some of those most heavily affected by deregulation, but there have been few victories in the arena of policy. The living-wage movement is a noticeable exception, however. It began in the early 1990s as an attempt to counter the direct and indirect effects of labour market deregulation. Living-wage laws require employers receiving public money to pay their workers a higher minimum wage and in some cases to provide basic employment benefits. Now in force in over 100 municipalities, living-wage ordinances suggest that an alternative to recent practice in U.S. labour market policy is possible, at least at the municipal level.

But do these ordinances really offer a viable and effective alternative to labour market deregulation? Can they counter the trends of contracting out, falling wages, and other negative labour market trends in the United States and elsewhere? Do they hold employers and economic-development planners accountable for wage inequality and low wages? Can they fit into a broader strategy of rebuilding union membership and power?

This chapter attempts to answer these questions. The first section provides background on U.S. national and municipal labour market deregulation. The second describes the living-wage movement, and the third reviews research on the ordinance's impact on labour market outcomes. The fourth examines the potential of living-wage ordinances to affect employers and workers, through a case study in Los Angeles, which passed its ordinance in 1997. The fifth assesses the movement's significance to broader debates over labour market deregulation.

LABOUR MARKET DEREGULATION: THE U.S. CASE

To understand the political climate in the U.S. cities and counties with living-wage campaigns, one must first situate those efforts in the wider context of municipal and national labour policy. The living-wage movement sits at the intersection of two trends: the rise in the number of working poor and the decline in the ability or willingness of local, state, or national governments to enact pro-labour policy.

Although the United States passed a federal minimum-wage law in 1938 (as part of the Fair Labour Standards Act), the law did not include automatic indexing with inflation. Congress must approve any increase in the federal minimum wage. In the 1940s and 1950s, when the labour movement enjoyed greater density and more political power, the federal minimum wage went up regularly, roughly keeping pace with average manufacturing wages. The minimum wage peaked (in real terms) in 1968, however, and was increased only a few times thereafter. By the early 1990s, the real value of the minimum wage had fallen far below its historic level and also far below the amount necessary to allow a full-time worker to earn enough to reach the federal poverty threshold.[1]

At the same time, many municipal governments were facing serious fiscal crises brought on by the recessions of the 1970s and 1980s, by large cuts in federal funding, and by a movement of residents and firms to the suburbs, eroding the tax base (Lemann, 1994). In response, city managers pursued a three-pronged strategy to attract business and to cope with shrinking tax revenues. Improving a city's "business climate" would encourage employers to create jobs, thereby increasing prosperity for residents and the cities themselves. One part of the strategy involved the creation of public–private business assistance organizations and city offices of economic development. For example, most cities have Private Industry

Councils, funded by government and private business, that assist unemployed workers to find jobs. Also common are initiatives such as the Philadelphia Mayor's Business Action Team, which uses city resources to provide technical, legal, and other assistance to business owners. By 1990, there were 15,000 to 18,000 similar public and private organizations around the country devoted to promoting local economic development (Levy, 1990).

Another part of this strategy involved establishment of a wide range of subsidies and incentives offered to firms, such as tax abatements, subsidized and guaranteed loans, industrial property management, land acquisition and clearing, streamlining building regulations, and the building and/or improvement of roads, parking, and airports (Luce, 1999).

A third part of the strategy included creating an image of a city without business regulation or an expensive or troublesome workforce. Mayors began downsizing public government to reduce payrolls, attacking public-sector unions, and privatizing city services (through outright privatization and/or contracting out) – allegedly to lower city budgets but also to provide lucrative contracts to the private sector. It is difficult to locate comprehensive data describing the magnitude or impact of these trends, but anecdotes suggest some of the trend of the 1980s. For example, in Toledo, Ohio, "government streamlining" resulted in the city's laying off 40 per cent of its workforce between 1979 and 1982. Newark, New Jersey, reduced its workforce from 10,000 to 4,000 in the 1980s (Kurtz, 1988). After federal cuts hit cities in the early 1980s, Phoenix implemented its first layoffs in over 25 years (Bumiller, 1983).

Government data suggest that the downsizing of the 1980s may have reversed in the 1990s. In fact, the Bureau of Labor Statistics (BLS) lists local and state governments among the top-ten growth industries for the decade, mostly because of simple population growth. However, the data in most places show the main employment growth in law enforcement and public education, with jobs in administration and other services cut, outsourced, or restricted by hiring freezes (Walters, 1998). BLS projections for 1998 to 2008 predict increases in local-government employment (excluding education) in all occupations averaging 12 per cent – in tandem with population growth and service needs. However, this includes a 44 per cent increase in corrections officers, 34 per cent in police and sheriffs, and only 0.8 per cent in cleaning and building services, janitors, and food-service workers. For other municipal service occupations, the BLS predicts a loss of jobs, including some often contracted out or filled with temporary workers: bookkeeping clerks, data entry, secretaries, and file clerks (Bureau of Labour Statistics, 2001).[2]

Elliott Sclar (1997) argues that the "urge to privatize" has grown sharply since the early 1980s, as part of an ideological shift towards a weaker state and a stronger "free market." While there is little empirical research on contracting trends, the data that do exist show that contracting out of services increased sharply in the late 1980s and early 1990s. A private research organization, the Mercer Group, surveyed large cities in 1996 and found that between 1987 and 1995 they substantially increased the amount of services contracted out. For example, in 1987, these cities contracted out 52 per cent of their janitorial services. By 1995, the figure was 70 per cent. As Cranford notes in this volume, this same period saw a dramatic drop in the wages of janitors. In Los Angeles, janitors were earning about $12 per hour in the 1970s but less than $5 per hour by the early 1990s.

The Mercer Group's study found other services affected as well. Contracting out for street maintenance rose from 19 per cent to 38 per cent; for solid-waste collection from 30 per cent to 50 per cent; and for data-processing operations, from 16 per cent to 31 per cent (Zachary, 1996). Reports from the National League of Cities show that the pace of contracting out slowed somewhat in the later 1990s as cities reported better financial health, but, in 2000, 28 per cent of cities still reported contracting out of new services to cut costs (Pagano and Shock, 2000).

Whether or not contracting out results in savings is not clear. Some cases show that promised savings have not materialized because of corruption, mismanagement, added costs of contract oversight, or other factors (Sclar, 1997).

Other municipalities find contracting out cheaper than performing the service in-house. However, this is the case not usually because of greater efficiency attained by managerial expertise, but because contractors pay lower wages and/or benefits. For example, the Chicago Institute on Urban Poverty studied the impact of privatization on 10 job titles in Chicago from 1989 to 1995. It found wages and benefits dramatically reduced in each of the entry-level positions. The average wages and benefits for security guards fell 49 per cent after privatization. Parking-lot attendants suffered least with a 25 per cent drop in wages and benefits. Some contractors did not reduce wages but forced fewer employees to do the same amount of work, resulting in job speed-up (Pollin and Luce, 1998). A study of eight services in the Los Angeles area found that many contractors paid wages similar to those given to municipal employees, but that the private contractors hired fewer workers to do the same job, relied more on part-time workers, terminated employees more frequently, and used more capital equipment (Rehfuss, 1989).

Whether wages were cut or working conditions were intensified, the end result was the same. As municipal managers pursued labour deregulation in the hopes of creating a friendly business climate, workers suffered because of weakened public-sector unions and a reduction in the number of high-wage, stable jobs. Unable to win a higher federal minimum wage because of political resistance to raising costs for businesses, and lacking power in municipal wage-bargaining because of threats of privatization, activists turned to their local governments to pass living-wage ordinances.

THE LIVING-WAGE MOVEMENT

It is in this context that the modern living-wage movement emerged.[3] The idea was not new; similar laws that require federal, state, or local contractors to pay a "prevailing wage" existed for most of the twentieth century (including Davis–Bacon laws and the Federal Service Contract Act). The prevailing-wage model is similar to Canadian "fair wage" policies, in that they require firms with public construction contracts to pay the going market wage in a unionized industry – in essence, the union wage. The policy – designed to "take wages out of competition" – allows contractors to compete on quality and efficiency rather than on low wages. However, prevailing-wage laws are effective only in industries with high union density and high wages. In services, the going market rate is usually close to the minimum wage. Rather than requiring contractors to pay the prevailing local market wage, living-wage ordinances mandate wages at a particular level, usually set to bring a family of three or four up to or above the poverty level.

As of this writing, over 100 city municipalities have passed such ordinances, and only a handful have defeated them. Living-wage campaigns are ongoing in another 70 or more localities. Most ordinances govern cities or counties, but a few apply to other levels of government, such as the Milwaukee County School Board and the San Diego Metropolitan Transit Development Board. The living-wage movement has also entered the education sector, as university students have begun to campaign for living wages for university employees and employees of firms with university contracts.[4]

Living-wage campaigns and ordinances differ greatly along a variety of dimensions, including the firms and workers covered by (or exempted from) the ordinance and the wage and benefit levels mandated. The ordinances differ so widely partly because the movement is heterogeneous and decentralized: it has no umbrella national organization and no central leadership co-ordinating the legislative language and demands. The national Association of Community Organizations for Reform Now (ACORN) has played a large role through individual campaigns and through its National Living Wage Resource Center. The AFL–CIO has endorsed the living wage as part of its "America Needs a Raise" campaign

and pushed local Central Labour Councils to take part. However, in each
city, local coalitions of community, labour, and religious organizations
and individuals organize the campaigns.

As a result, each ordinance addresses the priorities of coalition members
as well as reflecting local politics. While the first laws in the early 1990s
applied to firms receiving financial assistance or service contracts from
cities, the concept now includes city and county employees, firms holding
city leases or concession agreements (such as a company selling food at a
city-owned airport), and/or subcontractors of affected firms.

The ordinances also range in coverage. Some, in small cities such as
Jersey City, New Jersey and Somerville, Massachusetts, cover only a few
dozen workers. Los Angeles County's is expected to cover 10,000, and San
Francisco's, 21,000. However, a few recent campaigns have attempted to
expand the scope of ordinances. In March 2003, the city council of Santa
Fe, New Mexico, approved a living wage of $8.50 (to rise to $10.50 by
2008) for *all* employers within city limits with 25 or more employees. Geo-
graphically-based ordinances could significantly increase the number of
workers covered.[5]

In most cases, the ordinances affect those types of low-wage jobs that
have tended to be privatized or contracted out in recent years: bus drivers
and monitors, janitors, parking attendants, and security guards. In some
cities they also cover temporary and part-time workers, and a number
include non-profit service workers.

The living-wage level in ordinances varies, depending on the political
power of the local living-wage coalition. On the low end, some ordinances
tie the wage to the poverty level for a family of three, which amounted to
approximately $6.97 per hour in 2002. On the higher end, some set it at
some *multiple* of the federal poverty level for a family of four. In 2002, the
average wage won was $10.46, plus health benefits.

Most of the ordinances are indexed – to the federal poverty level, to the
consumer price index, or to some other measure of regional cost of living.
This arrangement presents a strong advantage over federal and most state
minimum-wage legislation, which only new laws can adjust. A number of
ordinances require employers to provide either health benefits or an additional dollar or two per hour to cover health insurance.[6] A few mandate
paid and/or unpaid days off – typically 12 paid and 10 unpaid days per
year.

Other provisions may include use of community hiring halls, which
require recipients of economic subsidies to use local, certified hiring halls
when searching for new employees. A few cities have a "labour peace"
clause, which enables the municipality to deny a contract or subsidy to a
company with a poor record of labour relations. Other campaigns have
included companion "worker-retention" language, which allows employ-

ees to keep their jobs should the city decide to give the contract to another firm. This means that if a contractor receives a penalty for non-compliance and cannot obtain further contracts, the city does not punish the employees as well.

ORDINANCES TO FIGHT DEREGULATION

It is clear that the living-wage movement has generated tremendous support from a range of organizations, but how successful are the ordinances in practice? Although there are now dozens of them in place, there is little evidence about their impact on workers, employers, and communities and on labour markets in general. There are several reasons for this absence. First, enactment can take time. Even after enactment, the ordinances do not cover employers until new contracts come up for bid or the city grants new subsidies. Phasing in can take years: some of the largest concession agreements covered by the Los Angeles ordinance of 1997 are ten-year contracts renewed earlier in 1997, and hence will remain in effect for several years.

Second, implementing the new law can be difficult. For example, after Boston passed an ordinance in 1997, business groups threatened to sue the city if it enacted certain disclosure provisions. The municipality worked with a task force for over a year to amend the ordinance and adopt much less stringent regulations. Implementation of the early Michigan ordinances (in Detroit, Ypsilanti City, and Ypsilanti Township) was also held up; employer organizations mobilized state representatives to introduce a state law to outlaw the municipal wage ordinances.[7] With this legislation pending, the cities and employers have been slow in implementing the living-wage ordinances.

Finally, in some cities, the implementation process itself is unclear. With no one person or department in charge of administering the law, implementation can fall through the cracks. In these instances, appropriate records are not collected from employers, and the data for assessing the effect of the ordinance does not exist.

None the less there have been a few impact assessments, including reports on Baltimore, Boston, Chicago, Detroit, Los Angeles, the Lower Rio Grande Valley, (Texas), and San Jose. These initial reports have similar findings, summarized here.

Limited Coverage

First, as we saw above, the ordinances cover a small number of workers. In some cities the absolute number may be large but still quite small relative to the overall number of low-wage workers. For example, the Los Angeles

County ordinance covers about 10,000 employees, out of approximately 1 million low-wage workers. Weak implementation exacerbates the problem of limited coverage. Where cities do not enforce the law or allow for exemptions, even fewer workers actually receive wage increases.

Reduction in Poverty

Although few workers have coverage, the raises and benefits can be significant to many of them. Comprehensive statistical data are not available, but anecdotal evidence gathered from interviews in several cities suggests that at least for some people the raise is noteworthy. Pre-enactment impact studies in Los Angeles and Miami–Dade found that, even though workers' incomes are not likely to rise in proportion to the wage increase (because of a decrease in subsidies and an increase in taxes), the net result is still an increase in disposable income. For example, the living-wage increase and benefits would give a family of four in Miami–Dade a 14 per cent increase in disposable income (Nissen, 1998). In addition, the proportion of that income coming directly from the workers' earnings would rise from 63 to 81 per cent.

Some workers commented that the raise is not enough to lift them out of poverty, because in some cities the ordinances do not include health insurance and because many low-wage earners cannot find full-time, year-round work (Niedt et al., 1999). Even the highest living wage won to date is not enough to move a wage earner up to the poverty line if he or she has only part-time or seasonal work.

Another study, by Neumark and Adams (2000), examines the effect of the laws on workers' incomes. The authors use Current Population Survey data to analyse the impact of living-wage ordinances on cities that have enacted them since 1996, as compared to selected control-group cities. They conclude that "living wage ordinances boost wages of low-wage workers" and that they may modestly reduce urban poverty. However, Brenner, Wicks-Lim, and Pollin (2002) have criticized these findings, because the authors use data from a government survey, not from covered workers. Therefore their results may not be accurate.

Small Cost to Firms and Cities

In contrast to the significant wage gains for workers, evidence to date suggests that living-wage ordinances cost affected businesses little. Coverage is small, and implementation can be weak, and at any rate the wage gains do not represent a large budget item for most firms. This is true for most private firms, as well as for non-profits (Reynolds and Vortkamp, 2000).

Similarly, costs to cities have been relatively low. Sander and Lokey

(1998) found that in Los Angeles, in cases of competitive bidding for a contract, firms did not tend to pass on the costs of the wage increase to the city. But even when they did so (for example, when there was no bid competition or with some non-profit providers), the costs did not much affect municipal budgets. A few cities that allocated budget lines to cover increased contract prices found that they did not have to spend the expected cost. Milwaukee set aside $140,000 to cover costs in the first year of implementation but spent only about $10,000 (Luce, 1999). The Pasadena ordinance was predicted to cost the city about $2 million but used up only $220,000 (Ruggles, 2000).

Similarly, Osterman (2000) discovered that living-wage ordinances in schools and other public entities in the Lower Rio Grande Valley of Texas resulted in relatively small budgetary increases. For example, "for the McAllen schools the total wage increase (including the ripple effect) represented a 2.5 percent increase in their wage costs and a 1.4 percent increase in their operating costs," Osterman writes. "For most other school districts the burden was even lower."

Yet some firms and cities faced sizeable costs. Reynolds and Vortkamp (2000) found that up to one in four non-profits covered by the Detroit law encountered "significant financial problems in implementing the living wage requirements." However, even in these cases the problems were likely to be administrative rather than financial, because of restrictions on certain funds in the non-profits' budgets. Other prospective studies note the existence of "high-impact" firms, which some cities have chosen to exempt. Other municipalities simply paid for a large part or all of the wage increase, relieving the firm of the burden.

Some Evidence of Ripple Effects

One potential outcome of a living-wage ordinance is a "ripple effect" – that is, wage increases going to workers not directly covered by the living-wage laws. Since the ordinances cover only people working on a city contract or on a subsidized property, the increase may lead other employees in the firm to ask for higher wages – both workers at the same wage level who are not on the contract and those earning more. This is the direct ripple effect. In addition, some living-wage opponents fear (and advocates hope) that the living wage will spread outside affected firms, creating upward pressure on wages in the entire region or industry – the indirect ripple effect. Osterman (2000) finds ample evidence of direct and indirect ripple effects in the Lower Rio Grande Valley. Ordinances passed in that area covered approximately 4,500 workers, an additional 1,800 people received a direct–ripple effect wage hike, and another 1,000, indirect increases.

Some Evidence of Efficiency Wage Gains

Living-wage laws are relevant to the determination of "efficiency wages" – that is, the effect of wage increases on productivity, turnover, and absenteeism. Many researchers speculate that living-wage increases could affect all three variables, and there is growing evidence that this is the case. Employers in Baltimore have reported that living-wage increases have reduced turnover, lowering recruitment and training costs. Anecdotal reports from other cities suggest similar effects. For example, George Corti, owner of a security-guard firm in Tucson, Arizona, observed that the living-wage ordinance substantially reduced turnover among his employees. In Boston, Diane Collins, responsible for the security-guard contract at the Library Business Office, said that she felt that higher wages have brought about positive changes. "The guards seem a little happier than the batch that was here before," Collins stated. "Plus, they seem to be here longer. Before the living wage, you'd see new faces all the time. With higher wages, the guards seem to take the work more seriously and provide better service" (Brenner, 2003).

Mixed Results on Job Loss

Perhaps the most contentious issue is whether these laws result in job loss. Opponents have two arguments: higher wages will result in across-the-board layoffs, and employers will replace their existing workforce with a higher skilled group, resulting in net job loss for the most disadvantaged workers. So far, there appears to be little support for either claim. While Sander and Lokey (1998) detected some overall job loss following the living-wage ordinance in Los Angeles, the numbers were small. In 17 of 30 businesses, "employment levels dropped modestly, if at all." Five of the 30 firms met the cost of the ordinance by reducing the scope of the contracted services, and "in these cases, workers were laid off or reassigned to other jobs." The end result is a total drop in employment on city contracts of about 3 per cent.

Osterman (2000) reports that none of the school districts or other administrative bodies adopting ordinances in the Lower Rio Grande Valley reduced staff in response to the higher wage level.

Some Reduction in Contracting Out

The living-wage laws may halt or even reverse the contracting out of city services. So far, there have been a few examples of services being brought back in-house, into higher-paid unionized jobs. In San Jose, California, union members used the ordinance to help prevent the privatization of city water services. Overall, while some advocates argue that their ordinances "put a chilling effect" on privatization efforts, others have not seen much impact (Luce, 1999).

The overall result of the impact research done to date suggests that the costs of the ordinances to businesses and cities are typically low, while the benefits to workers are generally high. In addition, the ordinances can increase business efficiency, encourage competitive bidding on contracts (which keeps costs down and discourages corruption), and generate ripple effects to other workers. However, only further research can verify (or not) these findings and uncover unforeseen negative consequences.

A CASE STUDY:
LIVING WAGES IN LOS ANGELES

Given the ordinances' small positive impact on labour market trends, how do we assess the overall effectiveness of the living-wage movement? In particular, how does it hold up to the criticism that it does not go far enough in advancing workers' interests? Can it hold private employers sufficiently accountable for poverty among low-wage service workers? Is it ultimately ineffective because it touches only a limited number of workers? And does it hurt workers by interfering with unionization and collective bargaining? Case studies of living-wage struggles can perhaps best answer these questions.

The campaign in Los Angeles provides one example of how the movement can spread beyond a narrow policy proposal to affect a regional labour market (Cranford's chapter in this volume provides a similar and complementary case study of new organizing initiatives in the Los Angeles area). The campaign had its roots in a 1995 effort to pass a Worker Retention Ordinance. The L.A. Alliance for a New Economy (LAANE)[8] – a research and organizing group founded with support from the Hotel Employees and Restaurant Employees Union (HERE) – fought for and won a city ordinance that allowed service contract workers to keep their jobs if a new firm was awarded an existing city contract.

Out of this success, LAANE forged alliances with community, labour, and faith-based organizations in the area, which culminated in the L.A. Living Wage Coalition. The coalition won a living-wage ordinance in 1997, mandating a wage of $7.25 an hour plus health benefits for service contract workers, as well as for employees of city concessionaires, subcontractors, and subsidy recipients.

LAANE built relations among various local constituencies,[9] and won higher wages for those workers directly covered. But if it had stopped there, it would have helped only about 8,000 workers – a small proportion of the city's low-wage labour force. Instead, it continued its momentum. First, it ensured implementation and monitoring. It hired staff to monitor upcoming city contracts, noting whether potential bidders were unionized, anti-union, or potentially open to card check/neutrality agreements. LAANE then used the ordinance to lobby the city to award contracts to pro-union, pro-living wage employers, not to those unwilling to pay or hostile to unions. It was instrumental in getting city council to deny a bid from anti-union Host Marriott to run airport concessions at a new airport terminal. Instead, the bid went to a competing firm, CA-1, which had signed a card-check agreement with HERE.

LAANE also engaged in ambitious research, releasing regular studies on city agencies not yet subject to the ordinance. Through this and ongoing monitoring efforts, it paid close attention to upcoming subsidy arrangements. In the case of a major development proposed for the Hollywood area, it successfully pressed city council to place additional stipulations on public subsidies, including living wages for all employees of the builder and its contractors, a living-wage incentive program for tenants, and seed money for a workers' health care trust fund.

During this period, the L.A. Living Wage Coalition remained active and took the campaign to new areas. In 1999, it won an ordinance for the County of Los Angeles, covering 10,000 workers. Pasadena and West Hollywood also passed ordinances. In 2000, LAANE helped launch a new campaign in nearby Santa Monica. Working with community groups, unions, and Green representatives on city council, it put forward a proposal to extend the living wage to new territory. In July 2000, council passed an ordinance covering large private businesses in that city's downtown tourist district. Thousands of hotel, restaurant, and retail workers would have seen their wages go up to approximately $10.50 an hour plus benefits. However, the business coalition that opposed the ordinance was able to get an initiative onto the ballot in November 2002 to rescind the living wage. The Chamber of Commerce and its allies spent millions of dollars to defeat the campaign. They employed a variety of tricks, including disseminating deceptive "Democratic voter guides" and "pro-choice voter guides" advocating a vote against the living wage. The ordinance lost narrowly, by 49.02 per cent to 50.98 per cent.

None the less LAANE and the L.A. Living Wage Coalition intend to push the movement as far as they can, looking for any leverage to force all employers to pay higher wages.

Some union organizers have expressed reservations about the movement, suggesting that a higher wage won through legislation discourages workers from joining unions. But the Los Angeles case shows otherwise. Several unions helped pass the law, and have been working since then to use it as an organizing tool. For example, the ordinance served as a rallying point to organize workers at the Los Angeles International Airport (LAX), kicking off the "Respect LAX" organizing drive in 1998 with the support of the national AFL–CIO. Although the intention of the original ordinance was to cover subcontracted airport employees, the city did not interpret the law as such, and only active lobbying by the Living Wage Coalition forced city council to add in the airport workers. Workers could see that passing an ordinance was not enough: it took a union to enforce the law, as well as to win provisions such as grievance rights and job security. Today, the ordinance covers a majority of workers at LAX – and union members.

In addition, LAANE worked with the Los Angeles County Federation of Labour to pass a Responsible Contractor Ordinance (RCO) in 2000. The RCO strengthened the living-wage ordinance by requiring city council to review employers' past labour practices before awarding new contracts, leases, or financial assistance. The RCO, gave council a legal basis to deny contracts to known labour-law violators or union busters.

Has the Los Angeles effort help spread living wages throughout the region? Los Angeles is now the U.S. city with the fastest growth in union membership, with tens of thousands of workers joining each year over the past few years. The living-wage campaign cannot take all the credit, but its momentum has certainly added to the broader workers' rights movement in Los Angeles. Harold Meyerson, editor of the *LA Weekly*, credits it as one of the most powerful political forces in the city, even shaping the 2001 mayoral race (where most of the 15 candidates in the primary competed to present themselves as the most living-wage, labour-friendly candidate). Meyerson compares the movement to the period before the New Deal, when activists unable to win national social legislation worked in cities and states, passing minimum-wage, health-and-safety, and child-labour laws and building momentum towards the federal New Deal (National Public Radio, 2001). Los Angeles is at the forefront of this new movement, setting the standard for other cities to follow.

Los Angeles represents a particularly successful case, and not all living-wage campaigns have achieved victories of this magnitude. But it is not the only place where living-wage organizing has expanded to include new union organizing, the passage of other pro-union or pro-worker legislation, and efforts to expand protection for workers in the broader private sector.

IDEOLOGICAL IMPLICATIONS
AND LESSONS FOR OTHER PLACES

While existing research shows that living-wage ordinances have had a relatively small impact on the American labour market, the Los Angeles campaign makes it clear that the movement can pose an enormous challenge to standard deregulation ideology. While advocates do not frame their struggle explicitly as one against labour market deregulation, their language is indicative of growing resistance to deregulation. For example, their arguments about a community's responsibility to working people, residents' desire to stop giving businesses free rein over city money, and interest in developing new strategies of economic development all suggest growing public willingness to reject the deregulation model.

The first campaign in Baltimore began as a response to the city's economic-development strategy. Clergy members in Baltimoreans United in Leadership Development (BUILD) had been persuaded to support the city's redevelopment programs in the 1970s and 1980s. By the early 1990s, however, poverty among residents, including those with jobs, was still a serious problem. In early 1993, when city leaders began a $165-million bond drive to renovate the convention centre, BUILD launched the "Social Compact Campaign" to demand that civic development benefit low-income residents. Organizers demanded in particular creation of more full-time, year-round jobs with benefits and living wages, funds for training, and advancement opportunities in jobs created with public money, especially for African Americans.

Officials in many cities have also argued that municipal governments need to stop contracting out services at the expense of workers' wages. As Los Angeles City Council member Jackie Goldberg stated, it does not take managerial genius to provide services at a lower price than the government when all you do is slash wages (Luce, 1999). In their study of corporate accountability, the non-profit research organization Good Jobs First discovered that some economic-development officials wanted to move away from "subsidizing the dead-end, poverty-level jobs" (LeRoy, Hsu, and Hinkley, 2000). City council member Erik Sten in Portland, Oregon, "indicated his pleasure in being able to sponsor a direct bottom–up economic development ordinance, rather than a business subsidy which relies on 'trickle down'" (Jobs with Justice, 1998).

Some business operators agree with this approach, as well. A small business owner in Albuquerque, New Mexico, commented on the state's business-subsidy programs: "So much industry comes into New Mexico and the people at the lower level never get the benefit from it. The chamber feels a lower pay scale will attract more industry. They don't have a feel for what it takes to support yourself at the lower level" (Gibbs, 1999). According to management consultant Peter Bernstein, outsourcing trends beginning in the 1980s led to the replacement of higher-paid city and union workers by lower-paid, private-sector workers. Bernstein notes that this laid the foundation for the living-wage campaign in Chicago: "It's the idea of share the wealth, share the patronage. As long as the city is giving out money, let's spread it around a little bit" (Hirschman, 2000).

More important, other business operators support the living-wage concept because they feel that current economic-development strategies are unfair. Far from creating an "even playing field," civic deregulation often reduces costs only for particular firms. Governments that subsidize employers, through tax abatements, credits, low-interest loans, or lucrative contracts, allow them to pay low wages and give them a competitive advantage over smaller or less politically connected firms. Small Business Owners of Washington State (SBOWS) attempted to convince other business owners to support that state's minimum-wage law. It argued that since small businesses and other taxpayers do not receive the tax breaks given to large businesses, they "often end up paying for government subsidies (medical and food assistance, Earned Income Tax Credit) to employees who aren't earning enough at their jobs to support themselves and their families" (Kraut, Klinger, and Collins, 2000).

The fact that so many activists and elected officials and some business people are arguing for the ordinances, by pointing out the inadequacy of current market-oriented labour market policy, provides a lesson for other countries. Although deregulation has been the dominant political and corporate strategy in the United States, many sectors are now rejecting its logic and fighting back. The living-wage movement shows that such resistance has located points of leverage to counter the trend.

The impact of the ordinances is small, but there is great potential. The concept has advocates elsewhere, looking for openings to establish new forms of labour market regulation. Besides local living-wage ordinances, many are now targeting other types of legislation, including the five mentioned below.

First, legislators in a number of U.S. states as well as in the federal government are attempting to apply the living-wage requirement to state or federal service contracts. This would substantially increase the number of workers covered by such laws. The Guiterrez bill, in the U.S. Congress, for example, would provide raises to approximately 200,000 workers working on federal contracts (Brocht, 2000).

Second, dozens of localities are legislating corporate accountability, attaching job-quality standards to economic-development incentives. They resemble living-wage ordinances in prescribing wage levels, health and retirement benefits, and full-time employment requirements for public subsidies (LeRoy, Hsu, and Hinkley, 2000).

Third, the Union of Needlepoint, Industrial, and Textile Employees (UNITE) is pushing for procurement ordinances. Unlike living-wage ordinances, they would apply to municipal goods contractors, such as the companies that produce uniforms for police and other city employees. A number of centres have passed such ordinances, including most recently New York City, where council overrode a mayoral veto by 44 to 4. Since many municipalities spend more on the purchase of goods than on services, these laws could also expand the scope of the living-wage movement and also target different kinds of workers and industries.

Fourth, building trades unions are promoting responsible employer language ordinances. These apply to government contracts covered by prevailing wage agreements and therefore do not address wages. Instead, building contractors doing city business must provide health benefits, establish local hiring procedures, and use a state-certified apprenticeship program.

Fifth, the recent anti-sweatshop movement is another example of the use of local leverage to raise labour market standards (see the chapter by Wells in this volume). Like the living-wage movement, it targets a "middleman" – the university as a licenser of goods – to fight the downward spiral of wages and working conditions of private-sector employers.

All these movements and campaigns, together with the living-wage movement, show the growing U.S. opposition to the detrimental effects of labour market deregulation. They also demonstrate the increasing ingenuity of activists' methods, despite the prevailing ideology.

CONCLUSION

The goal of this chapter was to evaluate the impact of the living-wage movement on workers and firms and to situate this initiative in the context of larger debates over labour market deregulation. It is still too early to state definitively what effects the ordinances are having on wages, employment, contracting, and subsidy patterns. However, the mere existence of such laws, along with the supportive statements of activists, city officials, and even some business people, suggests growing resistance to municipal economic development based on deregulation.

Is the success of the living-wage movement based on the U.S. economic expansion of the 1990s? These ordinances are more likely to pass when the economy is strong. But even an economic boom is no guarantee that workers will share in the gains. Therefore living-wage advocates must pass ordinances institutionalizing gains, especially when they include wage indexing. But what will happen when the economy weakens? Since the U.S. recession of 2001–2, the movement has slowed only moderately. There were still 20 new ordinances passed in 2002, and activists continue to push for higher wage levels and broader coverage.

The living-wage movement is only a small step towards larger labour market reforms. The coverage is small and the wage gains are modest. Even where ordinances pass, there is no guarantee that city administrators have changed their perspective. For example, regardless of their endorsement of living-wage ordinances, city councilors may still support large subsidies for hotel development. Overall, however, this movement represents a growing constituency that not only rejects the logic of deregulation but is also working to fight it.

NOTES

1 The U.S. Census Bureau sets the federal poverty threshold annually. It initially did so by determining the average cost for a basket of food with the necessary calories for different family types and multiplying this by three. Since 1969, it has simply adjusted this number for inflation. Most experts find this method outdated, and would set subsistence thresholds at somewhere between 125 per cent and 150 per cent of current levels.

2 Of course, outsourcing is not the only cause of slow or negative job growth. Factors such as computerization have played a role as well.

3 For information on the historical use of the term "living wage" and on struggles for living wages in the earlier part of the century in the United States, see Glickman, 1997.

4 Students at the University of Wisconsin – Madison passed a referendum mandating a higher wage for all university employees, and students at Wesleyan College held a sit-in and won an agreement that entitled all direct and sub-contracted employees to a living wage plus benefits. Campaigns are under way at many other universities. The chapter by Wells in this volume reports on similar campaigns by university students for anti-sweatshop purchasing policies in the university sector.

5 Other attempts at geographically based ordinances have either been defeated by ballot initiative or challenged legally. The Berkeley (California) Marina has so far (as of 2003) withstood legal challenge. New Orleans's city-wide minimum wage, passed by voters in February 2003, was struck down by the Louisiana State Supreme Court that same year. (The court upheld the state's right to outlaw the city wage law).

6 Federal law (ERISA) prevents cities from passing laws that would mandate

health-insurance benefits. Employers must have the option to pay a higher wage if they do not wish to provide benefits.

7 The Michigan law would also outlaw a variety of municipal laws, from prevailing wages to consumer protection. While it has not passed, other states, including Arizona, Colorado, and Louisiana, did forbid municipalities from setting local minimum wages. Utah recently explicitly outlawed living-wage laws for local service contractors.

8 LAANE was originally the Tourism Industry Development Council, or TIDC. It became LAANE in 1998.

9 The L.A. Living Wage campaign helped to found Clergy and Laity United for Economic Justice (CLUE) – an interdenominational group working to support workers' rights.

REFERENCES

Bernstein, Jared. 2000. *Viewpoints: Higher Wages Lead to More Efficient Service Provision.* Washington, DC: Economic Policy Institute.

Brenner, Mark D. 2003. "The Effect of Living Wage Ordinances on Covered Contracts." Draft report. Political Economy Research Institute, University of Massachusetts – Amherst.

Brenner, Mark D., Jeannette Wicks-Lim, and Robert Pollin. 2002. *Measuring the Impact of Living Wage Laws: A Critical Appraisal of David Neumark's* How Living Wage Laws Affect Low-Wage Workers and Low-Income Families. Working Paper Number 43. Political Economy Research Institute, University of Massachusetts – Amherst.

Brocht, Chauna. 2000. *The Forgotten Workforce.* Washington, DC: Economic Policy Institute.

Bumiller, Elisabeth. 1983. "Two Mayors' Tales of Two Cities; Toledo's DeGood, Phoenix's Hance in Worst of Times," *Washington Post,* 28 Jan., D1.

Bureau of Labor Statistics. 2001. National Industry-Occupational Matrix. www.bls.gov/asp/oep/nioem/empiohm.asp

Epstein, Edward. 2000. "Cost of Living Wage Proposal Not Clear, Budget Analyst Says," *San Francisco Chronicle,* 8 Aug., A16.

Gibbs, Jason. 1999. "Local Businesses Support Living-wage Proposal," *Albuquerque Tribune,* 23 Sept., A5.

Glickman, Lawrence. 1997. *A Living Wage: The Making of a Consumer Society.* New York: Monthly Review Press.

Hirschman, Carolyn. 2000. "Paying Up," *HR Magazine* 45 (7), 35.

Jobs with Justice, Portland Chapter. 1998. "Living Wage Supporters Pack Hearing," press release, 13 Feb.

Kraut, Karen, Scott Klinger, and Chuck Collins. 2000. *Choosing the High Road: Businesses That Pay a Living Wage and Prosper.* Boston: Responsible Wealth.

Kurtz, Howard. 1988. "Learning to Live with Less; Budget Cuts Have Limited Impact in Newark," *Washington Post,* 1 June, A1.

Lemann, Nicholas. 1994. "The Myth of Community Development," *New York Times,* 9 Jan., 27.

LeRoy, Greg, Fiona Hsu, and Sara Hinkley. 2000. *The Policy Shift to Good Jobs: Cities, States and Counties Attaching Job Quality Standards to Development Subsidies.* Washington, DC: Good Jobs First.

Levy, John M. 1990. *Economic Development Programs for Cities, Counties and Towns.* New York: Praeger Publishers.

Luce, Stephanie. 1999. "The Role of Secondary Associations in Local Policy Implementation: An Assessment of Living Wage Ordinances." PhD dissertation, University of Wisconsin – Madison.

Merrifield, Andy. 2000. "The Urbanization of Labor: Living-Wage Activism in the American City," *Social Text* 18 (1), 31–54.

National Public Radio. 2001. *The Connection.* 7 May.

Neumark, David, and Scott Adams. 2000. "Do Living Wage Ordinances Reduce Urban Poverty?" National Bureau for Economic Research, Working Paper 7606. Cambridge, Mass.

Niedt, Christopher, Greg Ruiters, Dana Wise, and Erica Schoenberger. 1999. *The Effects of the Living Wage In Baltimore.* Working Paper No. 119, Washington, DC: Economic Policy Institute.

Nissen, Bruce. 1998. "The Impact of a Living Wage Ordinance on Miami–Dade County." Miami: Center for Labor Research and Studies, Florida International University.

Office of Equality Assurance, City of San Jose. 1999. "City of San Jose Living Wage Policy Six Month Evaluation Report."

Osterman, Paul. 2000. *Report on the Impact of the Valley Interfaith Living Wage Campaign.* Cambridge, Mass.: MIT Sloan School of Management.

Pagano, Michael A., and David R. Shock. 2000. *City Fiscal Conditions in 2000.* Washington, DC: National League of Cities.

Pollin, Robert, and Stephanie Luce. 1998. *The Living Wage: Building a Fair Economy.* New York: New Press.

Rehfuss, John A. 1989. *Contracting Out in Government.* San Francisco: Jossey-Bass Publishers.

Reynolds, David, with Jean Vortkamp. 2000. *Impact of Detroits Living Wage Law on Non-Profit Organizations.* Detroit: Center for Urban Studies and Labour Studies Center, College of Urban, Labor and Metropolitan Affairs.

Ruggles, Rick. 2000. "Wage Law's Cost to City Unclear," *Omaha World-Herald,* 8 March, 1.

Sander, Richard. 1998. "Memorandum to the Personnel Committee, Los Angeles City Council." 20 May.

Sander, Richard, and Sean Lokey. 1998. "The Los Angeles Living Wage in Operation: The First Eighteen Months." Report Presented to Los Angeles City Council, 16 Nov.

Sclar, Elliott. 1997. *The Privatization of Public Service: Lessons from Case Studies.* Washington, DC: Economic Policy Institute.

Walters, Jonathan. 1998. "Did Somebody Say Downsizing?" *Governing Magazine,* Feb., 17.

Weisbrot, Mark, and Michelle Sforza-Roderick. 1996. *Baltimores Living Wage Law: An Analysis of the Fiscal and Economic Costs of Baltimore City Ordinance 442.* Washington, DC: Preamble Center for Public Policy.

Zachary, G. Pascal. 1996. "Beyond the Minimum Wage," *In These Times.* 5 Aug., 27–9.

15

Gendered Resistance:
Organizing Justice for Janitors
in Los Angeles

CYNTHIA J. CRANFORD

Employers are increasingly distancing themselves from workers through the use of subcontracting, labour market intermediaries, and self-employed contractors. This restructuring marks a break with the post–Second World War compromise between labour and capital, mediated by the state, which secured a "family wage" for (white, citizen) male industrial workers but never included most women and many immigrant and racialized men. Economic restructuring transforms social reproduction, as employers seek to minimize their contributions to the health and social welfare of workers and their families, and as governments deregulate, or regressively reregulate, labour migration. These restructurings loudly announce the need to move beyond the industrial unionism that emerged from the post-1945 compromise. Indeed, they have prompted a return of some unions to their social-movement roots.

In this chapter, I examine workers' collective efforts to posit an alternative to the restructuring of both production and social reproduction through a case study of the commercial cleaning industry in Los Angeles.[1] The negative impact of restructuring on workers and their families is particularly visible in the United States, where labour market regulation and social-welfare provision are the weakest among industrialized nations (Meulders and Wilkin, 1987; Stanford, 1996). Los Angeles janitors work for companies that compete for short-term contracts with building owners. They are immigrant women and men predominantly from Mexico, El Salvador, and Guatemala, and many are (or have been) undocumented, with no legal right to live or work in the United States. Over half of them are women (Cranford, 1998). After a decade of deunionization in the 1980s,

in the 1990s the Justice for Janitors (J4J) campaign of the Service Employees International Union began to reorganize the industry. Some observers
have described the J4J campaign as a success story that marks a renewed
"community unionism" and a "mini-movement" that could revitalize U.S.
labour (Banks, 1991; Lerner, 1991; see also Milkman, 2000; Waldinger et
al., 1998).

I argue that the J4J strategy is gendered, and I show how its gendered
resistance contributes to the movement's widely heralded success. In the
first section, I review trends in restructuring and resistance in the United
States in general and in California in particular, and I introduce the concepts that guide this analysis. The second section describes the organizing
strategies of J4J in Los Angeles. I illustrate the gendering of its strategy
through its active recruitment of women into grass-roots and formal leadership alongside men. The third section provides an ethnographic
account of the janitors' gendered challenge to the building owners' distancing strategy during their recent Year 2000 campaign, which focused
on public actions and the mobilization of community and political
support. I argue that the leadership of immigrant women workers alongside men strengthened the effort to require building owners to contribute
to the health and welfare of the immigrant workers and their families. Furthermore, the visible leadership of immigrant women focused attention on
the social welfare of families in a way that did not reproduce unequal relations of social reproduction – as occurred all too often with unions in the
past.

RESTRUCTURING AND RESISTANCE

Economic and Political Restructuring

The break with the postwar compromise between labour and capital is
often described as employers' search for greater labour market "flexibility." However, the term "flexibility" can refer to various processes at different levels of analysis (Atkinson, 1987; Macdonald, 1991; Meulders and
Wilkin, 1987). Furthermore, the term is arguably ideological – in contrast
with rigidity, "flexibility" has a positive connotation. Employers often
invoke it to justify their calls for deregulation or reregulation in favour of
business interests or a broader neoliberal agenda (see the introduction by
Stanford and Vosko in this volume).

Understanding restructuring, and resistance to it, first requires a clear
definition of terms. What Atkinson (1987: 90–1) has called "distancing"
differs from various forms of "flexibility." Distancing is the displacement of
employment contracts with commercial contracts, through subcontracting, use of labour market intermediaries, and the use of "self-employed"

contractors. The workers are not (legal) employees of the client firm, although they may be (legal) employees of the subcontractor or intermediary. Rather than organizing its own workforce "flexibly," the firm seeks to specialize in core areas and contracts out work that other organizations or individuals can produce at lower cost. Distancing provides employers with "wage flexibility" – that is, the ability to adapt wage levels or distributions, including adjustments both to the direct wage and to employers' contributions and levies (Meulders and Wilkin, 1987). This power to reduce the wage bill is arguably not a form of "flexibility" at all, but more akin to what Sassen (1995) has called "informalization" – a process whereby employers distance themselves from responsibilities encoded in labour legislation, such as minimum wages and contributions to social security.

Distancing presents pressing problems for union organizing. Crafted in 1935 to suit the needs of predominantly male industrial workers, the U.S. National Labor Relations Act (NLRA)[2] assumes a direct employment relationship with a single employer at a single, generally large and formal worksite. This results in several problems for workers who fall outside this norm (DuRivage, Carré, and Tilly, 1998). First, the NLRA defines the bargaining unit via a narrow definition of community of interest that generally corresponds with a single worksite and often fragments workers further within worksites. Small bargaining units limit the resources available to represent workers and workers' power at the bargaining table. Second, the NLRA does not well suit workers with joint employers, such as those working directly for subcontractors that have a commercial contract with a client firm. Unlike many industrialized countries, U.S. labour law does not require the successor company to hire the previous employees. The NLRA treats most client firms as "neutral secondary employers," does not insist that they bargain in good faith with workers, and prohibits "coercive" action against them, such as picketing (Fisk, Mitchell, and Erickson, 2000). However, "secondary employers" have significant control over the wages and working conditions of the people at the bottom of the subcontracting chain, and hence are not really "neutral." Finally, high-turnover workforces have difficulty unionizing because, with a few exceptions, the NLRA assumes long-term attachments to a single employer (DuRivage, Carré, and Tilly, 1998: 268–9).

The structural mismatch between the social relations of work and labour-relations law combines with labour-relations policies and procedures to make unionization difficult for a growing number of workers (Friedman et al., 1994). The level of employer hostility to labour is unique in the U.S., although growing elsewhere as well, and includes both legal and illegal strategies (Clawson and Clawson, 1999; Friedman et al., 1994). U.S. labour law allows employers considerable leeway to oppose employees' decisions to unionize, through extensive appeals and technical refusals to bargain (Fisk, Mitchell, and Erickson, 2000). Decisions by courts and administrative judges have also expanded employers' rights (Brody, 1997). In addition, given the lack of enforcement of labour standards (a trend that became clear under President Ronald Reagan in the 1980s), employers increasingly use *illegal* methods to prevent unionization or to deunionize workplaces. Unfair Labour Practice (ULP) charges brought by workers and unions against employers, which include hindering workers from forming a union, increased in the 1980s and 1990s (Bronfenbrenner et al., 1998). Within this context, Green and Tilly (1987: 487) refer to reliance on National Labor Relations Board (NLRB) elections, where a union must gain majority support at a single worksite, as the "fetishism of the 51 percent." Indeed, unions won only 48 per cent of NLRB elections in 1990. Even when a majority of workers voted for the union, only one-third of elections resulted in collective-bargaining agreements because of employers' persistent appeals (Crump, 1991: 33).

The use of workers who lack rights (such as undocumented and off-shore workers) also allows firms to externalize employers' responsibilities, furthering informalization (Sassen, 1995). An accurate count of undocumented U.S. residents is difficult, since the census does not ask about legal status. Estimates of their numbers ranged from 7 million to 8.5 million in 2000 – over half from Mexico, and another one-quarter from other Central and South American countries and the Caribbean (Fix and Passel, 2001). The least regulated jobs in California were dependent on undocumented immigrant women and men, particularly in household, hotel, and building cleaning; food services; and garment sewing (Cornelius, 1989; Marcelli and Heer, 1997). In Los Angeles, Latina immigrants, particularly those who arrived in the 1980s, were over-represented in low-wage service occupations (Cranford, 1998). While the Immigration Reform and Control Act (IRCA) of 1986 makes it illegal for employers to hire knowingly an undocumented worker, and for those unauthorized to enter the United States to work, the NRLA does not limit their access to collective bargaining. The policy has been that administrative bodies concerned with protecting workers' rights, such as the NLRB and the Equal Opportunity Employment Commission, do not share information with the Immigration and Naturalization Service. However, in practice employers draw on workers' undocumented status to stop unionization drives, and the U.S. Supreme Court has recently strengthened their ability to do so. The NLRB awarded back pay to an undocumented immigrant who had been fired for engaging in union activity. However, the Supreme Court overruled the NLRB's decision, arguing that awarding back pay to an undocumented immigrant ran counter to the IRCA.[3] The precarious legal status of individual workers reinforces the effect of supply-side deregulation and points to the relationship between economic restructuring and the restructuring of social reproduction.

Restructuring Social Reproduction

Social reproduction is the "mental, manual and emotional labour involved in the maintenance of life on a daily basis and intergenerationally" (Laslett and Brenner, 1989: 382–3). The organization of social reproduction changes over time and varies among groups. As capital took over the production of goods, a normative family form developed, characterized by a male breadwinner and a female homemaker. This ideal was not attainable for many women and men. However, the ideology of domesticity defined women who did work for pay as secondary earners; they had insecure jobs with less pay, reinforcing their dependence on male wages and denying them leverage to shift some of the unpaid work to men (Hartmann, 1976).

Working-class struggles to unionize and gain security in collective agreements also involved social reproduction and included many actors. May (1985) argues that the "family wage" was initially a broad-based class strategy supported by working-class women and men that did not include calls to exclude women from industry. However, middle-class reformers, politicians, and large employers such as Henry Ford began to call for the family wage for a breadwinning father to support a stay-at-home mother, within the context of the middle-class, Eurocentric ethos of Americanization. The American Federation of Labour (AFL) unions, and their predominantly male members, accepted this logic of male privilege in order to gain broad support and consolidate organizing gains. A similar familism framed the post-1945 compromise between the industrial unions and employers, mediated by the state. This era also saw more of the work of social reproduction move into the public sphere. Both the private and the public sectors hired women to do this paid reproductive work, ranging from social work to food services (Glenn, 1992).

Racial-ethnic and immigrant U.S. women always worked for pay, albeit in casual and menial jobs. Racial-ethnic men did not earn a family wage, in part because trade unions either excluded or marginalized them. Unlike white working-class women, racial-ethnic women were defined primarily as units of labour; their position in production took precedence over the standard of living of their families (Glenn, 1992). This is clear when one looks to migrant labor, which externalizes the costs of social reproduction to the sending nation (Burawoy, 1976). In the United States, Mexican men were recruited to work as farm labourers on short-term contracts through the Bracero program (1942–65). Mexican women and children could not migrate under this program, although women and men continued to migrate without legal authorization (Hondagneu-Sotelo, 1995).

With the break in the postwar accord, new struggles surfaced over social reproduction characterized by shifting responsibilities of states, markets, and families (Vosko, 2002). Again the role of immigrant labour is revealing. As more immigrant families have settled in the United States, the state and employers have sought to evade the costs of their social reproduction. The IRCA of 1986 introduced sanctions against employers for hiring undocumented immigrants, increased the budget for stopping clandestine crossings at the U.S.–Mexican border, and gave amnesty to some undocumented workers.[4] Despite the amnesty, the act was a reaction to the settlement of undocumented workers that followed the legalization of braceros and family reunification measures in the Immigration Act of 1965 (Hondagneu-Sotelo, 1995). However, the IRCA failed to stem undocumented migration and settlement.

The early 1990s brought a renewed focus on undocumented immigrants' use of social services as part of the neoliberal project of rolling back the welfare state. Politicians and community groups began to construct immigrants as people who wanted to benefit from the U.S. social-welfare system. The migration of women and children had solidified settlement, and they became the targets of a new xenophobia that demonized the reproduction of Mexican immigrant families (Hondagneu-Sotelo, 1995). This focus on immigrants as burdens to the state reached its peak in 1994 with California's Proposition 187, which would have denied education, health care, and other social services to undocumented immigrants and their children, even if U.S.-born. Questions of constitutionality blocked Proposition 187 in the courts, yet in 1996 Congress passed the Illegal Immigration Reform and Immigrant Responsibility Act, which cut welfare benefits to *legal* immigrants across the country. In 1998, California voters ended bilingual education through Proposition 227, coupling anxieties about English as the official language with an effort to evade the costs of educating immigrant children.

In short, both the state and employers have sought to distance themselves from the costs of workers' health and social welfare through subcontracting and the exploitation of undocumented workers. Justice for Janitors is one example of resistance to this restructuring.

Revival of the U.S. Labour Movement

A combination of local grass-roots mobilization and a change in leadership of the AFL–CIO has resulted in a new wave of U.S. labour organizing, which is particularly strong in Los Angeles. The new unionism includes non-contract organizing among community-based workers' centres and associations of day labourers, garment workers and domestic workers; the living-wage campaigns described by Luce in this volume; and the organizing of

HERE, SEIU, and other unions for recognition and collective agreements through direct pressure and mass action (Bonacich et al., 2000; Hondagneu-Sotelo and Riegos, 1997; Johnston, 1994; Milkman, 2000; Turner, Katz, and Hurd, 2001; Wilton and Cranford, 2002).

Andy Banks (1991) outlines six elements in this new wave of labour organizing. The first element is that "employer acquiescence to the union" represents success. Rather than holding elections monitored by the NLRB, unions seek recognition and neutrality agreements through direct pressure. Organizing outside the law requires expensive strategic campaigns – the second element – and a broad-based support movement (see also Luce in this volume). The third element consists of intensive rank-and-file campaigns, in which union members help to organize the unorganized mainly on a volunteer basis (also Lerner, 1991). Because of the concentration of women, immigrants, and racial-ethnic groups in most low-wage service-sector jobs, involvement of workers also helps to diversify the (often white male) leadership of union organizing drives. This in turn helps to recruit non-union workers as well as community allies. Coalitions between unions are the fourth element, and alliances with religious and community groups are the fifth. Significantly, religious and community groups do not fall under restrictions of U.S. labour law prohibiting action (such as picketing) against secondary employers. The sixth element is waging campaigns in the court of public opinion, so that they "embody the crusading zeal common to most popular movements" (Banks, 1991: 20).

In addition to organizing for union recognition, contract campaigns have also returned to the use of mass-action tactics. Because employers can permanently replace (economic) strikers under U.S. labour law, most strikes throughout the 1980s and 1990s required a significant mobilization of community and political support (Breecher and Costello, 1990). As economic disruption alone has lost its power, unions increasingly seek to mobilize broad public pressure during strikes through coalitions (Clawson and Clawson, 1999).

New organizing and innovative bargaining strategies are limited to a small number of unions, and traditional "business unionism" remains strong in the U.S. labour movement; new organizing reflects potential rather than widespread change (Delgado, 2000; Milkman, 2000; Sherman and Voss, 2000). The potential to revive U.S. labour is particularly evident in the "immigrant unionism" of Los Angeles (Milkman, 2000).

RESTRUCTURING AND RESISTANCE AMONG LOS ANGELES JANITORS

The commercial real estate janitorial industry in Los Angeles is a microcosm of broader trends in economic restructuring and the restructuring of

social reproduction. In turn, the Los Angeles Justice for Janitors movement is emblematic of a new wave of organizing and a clear instance of
new struggles over social reproduction.

Restructuring of Commercial Cleaning

In the late 1940s Local 399 of the Service Employees International Union
(SEIU) unionized the cleaning of high-rise buildings in the commercial
real estate industry in Los Angeles. The janitorial workforce consisted predominantly of African-American male migrants from southern U.S. states
employed directly by the building owners. By the late 1970s, unionized
janitors were earning up to $12 an hour and had benefits that included 11
days of paid holiday per year and full medical, dental, vision, and prescription coverage (Mines and Avina, 1992). However, new organizing did
not keep pace with the growth in commercial real estate or with building
owners' distancing strategies.

In the 1970s, building owners began to subcontract cleaning to a
growing number of non-union companies. During the real-estate boom of
the early 1980s, they made a concerted effort to deunionize the industry
by creating competition among non-union cleaning companies. This
"bidding war" resulted in a 42 per cent reduction in cleaning costs
between 1979 and 1993 (Service Employees International Union [SEIU],
Local 399, 1995: 10) as non-union companies won the contracts in new
developments and long-time building owners switched from union to non-
union contractors (Waldinger et al., 1998). The union estimated that
while one-third of janitors in Los Angeles were unionized in 1977, by 1985
SEIU represented only 8 per cent of janitors in Los Angeles (SEIU, Local
399, 1995).

In the early 1980s, SEIU Local 399 tried to organize cleaning companies
through the workplace-based election process of the NLRB. It won elections
at a few buildings; but cleaning companies in response turned over their
entire workforce and hired non-union workers. In addition, if a cleaning
company did recognize the union, the owner could terminate its contract,
replacing it with one of the many non-union companies competing for
bids. The proliferation of non-union competition also rendered strikes
ineffective, and the union increasingly made concessions at the bargaining
table (Mines and Avina, 1992).

The non-union cleaning companies won cleaning bids by informalizing
the recruitment and labour processes. They hired recently arrived, predominantly undocumented Latina/o immigrant women and men in an
effort to lower labour costs. Los Angeles janitors are members of a new
cohort of Latino immigrant workers within which women are well represented. They include Salvadorans and Guatemalans who left home in the

late 1970s and 1980s because of civil war and economic depression. They include as well Mexicans predominantly from the new streams of migrants who left urban areas during the economic crises of the 1980s and early 1990s. Upheavals in gender relations that have come with these economic and political changes have propelled the migration of more single bread-winning mothers who are well represented among Los Angeles janitors (Cranford, 2001: chap. 3).

Cleaning contractors offered competitive bids to the building owners by violating labour laws. They paid the immigrant workers less than the minimum wage through violations of wage and hourly-pay regulations, as well as through paying by the piece rather than by the hour. They did not compensate workers for training periods and encouraged them to bring family members to help finish the work without pay. Finally, they paid the workers in cash to avoid making contributions to social-security and unemployment insurance, as well as to avoid IRCA fines for hiring undocumented workers (Cranford, 2001: chap. 3). The informalization of recruitment and labour processes by cleaning companies, coupled with the distancing strategies of building owners, evoked innovative strategies of resistance.

Organizing Justice for Janitors

The Justice for Janitors (J4J) organizing model has received much attention (Lerner, 1991; Walginder et al., 1998; Wial, 1993). The strategy abandoned the worksite-based NLRB election process and instead sought to organize janitors on a geographical basis. The building owner's ability to sever the contract with the cleaning contractor in the event of a unionization drive, coupled with the growth in non-union cleaning companies, required the union to take wages out of competition in strategic commercial real estate markets.

While in other regions of the country J4J organized entire cities, it was necessary to split the sprawling Los Angeles metropolis into "mini-cities" of concentrated commercial real estate, such as Downtown and Century City. Beginning in 1988, organizing drives moved from mini-city to mini-city. Without mechanisms in the law for broader-based bargaining, and given the building owners' NRLA status as "neutral secondary employers," janitors and their supporters pressed cleaning contractors to recognize the union and pressed building owners to use union contractors through public mass action.

This organizing was very expensive and labour intensive. Key ingredients of its success included corporate research, financial support from the international union, active participation by militant immigrant workers, and mobilization of community support (Waldinger et al., 1998). In a seven-year period (1988–95), J4J organized over 8,000 workers. By 1995 the union had negotiated a master contract that covered 8,500 janitors employed by 18 cleaning companies operating across Los Angeles County.

Less recognized, however, has been how J4J gendered its organizing activities. This was essential to the campaign's ability to consolidate its gains, both in new organizing and in collective bargaining (Cranford, 2001: chap. 4). In particular, J4J's Year 2000 campaign focused on strengthening the union through growth from new organizing, in order to protect currently unionized buildings from going non-union and to advance wages and benefits for union janitors in a new contract. The campaign began with organizing drives concentrating on those building owners most likely to switch to non-union contractors and culminated in a county-wide strike over contract negotiations.[5] Contract demands focused on family health insurance and living wages for suburban janitors.

Campaign strategy included a concerted effort to develop leadership among women janitors. From the beginning, women had been active in the militant, grass-roots organizing in the streets. J4J was and still is a "family affair," to quote a Latina organizer, which involves children and entire families. However, when janitors began to take formal leadership, it was men who dominated the union local. Bringing women into formal leadership required a gendering of recruitment to consider behind-the-scenes forms of leadership through networking, as well as organizing resistant male partners and incorporating children into union activities. Incorporating women's voices also necessitated structuring the work of the gender-integrated committees in a participatory way that recognized both women and men's contributions (Cranford, 2001: chap. 4).

The results of this gendered recruitment appear in Table 15.1. Significantly, women were well represented on the Year 2000 committee, which directed the more specialized organizing and political committees. Women make up approximately 50 per cent of janitors and are thus still slightly under-represented in leadership positions. In the past, the executive board and the negotiating committee were roughly 80 per cent men, and shop stewards, roughly 70 per cent (Cranford, 2001: chap. 4).

Including women's voices ensured that, as the local (now SEIU Local 1877[6]) began to focus on consolidation, it remained wedded to a broader unionism that addressed relations of social reproduction. The downtown workers who were organized first won family health insurance in the 1995 contract, and many then became keen for larger wage increases. However, the new women in leadership were less willing to trade off higher wages for family health insurance, which suburban workers had still not secured. These women were also aware that the women in the broader membership ranked family health insurance as their most important issue (Cranford, 2001: chap. 4). This interest in health insurance reflected the fact that

Table 15.1   Leadership positions, by gender, SEIU, Local 1877, 1999

Position	Women	Men	% women
Executive board*	5	6	45
Shop stewards*	124	168	42
Committees			
Leadership	4	7	36
Negotiating*	10	14	42
Organizing	14	17	45
Political	3	7	30
Year 2000	10	11	48

*Elected positions.
Source: Service Employees International Union, Local 1877.

women do much of the work of social reproduction. This is particularly the case for immigrant women in the United States, where that unpaid effort includes navigating the drastically under-funded public health-care system and the many private clinics – sometimes even travelling to Mexico for less expensive medical care (Hondagneu-Sotelo, 1995). This quote from Eva, a married mother of two, is representative of what I heard during my field-work: "More than anything, the participation of the women is very important. We have to go forward. And we have a lot of ideas. As mothers, as women, we feel the necessity of the children. Fathers, they think about the wallet, the money ... The women take the children to the doctor and they see how much it costs. And that's why we are fighting for health insurance." Eva looked at the broader work of social reproduction, including taking children to the doctor, and linked this work to women activists' struggle for employer-sponsored health insurance. An ethnographic account of J4J resistance illustrates how the leadership of women contributed to J4J's success.

THE GENDERED RESISTANCE
OF JUSTICE FOR JANITORS

One cannot attend a J4J action or meeting without hearing the slogan: "It's in the streets where we win." An account of J4J street protests, where women's grass-roots and formal leadership come together, reveals the gendered resistance of the campaign.

The street protests link building owners to cleaning contractors in order to press the former to take some responsibility for the janitors' health and welfare. This effort uses three tactics simultaneously: legal action, direct action, and symbolic action. Two forms of legal action are central to J4J campaigns. First, the union may file legal suits against non-union cleaning companies for violations of labour standards, such as wage, hour, and occupational health-and-safety regulations, and for sexual harassment and racial discrimination. These suits can cost the contractors thousands of dollars, which pressures the larger ones to negotiate and drives the smaller ones out of business. Second, J4J files Unfair Labour Practice (ULP) suits with the NLRB against the companies for interfering with workers' rights to organize a union. One journalist called J4J's legal action its "hard currency" (Gardetta, 1991: 19). However, J4J must link legal action to the building owner, which holds the ultimate responsibility to improve wages and working conditions.

To connect unfair labour practices and violations of labour standards to the owner must combine legal and direct action. It relies on a U.S. Supreme Court decision (*De Bartalo*), which found that free speech rights override the NLRA, allowing unions to target secondary employers by "non-coercive" tactics. While the law defines picketing as "coercive," freedom of speech protects leafleting or holding rallies in public space (Fisk et al., 2000). Janitors occupy the city's public spaces – the streets, intersections, and sidewalks. In addition, J4J actors will invade the building owner's private, corporate property. Lupe, a long-time worker-activist, emphasized the potential of direct action: "If we do not go public, who is going to know us? It's necessary that we take the struggle into the streets, and what happens happens. Without risk, there is no action, nor recognition." As Lupe explains, this spatial transgression challenges the "socio-spatial order" of the Los Angeles streets (Wilton and Cranford, 2002). In these public protests, janitors emerged from the night shift and inserted themselves into spaces generally occupied by tenants, customers, and building owners during the lunch hour.

Because of the lack of legal responsibility assigned to building owners by collective-bargaining law, J4J actors also focus public attention on the owners' moral responsibility by means of a tactic akin to what Bourdieu (1999) calls "symbolic action" – discursive acts of resistance meant to disrupt taken-for-granted ideas. Central to the concept is inserting the social dimension into the solely economic arguments of neoliberalism. The janitors' symbolic action sought to present unionism as an issue of social justice through what I refer to as "immigrant familism," which presents unionism as a way to achieve upward mobility "for the family" and "for the children" of the immigrant community, and constructs workers' rights as synonymous with immigrants' rights. Through women's active leadership, immigrant familism recognizes single-mother, dual-couple, and extended families, as well as nuclear families, and emphasizes that most women janitors are breadwinning mothers. As a result, it not merely garners sympathy and support and morally presses the building owner. It also resonates with the women janitors as part of a broader struggle of immigrant families to reproduce themselves and their families socially within a political context that has little regard for their standard of living (Cranford, 2001: chap. 4).

Symbolic action used jointly with legal and direct action can also target the building owner. Speeches made in public spaces or to the press, text on flyers, street theatre, and other symbolic acts are more likely to be interpreted as free speech rather than as threatening speech. Elena, a Mexicana janitor, stressed the moral currency of immigrant familism combined with direct action as a "family affair": "It's necessary that we're publicly against the building owners because it is our manner of communication. In addition, it's good when the building owners, the contractors and the press see the children at the marches." An ethnographic account of the public protests illustrates how combining direct and symbolic action that targets building owners, with legal action against the cleaning contractors, presses the owners to contribute to the janitors' health and welfare. A series of actions during the Year 2000 campaign surrounding one of the buildings targeted for organizing is an illustrative case. The owner had recently cancelled the contract with a union cleaning company and contracted with a non-union firm that brought in new workers. The union janitors were about to receive full family health insurance. Owners such as this one were the targets of the Year 2000 campaign.

At one action by 50 workers (29 of them women), 7 children, several union staffers, and me, we collected our picket signs declaring "Unfair Labour Practice" against the cleaning company and began picketing on the thin, public sidewalk. However, in less than five minutes, we moved the line onto the private property close to the glass door entrance. As we passed by the doorways, janitors whistled, hit their palms against the picket signs, and shook their seed-filled pop cans. As a male worker opened the door for a tenant to enter, a long-time woman union member added a louder intonation to her chanting, projecting Spanish into the corporate lobby. After about 20 minutes of picketing in this private area, we moved back to the public spaces surrounding the building. As the traffic light turned green, union members and union staffers stood in between the traffic and the rest of us to keep the cars at bay as we blocked traffic.

Over several months, repeated occupation of the public spaces surrounding this building and transgression into the private space closest to the entrance elicited a response from the building owner. During one protest, he stormed in and out of the building several times, walked across the street to talk to the police, and made several calls on a cell phone. During a rally on the "private" planters, the lead organizer referred to the owner's frantic appearance and told the janitors that the owner was probably upset to see so many Latinos in front of his building during the daytime, when the tenants were present. "We need to give him a clear message that 'we are here and we are not leaving!' (*aqui estamos y no nos vamos!*)." This immigrant-rights slogan surfaced constantly during protests calling for an amnesty for undocumented workers in the 1980s, as well as in protests against Proposition 187 in the mid-1990s, to lay claim to a space that one is denied a right to inhabit. Here this slogan referred to the racialized and gendered class relations in the building services industry. Conceptually, it challenges the owners' efforts to externalize the costs of social reproduction.

The janitors' calls for the owner to take some responsibility for their standard of living gained strength from women janitors' public leadership at both the grass-roots and leadership levels. Women made this link through both familist symbolic action and simultaneous protesting and mothering – a common sight at J4J demonstrations. For example, during another protest at this same building, union member Alicia was carrying her 1½-year-old niece, whom she cares for most afternoons. After a while, she left the picket line to hand out flyers to customers and tenants. At one point, she was holding the baby in one hand and extending the other hand inside a sport-utility vehicle to give a flyer to a Euro-American businessman who had left the building. With this act, Alicia asked him to call the owner and insist on health care and living wages for the building's cleaners and their families. Her simultaneous caring and activist work emphasized the urgency of her request by making visible the costs of raising children. As well, women workers' active participation in public leadership ensured that attention to social reproduction did not reinforce gendered inequalities in the work of organizing (May, 1985).

The strike that culminated the Year 2000 campaign, like most U.S. strikes, required coalitions with non-labour groups and mobilization of widespread support. Recognizing the coalition's emphasis on racialized class polarization in Los Angeles, Spanish-language newspapers printed the common saying during the strike: "*Que limpien los ricos. Estamos en huegla!*" (Let the rich clean. We're on strike!) The press also recognized women's leadership, calling J4J "The New Women's Movement" (Treviño, 2000). That leadership helped to press building owners to assist in workers' social reproduction.

The strike followed a breakdown in negotiations for the new union contract. The union asked for full family health insurance and yearly raises of $1 per hour for janitors across the metropolis. The contractors offered a first-year 50-cent raise to janitors in the highly unionized urban core but wanted to freeze janitors' wages in the less unionized suburban areas. Furthermore, the Building Owners and Managers' Association argued that it had no part in the negotiations between janitors and cleaning contractors. Because of nearly two years of solidarity-building between the relatively more privileged workers in the urban core and those in the suburban areas, janitors voted to go on strike.

Janitors and their supporters combined nighttime picket lines with mass demonstrations. Janitors led an all-day "pilgrimage" from the immigrant neighbourhoods of central Los Angeles to the wealthy west side. The day after the initial walkout, over 3,000 janitors and supporters occupied the downtown business district and held a sit-in at a busy intersection. They combined short-lived occupations of intersections and blockages of freeway entrances and exits with drawn-out acts of civil disobedience leading to arrests.

Because of the janitors' months of mobilizing work, other unions, religious leaders, local politicians, and community supporters joined them in the streets. The Los Angeles Federation of Labor raised money for the strike fund and mobilized members of other unions to help maintain nighttime picket lines and run the food bank. As Teamsters UPS drivers refused to deliver packages to law firms and doctors' offices, and sanitation workers would not pick up the trash from the parking lots, pressure on the building owners mounted. This solidarity was an important step away from traditional business unionism. Additional moral pressure came from the support of religious clergy and laity, who held a Palm Sunday mass and a Seder meal to emphasize the janitors' cause as a just one. Strong support came also from city, county, and state politicians, a reflection of the coalitions against anti-immigrant initiatives spearheaded by this and other immigrant-dominated union locals. City council passed a resolution urging owners to intervene and prevent a strike. As janitors marched to the county offices, blocking the downtown exits of a major freeway on the way, the county supervisors also passed a resolution in support. Several politicians participated in an act of civil disobedience by over 40 people.

Women workers active on the committees leading the campaign gave public speeches alongside men activists and other supporters. Their public leadership ensured that familist symbolic action did not reinforce gendered inequalities in social reproduction. Unions and other social movements have always been sites of struggle over social reproduction. When men are the public leaders, their interests in preserving a gendered division of unpaid work are often those on display (García, 1997). This is even more likely in broad mobilizations that include politicians and other middle-class allies (May, 1985) and generally rely heavily on symbolic action.

Some male leaders expressed traditional immigrant familism, yet in many instances women leaders made their own links between production and social reproduction. The Vice-President of SEIU, Eliseo Medina, is representative of traditional immigrant familism. He told one large rally: "The majority of us have come to this country for a better future for our

families and our children. And no [building] owner or [cleaning] contractor is going to take this dream away from us." Here Medina links the
American dream of upward mobility for the family with labour organizing.
He does not refer specifically to a male-breadwinner family but does not
emphasize that both women and men janitors are breadwinners. In contrast, when women delivered a familist message, both their words and their
embodied presentation emphasized the breadwinning motherhood more
common in the industry. Consider how Cecelia, a single mother of two,
explained to SEIU Local 1877's newspaper why she joined the union: "I
want health insurance. I hurt my back and I can't afford to see a doctor ...
I want to earn enough to finish putting my daughters through college.
Sometime I won't buy myself a pair of shoes because they need money for
books, but I tell them to keep studying. I don't want them to go through
the same things I have to put up with at work." Cecelia's message also went
out over the Spanish-language TV station. Her symbolic action incorporated traditional immigrant familism focused on upward mobility for the
children but also asserted a political motherhood that linked production
to social reproduction and connected improvements in both realms to
labour organizing.

Through an alliance of labour, religious, and political support, janitors
were able to press the building owners to take some responsibility for their
health and welfare. Partly because of mass mobilization, a key real-estate
investment trust that owns buildings in both Los Angeles and Orange
County switched to a union contractor. By the third week of the strike,
widespread public and political support pressed owners to call the contractors back to the table, and they negotiated a new contract with the
union. The new three-year contract secured family medical insurance for
suburban janitors and added a broader package of dental coverage, as well
as additional paid vacation and sick days. While it did not achieve complete urban–suburban wage parity, all janitors will earn wages above those
called for by the city's "living wage" ordinance (described by Luce in this
volume). The contract includes a no-speed-up clause that will mitigate violations of wage and hour laws. It also protects undocumented workers,
requiring employers to call the union if they know of an immigration
agent on or near the premises or know of an audit by the Social Security
Administration. There will also be protections implemented for workers
who lawfully change their names or social security numbers when legal-
ized. The leadership of women was key to this success.

CONCLUSION

Justice for Janitors consolidated its organizing gains by gendering its strategy. Since the movement's beginning, women have been leaders in the

grass-roots organizing. The Year 2000 campaign marked their movement into formal leadership, reflecting a concerted effort to gender the movement's recruitment criteria and practices. As well, the new women leaders ensured continued emphasis on a broader unionism concentrated on a key aspect of social reproduction: family health care.

An ethnographic account of the public protests surrounding the organizing drives and the strike illustrates how the janitors and their allies are challenging not only economic restructuring, but also the restructuring of social reproduction. Using a combination of legal, direct, and symbolic action, janitors and their allies pressed building owners to help pay for the health and welfare of the service workers and their families. Anti-immigrant stereotypes in California depict immigrant women and children as economic burdens on the state, but the janitors' symbolic action shows the building owner as the public charge. The grass-roots and formal leadership of women workers alongside men strengthened the claims about health and welfare. Through both direct and symbolic action, women linked wage earning and union leadership to mothering, making visible the relationship between production for the market and social reproduction. The leadership of immigrant women janitors ensured a broader look at social reproduction that challenged building owners' distancing strategies as well as the cleaning companies' efforts to informalize labour relations.

The women members' unpaid work of social reproduction shaped their activism and contributed to a broader unionism. In turn, the family health care and living wages guaranteed in a union contract have mitigated some of women's unpaid work. However, unlike many women-dominated locals in professional sectors, this local has not yet addressed child care in collective agreements. If the union were to bargain for child care, it would provide a stronger challenge to inequalities in social reproduction. However, even sustaining the gains accrued thus far may be difficult.

Employers are increasingly challenging direct action and other nontraditional organizing strategies in court (Fisk et al., 2000). Only changes in labour laws that compel building owners to bargain with the janitors will assure workers a better standard of living. Changes in immigration policy are also essential. While SEIU and other unions have been pushing for a new amnesty for undocumented workers, repercussions in the wake of the 11 September, 2001 attacks on the United States make an amnesty unlikely. In addition, the U.S. Supreme Court has recently limited undocumented workers' ability to exercise the freedom of association accorded to legal residents and citizens.

In Justice for Janitors, a conscious gendering of class resistance created a powerful unionism able to link social reproduction to production, but further challenges to unequal gender relations will require more structural change. Justice for Janitors and other islands of community unionism are crucial to creating the political will necessary for those broader changes.

NOTES

1 This study is based on fieldwork from September 1997 to September 1999 and on follow-up interviews during the March 2000 strike. I participated in training sessions, strategy meetings, and demonstrations; worked as a janitor for two months; analysed U.S. census economic and demographic data pertaining to this industry; consulted extensive press coverage on the movement; conducted 35 in-depth interviews with women janitors and 7 interviews with women members of union staff; and engaged in numerous shorter conversations with both women and men janitors and staff. The names used in this chapter are pseudonyms.

2 The National Labour Relations Act (NLRA), 1935, was amended by the Taft–Hartley Act, 1947, and the Landrum–Griffin Act, 1957.

3 See *Hoffman Plastic Compound, Inc. v. NLRB.*

4 The Immigration Reform and Control Act (IRCA), 1986, gave residency to those who had continuously lived "illegally" in the United States since January 1982 or who had worked a minimum of 90 days in U.S. agriculture between May 1985 and May 1986.

5 The campaign was shaped by a set of compromises in the 1995–2000 union contract. Three months before the expiration of that contract, suburban janitors would receive a raise of 40 cents per hour and family health insurance (costing roughly $2 per hour per janitor). It was assumed that cleaning contractors would pass these costs on to building owners.

6 After the 1995 signing of the contract, an internal leadership struggle resulted in the international union imposing an 18-month trusteeship. In the spring of 1997, the janitors voted to leave Local 399, which included health-care workers, and join Local 1877, a local of janitors in central California. See Cranford, 2001, for an account of this transformation.

REFERENCES

Atkinson, John. 1987. "Flexibility or Fragmentation? The United Kingdom Labour Market in the Eighties," *Labour and Society* 12 (1), 87–105.

Banks, Andy. 1991. "The Power and Promise of Community Unionism," *Labour Research Review* 18, 16–31.

Bonacich, Edna, and Richard P. Appelbaum, with Ku-Sup Chin, Melanie Myers, Gregory Scott, and Goetz Wolff. 2000. *Behind the Label: Inequality in the Los Angeles Apparel Industry.* Berkeley: University of California Press.

Bourdieu, Pierre. 1999. *Acts of Resistance against the Tyranny of the Market.* New York: New Press.

Breecher, Jeremy, and Tim Costello, eds. 1990. *Building Bridges: The Emerging Grass-roots Coalition of Labour and Community.* New York: Monthly Review Press.

Brody, D. 1997. "Labor Elections: Good for Workers?" *Dissent* (summer), 71–7.

Bronfenbrenner, K., S. Friedman, R. Hurd, R. Oswald, and R. Seebers, eds. 1998. *Organizing to Win: New Research on Union Strategies.* Ithaca, NY: ILR Press.

Burawoy, Michael. 1976. "The Functions and Reproduction of Migrant Labor: Comparative Material from South Africa and the United States," *American Journal of Sociology* 81 (5), 1050–87.

Clawson, Dan, and Mary Ann Clawson. 1999. "What Has Happened to the US Labor Movement? Union Decline and Renewal," *Annual Review of Sociology* 25 (August), 95–119.

Cornelius, Wayne. 1989. "The U.S. Demand for Mexican Labour," in Wayne Cornelius and Jorge Bustamante, eds., *Mexican Migration to the United States: Origins, Consequences, and Policy Options.* San Diego: Center for U.S. Mexican Studies, University of California, San Diego, 25–46.

Cranford, Cynthia. 1998. "Gender and Citizenship in the Restructuring of Janitorial Work in Los Angeles," *Gender Issues* 16 (4), 25–51.

– 2001. "Labour, Gender and the Politics of Citizenship: Organizing Justice for Janitors in Los Angeles." Doctoral dissertation, University of Southern California, Los Angeles.

Crump, Joe. 1991. "The Pressure Is On: Organizing without the NLRB," *Labour Research Review* 18 (fall/winter), 33–43.

Delgado, Héctor L. 2000. "The Los Angeles Manufacturing Action Project: An Opportunity Squandered?" in Ruth Milkman, ed., *Organizing Immigrants: The Challenge for Unions in Contemporary California.* Ithaca, NY: ILR Press, 225–38.

DuRivage, Virginia A., Françoise J. Carré, and Chris Tilly. 1998. "Making Labor Law Work for Part-time and Contingent Workers," in Kathleen Barker and Kathleen Christensen, eds., *Contingent Work: American Employment Relations in Transition.* Ithaca, NY: ILR Press, 263–80.

Fisk, Catherine L., Daniel J.B. Mitchell, and Christopher Erickson. 2000. "Union Representation of Immigrant Janitors in Southern California: Economic and Legal Challenges," in Ruth Milkman, ed., *Organizing Immigrants: The Challenge for Unions in Contemporary California.* Ithaca, NY: ILR Press, 199–224.

Fix, Michael E., and Jeffrey S. Passel. 2001. *US Immigration at the Beginning of the 21st Century.* Testimony before the Subcommittee on Immigration and Claims Hearing on U.S. Population and Immigration, Committee on the Judiciary, U.S. House of Representatives. www.urban.org

Friedman, S., R.W. Hurd, R.A. Oswald, and R.L. Seeber, eds. 1994. *Restoring the Promise of American Labor Law.* Ithaca, NY: ILR Press.

García, Alma, ed. 1997. *Chicana Feminist Thought: The Basic Historical Writings.* London: Routledge.

Gardetta, Dave. 1991. "True Grit: Clocking Time with Janitors Organizer Rocio Saenz," *LA Weekly* 14 (35).

Glenn, Evelyn Nakano. 1992. "From Servitude to Service Work: Historical Continuities in the Racial Division of Paid Reproductive Labour," *Signs: Journal of Women in Culture and Society* 18, 1–43.

Green, James, and Chris Tilly. 1987. "Service Unionism: Directions for Organizing," *Labour Law Journal* 38 (8), 486–95.

Hartmann, Heidi. 1976. "Capitalism, Patriarchy, and Job Segregation by Sex," in M. Blaxall and B. Reagan, eds., *Women and the Workplace: The Implication of Occupational Segregation*. Chicago: University of Chicago Press, 137–70.

Hondagneu-Sotelo, Pierrette. 1995. "Women and Children First: New Directions in Anti-Immigrant Politics," *Socialist Review* 25 (1), 169–90.

Hondagneu-Sotelo, Pierrette, and Cristina Riegos. 1997. "Sin organización, no hay solución: Latina Domestic Workers and Non-traditional Labor Organizing," *Latino Studies Journal* 8, 54–81.

Johnston, Paul. 1994. *Success While Others Fail: Social Movement Unionism and the Public Workplace*. Ithaca, NY: ILR Press.

Laslett, Barbara, and Johanna Brenner. 1989. "Gender and Social Reproduction: Historical Perspectives," *Annual Review of Sociology* 15, 381–404.

Lerner, Stephen. 1991. "Lets Get Moving: Labor's Survival Depends on Organizing Industry-wide for Justice and Power," *Labor Research Review,* 18, 1–15.

MacDonald, Martha. 1991. "Post-Fordism and the Flexibility Debate," *Studies in Political Economy* 36 (fall), 177–201.

Marcelli, Enrico, and David M. Heer. 1997. "Unauthorized Mexicans in the 1990 Los Angeles County Labour Force," *International Migration* 35 (1), 59–83.

May, Martha. 1985. "Bread before Roses: American Workingmen, Labor Unions and the Family Wage," in R. Milkman, ed., *Women, Work and Protests: A Century of U.S. Women's Labor History*. London: Routledge, 1–21.

Meulders, Danièle, and Luc Wilkin. 1987. "Labour Market Flexibility: Critical Introduction to the Analysis of a Concept," *Labour and Society* 12 (1), 3–17.

Milkman, Ruth. 2000. "Immigrant Organizing and the New Labor Movement in Los Angeles," *Critical Sociology* 26 (1/2), 59–81.

Mines, Richard, and Jeffrey Avina. 1992. "Immigrants and Labor Standards: The Case of California Janitors," in J.A. Bustamante, C. Reynolds, and R.H. Ojeda, eds. *U.S.–Mexico Relations: Labor Market Interdependence*. Stanford, Calif.: Stanford University Press, 429–48.

Sassen, Saskia. 1995. "Immigration and Local Labor Markets," in Alejandro Portes, ed., *The Economic Sociology of Immigration: Essays on Networks, Ethnicity and Entrepreneurship*. New York: Russell Sage, 87–127.

Service Employees International Union (SEIU), Local 399. 1995. *A Penny for Justice: Janitors and L.A.'s Commercial Real Estate Market*. Los Angeles.

Sherman, Rachel, and Kim Voss. 2000. "'Organize or Die': Labor's New Tactics and Immigrant Workers," in Ruth Milkman, ed., *Organizing Immigrants: The Challenge for Unions in Contemporary California*. Berkeley: University of California Press, 81–108.

Stanford, Jim. 1996. "Discipline, Insecurity and Productivity: The Economics behind Labour Market 'Flexibility,'" in Jane Pulkingham and Gordon Ternowetsky, eds. *Remaking Canadian Social Policy: Social Security in the Late 1990s*. Halifax: Fernwood Publishing, 130–50.

Treviño, Joseph. 2000. "Janitor Power: The New Women's Movement," *LA Weekly* (28 April–4 May).

Turner, Lowell, Harry C. Katz, and Richard W. Hurd, eds. 2001. *Rekindling the Movement: Labor's Quest for Relevance in the 21st Century*. Ithaca, NY: ILR Press.

Vosko, L. 2002. *Rethinking Feminization: Gendered Precariousness in the Canadian Labour Market and the Crisis in Social Reproduction*. 18th Annual Robarts Lecture, York University, 11 April. Toronto: Robarts Centre for Canadian Studies, York University.

Waldinger, Roger, Chris Erickson, Ruth Milkman, Daniel J.B. Mitchell, Abel Valenzuela, Kent Wong, and Maruice Zeitlin. 1998. "Helots No More: A Case Study of the Justice for Janitors Campaign in Los Angeles," in K. Bronfenbrenner, S. Friedman, R. Hurd, R. Oswald, and R. Seeber, eds., *Organizing to Win: New Research on Union Strategies*. Ithaca, NY: ILR Press, 102–20.

Wial, Howard. 1993. "The Emerging Organizational Structure of Unionism in Low-Wage Services," *Rutgers Law Review* 45 (summer), 671–738.

Wilton, Robert, and Cynthia Cranford. 2002. "Toward an Understanding of the Spatiality of Social Movements: Labor Organizing at a Private University in Los Angeles," *Social Problems* 49 (3), 374–94.

16

Labour's Current Organizational Struggles in Argentina: Towards a New Beginning?

VIVIANA PATRONI

Despite a quarter-century of political turmoil and far-reaching policy shifts, Argentina has failed to produce a viable pattern of economic and political development.[1] Argentina initially attempted after 1976 what became known in Latin America as "neoliberalism."[2] Following the end of the dictatorship in the 1980s, a debate originally over the nature and stability of democracy gave way to growing concern with the magnitude and implications of economic decline. During the 1990s the government consolidated neoliberalism. The subsequent crisis that unfolded in 2001 reflected not only the failure of neoliberal restructuring, but also government's increasing detachment from public demands for a resolution to the most pressing social problems that emerged under neoliberalism.

Market reform in Argentina has dismantled labour legislation, motivated by the premise that more flexible labour relations would help create jobs. However, unemployment has reached unprecedented levels since the 1990s, even during periods of economic growth. Moreover, the flexibility in labour regulation has led to a greater incidence of precarious and informal employment. The arduous conditions faced by large segments of the population constitute the most tangible shortcoming of the neoliberal economic model, and also its most serious challenge. Given the magnitude of the problem, the debate about these conditions has sparked a broader questioning of current policies.

This process has transformed key social and political actors. Changes within the Peronist party[3] (the Justicialista Party, PJ) indicate the pervasiveness of "market-friendly" policies. The PJ's zealous dismantling of labour legislation that dated back to the initial Peronist policies of the

1940s reveals the party's reorientation. But it also indicates the changing position of labour – specifically the General Confederation of Labour (CGT), once the "backbone" of Peronism – within the party and within society.

It is in the context of the traditional labour movement's weakening position within the Peronist party that this chapter considers the emergence of alternative expressions of working-class organization. In particular, it looks at the Central of Argentinean Workers (CTA), founded in the early 1990s. The CTA's organizational efforts have helped generate a new structure for the growing numbers of people unemployed, underemployed, or in precarious work conditions. In this respect, the CTA has transcended traditional patterns of labour organizing, reaching out to sectors that are increasingly excluded from the benefits of economic growth. The CTA's capacity to organize such sectors has transformed it into an increasingly viable alternative to neoliberalism, both as a union force and as a political referent.

Equally important, the CTA's organization of new sectors might give it the strength to challenge the traditional Peronist labour leadership and its anti-democratic and bureaucratic practices.

To set the background for this discussion, the first section considers the continuing economic crisis faced by Argentina and its implications for labour markets. The second section discusses the recent experience of the Peronist labour movement, particularly its internal conflicts and its responses to reforms since the 1990s. The third examines labour organization under neoliberalism. The final three sections assess the implications and possibilities of the alternative organizational and political model proposed by the CTA. The conclusion raises questions regarding the CTA's prospects for helping to construct a more democratic unionism and a more just society.

THE ECONOMIC CONTEXT FOR NEOLIBERALISM

The military coup of 1976 closed a long phase in the modern history of Argentina. Beginning early in the century, the country grounded industrialization on generating substitutes for imports as the dominant source of economic growth in the country. While the program of neoliberal reforms implemented by the military from 1976 on dismantled key aspects of import-substituting industrialization, it failed to consolidate an alternative model of development. In fact, 25 years later, Argentina still lacks even the elements of a viable alternative program for economic growth.

The military's neoliberal reforms aimed at addressing the increasing social and political tensions that had accompanied economic growth since the mid-1960s (Nochteff, 1998: 30). Labour, particularly its more radical and combative sectors, had been central to these conflicts, challenging not only the structures of power fostered by development but also the place of the traditional labour leadership within them. The military blamed the way in which industrialization had emerged under protectionism for the power of labour unions. In effect, a captive domestic market had allowed producers to raise prices to cover the costs of concessions extended to labour. The military therefore sought to limit labour's push for higher wages by forcing capital to adjust to trade liberalization. The workings of the market, imposing its discipline on labour and on capital, would curb the capacities of organized labour (Canitrot, 1981: 133).

The policies of the military regime sharply reduced real wages, while intense political repression made opposition practically impossible. At the same time, however, reform also destroyed some industrial sectors, particularly small- and medium-sized firms. The overall impact was a marked decline in industrial output, from 28.2 per cent of gross domestic product (GDP) in 1974 to 25.3 per cent in 1978 and 22.4 per cent in 1982.[4] This structural transformation – deindustrialization, accompanied by unemployment and growing heterogeneity in labour markets – altered the context for labour struggles in Argentina (Patroni, 2001: 266).

The return to democracy in 1983 failed to improve living standards and to renew economic growth and ushered in unprecedented hardship for most Argentineans. President Raúl Alfonsín (1983–89) could not solve the pressing foreign debt (inherited from the military regime) or control inflation, culminating in the hyperinflation of 1989. This experience, and a repeated episode in 1991, created the atmosphere in which Peronist President Carlos Menem (1989–99) could impose further neoliberal reforms. This package included privatization, further liberalization of financial markets, and trade liberalization. Central to this program was the attempt to control inflation, the chronic Argentinean malaise. It is there that Menem achieved his key victory – the Convertibility Law.[5] He also further deregulated labour markets.

The neoliberal reforms have profoundly worsened working conditions, income distribution, the level of employment, and poverty, as a few figures can show. Poverty increased exponentially during the 1990s, affecting 35.4 per cent of the population in October 2001 and over 54 per cent a year later (*Pagina 12*, 2002). While in 1974 "official" unemployment afflicted only 3.4 per cent of the labour force, the figure had reached 18.3 per cent by the last quarter of 2001 and continued to climb during 2002. If we include underemployment, 34.6 per cent of the labour force experienced employment problems in October 2001. The changes were also dramatic in income distribution. The income of the lowest quintile fell from 4.5 per cent of all income in 1990 to 3.8 per cent in 1998, while that of the highest quintile increased from 50.6 per cent of the total to 54.25 per cent. By the late 1990s real salaries were still 23 per cent below their 1986 level and 30 per cent below the level of 1980 (Mancebo, 1998: 187). Conditions of work have changed dramatically for those who still have an occupation. The "flexibilization" of labour regulations has created large groups of people who work fewer hours than they desire (the underemployed), lack permanent positions (the temporarily employed), work without any social provision (the unofficially employed), or work in the informal economy. This growing uncertainty has devastated family incomes, and many women from the most vulnerable sectors have joined the labour force (Mancebo, 1998: 188).

THE PERONIST LABOUR MOVEMENT AND POLITICS

Before we examine how these structural transformations affected traditional and emerging working-class organizations, this section briefly reviews the evolution of organized labour, especially its relationship to Peron and the Peronist movement. The labour movement grew enormously during Juan Peron's two presidential terms, from his electoral victory in 1946 until a military coup overthrew him in 1955. From approximately half a million members in 1945, union membership grew to 2.5 million in 1954. Moreover, with compulsory collection of dues, unions became financially powerful, able to provide handsome salaries and other benefits for their leaders; a new sense of prestige was attached to such positions. Union leaders also gained access to political appointments and elected office.

Labour's new power allowed it to become central in the political conflicts that followed Peron's downfall (Gaudio and Thompson, 1990). Since Peronism was loosely organized, once the military outlawed it after 1955, only the labour sector retained real organizational capacity. Thus some key unions became major players within Peronism. Moreover, because the party was banned from presidential elections, unions also became the main brokers of the Peronist vote.

The country's most conservative forces after 1955 wanted a return to the conditions prior to Peronism, particularly a curtailment of union power. However, even the anti-labour military regime did not attempt a frontal attack on union bureaucracies. In fact, faced with their enormous influence within Peronism, their social power, and their control over their rank and file, most post-populist regimes (at least until 1976) actually tolerated an increase in union power.[6] Legislation reinforced their corporatist power, in particular compulsory affiliation, the principle of a single union per trade, and a legislated monopoly of representation for the CGT. Moreover, in the late 1960s the military regime entrenched unions' financial power by institutionalizing their right to control and administer health-care services (*obras sociales*) for their members (Moreno, 1993: 53–6).

The corporatist[7] relationship between state and organized labour led labour leadership to limit democratic participation within unions. Labour organizations became increasingly authoritarian and hierarchical, with their main function being to intervene with and negotiate within the upper echelons of business and politics. They used fraudulent electoral practices, single electoral lists, or sometimes simply open intimidation to hold on to power. Their most extreme actions involved violent persecution of left-wing supporters, both real and imagined, in the years before Isabel Perón's administration collapsed in 1976 (Halperin-Donghi, 1998: 25–6). This period was the culmination of a long process, interrupted only for a few years after Juan Peron's downfall in 1955, which saw unions become undemocratic, bureaucratic, and openly coercive.[8]

As political conflict deepened and Peronism broadened, the unions faced challenges from left-wing alternatives. From the late 1960s until the mid-1970s, the Peronist party (in power again 1973–76) and labour movement became increasingly violent. Yet the worst repression of progressive labour forces came under the military regime after 1976. The state widely used disappearances, torture, imprisonment, and executions to create terror and attempt to eliminate opposition to neoliberalism.

The return of democracy in 1983 posed new challenges to the traditional labour movement. The Justicialista Party lost political power (Gutierrez, 2001) and this reflected broader changes that eventually led to the emergence of alternatives to the CGT. Paradoxically, probably the key variable in accelerating the crisis within the labour movement was Peronism's return to power in 1989.

LABOUR ORGANIZATIONS AND NEOLIBERALISM

Restructuring in Argentina from the 1980s on transformed the context of corporatism. Peronist labour organizations could not prevent a decline in living standards for most workers, including the dramatic erosion of real wages and ever more precarious working conditions. While the CGT ultimately supported most of the legislative changes that reduced protections for workers, the core of the legal framework securing its own power remained untouched, but this success cost it dearly in terms of legitimacy. None the less, the CGT did call for several general strikes after 1996, partly to assert its right to negotiate with the government over labour legislation and partly to protect its own prerogatives, such as its administration of health care services.

Similar calculations guided the government with respect to its labour allies. Sensitive to the delicate political balance that permitted his restructuring policies, President Menem did not push for reforms that were not essential to his broader objectives. While his relations with the CGT were at times quite tense, he invested considerable political effort in avoiding a final rupture with it, especially after his party's defeat in the congressional elections of 1997. The new labour laws passed by Congress in September 1998 reaffirmed industry-wide collective agreements and protected union health-care programs from private competition.

Avoiding further friction with labour became crucial for Menem during the last year (1998–99) of his presidency. As in the congressional elections of 1997, in 1999 the two major opposition parties – the Radical Party and FREPASO (Front for a Nation in Solidarity) – ran together again under the Alliance ticket. The presidential victory of the Alliance's Fernando de la Rúa in October 1999 was predictable, although it would prove ephemeral.

After the Peronist defeat, strong internal disagreements surfaced in the CGT over renegotiation of its position within the PJ and over the terms for both negotiation and conflict with the non-Peronist government. Differences reached a critical point as the new president pushed for a new labour law, and the CGT split. This schism reproduced traditional divisions, between one group willing to negotiate and another more reliant on confrontation. The "official" CGT was keen on dialogue with the Alliance government, but it called for several general strikes and supported other opposition activities. Currently led by Rodolfo Daer, this sector of the CGT represents orthodox Peronism, and several of its unions advocate the "business unionism" now prevalent in newly privatized sectors. Clearly, this form of unionism faces the most serious lack of popular legitimacy: its relationship to the former Peronist government renders its discourse on workers' rights painfully hollow. Moreover, while Daer can still mobilize large sectors of the working class, he has found it increasingly difficult to adjust to the new wave of labour militancy since 2001.

The other faction, led by Hugo Moyano and known as CGT "*rebelde*" or "*disidente*" (dissident), descends from the Movement of Argentinean Workers (MTA), founded in 1994. It remained within the CGT during Menem's presidency and retained strong connections to the Peronist party. However, its more active opposition to the reforms of the 1990s helped to sustain its stronger claim to workers' interests. Much of its organizational strength derives from the influence of some of its member unions, mostly in services and transportation, which restructuring has affected less. Moyano's very active presence within labour opposition to De la Rúa's adjustment programs has given him important political clout. This process also led him into common actions with more radical labour alternatives – most notably, the CTA and the Combative Class Current (CCC), another key organization of the unemployed. None the less, these alliances were limited to specific events, and Moyano does not seek more organic links with these forces.

A more militant stance can, however, be compatible with corporatist tradition. Moreover, Moyano's calculations regarding mobilization and negotiation derive from his faction's capacity to influence outcomes within the PJ. A public debate regarding the possible reunification of the two CGTs in the last half of 2001 coincided with such a period of realignment and redefinition within the party (*Página 12*, 2001b). However, the subsequent political crisis of December 2001 and the presidential campaign in 2003 made clear the party's fragmentation and the diverging interests of the two CGTs. Given very high levels of uncertainty in Argentina, Moyano is more likely to remain very cautious about any consolidation either within the party or outside.

Both CGTs faced threats from the government's direct attack on sources of their traditional power (such as the legislated deregulation of the health-care system) and from the growth of alternative labour organizations, particularly the CTA. The CGT has faced similar conditions before, including internal divisions and the emergence of more radical alternatives. But conditions today are fundamentally different. First, the high incidence of unemployment and underemployment and the growth of precarious and informal employment have reduced the power of unions, especially in industry. Second, the CGT's weaker position within the Peronist party has also left a political vacuum within the union leadership.

However, for both CGT factions the key dilemma is the evaporation of the discourse that defined Peronism as a working-class struggle. It was a Peronist government that transformed the context for the shared collective memory that underlay working-class political identity (James, 2000). But if weakening social and political identities threaten traditional labour organizations, they are also the context for new labour alternatives. The CTA's experience thus becomes relevant and promising, as we see next, despite the negative legacies of Argentina's traditional unions.

BUILDING AN ALTERNATIVE: THE CTA AND NEW COLLECTIVE IDENTITIES

The CTA's origins date back to the decision in 1992 by large public-sector unions, in particular the Association of Public Workers (ATE) and the Central of Education Workers (CTERA), to abandon the CGT. These unions, and others associated with the CTA, have strong historical connections to more independent and combative alternatives within the labour sector. Besides questioning the CGT's viability as a channel to confront neoliberal policies, the CTA has advocated greater independence from political parties and the state and a search for new and more timely forms of organization. Autonomy had been a central goal for the ATE since the

1980s, when Victor De Gennaro, now the CTA's leader, became its secretary general.

The perception that the close connection with the state and the party hampered Peronist unionism has unified the ATE and the CTA. As we saw above, the impressive institutional role acquired by labour directly reflected the state's power over it. This relationship with the state and the party conditioned labour demands and transformed unions. To escape this problem, the CTA has emphasized that political autonomy is an essential feature of the alternative labour movement. Moreover, it believes that emerging labour alternatives must help construct a new political force able to represent people excluded from current structures. It understands that a real alternative must emerge outside traditional politics. It now needs to identify such a political force, how to build it, and the CTA's role in it.

From the start the CTA has defined politics as an effort to mobilize and to construct an alternative to neoliberalism.[9] Such a movement is the first step in overcoming the crisis of representation that permeates Argentina's government, parties, and union movement (Lozano, 2000: 6). Thus the CTA identifies the crisis in the labour movement also as a political crisis, expressed by the lack of alternatives (political in general and electoral in particular) to represent the majority of the population. However, this characterization has not hindered several CTA leaders' political involvement, which has in turn sparked internal controversy.

The CTA has always defined itself as a social movement aimed at consolidating a new awareness of the sources of working-class problems and at presenting an alternative to dominant ideas about the primacy of markets and the incontestability of globalization. However, how to generate political alternatives has remained unclear. During the 1990s, this tension expressed itself as a choice between linking diverse social movements and constructing a political party (Novick and Tomada, 2001: 102). In its most recent congress in December 2002, the CTA decided to work towards a "Social and Political Movement," but more recent tensions will test its new capacity as a political actor.

The CTA looks at the working-class crisis in terms of its own collective political identity and seeks to articulate a "new thought" – a counter-hegemonic discourse that could construct new social subjects and identities.[11] The contestation of democracy under conditions of generalized social exclusion has been central to the CTA's activity and has been the organizing principle behind a number of key struggles. As the CTA defines the scope for new political alliances, its effort to build truly representative forms of organization will determine the future role of that organizing principle.

Problems and tensions within the CTA's political perspectives do not reduce the innovative nature of its efforts to constitute a new unionism. It

has opened a debate and departed markedly from Peronist union traditions. Its methods show its capacity for innovation and its potential for
becoming a pivotal force in constituting new forms of working-class organization.

ORGANIZING THE WORKERS OF THE NEW CENTURY

The CTA has developed direct or individual forms of affiliation in response
to the working class's weakening structural position and the increasing
fragmentation of workers' reality. This alternative organizing approach
may become an effective response to the growing individualization of the
experience of most workers under neoliberalism. Specifically, it is an
attempt to create a new unity and common identity among workers,
including the unemployed and those who work under precarious conditions. The CGT has tended to target the unemployed and underemployed
as possible sectors to organize and has consistently emphasized the traditional formal workforce as the main constituency for unions. The CTA
traces the antecedents for the incorporation of these new and growing
labour market sectors to the traditions of working-class organization and
in so doing reclaims a fundamental aspect of workers' history.[12]

From a pragmatic perspective, direct affiliation has also been a response
to the serious decline in union membership. Rising unemployment and
the increase in precarious forms of employment have deeply cut into
union membership. As Clarke's paper in this volume shows for South
Africa, adverse conditions in labour markets have reduced unions' capacity to struggle for increased regulation of working conditions. Direct affiliation to the CTA becomes a viable alternative for all those workers who
cannot join a traditional union. CTA members thus represent a wide range
of work experiences, including the unemployed, the underemployed, the
self-employed, retirees, and workers in the formal sector.

Because of its capacity to organize all types of workers, the CTA has also
become invaluable to the growing number of women in the labour market,
who particularly experience unemployment and precarious employment.
Negative trends in employment relationships have also undermined the
struggle to change policies that continue to reproduce gender discrimination in pay (Camusso, 2000). Women's growing participation within the
CTA has prompted initiatives to foster a specific organization of women
and to participate in national forums on women's issues. Women have also
played a crucial role in some of the federations affiliated to the CTA (discussed below) and have secured changes in CTA structures to gain better
representation in leadership.

Workers in the formal sector can also take individual membership in the
CTA. This has been the subject of controversy, since it may weaken existing

union structures. None the less, the CTA's objective in recruiting individual members in already-unionized workplaces has been to organize workers to contest union elections and introduce the union as a collective affiliate of the CTA.

Within the CTA, workers organize according to labour market experience. The CTA has groups for the unemployed, for retirees, and for workers in similar sectors of production. These organizations reflect the CTA's goal to articulate sector-specific demands and to provide some of the benefits of union membership. All CTA members, whether affiliated individually or through their unions, have an individual and secret vote for the central's leadership.

As a response to neoliberalism's segmentation of working-class experiences, and to the restructuring of capital, the CTA has also fostered the organization of sectoral federations. While specific unions may continue to be central in the fight for sectoral demands, these federations may serve as intermediate organizations with the capacity to generate broader responses. For example, the Federation of Industrial Workers encompasses workers from all industrial sectors and aims to elaborate an alternative to deindustrialization. Other federations cover health, education, and energy.

Probably the most innovative of such bodies is the National Federation of Workers for Land, Housing, and the Habitat (FTV). Organized on territorial lines, it is the most heterogeneous and brings together constituencies generally ignored by traditional unions – landless peasants, First Nations, shanty-town dwellers, tenants' associations, and neighbourhood associations – organizing around issues related to the cost and delivery of newly privatized public services. It also includes the employees of state housing institutions. From its very origins, unemployment was a common experience of many FTV members. As unemployment worsened in the 1990s, the federation became a central organization in the growing movement of the unemployed.

One of the most effective organizing principles of the FTV (and of the whole CTA) has been that "the neighbourhood is today the new factory in Argentina, and we are all workers."[13] Given the experience of its members, the "neighbourhood factory" evokes not only a site of struggle, but also a place to forge political identities. Moreover, members' identification as workers is also a vivid reminder of the contingent nature of employment in Argentina.

THE SHAPE OF NEW STRUGGLES

The reality of unemployment and informal employment means that traditional forms of working-class struggle – particularly strikes and general

strikes – do not have their traditional impact.[14] Moreover, many CTA organizations focus on issues not directly related to labour conflicts. Thus there
has been a growing emphasis on new forms of mobilization and struggle
that reflect the reality of participants. The disruptions of highways and
bridges, land occupations, demands for reduced public-service tariffs, and
demands for unemployment insurance and work programs have become
fundamental strategies. The FTV has been prominent in leading these
innovative struggles since the late 1990s, becoming one of the most important organizations of the unemployed.

In recent years the *piqueteros* – the participants in this new style of political activism – have become a much-talked-about example of the erup-
tion of "new social subjects" in politics.[15] Roadblocks became typical in
mass protests in several regions hit very hard by the privatization of
public enterprises that had provided the main source of employment.
One of the best examples is the community mobilization in General
Mosconi, in the northern province of Salta. The main employer had
been Argentina's public petroleum company, YPF. Other roadblocks
were central in organizing mass demonstrations against delayed wage
payments to public-sector employees, as provincial governments faced
increasing fiscal problems. Progressively, *piquetes* became the most
common form of protest in the poorer areas around Buenos Aires, hit
hardest by unemployment.

While in the 1990s the unemployed and poor communities were
primary actors in these roadblocks – one of the few available forms of
protest – workers in the formal sector and students have also been key participants. Moreover, many roadblocks featured marches, involving a range
of social sectors and political organizations, and general strikes. Thus
there has been integration of different forms of protest.

The implementation of public work programs (initially known as Plan
Trabajar and since 2002 as Programa Jefes y Jefas de Hogar) or their extension and renewal has been a major demand of most roadblocks. These programs provide small, temporary subsidies to participating workers in
exchange for work on public projects. The protests have been successful in
obtaining this limited form of government action, but not in reorienting
broader government policies on unemployment.

However, the CTA has tried, with other groups, to provide the roadblocks
with broader political objectives and to co-ordinate regional struggles at
the national level. It helped organize three consecutive weeks of protest
during July and August 2001 (involving roadblocks, demonstrations in
downtown Buenos Aires, public-sector and teachers' strikes, and other
forms of community-based protests, such as blackouts and "*cacerolazos*," or
pot banging). This program of popular protest was a response to the De la

Rúa government's adjustment plan, aimed at a "zero deficit" (implying a reduction in public-sector salaries and pensions and cutbacks in other areas of public spending). These days of protest legitimized the role of organizations for the unemployed. However, internal divisions run deep. One line dividing the experience of movements of the unemployed is their part in the distribution of social assistance. As with the FTV, this function has placed some organizations as intermediaries between the government and their own grass-roots members, with the obvious potential for patronage and weaker political impact.

Probably the CTA's first and more complete attempt to organize a coalition to challenge the overall framework of neoliberal policies involved the formation of the National Front Against Poverty (FRENAPO). The Front's core strategy – sustained during 2001 by a number of major public events – was to call for a national referendum on the creation of a national employment- and training-insurance system (*seguro de empleo y formación*). This had been one of the CTA's key demands for several years, so its ability to mobilize a number of social forces – most notably, human rights organizations, student associations, and unions – was a sign of its increasing social and political influence. The request for a referendum did not gain official support, but an unofficial referendum took place in December, with results that encouraged the organizers: while FRENAPO had set its target at 2 million votes, approximately 3.1 million Argentineans took part. These results indicate both the very high levels of discontent in Argentina and an obvious willingness to express it actively.

On 19 and 20 December, 2001, massive public opposition, violent protests, and a financial and banking crisis forced the De la Rúa government from power. A new Peronist regime led by Eduardo Duhalde eventually took office. The pace of social conflict during 2002 imposed new challenges on the CTA, increasing the pressure to define more clearly its political role. As we saw above, its decision in December 2002 to build a more explicitly political movement represents a new way of conceiving the role of a labour organization, but it certainly also raises problems. There are a number of issues still unresolved within the CTA, particularly its capacity to unify the struggles of different sectors of the working class.

In moving towards its new role as a political movement, the CTA has defined this problem in the context of a broader dilemma – namely, the political vacuum left by the legitimacy crisis of traditional parties and institutions. Even as the CTA, a new alternative for union organizing, has allowed various labour sectors to organize and to respond to the drastic deterioration of living and working conditions over the last 25 years, becoming a political force may be difficult, all the more so after the presidential election of May 2003.

CONCLUSION

Quite clearly, novel methods in unionism may not always be viable. None the less, the CTA has been successful in building its credibility, in the eyes of large sectors of the population, as a legitimate organizational option in the search for an alternative to the corporatist practices so prevalent in the history of unionism in Argentina. More specifically, its ability to incorporate the growing sectors most excluded by neoliberalism has given it the basis to challenge both the policies that intensified poverty and marginalization and its most important competitors within the labour movement.

However, the CGT still has a number of opportunities to regain relevance, particularly with the return of Peronism to power since December 2001. Reunification of the two CGT factions would inject the organization with new dynamism and credibility. While the CGT's traditional basis of legitimacy may have weakened through the 1990s, it still possesses considerable organizational capability and, with that, political influence.

Besides its challenge to the CGT, rooted in shifting working-class political identities, the CTA does not have a clear strategy towards traditional labour organizations. It is also not clear how these emerging identities relate to previous forms of political identification. This seems particularly relevant as exclusion was central to the Peronist expression of working-class political identity. Other problems are posed by relying on "exclusion" as a basis for the construction of social identity. The experience of exclusion is not necessarily a unifying force or the basis for enduring solidarity. Moreover, there are many alternatives through which those excluded might envisage their inclusion – not all of which presume collective action. Similarly, an identity of exclusion, and the instability and vulnerability that it implies, do not necessarily lend themselves to a focus on transforming democratic participation. In summary, while exclusion might provide a common experience through which large sectors of the population construct new and common identities, this outcome is certainly not the only possibility. The outcome will depend on which particular meaning "exclusion" acquires, as a new political discourse emerges from the concrete practices and conflicts of Argentina's dynamic and unstable political environment.

Ironically, however, this uncertainty probably highlights the CTA's weakest point. The CTA seems to understand that the "construction of power" is a long-term process, through which the accumulation of shared experiences can become an effective counter-hegemonic discourse. However, this does not necessarily resolve the immediate political dilemmas faced by the sectors that it wants to attract to respond to the political demands of the moment. Yet mobilization and protest by themselves do not generate greater participation and commitment unless they are part and parcel of a broader and reachable objective.

None of these problems, however, need become a dead end for the CTA. It has already helped reconstitute belief in possible and viable alternatives to neoliberalism. And it has helped organize the process of building a broad and strong political movement motivated by that belief. The CTA has become a major new option, both for labour and for the broader sectors that it has included in its struggles. Its main challenge now will be to define its scope for political alliances while fostering more democratic alternatives for labour organizing and participation.

NOTES

1 Financial support from SSHRC and IDRC allowed me to undertake this research project, including fieldwork in Argentina during 2001 and 2002. I would also like to thank Leah Vosko and Jim Stanford for very helpful comments on an earlier version of this chapter and Ruth Felder for her research assistance.

2 Neoliberalism has involved market deregulation, trade and financial liberalization, and privatization of state-owned firms.

3 This party emerged in Argentina after the rise of Juan Domingo Peron to power in the mid-1940s. Central to Peronist policies since then have been support for union demands and expansion of state expenditures in health care, education, and other social services. Peronism also represented the legitimization of labour as a social actor and the incorporation of previously marginal sectors of the population. Until the 1990s, Peronism stressed domestic markets in the process of economic growth.

4 This structural change affected various industrial branches differently. The sectors more affected were those more vulnerable to foreign competition. Thus, for instance, between 1976 and 1982 production of textiles, clothing, and footwear fell by 35 per cent, furniture by 40 per cent, and metallic products, electrical equipment, and transport material by 30 per cent (Kosacoff and Azpiazú, 1989: 16).

5 Through the Convertibility Law the government set a fixed parity between the dollar and the domestic currency. It also established that the monetary base must be guaranteed 100 per cent by reserves, either in foreign currencies or in gold.

6 See, for example, Cavarozzi, 1984.

7 "Corporatism" is "a system of interest representation in which the constituent units are organized into a limited number of singular, compulsory, noncompetitive, hierarchically ordered and functionally differentiated categories,

recognized or licensed (if not created) by the state and granted a deliberate representational monopoly within their respective categories in exchange for observing certain controls on their selection of leaders and articulation of demands and support" (Schmitter, 1974: 93–4).

8 One of the best accounts of union struggles during this critical period appears in James, 1988.

9 Victor De Gennaro, secretary of the Congress of Argentinean Workers, defines power as "not something abstract. On the contrary, it is something very concrete: it's the capacity to organize our own forces in order to do what we believe needs to be done; that is power" (Rauber, 1999: 61).

11 Interview with Claudio Lozano (Rauber, 1999: 140).

12 Moreover, De Gennaro suggests that the CTA's experience would be difficult to duplicate in another country that lacked the same traditions of class struggle (Rauber, 1998: 292).

13 Interview with Luis D'Elía, Buenos Aires, April 2001.

14 There were many general strikes in Argentina during the 1980s and 1990s. They were quite effective in gaining support from large groups of workers.

15 Since the late 1990s there has been an exponential increase in roadblocks – a sign of both the mounting economic crisis and rising levels of organization. In the first half of 2001 there were 71 per month – almost twice as many as in 2000 and three and a half times as many as in 1999. In 1998 there were on average only four roadblocks per month; *Pagina 12*, 2001a.

REFERENCES

Camusso, Cristina. 2000. "La tercera jornada," *Le monde diplomatique, Edición Cono Sur,* 15.

Canitrot, Rodolfo. 1981. "Teoría y práctica del liberalismo. Política inflacionaria y apertura económica en la Argentina, 1976–1981," *Desarrollo económico* 21 (83), 133.

Cavarozzi, Marcelo. 1984. *Sindicatos y política en Argentina.* Buenos Aires: CEDES.

Gaudio, Ricardo, and Andrés Thompson. 1990. *Sindicalismo peronista/gobierno radical. Los años de Alfonsín.* Buenos Aires: Fundación Friedrich Ebert.

Gutierrez, Ricardo. 2001. "La desindicalización del Peronismo," *Política y Gestión* 2, 93–112.

Halperin-Donghi, Tulio. 1998. "The Peronist Revolution and Its Ambiguous Legacy," *Occasional Papers Series,* no. 17. London: Institute of Latin American Studies, University of London.

James, Daniel. 1988. *Resistance and Integration: Peronism and the Argentine Working Class, 1946–1976.* Cambridge: Cambridge University Press.

– 2000. *Doña María's Story: Life History, Memory, and Political Identity.* Durham, NC: Duke University Press.

Kosacoff, Bernardo, and Daniel Azpiazú. 1989. *La industrial Argentina: Desarrollo y cambios estructurales*. Buenos Aires: Centro Editor de América Latina.

Lozano, Claudio. 2000. "Escenario político, económico y social de la Argentina." Buenos Aires: IDEP y CTA, June.

Mancebo, Martha. 1998. "El nuevo bloque de poder y el nuevo modelo de dominación (1976–1996)," in Hugo Nochteff, ed., *La economía Argentina a fin de siglo: Fragmentación presente y desarrollo Ausente*. Buenos Aires: Eudeba.

Moreno, Omar. 1993. "La ultima oportunidad del sindicalismo Argentino," in Holm-Detlv Kohler and Mandred Wannoffel, eds., *Modelo neoliberal y sindicatos en América Latina*. Mexico: Fundación Friedrich Ebert.

Nochteff, Hugo. 1998. "Neoconservadorismo y subdesarrollo. Una mirada a la economía Argentina," in Hugo Nochteff, ed., *La economía Argentina a fin de siglo: Fragmentación presente y desarrollo Ausente*. Buenos Aires: Eudeba.

Novick, Marta and Carlos Tomada. 2001. "Reforma laboural y crisis de la identidad sindical en Argentina," *Cuadernos del CENDES* 18 (47), 79–110.

Página 12 (Buenos Aires). 2001a. "Aumenta el Riesgo-piquete," 23 June. www.pagina12.com.ar/2001/01–06/01–06–23/pago4.htm

– 2001b. "Y ya lo ve, y ya lo ve, habrá una sola CGT, pero será recién en el 2002," 26 Sept. www.pagina12.com.ar/2001/01–09/01–09–26/pag 18.htm

– 2002. "Más de la mitad afuera de la mesa." 28 Dec.

Patroni, Viviana. 2001. "The Decline and Fall of Corporatism? Labour Legislation Reform in Mexico and Argentina during the 1990s," *Canadian Journal of Political Science* 34 (2), 249–74.

Rauber, Isabel. 1998. *Una historia silenciada*. Buenos Aires: Pensamiento Jurídico Editora.

– 1999. *Tiempos de herejías*. Buenos Aires: Instituto de Estudios y Formación CTA.

Schitter, P.C. 1974. "Still the Century of Corporatism?" in F.B. Pike and T. Stritch, eds., *The New Corporatism: Social–Political Structures in the Iberian World*. Notre Dame, Ind.: University of Notre Dame Press.

Critical Times for French Employment Regulation: The 35-Hour Week and the Challenge to Social Partnership

STEVE JEFFERYS

Why regulate capitalism? The British socialist philosopher and historian R.H. Tawney (1929: 251) put the case succinctly: "Power over the public is public power; nor does it cease to be public merely because private persons are permitted to buy and sell, own and bequeath it, as they deem most profitable ... The question ... is whether the public possesses adequate guarantees that those [economic movements] which are controllable are controlled in the general interest, not in that of a minority."

While this chapter is about France, it is also about the fundamental issues raised by Tawney. For the conflict sparked by the French government's 35-hour laws is directly about whether private buyers and sellers of labour power should exercise the "power" to determine how long people work or whether it should be "controlled in the general interest."

In 1996 France had the world's fourth-largest economy. Its 22 million economically active workers produced just slightly more output (at purchasing-power parity) than did Britain's 26 million. When an economy of such a size appears to counter the global trend of deregulation, it presents a key case study in the debate between free marketeers and those who believe, with Tawney, in regulation of "power over the public."

In June 1998 and January 2000 the French National Assembly cut the "legal" working week by four hours to 35 hours. These were the sixth and seventh laws passed on the issue since 1981. Most French employers were angry: not only did the reduction seem excessive, it also ran counter to the general deregulation occurring in most of France's competitors. It would, they claimed, trigger an exodus of jobs from France. However, unemployment has fallen significantly since passage of the laws, and by the end of

2000 the 35-hour laws had led to an average two-hour reduction in average weekly working hours in firms with 10 or more workers.

Does the French case show that it is still possible to control global capitalism? And if so, can the nation state still exercise that control? This chapter illustrates the same arguments raised by Broad, MacNeil, and Gamble and by Luce elsewhere in this volume – namely, that there is no simple answer. The industrial and political mobilizing capacities of capital and labour ultimately decide the outcomes of these struggles. The first section of this chapter sets out the evolution of French regulation and its working-time laws. The second examines capital and labour's ambivalent responses to the 35-hour laws.

THE EVOLUTION OF STATE REGULATION

The national specificity of France derives essentially from its geography. Its soil and climate provided huge agricultural surpluses from both grape and grain, while the gradual formation of the nation-state from the ninth to the sixteenth centuries bequeathed a strong state untainted by a Magna Carta or a Protestant revolution. The wealthiest European country from the seventeenth to the nineteenth centuries, it both straddled key North–South trade routes and faced west towards the New World. This combination of rich agriculture and rich trade produced a wealthy but dispersed ruling elite whose tastes mimicked the aristocracy – in wanting both fine, hand-crafted consumer goods and a role in exercising centralized political power. The result was not just the French Revolution and a continuing presence of the state as a key arbiter and regulator of economic and social relations. It was also a particularly slow transition from a peasant economy to a peasant–worker economy and finally to a worker–peasant economy. This had major consequences for social and political life in the nineteenth and twentieth centuries: none of France's major social classes – the aristocracy and the church, financiers and industrial capitalists, rich peasants and rural and urban working classes – developed sufficient coherence and co-ordination to dominate society and its institutions. In place of such domination, the state (senior civil servants and generals) negotiated continuity and compromise between competing class interests (Jefferys, 2003).

Centralized regulation of labour mobility, pay, and working hours thus has a long history in France. While the state often changed form, it had three main motives for intervening in trade, production, and employment relations: to ensure its own survival (at risk during times of war and uncontrolled labour unrest); to increase tax revenues through "modernizing" production (often in response to Britain's growing economic hegemony); and to cement alliances with pressure groups to create or strengthen its political legitimacy. Until 1944 the dominant view was that the state should regulate relations between an employer and its workers only in an emergency or to protect the morally vulnerable. Since then, the Keynesian view – that the state should intervene preventively to *avoid* emergencies – has dominated, sustained by *dirigist* politicians and capitalist employers, most of whom benefit directly from the presence of that strong centralized state.

Regulation from the Fourteenth to the Nineteenth Centuries

How did this acceptance of centralized state regulation of economic and social life come about? Interventions began after the Black Death of 1349, when, to cope with the resulting tight labour market, royal ordinances limited workers' mobility. From the mid-fourteenth until the eighteenth centuries, "vagabonds" (the unemployed) could receive sentences of hard labour (for five years, ten years, or life) and in the sixteenth century even execution. In the 1660s Louis XIV's finance minister, Jean-Baptiste Colbert, invested in 400 manufacturers to reduce France's dependence on imports of high-quality goods and military supplies; many of their workers were forced labourers (Castel, 1995: 126). Forced labour was extensive: between 1768 and 1772 nearly 112,000 "vagabonds" were captured (a per-head bonus was paid for each captive) and set to work, many on the Physiocrat Turgot's national road network for stage-coachs (Castel, 1995: 98).

The *ancien regime* also modernized France to compete with the industrial revolution taking place in Britain. It encouraged workhouse production for the market and promoted new forms of behaviour appropriate to market discipline. In particular, it reinforced employers' power through the worker's passbook, or *livret ouvrier*. Introduced in 1749, this was an attempt to "fix" highly mobile artisans and early industrial workers to their particular employers. Workers had to finish the job for which they had been hired and give eight days' notice before leaving. The system of temporary certificates gave way in 1781 to a permanent passbook, where the employer inserted both the dates of the workers' employ and any outstanding fines still owed. This method of controlling workers' mobility and earnings ended temporarily during the French Revolution, but Napoleon Bonaparte reinstated it in 1803, and in 1813 the maximum imprisonment for working without a passbook increased to six months.

Napoleon also re-established in 1806 a system of industrial courts to hear disputes between employers and workmen – the *Prudhommes* – although two years earlier his Civil Code had stipulated that, in the event of a conflict, the employer's word should be accepted. Under Napoleon III in 1854 and 1855 the passbook became an "internal" passport for workers: the *livret ouvrier* became compulsory for both male and female workers and was now to be held by the worker rather than by the employer so that he or she could produce it whenever asked (Dewerpe, 1989: 92–94). It dropped out of use late in the century in the face of acute labour shortages, but controls on immigrant workers introduced in 1888 and 1893 obliged them to register with the police every time they moved house and forbade employers from hiring unlisted workers (Schor, 1996).

In the French Revolution the state reinforced employers' power and contractualized the employment relationship. In 1791 it broke up the guilds, banned workers' associations and strikes, and imposed "free" contracts between individual workers and employers. Though modified in 1864, this ban remained until 1884, when trade unions finally received independent legal existence (Soubiran-Paillet, 1999). But from the 1890s on, as centrist politicians began to note the socialists' growing electoral strength and the unions' increasing presence, the state began to intervene more frequently, collecting labour statistics, in 1906 setting up the Ministry of Labour, and in 1910 consolidating all labour laws into a Labour Code that still lies on the desk of every French manager responsible for hiring and firing.

Working Time in the Nineteenth and Twentieth Centuries

The area of state intervention in the labour market with the biggest impact before the Second World War concerned working time (Jefferys, 2000). This was an issue around which alliances of moralists, natalists, militarists, reformers, trade unionists, and socialists could form with relative ease. Fear of the rioting poor led to an 1841 law making it illegal for children under 7 to work in textile factories and restricting the working hours of children from 8 to 12 years old to a maximum of 12 hours per day. In 1874 the legal minimum working age for all children went up to 12, night work became illegal for all under 16, and children could work only six days a week (Bordeaux, 1998). In 1892 all workers under 18 and all women employed in manufacturing were limited to a maximum 11-hour day and excluded from night work (Viet, 1998) – the latter protection finally abrogated only in 2001, because of the European Union's law on equality. In 1900 the maximum working day for women and children fell to 10 hours. Although a general strike for the 8-hour day called by the Confédération générale du Travail (CGT) on 1 May 1906 was defeated, a new law later that year extended the 10-hour day to men and gave them Sundays off (Jefferys, 1997).

Immediately following the First World War, regulation on working time finally broke from the British model. The French state's interest in catching up with its rival made it henceforth consistently more interventionist than the British – and it often used direct legislation on working time when it wished to reform collective bargaining.

Thus, in the face of a huge upsurge in trade unionism, the state issued legal directives in the immediate postwar period imposing the results of sectoral collective bargaining on groups of employers and unions and legislated the long-demanded 8-hour day (for a maximum 48-hour week).[1] Collective bargaining between employers and unions would now regulate working-time patterns. In 1936 a mass wave of factory occupations led the Popular Front government to strengthen the collective-bargaining machinery of 1919. New laws created the core of the contemporary system of industrial relations, and once again forced employers to the bargaining table by implementing a "legal" 40-hour week and two weeks of paid holiday (Didry, 1998).

The period immediately after the Liberation in 1944 saw pervasive state regulation. This built in part on the corporatist experience of the Vichy government (Crom, 1995). But in the main it arose from the requirements of running a war-devastated economy in a radically new political context. The Communist Party (PCF) had emerged as the largest party in the first postwar elections; the Allied victory had boosted support for democratic state planning and nationalization; Charles De Gaulle believed firmly in state intervention to rebuild France. Laissez-faire ideology and the French employing class were on the defensive following the interwar failures of neoliberalism, the 1940 defeat of France, and employers' widespread collaboration with the German occupiers. Between 1944 and 1950 the government implemented widespread nationalization, included the right to strike in the constitution of the Fourth Republic, institutionalized national and sectoral collective bargaining via Works Councils, established a national Planning Commission in 1946, and imposed the First Plan for 1947–51. It introduced regulatory controls in four key areas of labour policy – a national minimum wage, sectoral bargaining that could be extended to all workers, redistributive social welfare and pensions, and "standard" working time laws. This legacy inhibited the growth of income inequalities in the 1980s and 1990s (OECD, 1996a).

In the 1960s, the Gaullist government extended state regulation to impose "wage norms" in an attempt to restrain inflation by holding down incomes – a policy that surfaced again in the late 1970s. Later, a joint employer–government committee was created to monitor the top 100 French companies under threat of denial of government contracts and tax breaks if they defied the guidelines. If other companies contravened the directives they would receive a three-month price freeze and only gradual price rises for the following year (Jefferys and Contrepois, 2001). These restraints on incomes helped provoke the mass mobilization from May–June 1968 to the mid-1970s that markedly improved workers' lives. Compensation to employees as a proportion of gross domestic product (GDP) rose from 44.5 per cent in 1960 to a high of 56.7 per cent in 1982

(OECD, 1998), and benefits from the jointly managed welfare system grew as a proportion of household disposable income from 19.3 per cent in 1960 to 35.3 per cent in 1983 (Ambler, 1991). Meanwhile, working time, which had increased during the reconstruction and boom of the 1950s and 1960s, finally began to fall again, helped by new laws extending legal annual holidays.

State Regulation in the 1980s and 1990s

After the socialist François Mitterrand won the presidency in 1981, regulation increased massively[2]. The government made huge investments in research in state industries, increasing them by 25 per cent each year from 1981 to 1984, while also backing struggling private-sector employers in sectors like machine tools, textiles, shipbuilding, and paper (Stoffaës, 1991: 463–4). These investments, combined with the cumulative impact of the European Union's (EU's) Common Agricultural Policy on expanding agri-business, meant that a whole raft of large companies experienced direct benefits from expanding state intervention.

For employers, however, the negative side of regulation was the reform of industrial relations. The Auroux Laws of 1982 included a 39-hour week, a requirement that half of all overtime worked in excess of 130 hours per year be compensated by extra time off, and five weeks' annual holiday. Procedural reforms also gave workers the right to free "expression" inside the workplace, established Health and Safety Committees, and obliged employers to negotiate every year on wages and working conditions with their employees (Guedj and Vindt, 1997). The individual firm or establishment became the level at which to negotiate change, and, to encourage employers to decentralize negotiations, the government allowed significant exemptions from common work rights if agreed to in firm-level bargaining.

By 1986 the political context had changed significantly. Mitterrand had turned away from Keynesianism, and a right-wing majority was returned to the National Assembly. Prime Minister Jacques Chirac privatized part of what had been nationalized in the early 1980s. However, neither this nor later privatization after 1993 reduced the number of workers directly employed by the state. Total public-sector employment remained steady at about 5 million, before rising again after 1988, when Mitterrand received a second seven-year term. By 1996 it had reached 5.5 million, and it stands still higher today (Institut national de la Statistique et des Études économiques [INSEE], 2000), reflecting the sector's continuing importance.

From 1986 on, working-time regulation encouraged enterprise-level flexibility within *optional* frameworks. In 1987 legislation freed firm-level

negotiations from any link with a sectoral agreement and permitted annu-
alization and more flexible opening hours *without* reductions in working
hours. In 1993 another law allowed businesses to negotiate weekly hours
ranging from zero to 48 hours in exchange for shorter hours that could
reduce work by as little as one minute per week. It also gave them strong
incentives to hire more part-time workers. The Robien Law of 1996 provided financial inducements to firms that increased flexibility by reducing
working time, whether or not by company-level collective agreement
(Goetschy, 1998). It would appear that all these laws passed between 1982
and 1996 "had in common less the intention of imposing time norms than
of opening negotiating spaces" for "time flexibility [to become] the counterpart to any reduction in hours" (Thoemmes and Terssac, 1997: 54).

The 35-Hour Laws of 1998 and 2000

What of the Aubry laws of 13 June 1998 and 19 January 2000? Do they too
essentially press work reorganization and reform of industrial relations on
French capitalism to make it more competitive and profitable? Certainly
the volume of collective bargaining increased at the firm level, up from
11,800 agreements reached in 1997 to 31,000 in 1999 (Direction de l'Animation de la Recherche, des Etudes et des Statistiques [DARES], 2000:
40). The laws also seem to have lowered wage expectations. A large-scale
survey of workers who had been on 35 hours for at least a year found that
just over one in 10 (12 per cent) had wages reduced as a result, 48 per cent
experienced wage freezes, 5 per cent had lower wage rises than would have
been the case without the 35-hour agreement, and only 31 per cent
retained their former wages and experienced no "wage moderation"
(DARES survey quoted in *Le Monde,* 15 May 2001). A variety of methods
enhanced temporal flexibility. One survey found that 30 per cent of a
sample of 1,000 firms with more than 20 workers regularly employed temporary workers, and this proportion rose to 34 per cent among businesses
(making up 43 per cent of the total sample) that had implemented the 35-
hour week (*Le Monde,* 27 June 2000). An analysis of the first 22,500 agreements reached between June 1998 and August 2000 showed that the most
common implementation methods were annualized hours regimes (in 54
per cent) and free-floating additional rest days (in 50 per cent of agreements; *Premières synthèses,* November 2000). Not surprisingly, workers were
divided on these changes: the DARES survey found that 28 per cent
believed that their working conditions had deteriorated; 46 per cent, that
they had not changed; and 26 per cent, that they had improved (*Le Monde,*
15 May 2001).

Ongoing negotiations and contentious issues led to more open conflict
as the new laws were implemented. From 1998 to 1999 "local" private-

sector strikes rose by 5 per cent. Changes in working time were responsible for 25 per cent of those strikes in 1999, up from 12 per cent in 1998 (DARES, 2000: 224). Often these conflicts involved manual workers having to be on the job Saturdays as a result of "annualized" hours – for example, under Michelin's 2001 agreement employees must work 15 Saturdays each year.

Although the Aubry laws clearly allow employers to reorganize work, the overall picture is more ambiguous. Shorter hours actually created some jobs. It is difficult to gauge what proportion of the one-million drop in unemployment since Socialist Lionel Jospin's election as prime inister in 1997 was the result of the 35-hour laws. The government claimed that the laws saved or created up to 287,000 jobs (*Le Monde*, 15 May 2001). At least one respected French labour economist, Michel Husson, finds evidence of up to 500,000 new jobs created between March 1997 and March 2001 (Husson, 2002); another sees hardly any (Pisani-Ferry, 2001). In December 2000 the Ministry of Labour reported that 60 per cent of the positions generated by the 35-hour week were permanent (as opposed to short-term, contractual posts), and the INSEE has suggested that since 1998 the overall balance of new posts has reversed – from being two-thirds short term to two-thirds permanent today. The government estimates that since June 1998 50,000 part-timers have switched to full time (quoted in *35 heures la dépêche*, 10 May 2001).

The overall balance sheet is also difficult to judge because the Aubry measures are more far-reaching than most previous working-time regulations: the size of the hours reduction is much greater than the one hour of 1982, and these regulations are universal. Many businesses will find loopholes or defy the laws. But the laws initially required that all enterprises with over 20 staffers implement the shorter work-week on 1 January 2000, and small firms on 1 January 2002. A problem for the (outgoing) Jospin government in the presidential and parliamentary elections of April–June 2002, however, was that employers' opposition and the postponing of implementation for small firms meant that by the time of the 2002 elections the legislation had affected only one-third of all employees.

Yet the economic context since 1998 has been favourable, whereas the 39-hour week started in a politically induced recession. The 35-hour week, and particularly the second Aubry law, which introduced a "legal" working year of 1,600 hours, has already affected many people's lives. The changes in normal working hours for full-timers in firms with ten or more workers appear in Figure 17.1.

By the end of 2000, average agreed working hours for full-time workers in all such businesses had fallen to 36.6 hours, or down more than two hours from the average from 1993 to 1998 (*35 heures la dépêche*, 10 April 2001). Those employees most favourable to the shorter working week are

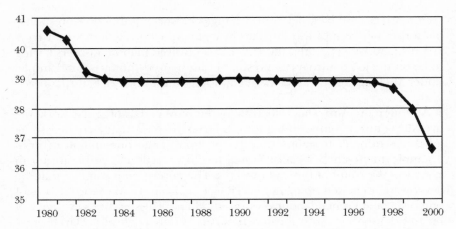

Figure 17.1   Average working hours per week, full-time workers in firms with 10 or more employees, France, fourth quarter, 1980–2000

those eligible to take the cuts as extra whole days off. Thus the principal immediate beneficiaries are the growing numbers of white-collar workers and managers whose overtime hours never counted and who can now take an extra ten days of holiday per year. According to French hoteliers, these people are now taking more "mini-breaks" than ever before. More than half the managers affected for at least one year have taken at least one mini-break away as a result, compared to just 13 per cent of manual and clerical workers (*Le Monde*, 15 May 2001).

Little wonder, then, that reduced working time has become more popular. In November 2000 a national opinion poll reported overall approval at 61 per cent (compared to 30 per cent who disapproved), with managers (64 per cent), the unemployed (72 per cent), and technical and professional white-collar workers (74 per cent) being most supportive. Overall 71 per cent of those questioned believed that the laws improved the quality of life, as did 87 per cent among employees already working 35 hours (quoted in *35 heures la dépêche*, Feb. 2001). In the DARES survey (covering those with at least a year on 35 hours) 69 per cent of managers reported better quality of life, compared to just 49 per cent of unskilled workers (*Le Monde*, 15 May 2001). Little wonder, too, that the strongest opposition comes from employers in industry and commerce (41 per cent approval).

But it is not only the employers who find the new laws problematic. The laws have also created challenges as well as opportunities for French unions, and we now turn to the laws' impact on the mobilizing capacities of both employers and unions.

DIVISIONS IN UNITY: LABOUR AND CAPITAL
IN THE FACE OF THE 35-HOUR WEEK

The 35-hour laws have offered both a threat and an opportunity to French employers and workers. They have mobilized and demobilized, united and disunited, both employers' associations and the unions. To explain these developments requires a closer look at the context.

French industrial relations experienced a stable trajectory through much of the 1980s and early 1990s. Before the wave of public-sector strikes in 1995, most commentators agreed that "normalization" was taking place. Its principal elements were a declining significance for national and sectoral collective bargaining, a slow decline in union membership, a drop in the numbers of strikes and days lost, particularly in the private sector, and (since the tearing down of the Berlin Wall in 1989) a rapprochement between the leaderships of the two largest trade-union confederations (the CGT and the Confédération française démocratique du Travail, or CFDT). Even after 1995, with the possible exception of the decline in union membership (which appears to have bottomed out), these trends resumed.

Yet the strike movement of October–December 1995 and the extent of support for the public-sector workers protesting against reductions to their pensions (Béroud and Mouriaux, 1997; Jefferys, 1996) revealed that workers could still articulate or channel *class* interests through the union confederations, which, though enfeebled and divided, still provided legitimacy to the protests and a "lattice-work of organization" (Shorter and Tilly, 1974). They expressed themselves politically, and the strike wave affected the Parti Socialiste (PS), which had just seen the narrow defeat of its presidential candidate. Then, in October–December 1995, after Chirac had veered back to the political right, a mass movement protested the government's attack on pension rights. These experiences, as well as the need to secure an electoral arrangement with the Parti Communiste français (PCF), insulated the PS and the group around its leader, Lionel Jospin (a former Trotskyist), from pressures to abandon a redistributive agenda to which the British New Labour Party had already succumbed. Instead, the PS's 1997 election platform promised a 35-hour week to create new jobs and enhance workers' quality of life.

The election of a coalition government with PS, PCF, and Green ministers did not imply any deep radicalization. As in Britain, the left's 1997 victory was partly a result of government actions. President Chirac, to his credit (and unlike the Austrian conservatives in 2000), refused to allow the Gaullist Party to make an electoral deal with the neo-fascist National Front. Alain Juppé, his prime minister, remained highly unpopular for having spearheaded the government's rightward turn. The mass mobilization of 1995 thus triggered events that brought a minority left government to power and subsequently established the new national-level labour law. The right parties' subsequent refusals to promise repeal of the 35-hours laws (a position that would have been politically unpopular) and doubts about their re-election chances in 2002 helped lead the French employers' association – the Conseil national du Patronat français (CNPF, or the *patronat*) – to re-evaluate its role and strategy.

Employers' Opposition and Disunity

Tension between large and small firms within the CNPF existed from its foundation in 1946. In 1965, a "Liberal Charter" section of the CNPF leadership proposed a shift away from dirigisme with a direct appeal to small and medium-sized employers. Yet growing social tensions and the explosion of 1968 effectively curbed this tendency (Brizay, 1975). Instead the CNPF became stronger, reinforcing *paritarism* – institutionalized pluralism and joint regulation of welfare with the unions, especially the non-Communist unions. The CNPF became more evidently the voice of France's major firms, all headquartered in Paris. Between December 1968 and March 1975, and with industrial conflict intense, the CNPF signed nine national agreements, covering such issues as reduced working time, the establishment of workplace union branches, and training (Sellier, 1984). Most of these agreements became part of the Labour Code, confirming the organic link between the social partners and the state.

In 1981 the nationalization program led the biggest private-sector employers to establish the Association française des enterprises privées (AFEP) as a ginger group within the CNPF. The CNPF then mounted a massive campaign against "additional charges" on business, organizing a mass meeting in December 1982 of 15,000 employers, who were joined by 6,000 construction employers (Weber, 1986). Many went on an investment strike and withdrew billions of francs from the economy. In 1983 the CNPF's president urged a meeting of 500 employers to profit from the presence of the left in power by "lowering workers' purchasing power" (quoted in Weber, 1986: 341). The CNPF now outflanked the more militant opposition being mounted by the two smaller national employers' organizations, while the government had to make a whole series of concessions.

By 1988, however, with Mitterrand narrowly re-elected, the CNPF's confrontational strategy looked to be dead. Its continuation risked further alienating big business from political power. Links between big business and government increased after the nationalizations of 1981 and the subsequent privatizations of 1986–87. Many individuals high up in formerly nationalized and now private companies were top civil-servant graduates from the Ecole nationale d'administration or from the other elite *grandes écoles.* They knew the top politicians personally and were ready to use their new influence within the CNPF to moderate its oppositional tone. By the early 1990s a new leadership at the CNPF was much more prepared to negotiate.

With the 1997 election of a socialist government, the pendulum swung back again. The "social" face of Jean Gandois, the CNPF's president from the nationalized steel industry, was already receiving criticism as neoliberalism spread. The head of insurance employers, Denis Kessler, openly started identifying the business opportunities that would follow restructuring of the welfare system on the basis of individual insurance- and pension-funds, rather than on the self-financing, redistributive basis established in 1946.

In this context, the tripartite meeting of 10 October 1997 called by Jospin on the 35-hour laws was decisive. The CNPF was furious because its total opposition to the 35-hour week did not carry enough weight; it did not receive the expected postponement of implementation and widespread exclusions. Gandois immediately resigned, calling for a replacement with a "killer" instinct to unite the increasingly disparate employer class – senior managers of overseas multinationals operating in France, top managers of French-based multinationals, and the bosses of small and medium-sized French firms – against new controls on capitalism.

The CNPF's next president, Ernst-Antoine Seillière, chief executive of the Wendel family-owned investment fund, was more representative of private capital. Closely supported by Kessler, who took overall responsibility for the CNPF's social policy, he decided to use its sudden unity to build a "new CNPF" as a different and more effective political organization. In Strasbourg in October 1998 the Mouvement des entreprises de France (Medef) was launched before an audience of 1,700 employers. Seillière declared: "We are changing the world ... Taboos, forbidden issues, statutes, certainties about acquired rights, laws and peremptory decrees no longer suffice to exorcise reality. It is our task, we the entrepreneurs, to bring back French society to the reality" (quoted in *Le Monde,* 29 Oct. 1998).

The Medef's new aims are now much closer to the Liberal Charter of 1965 than to tripartism. Its choice of "Mouvement" to replace the anachronistic "patronat" reflects a new and highly political agenda. In the absence of reliable conservative allies in the National Assembly or even in the presidency, the employers now stress the need to act on their own, even in defiance of a parliamentary majority and the law. The Medef thus prepared to "promote an entrepreneurial spirit by reiterating the messages, aspirations and ambitions of business people on the ground," to campaign for reform of the state "as an absolute priority," and to turn some areas of social welfare over to the private sector.

The Medef consists of 85 broad industrial associations (fédérations) and 600 affiliated trade organizations, but it also organizes in 165 regional associations. Overall it claims to represent between 700,000 and one million French firms and to have an annual income of 180 million francs (*Le Monde*, 3 April 2001). Its new structure includes a larger national executive (up from 36 members to 45) and stronger regional representation (up from 8 to 12) and stipulates that three-quarters of executive members be serving company heads. Its constitution reverts to the pre-1969 situation in making national intersectoral agreements the exception rather than the rule and in allowing any of the 22 sectoral federations to insist on a two-thirds majority of the executive before it negotiates nationally. As with the Confederation of British Industry (CBI), firms may now join the Medef directly, rather than only through sectoral federations (Bilous, 1998).

The Medef responded to the 35-hour week in several ways. It advised its sectoral associations to seek agreements with the unions that would weaken the previous national framework agreements on working hours by any means necessary, including threats to denounce sectoral bargaining in its entirety if their demands were not met. At the same time the Medef launched a huge public campaign against the 35-hour laws. Its smaller members worried that the shorter week would increase costs and lower profits, while its larger members ideologically opposed more government controls. In October 1999 it brought these two groups together in a huge, 25,000 person protest meeting against the "100 per cent old-fashioned Aubry law." Kessler, the protest's principal organizer, recalled that "this was the second time in 20 years that we have come together to say 'no' to dogmatism, 'no' to the seizure of social dialogue, and 'no' to an administered economy" (quoted in *Le Monde*, 6 Oct. 1999). The truck owners' federations, opposing a decree imposing a 39-hour limit on weekly hours, organized a blockade of major frontier crossing-points in January 2000 (*Le Monde*, 9 Jan. 2000).

Finally, Sellière and Kessler used the Medef's unity to extend the conflict to the welfare system. They criticized the existing system for occupying a huge financial space that could be privatized. Further, its redistributive, "pay as you go" structure means that the current generation of workers and their employers pay directly for those who are sick, unemployed, or retired. The rising numbers of retirees implies that either transfers will have to rise or benefit levels will have to fall. Some employers also wish to reform welfare because of its role in institutionalizing and legitimizing small unions.

The tradition of social partnership (paritarism) is the cornerstone of virtually all French welfare and collective bargaining. The institutions deal with sickness, industrial accidents, the family, and old age, as well as with adult training, supplementary pension funds, and unemployment insurance. A recent investigation confirmed that their role in joint management allowed unions to transfer funds for their own purposes, such as placing full-time union activists on mutual-fund payrolls. In the case of the Concierges' Pension Fund, the late Communist general secretary and a former general secretary of the CGT both received pensions despite never having paid in any contributions (*Le Monde*, 8 Jan. 2000).

Following a Medef general assembly on 18 January 2000, Sellière announced withdrawal as of 30 June 2000 from the Union nationale pour l'emploi dans l'industrie et le commerce (UNEDIC) – unemployment insurance. The last three-year agreement had expired at the end of 1999. The Medef would quit all other bi-partite welfare organizations as of 31 December 2000, unless the unions agreed to "refounding the French social system" (*Le Monde,* 20 Jan. 2000). Since neither the CFDT nor the government was willing to tolerate the risks that this strategy posed for the unemployed, the threat worked. The first UNEDIC agreement was eventually reached just days before the Medef's deadline, although only two of France's five trade union confederations – the CFDT and the Confédération française des Travailleurs chrétiens (CFTC) – signed. However, notwithstanding the signatories' continuing minority status, Jospin, in a late-night phone call to Sellière in September, agreed to enact the agreement rather than risk an all-out confrontation. The unions' disunity allowed the employers to end unemployment benefits as a "right" and obligated the unemployed to take work if it was offered to them.

The Medef later applied exactly the same strategy in negotiations on other parts of the French welfare system. However, divisions over confrontational tactics grew among employers. Thus, while the chair of Basse-Normandie Medef was happy that "at last the Medef is making its voice heard in the heart of a Colbertist France whose evolution is so difficult," he was not sure about a "long social confrontation": "We will have to find partners to sign the peace, or at the very least a truce" (*Le Monde*, 3 April 2001). An AFEP meeting of France's top 80 private employers on 7 February 2001 (following a united, 300,000-strong union demonstration two weeks earlier), told Sellière to abandon his call on employers to boycott payments to the supplementary pension schemes for early retirees aged 60 to 65. He did so two days later (*Le Monde*, 28 April 2001). Thereafter he was less confrontational, though leading the Medef out of joint management of the largest social-security fund in protest against government intervention.

In the build-up to the 2002 elections, Sellière switched tack to more open campaigning against the government and sought to strengthen the neoliberals within the Rassemblement pour la République (RPR), the dominant right-wing party. After that election and the surprise victories of

Chirac and the combined right in parliament, the Medef's strategy has
been to press the Raffarin government (whose first finance minister was a
member of its inner circle) to tear up the 35-hour laws and to reform
social security by cutting pensions and raising the retirement age. The
Medef still seeks accommodation with the CFDT, but not at just any price:
employers feel much stronger than they did between 1981 and 2002 and
much less ready to compromise (Jefferys, 2003: 186–208).

Disunity Among French Unions

Disunity is much more evident on the union side. The unions were initially
positive about the government's plans for the 35-hour week, but the
employers carefully exploited divisions, and undermined this unity. Thus
most of the sectoral agreements reached, and about 10 per cent of enterprise agreements, faced strong challenges from union federations that did
not sign. Collective bargaining thus highlighted the divisions between and
within union confederations.

Since the mid-1980s, each of the three major confederations has
responded to the decline in French trade unionism in a different way. The
CGT, traditionally closest to the Communist Party, began to emphasize its
independence from the PCF and to move closer to the CFDT, arguing that
unity could help recruit new members. The CFDT began to distance itself
from its own radicalism of the 1970s. In 1988 it excluded some sections,
which went on to form SUD, a new, more radical confederation (Coupé
and Marchand, 1998). Under Nicole Notat, the CFDT began to take centre-
right positions on several issues, including partial support for Juppé's
pension reforms of 1995. It argues that unions need to break away from
"struggle" and prove that they can help employers modernize. Finally,
some leaders of the smaller, traditionally anti-Communist Force Ouvrière
(FO) confederation had come under Trotskyist influence and became
more militant – as when General Secretary Marc Blondel publicly shook
hands with the CGT's general secretary in October 1995 at a one-day strike
against a proposed public-sector pay freeze. The FO strongly opposed any
reform of paritarism in which it had traditionally played a role disproportionate to its size, thanks to its closer relations with employers.

Formerly, workers saw these divisions as remote – based on political and
religious differences and played out on the national stage. But the combination of expanded negotiating opportunities coincident with a shrinking
trade-union movement has pushed these differences down to the grass
roots. The "mandating" element of the 1998 law slightly privileges the CGT
and the CFDT, the most visible unions. The two bodies campaigned for
further revisions of the French "representative" system to ensure legality
for only agreements signed by a "majority" union or unions and achieved

partial success with the Aubry law of January 2000. Financial incentives would be provided automatically only when agreements were signed with unions representing a *majority* of the workforce (as defined by votes in the previous Works Council elections), although minority signatory agreements could still become valid if ratified by the whole workforce.

French workers have had more exposure to inter-union conflict because negotiations over major changes in the organization of work have brought ideological differences into the open at the local level. The Michelin case provides an extreme example. Thus in Michelin's 35-hour agreement the overseeing federation overruled the local CFDT's opposition with the support of the confederation, which then called for a referendum that carried only thanks to the vote of non-union managerial workers. As a result, many local CFDT activists set up a SUD union that later received 18 per cent of the vote in the Works Council at Michelin's Clermont Ferrand site (against the CGT's 49 per cent and the CFDT's 12 per cent).

Many serious disagreements have occurred over the "refounding" of French welfare. This conflict often has a material base: the Medef has made it clear that it will support in joint management committees only unions that sign on to the reforms. While the CFDT has proved the most amenable, even it has recoiled from employers' efforts to individualize welfare. Thus between 1999 and 2001, as the Medef tackled reform after reform, it never knew whether it would find a union partner. The CGT and FO shifted from mobilizing against employers to trying to keep the CFDT from drifting too far into the employers camp. The same process was under way again in mid-2003, as the government proposed to increase years of pension contributions from 37 to 42 in the public sector and from 40 to 42 in the private.

CONCLUSION

This chapter has argued that the French state has consistently intervened to promote what it saw as the best interests of French aristocrats, businessmen, farmers, and capitalists, but that under pressure of mass worker mobilizations it has sometimes identified those "best interests" with protective regulation of employment, industrial peace, and improved working lives.

In the context of global deregulation, the controlled redistribution of leisure in favour of workers is a major achievement. In this respect, French working-time legislation is a touchstone, indicating the possibilities of restraining the spreading influence of American-style capitalism. However, hours of work are not the only element in the work–effort balance. If the move to shorter hours has helped dismantle what remains of the postwar social settlement, which in the 1980s and 1990s provided some protection from the ravages of neoliberalism, then the achievement's value would shrink considerably.

The provisional "lesson" from the early experience of the 35-hour laws is that global capitalism can still be "controlled in the general interest" (Tawney's phrase) at the national level. Yet the defeat of the Jospin government which introduced the 35-hour week; the legislation's unpopularity among many of the manual workers whom it was supposed to benefit; and the subsequent freezing of progress towards a shorter working week indicate the limits of such measures. By failing to offer a more universal benefit to workers (for example, through additional holidays which could be negotiated more flexibly and universally), the Aubry laws allowed employers to divide employees. Then, by trying to implement a weak law through a flawed bargaining system that allows minority unions to sign legally binding agreements with the employers, the government in effect allowed employers to decide the terms of this major potential advance. Government timidity in the face of world capitalism clearly limited the effectiveness of regulation. To realize a stronger combination of increased leisure and less work stress and insecurity would require widespread and united mobilization of workers. This latter element has thus far been missing in France, where the times remain critical.

NOTES

1 I wish to thank Sylvie Contrepois (Évry University and GERS Paris) for this argument.

2 New nationalizations included Saint-Gobain, Rhône-Poulenc, PUK-CGE, Thomson, two steel companies (and Sacilor Usinor), two arms firms (Dassault and Matra), 36 commercial banks (including CCF and CIC), and two financial giants (Paribas and Suez).

REFERENCES

Ambler, J.S. 1991. "Ideas, Interests, and the French Welfare State," in Ambler, ed., *The French Welfare State: Surviving Social and Ideological Change.* New York: New York University Press, 1–31.

Béroud, S., and R. Mouriaux, eds. 1997. *Le souffle de décembre: le mouvement de Décembre, 1995: continuités, singularités, portée.* Paris: Syllepse.

Bilous, A. 1998. *Change in the Employers' Camp – CNPF Becomes Medef.* Dublin: European Foundation.

Bordeaux, M. 1998. "Nouvelle et perimée: la loi du 19 mai 1874 sur le travail des enfants et des filles mineures employés dans l'industrie," in J.-P. Crom, ed., *Deux siècles de droit du travail,* Paris: Les Editions de l'Atelier, 45–59.

Brizay, B. 1975. *Le patronat.* Paris: Seuil.

Castel, R. 1995. *Les métamorphoses de la question sociale: une chronique du salariat.* Paris: Librarie Arthème Fayard.

Coupé, A., and A. Marchand, eds. 1998. *Sud: syndicalement incorrect/sud-Ptt une aventure collective.* Paris: Syllepse.

Crom, J.-P.L. 1995. *Syndicats nous voilà! Vichy et le corporatisme.* Paris: Les Editions de l'Atelier.

Direction de l'Animation de la Recherche, des Etudes et des Statistiques (DARES). 2000. *La négociation collective en 1999.* Paris: Editions législatives et ministère de l'Emploi et de la Solidarité.

Dewerpe, A. 1989. *Le monde du travail en France 1800–1950.* Paris: Armand Collin.

Didry, C. 1998. "La nouvelle jeunesse des conventions collectives: la loi du 24 juin 1936," J.-P.L. Crom, ed., *Deux siècles de droit du travail.* Paris: Les Editions de l'Atelier, 129–41.

Goetschy, J. 1998. "France: The Limits of Reform," in A. Ferner and R. Hyman, eds., *Changing Industrial Relations in Europe,* Oxford: Blackwell, 357–94.

Guedj, F., and G. Vindt. 1997. *Le temps de travail, une histoire conflictuelle.* Paris: Syros.

Husson, M. 2002. "Réduction du temps de travail et emploi: une nouvelle evaluation," *Revue de l'IRES* 1 (32), 79–108.

Institut national de la Statistique et des Etudes économiques (INSEE). 2000. *Tableaux de l'economie française: édition 2000.* Paris: INSEE.

Jefferys, S. 1996. "Down but Not Out: French Unions after Chirac," *Work, Employment and Society* 10 (3), 509–27.

– 1997. "The Exceptional Centenary of the Confédération Générale du Travail, 1895–1995," *Historical Studies in Industrial Relations* 3, 123–42.

– 2000. "A 'Copernican Revolution' in French Industrial Relations: Are the Times A'changing?" *British Journal of Industrial Relations* 38 (2), 241–60.

– 2003. *Liberté, Égalité and Fraternité at Work: Changing French Employment Relations and Management.* Basingstoke: Palgrave Macmillan.

Jefferys, S., and S. Contrepois. 2001. "The French State and Wage Determination", European Industrial Relations Association Congress. Oslo.

Organization for Economic Co-operation and Development (OECD). 1996a. "Earnings Inequality, Low-paid Employment and Earnings," *Employment Outlook* (July), 59–108.

– 1996b. *Historical Statistics: 1960–1994.* Paris: OECD.

– 1998. *National Accounts, Main Aggregates, 1960–1996.* Paris: OECD.

– 1999. *Etudes économiques de l'OCDE: France.* Paris: OECD.

Pisani-Ferry, J. 2001. *La bonne aventure. Le plein emploi, le marché, la gauche.* Paris: La Découverte.

Schor, R. 1996. *Histoire de l'immigration en France de la fin du XIXe siècle à nos jours.* Paris: Armand Colin.

Sellier, F. 1984. *La confrontation sociale en France: 1936–1981.* Paris: Presses Universitaires de France.

Shorter, E., and C. Tilly 1974. *Strikes in France 1830–1968.* Cambridge: Cambridge University Press.

Soubiran-Paillet, F. 1999. *L'invention du Syndicat (1791–1884): itinéraire d'une caté-gorie juridique*. Paris: Librarie Générale de Droit et de Jurisprudence.

Stoffaës, C. 1991. "La restructuration industrielle, 1945–1990," in M. Lévy-Leboyer and J.-C. Casanova, eds., *Entre l'état et le marché*. Paris: éditions Gallimard, 445–72.

Tawney, R.H. 1929. *Equality*. London : George Allen and Union.

Thoemmes, J., and J. de Terssac. 1997. "La négociation du temps de travail et les composantes du référentiel temporel," *Loisir et société* 20 (1), 51–72.

Viet, V. 1998. "Entre protection legale et droit collectif: la loi du 2 novembre 1892 sur le travail des enfants, des filles mineures et des femmes dans les établisse-ments industriels," in J.-P.L. Crom, ed., *Deux siècles de droit de travail*. Paris: Les Editions d'Atelier, 73–83.

Weber, H. 1986. *Le parti des Patrons: Le CNPF (1946–1986)*. Paris: Seuil.

18

How Credible Are International Corporate Labour Codes? Monitoring Global Production Chains

DON WELLS

Credibility is the critical element in codes of conduct. Without it, the promises contained in a code are hollow and the credibility of the company falters. (United States Department of Labor, 1996: 9)

It is not enough to establish tough rules. We must ensure that they are enforced, and that American consumers know they are being followed. That is why the apparel industry is forming a special association to make sure companies and contractors live up to the Code of Conduct, using independent monitors. (U.S. President Bill Clinton, quoted in Schilling, 2000: 234)

PRIVATE LABOUR CODE CAPITALISM AND TRIANGLE MANUFACTURING

We live in an era of market triumphalism marked by massive privatization of state assets and functions and the decline of state-centred Keynesian politics in most industrialized countries.[1] Under pressure from financial forces and economic organizations such as the International Monetary Fund, as well as from domestic elites, many governments in the South are shifting from state-centred import-substitution policies to export-oriented strategies and trade liberalization. They give far less emphasis to regulating foreign investment and far more to attracting it. In this context, globalization has come to mean decreasing state regulation of labour rights and standards.

For increasing numbers of workers around the world, especially in the South, private corporate labour codes are emerging as a partial substitute for this growing regulatory vacuum. Many transnational corporations (TNCs) that have been outsourcing production to low-wage, authoritarian regimes face mounting pressure from consumers, workers, and citizen activists to improve labour standards and to respect basic labour rights. This pressure is directed primarily at firms selling brand-name toys, sporting goods, small electrical appliances, apparel, athletic footwear, and other labour-intensive goods.

In response, and to pre-empt labour regulation under inter-state auspices, many TNCs have advocated "corporate social responsibility," centring on international codes of conduct.[2] The TNCs themselves monitor most of these codes. However, because of criticism that self-monitoring is not credible, given the conflict of interest that it entails, many TNCs are turning to non-governmental organizations (NGOs) to monitor these codes. Increasingly, this monitoring is taking place through multipartite organizations involving two or more kinds of actors (for example, NGOs, government agencies, and firms). Among the most prominent is the Fair Labor Association (FLA), a U.S. non-profit agency. Run by representatives of apparel TNCs, NGOs, and universities, the FLA monitors global labour conditions, mainly in the apparel and footwear industries. Its adequacy as a monitoring institution is the main focus of this chapter.

Much of the world's apparel and athletic footwear industry is structured around "buyer-driven" supply chains in which commercial capital, rather than industrial capital, is the major force (Gereffi, 1994). Major North American buyers are large manufacturer-merchandisers, such as Nike, Levi Strauss, and Gap Inc., and large retailers, such as Wal-Mart and J.C. Penney. For the most part, the merchandisers and mass retailers do not own the manufacturers that make the products. Instead, most manufacturers are contractors that produce directly or subcontract to other producers.[3] The big retailers and merchandisers retain the higher value-added functions of research, design, sales and marketing, and finance. They decide the designs, quality standards, and schedules for the producers.

Initiating "triangle manufacturing," they outsource production to newly industrializing countries (NICs), particularly Asia's "four tigers," Hong Kong, Singapore, South Korea, and Taiwan.[4] As union density and wages have risen in "first-tier" NICs, the third side of the triangle has emerged, as contract manufacturers in first-tier NICs have transferred orders to second-tier NICs, such as Indonesia and Thailand, and to other less developed countries (LDCs) in Asia, Central America, the Caribbean, Africa and eastern Europe, where labour standards are yet lower.[5] Suppliers there complete the triangle when they ship goods to Canada, the United States, the European Union, and other developed countries, which constitute the primary consumer markets for these products.

This triangle approach embodies layers of manufacturing colonialism that correspond roughly to the international economic hierarchy. At the macroeconomic level, this entails a core of "metropolitan" industrialized countries; a NIC, or *comprador* periphery; and a periphery of the periphery with super-low labour standards. Transborder networks blur centre–periphery distinctions (Mittelman, 2000: chap. 8).[6] At the microeconomic level, triangle manufacturing may involve, for example, a Chinese-owned firm[7] and a Korean plant manager in an export-processing zone in Vietnam or Indonesia. These relations emphasize subcontracting built around layers of patriarchy that construct women as especially flexible workers (Pearson and Seyfang, 2002; Standing, 1999). In general, higher-paid work, such as that of designers and pattern makers, takes place in the metropolitan core (for example, in New York, Los Angeles, or London), whereas the manufacture of garments, shoes, toys, and other products takes place in the peripheries. The power relation between retailers and brand companies in the global North, which control consumption outlets, and manufacturers in the South, is highly asymmetrical. However, some TNCs in the South have been moving up the value chain as full-service companies that carry out research, design, cutting, and other functions, as well as assembly (Gereffi, 1999; Kessler, 1999).

Triggered by growing competitiveness among retailers in Germany, the United Kingdom, the United States, and other major consumer markets, competition in the global apparel and other labour-intensive industries is becoming more intense, as labour standards in the export sectors of LDCs fall (Ross and Chan, 2002). This increasingly destructive competition among manufacturers in the South is largely the result of excess production capacity and growing saturation of consumer markets. Lacking adequate bargaining leverage against mass retailers, manufacturers engage in cut-throat contract bidding wars, leading to a downward spiral wherein lower wages and deteriorating working conditions transfer the burdens of competition to workers. Manufacturers in lower-labour-standard LDCs become "price takers" to contractors in first-tier NICs, which cater to scheduling and cost pressures from large retailers, such as Wal-Mart in the United States. Via "forward integration"[8] into their own retail stores (as well as by selling to other retailers), manufacturer-merchandisers such as Nike, Gap Inc., and Eddie Bauer further enhance control over their subcontracted manufacturers.

Labour costs are a small part of the cost to consumers. For example, wages for direct assembly represent only about 0.4 per cent of the cost of a U.S.$100 shoe made in Indonesia (Wick, 2003: 106). Nevertheless, the competitive fates of subcontractors often lie with small differences in labour costs in global industries where wages have become a source of international "comparative advantage" rather than a basis for local consumer demand.

It is contradictory for mass retailers to claim to support higher labour standards while refusing to ensure cost margins that would allow manufacturers to meet those standards. Given considerable volatility in consumer demand, there is enormous pressure, often on extremely short notice, for manufacturers to supply goods to contractors higher in the supply chain, and to mass retailers, according to very tight shipping schedules. Such just-in-time production pressures lead manufacturers, particularly those further down the supply chain, to demand what are often highly excessive work hours.[9] This degree of employment flexibility, which is illegal in most industrialized countries, is available through subcontracting to manufacturers in many LDCs. While this is a solution for retailers facing rapid changes in consumer demand, it is a problem for people who must work excessive hours and endure serious stress and employment instability as a result (Hong Kong Christian Industrial Committee, 2003b).

In effect, these triangular relations give large manufacturer-merchandisers considerable power over supplier factories. These relations assume outsourcing of both production and industrial relations to regimes with lower labour standards. Although factors such as transportation and communication infrastructure, and various bilateral and multilateral international trade arrangements,[10] also shape decisions about the location of such labour-intensive production, variations in labour standards are critical.[11] State regulation is weakening in most nations with higher labour standards as well, and since more and more workers in both types of regimes make concessions to mobile (or apparently mobile) capital, this "double outsourcing" (of both production and industrial relations) is becoming a key part of a broader, reciprocal lowering of global labour standards – "the race to the bottom." TNCs build their investment strategies on these uneven industrial relations and in turn reinforce them.

A "race to the top" is also possible. The same logic that allows brand-name producers to gain rents (revenues beyond costs of production that they could distribute to workers) also provide social activists and "conscience consumers" with leverage to raise labour standards. A major issue is whether this potential leverage over brand-name firms can help "ratchet up" the labour standards of generic producers (Fung et al., 2001).

MONITORING THE MONITORS

The first section of this chapter reviews the political context in which concern over TNC labour practices has emerged and reviews the criteria for these monitoring schemes to be minimally credible. The second describes the monitoring guidelines and activities of the Fair Labor Association, highlighting their many deficiencies. The third considers alternatives for improving working conditions in developing countries, including the development of meaningful and enforceable international labour standards and the parallel development of transnational union strategies.

This privatization of industrial relations has been a major focus of popular protest over the lack of citizen representation and transparency in shaping the new global political economy. The declining popular legitimacy in many liberal democracies of state-centred politics based on parties and electoral processes has gone hand in hand with the emergence of a new politics of civil society (Beck, 1992; Tarrow, 1998). Most significant has been the development of "new social movements" built around new information technologies and informal networks of transnational mobilization (Beuchler, 2000; Brecher et al., 2000; Castells, 2000; Keck and Sikkink, 1998).

This new politics revolves around a global citizenship of conscience constituents, the core of which consists of young, well-educated consumers who identify with and support (often similarly young) workers in developing countries. One of the largest and most influential components is the anti-sweatshop movement centred in the United States, Australia, and Europe. A recent survey found 43 U.S.-based anti-sweatshop groups, more than half of which were formed in the 1990s (Elliott and Freeman, 2001). Among the most prominent are groups that look at the labour practices of TNCs such as Nike, The Gap, Reebok, Wal-Mart, and Disney. Others focus on sweatshops in particular countries, such as Mexico, Burma, and China, or target sweatshop practices generally.

At the heart of this movement lie demands to regulate the labour standards of TNCs, particularly those in LDCs, but also in "global cities" such as Los Angeles, New York, and London. In the United States, the United Students Against Sweatshops (USAS), based on over 200 university and college campuses, constitutes the most significant student mobilization since the Vietnam War. Recent protests against the World Trade Organization (WTO) in Seattle, the World Bank in Washington, DC, and the Free Trade Area of the Americas (FTAA) in Quebec City, as well as major protests in Europe, all have the anti-sweatshop movement as a core component. The popular base of the movement extends well beyond student activists. According to several U.S. surveys, three of every four respondents state that they would avoid buying products if they knew that they were made under poor labour conditions (Kull, 1999; Marymount University Center for Ethical Concerns, 1999).[12]

Voluntary labour codes based on private monitoring are becoming a new U.S.-government policy to fill the vacuum around transnational production. As this vacuum has become increasingly politicized, corporations have made gradual accommodations. In 1991, Levi Strauss became the first TNC to introduce a corporate code of conduct. Today most major apparel and sporting-goods firms in the United States, and many in

Europe, have such codes. Recently this corporate self-regulation has been shifting to multilateral codes developed by non-profit agencies supported variously by corporations, labour-rights groups, and religious and other NGOs. The most prominent is the Fair Labor Association (FLA) in the United States, which is the subject of the case study below.

If these codes are to address this policy vacuum, the legitimacy deficits facing the U.S. and other governments, and consumers' aversion to buying goods produced under bad labour conditions, they require popular credibility. This credibility will depend not only on the labour standards that the codes enshrine but also on the codes' practical relevance to manufacturers' labour practices. Thus, the codes' credibility depends primarily on the monitoring of their standards. There is considerable evidence that corporate self-monitoring has not been effective (see, for example, Connor, 2001; Hong Kong Christian Industrial Committee, 2003a, 2003b; O'Rourke, 2002; Prieto and Bendell, 2002; Sethi, 2003). For example, in Los Angeles – a much-publicized centre of self-monitoring as an alternative to state regulation – the U.S. Department of Labor found only 44 per cent of self-monitored garment firms in compliance with legislated labour standards (Cleeland, 2000). Another Department of Labor survey found only 39 per cent of apparel firms complying with basic wage and hours laws. An earlier Department of Labor investigation found a similar prevalence of infractions (Bonacich and Appelbaum, 2000: 166). Other examples abound of TNC's failure to monitor and enforce their own codes effectively (see, for example, D'Mello, 2003; Schoenberger, 2000; Utting, 2003).

As an alternative to self-monitoring, minimally credible monitoring and enforcement of private labour codes require the following eight conditions:

- Monitors must be independent of the power of employers in the firms that they monitor.
- Monitoring organizations must involve workers meaningfully in the workplaces being monitored, as well as unions and labour-oriented NGOs.
- Monitoring must cover most of the global supply chain producing the goods to which the code pertains.
- Monitoring "benchmarks" need to be clear, specific, and qualitatively and quantitatively measurable.
- Monitors must use investigative methods (such as interviews and questionnaires) and measures (such as those relevant to wages, hours of work, and health and safety standards) that conform to rigorous, widely recognized social and natural-science standards.
- Detailed information about the monitoring processes used and the results of monitoring, specific to particular workplaces (including their exact locations), must be publicly accessible.

- Workers, employers, and third parties (for example, consumers, unions, professional and religious organizations, and citizens generally) must be able, without fear of retribution, to register complaints alleging non-compliance with codes to an impartial adjudicator.
- Firms must rectify deficiencies in compliance in a timely fashion; if they do not do so, there must be effective sanctions.

The rest of this chapter uses these criteria to evaluate the credibility of the FLA's monitoring and enforcement of its international code of labour conduct.

THE FAIR LABOR ASSOCIATION: HOW CREDIBLE?

The Fair Labor Association (FLA) is an agency created in 1998 by TNCs and NGOs under U.S. President Bill Clinton's sponsorship to promote "decent and humane working conditions" in the global apparel and footwear industries. Its purview has expanded to include a variety of other products manufactured for sale on its 179 member colleges and universities. Thirteen major TNCs belong to the FLA, including such well-known firms as Nike, Liz Claiborne, Reebok, Polo Ralph Lauren, Levi Strauss, Eddie Bauer, adidas-Salomon, and Phillips–Van Heusen. With U.S.$30 billion in sales, they produce in 3,000 factories around the world (Wick, 2003: 51). In addition, over 1,100 other firms supplying licensed goods (bearing the logo or trademark of a member college or university) have affiliated with the FLA. Six prominent human-rights organizations also belong.

The FLA was a response to a spate of publicity about the resurgence of sweatshops in the United States and about accelerating imports of goods made under sweatshop conditions, including child labour, forced labour, and illegally low wages and excessive overtime. The import share of apparel sales in the United States had jumped from 45 per cent in 1987 to over 60 per cent in 1997 (Bernstein, 1999). There was growing concern among apparel employers that the U.S. Congress would conduct public hearings into sweatshop abuses and push for government regulation of labour standards for the overseas production of U.S. firms. Despite revelations of massive violations in China, including incidents of child and prison labour, the U.S. government had approved that country's most-favoured-nation trading status. Vulnerable on this issue, and having barely won congressional approval of the North American Free Trade Agreement, the Clinton administration worried that bad publicity about sweatshops might undermine its trade agenda. The FLA was a strategic response.

The FLA's code standards reflect a mixture of strengths and weaknesses. However, its monitoring system has been the main object of criticism.

Member firms agree to co-operate with its monitoring of plants that make
their products. If it deems plants to be code-compliant, the businesses may
use an FLA "service mark"(or "no-sweat" label). Given consumer sensitivity
to sweatshop production, and the danger that this could pose to a firm's
brand image (which is their "real production," as argued by Klein, 2000:
16), the service mark can be pivotal to marketing strategies.[13] Yet its value
depends almost entirely on its credibility, which in turn relies on the rep-
utation of the FLA's monitoring and enforcement system.

Consider, first, the FLA's independence from the apparel firms. The
FLA's board has no representatives of workers or their organizations.
Instead, apparel firms and NGOs each have six representatives; affiliated
universities have three. From the outset, several NGOs on the board were
criticized for financial and organizational ties to apparel firms and other
corporations (Issel, 2000; Light, 1998). In addition, the FLA is highly
dependent on corporate funding.[14]

Especially damaging, the voting system gives the firms a veto over most
important board decisions. Most key decisions require "supermajority
votes" – at least two-thirds of the board's corporate members – on such
matters as selection of the board chair and the FLA's executive director;
amendments to the code; monitoring principles and procedures; accreditation criteria for monitors; and termination of membership of businesses
deemed insufficiently compliant. As well, the FLA itself, rather than an
external agency, accredits monitors. Until very recently, each firm directly
chose its "independent" monitoring agency from a list approved by the
FLA, paid the monitors directly, and helped select plants to be monitored.
A new policy, however, prohibits "independent" monitors from having any
business or financial relation with the companies being monitored. The
FLA now selects monitors and pays them directly from corporate funds. It
also selects the factories to be monitored. These recent changes ushered
in some much-needed improvements in monitoring credibility. Nevertheless, corporations still dominate the FLA's governance structure. Moreover,
most monitors are management-identified commercial auditing firms
whose other clients include businesses. Neither workers nor their representatives participate in the monitoring structures.

Consider next how much of a firm's supply chain the FLA monitors. In
an initial phase-in period, it monitors 10 per cent of a business's "Applicable Facilities," which may *exclude* up to 15 per cent of the firm's factories,[15]
including those with short-term contracts. According to the director of
Worldwide Responsible Apparel Production (the factory certification
program of the American Apparel Manufacturers Association), most sweatshop abuses occur in those facilities (Hong Kong Christian Industrial
Committee, 2003a: 7; Jeffcott and Yanz, 2000: 68). Also excluded is much
home-based work, where child labour tends to be more prevalent and

where conditions generally are thought to be even worse (Chen et al., 1999).

After this initial period, the FLA monitors an unspecified "random sampling"[16] of no more than 5 per cent of Applicable Facilities (Wick, 2003: 54). Based on monitoring this small fraction of each company's plants, the FLA certifies its brand(s) as eligible to advertise a no-sweat label. Even though the FLA monitors only a fraction of each firm's plants, the business can attach the label to goods made in unmonitored plants.

FLA guidelines advise monitors to interview a "representative sampling" of workers, based on a "variety of factors" – for example, a cross-section of factory functions and particular kinds of workers (such as migrant contract workers and union members). However, the FLA does not lay out specific sampling parameters, including either minimum numbers or proportions of workers to interview. It leaves sampling characteristics largely up to each monitor. Some discretion is defensible for complex issues being investigated, but less so for others. In particular, except for interviews with union leaders where the union is not recognized or there is no collective agreement, monitors decide whether to arrange off-site interviews. The guidelines advise them to conduct interviews in a way that ensures that workers will "not face retaliation or other negative consequences as a result of participation in the interviews." Nowhere is it clear how to ensure this.

The guidelines exhibit both strengths and weaknesses. They contain numerous useful suggestions for plant inspections. For example, monitors must consult with local human-rights, labour-rights and similar organizations that are knowledgeable about labour conditions and have workers' trust. Such consultations may help to identify potential code violations and to facilitate communication with workers. Monitors are also asked to use a variety of interview techniques, especially open-ended questions. Many questions and procedures in the FLA guidelines for monitors are clear and specific and indicate a culturally nuanced understanding of plant-level industrial relations. As well, the FLA now insists that all auditing visits to plants be unannounced.

But important weaknesses in method nevertheless weaken the guidelines. Although monitors' reports are standardized, monitors have considerable discretion in their choice of investigative methods, which are not publicly divulged. Comparisons become problematic when monitors use different methods, and credibility comes to depend more on the credibility of individual monitors.

The guidelines do not address the central question: why would workers provide accurate information? Monitoring provides considerable incentives for workers *not* to do so. Among other things, interviews with workers need not take place off-site. Nor is it clear how monitors could prevent managers from retaliating against outspoken workers. Furthermore, although the

guidelines urge monitors to consult "knowledgeable local sources" and
"consult regularly" with human-rights and other local institutions, these local
bodies need not play any role in actual monitoring. Thus, workers may well
not trust monitors who, as some of them report, seem to be "men in suits."

Some FLA compliance benchmarks are clear enough to enhance credibility; others are less clear. For example, the guidelines state that employers may not prohibit the hiring of married women, must not use physical
discipline, and must communicate disciplinary procedures clearly. Other
benchmarks are too vague. For example, employers must comply with
"applicable" but undefined health and safety laws, and many other benchmarks contain similarly vague terms, such as "applicable" and "appropriate." The FLA code itself is even more elliptical in this important area.[17]
Some benchmarks are self-contradictory. For example, those on forced
labour forbid employers to "bind workers to employment as a condition of
fulfilling terms of a debt to a third party or to the employer," yet the code
then allows wage advances (i.e., incurring a debt to employers).[18]

Consider next the FLA code on wages: "Employers shall pay the legal
minimum wage or the prevailing industry wage, whichever is higher."
According to a report on wages and benefits in the global apparel and
footwear industry released by the U.S. Department of Labor in December
1999, many countries have no minimum wage, and others have various
regional minimum wages (United States Department of Labor, 2000: I-38;
II-72). Many countries have no data on average industrial earnings, and
others lack data on average earnings for the apparel industry. In the
absence of the required data on wages, how can monitors know the FLA's
benchmark wage levels? How can the FLA enforce them?

The meaning of excessive overtime is also unclear. According to the
code, employers may require workers to work 60 hours a week (unless the
legal maximum in the host country is less). Firms may insist on more than
60 hours in "extraordinary business circumstances" – a "temporary period
of extra work that could not have been anticipated or alleviated by other
reasonable efforts." This definition is amenable to many interpretations.
Moreover, since employers need not pay any overtime premium (unless
local law requires it), the code encourages excessive overtime in an industry where it is already endemic.

What constitutes "non-compliance" with the code? This is another critical uncertainty that may undermine the credibility of the FLA's approach.
Although monitors must report "significant and/or persistent patterns of
non-compliance," the FLA has not defined this crucial concept, especially
in terms of how a firm might thereby jeopardize its FLA membership.

In 2002, in response to widespread criticism of its monitoring procedures,
the FLA's board approved several changes, including disclosure of monitoring information. Company names and product types are to be disclosed, as

well as the monitor's name and some summary information about any non-compliance and remediation. Such disclosure will increase transparency, allow for comparison of auditors' reports, and provide a basis for better, more thorough audits. However, except for plants producing licensed goods for FLA schools, reports do not disclose names and addresses of factories. This makes it difficult for anyone outside the FLA to verify compliance.

Furthermore, the FLA's complaint mechanism, whereby third parties, including workers, may report code non-compliance, remains unclear. Employers are to provide an unspecified "secure communications channel" for complaints and (again unspecified) protection for workers making complaints. Alternatively, third-party complainants may submit to the FLA's executive director "reliable, specific and verifiable evidence or information that the Alleged Noncompliance has occurred." That official (hired with the agreement of two-thirds of the firms on the board) investigates and adjudicates the complaints.

Finally, the FLA's protection of free-association and collective-bargaining rights is weaker than it appears. Almost all its covered factories lack independent unions. The FLA code does little to change this in many circumstances. Particularly in countries where independent unions are illegal,[19] the FLA has no remedy to enforce these rights. This has special relevance in Vietnam, for example, and even more in China, the world's leading exporter of clothing. In both countries unions are a state-controlled monopoly. Even in countries where unions are not illegal, they are often illegal (or their legality is not enforced) in export-processing zones, which assemble much of the world's apparel (International Labour Organization, 1998).

Nor do the guidelines effectively address employers' ability to relocate production to penalize workers who join unions. They state that employers "will not shift production or close a factory for the direct purpose of retaliating against workers who have formed or are attempting to form a union." Yet, since employers typically have several reasons for relocating production, most of them could easily appear to comply with the code while laying workers off for exercising labour rights. Although these basic rights lie at the core of the FLA code, failure to ensure them does not disqualify firms from being deemed compliant or from using the no-sweat label on their branded apparel.

CONCLUSION

The credibility of codes of conduct requires high standards in monitoring:

- independent monitors
- meaningful involvement of workers

- monitoring throughout each firm's supply chain
- clear and, as far as possible, measurable monitoring standards
- scientifically rigorous monitoring methods
- public disclosure of processes and results
- effective complaint mechanisms
- timely rectification of code deficiencies or application of effective sanctions

The FLA's monitoring and enforcement system, despite notable strengths in certain areas, is deficient in each of these criteria. Most fundamentally, corporate dominance of the FLA's governance structure continues to weaken the independence of monitors.

Monitoring based on other code models is more credible in relation to several of the above criteria. For example, the Clean Clothes Campaign (CCC) – a network of unions and NGOs in Europe – has created a foundation model that avoids the FLA's credibility problems. Its board consists equally of firms, industry associations, and employer federations, on one side, and of unions and NGOs, on the other. Monitoring involves unions and NGOs "at the highest level of decision making" (van Eijk, 1998). Since the foundation selects and pays monitors to audit the workplaces of member businesses, there is no financial link between the monitors and the firms that they monitor. Members disclose all factory locations to the CCC.

Another model with greater credibility is that of the Worker Rights Consortium (WRC) founded recently by United Students Against Sweatshops (USAS) – the main U.S. anti-sweatshop movement. Its major function is to enforce codes in plants producing logoed apparel for over 100 member universities and colleges. Because the WRC's board has equal numbers of representatives from university administrations, USAS, and labour-rights experts from the WRC's advisory board, and has no representation from businesses, corporations have no power in the WRC's governance structure or over monitors. In addition, because the WRC receives its funds from university and college fees, and from grants from philanthropic foundations, it has no direct financial links to firms. The WRC does not certify businesses as code compliant and thus avoids misleading consumers with false certification. Instead, it investigates plants in response to complaints and on a "proactive," spot-check basis. Monitoring teams include knowledgeable local NGOs and academic experts who interview workers confidentially, in their homes and communities. All monitors' reports are available publicly, and the WRC maintains a web-site database of the names and locations of factories producing apparel for member schools.

In comparison to the FLA, monitoring by the CCC and the WRC is much more credible, especially because of the role of organized labour and labour-oriented NGOs in their governing bodies. Unlike the FLA, the WRC does not use commercial auditing firms to verify code compliance. Since factory certification is not a WRC function, companies cannot use a no-sweat label for marketing purposes. Yet, whereas the FLA completed 185 "independent external monitoring audits" in fiscal 2001–02 (Durkee, 2003), the WRC completed just three and planned only 10–15 in 2002–03 (United Students Against Sweatshops, 2002). Effective monitoring needs to be constant, not occasional. None of these three models is able to provide this. Monitors' reports based on infrequent investigations risk reflecting the sweatshop equivalent of Potemkin villages.

The WRC's credibility derives from the capacity of independent, skilled NGOs that workers trust to do effective monitoring. That capacity is currently quite limited. A sweatshop investigator in China reports that "NGOs are exhausted tracing the locations of tens of thousands of subcontractors all over the world," and NGOs' work is "made particularly difficult by the TNCs that change their subcontractors at any time" (Kwan, 2000). This lack of comprehensiveness and capacity appears to be the WRC's Achilles' heel.

Ultimately, ongoing, efficient, and cost-effective monitoring will require collective agreements negotiated by independent unions possessing strong workplace representation. This is why the "enabling rights" of freedom of association and collective bargaining are so critical to raising labour standards. Even independent unions may not significantly improve labour standards. Despite their own solidarity and militancy, most workers in most LDCs where TNCs and local political and military elites are hostile to independent unions will need solidarity from unions, consumers, and activists in the North to achieve significant improvements. In the absence of this added support, codes will probably be consistent with non-union-ism or with dependent company unions and non-adversarial "associa-tional unionism."

Fung et al. (2001) have proposed a "Ratcheting Labour Standards" approach, in which transparent monitoring and other conditions would encourage TNCs to compete with each other in raising labour standards. Yet beyond image-conscious firms, it is unclear what the incentives for such competition might be. Other observers argue that businesses have such incentives because higher labour standards increase productivity. However, there is little evidence of such a linkage in most of the global apparel and other relatively low-skill, labour-intensive global industries. Thus, if labour standards are to improve beyond the global supply chains of large TNCs with brand-name commodities, they will need enforcement at the sectoral level rather than at the firm level. A partial model for nego-tiating sectional labour standards is the "framework agreement" approach, negotiated between individual TNCs and global union federations.

In addition to the kinds of pressures generated by labour-code campaigns, more forceful efforts to improve labour conditions in LDCs will require the development of transnational unionism, with information exchange, building of technical capacity, international strike support, and eventually transnational collective bargaining (Ramsay, 1997; Wells, 1998). This does not mean unions in one country negotiating on behalf of workers in another. Rather, in place of increasing competition between transnational corporations and the resulting competition among workers, new forms of international labour co-operation and mutual solidarity are necessary. Some of these forms are now emerging (Anner, 2000; Wilson, 2000; Zinn, 2000).

Labour-code campaigns have arisen because governments and state-centred international institutions have failed to protect global labour rights and standards within the international trade regime. These campaigns are not an effective substitute for legislated, state-centred international regulation of industrial relations. However, because codes of conduct are a focus of political mobilization and "consciousness raising," and because these campaigns have developed sufficient leverage to improve labour standards in some cases, they can help to slow the international "race to the bottom" in labour rights and standards. The task now is to build bridges between the codes and domestic and international labour legislation to construct a new architecture of effective and comprehensive international labour regulation.

NOTES

1 I am grateful to the following for helpful information and comments: Sam Bain, Jeff Ballinger, Trim Bissell, Tim Connor, Jonathan Eaton, Ruth Frager, Josh Greenberg, Pharis Harvey, Bob Jeffcott, Graham Knight, Shawn MacDonald, Simon Pestridge, Kate Pfordresher, Sonia Singh, Jim Stanford, Ian Thompson, Amanda Tucker, Leah Vosko, and Lynda Yanz. Funding for this research came from the Social Sciences and Humanities Research Council of Canada.

2 In the 1970s, the International Chamber of Commerce, the International Labour Organization, the Organization for Economic Cooperation and Development, and the United Nations drafted codes of conduct that were voluntary, not legally binding, and largely ineffective at regulating international labour standards.

3 In rare cases (for example, Levi Strauss and New Balance), some production still takes place in-house, with the bulk subcontracted.

4 For European companies, Tunisia was also a major destination for capital in the wake of factory closings in the 1960s and 1970s.

5 Wage levels vary considerably in the South. For example, whereas South

Korean wages in the footwear industry are about U.S.$6 per hour, labour costs in the Philippines and Bangladesh are below U.S.$1 per hour, and in India 25 cents (U.S.) per hour. (D'Mello, 2003: 30). Other factors shaping location of such production include labour laws (especially regarding working hours), corruption, transportation and communication infrastructure, proximity to consumer markets, and trade policies – for example, tariffs and quotas under the North American Free Trade Agreement, the Multi Fiber Agreement of the World Trade Organization, and various bilateral trade arrangements, such as the Generalized System of Preferences (Tsogas, 2001: chap. 5).

6 Prominent examples include the Indonesia–Malaysia–Singapore growth triangle, the Southern China growth triangle (linking Hong Kong and Guangdong province), and the Greater Mekong subregion polygon (incorporating Cambodia, Laos, Myanmar, Thailand, Vietnam, and Yunnan province in China).

7 The apparel industry in all East Asian countries except Japan and Korea is dominated by ethnic Chinese networks rather than by individual firms. The networks typically emerge around informal trust relations that do not entail long-term obligations to suppliers (Appelbaum, 1998: 183–5).

8 Forward integration, exemplified by Nike's opening up its own retail outlets as well as selling to other retailers, entails a shift of power from production contractors to the forward integrators. Private labels give their owners more sway over both manufacturers and retailers.

9 This competitive cost dynamic is not exclusive to apparel. For example, interviews with senior managers of Chinese factories that produce toys for export confirm that, while the prices paid by retailers have been declining for several years, the manufacturers have had to absorb all the costs of compliance with corporate codes imposed by the retailers. Some managers estimate that this has increased their direct labour costs by from 20 per cent to 68 per cent (Hong Kong Christian Industrial Committee, 2003b: 4).

10 In particular, despite trade liberalization under the General Agreement on Tariffs and Trade and now the World Trade Organization, the Multi-Fibre Arrangement (MFA) sets quotas for the importation of textiles and clothing from any country. The MFA is to be phased out by 2005. Also, some bilateral trading arrangements have labour standards associated with them (Tsogas, 2001: chaps. 5 and 6).

11 Variations in labour standards figure particularly prominently in the sourcing decisions of industries and subsectors that are labour intensive, use unskilled labour, and face volatile demand in competitive markets.

12 About three-quarters said that they felt morally obligated to help improve working conditions and would pay $5 more for a $20 garment if they knew that it had not been produced in a sweatshop (Kull, 1999).

13 Yet it is unclear how many of the firms intend to use the label (Sweeney, 2000: 259).

14 The FLA also receives funding from the U.S. government and fees from its
    university and college affiliates.

15 Up to 15 per cent of factories making goods for an FLA firm for 6 months or
    less in 24 months, and those whose manufacture for FLA business is 10 per
    cent or less of its total production, are not considered "Applicable Facilities"
    and hence are excluded from independent monitoring.

16 This sample is not random, since selection also involves assessment of "risk
    factors."

17 The code requires employers to "provide a safe and healthy working environ-
    ment to prevent accidents and injury to health arising out of, linked with, or
    occurring in the course of work or as a result of the operation of employer
    facilities." By contrast, benchmarks based on conventions and recommenda-
    tions of the International Labour Organization or on those of the American
    Conference of Government Industrial Hygienists provide useful specificity.

18 The FLA requires that advances "not exceed three months pay or legal limits,
    whichever is less."

19 Export processing zones in Bangladesh, Malaysia and Pakistan deny the right
    to organize unions (Jeffcott and Yanz, 2000: 14).

REFERENCES

Anner, Mark. 2000. "Local and Transnational Campaigns to End Sweatshop Prac-
    tices," in Michael Gordon and Lowell Turner, eds., *Transnational Cooperation
    among Unions*. Ithaca, NY: Cornell University Press.

Appelbaum, Richard. 1998. "Future of Law in a Global Economy," *Social and Legal
    Studies* 7 (2), 171–92.

Beck, Ulrich. 1992. *Risk Society*. London: Sage Publications.

Benjamin, Medea. 1999. *What's Fair about the Fair Labor Association?* San Francisco:
    Global Exchange, Feb. www.globalexchange.org/economy/corporations/sweat-
    shops/fla.ht

Bernard, Elaine. 1997. "Ensuring That Monitoring Is Not Coopted," *New Solutions*
    7 (4) 10–12.

Bernstein, Aaron. 1999. "Sweatshop Reform," *Business Week*, 3 May.

Beuchler, Steven. 2000. *Social Movements in Advanced Capitalism*. New York: Oxford
    University Press.

Bonacich, Edna, and Richard Appelbaum. 2000. *Behind the Label: Inequality in the
    Los Angeles Apparel Industry*. Berkeley: University of California Press.

Bonacich, Edna, et al., eds. 1994. *Global Production: The Apparel Industry in the Pacific
    Rim*. Philadelphia: Temple University Press.

Brecher, Jeremy, et al. 2000. *Globalization from Below*. Cambridge, Mass: South End
    Press.

Castells, Manuel. 2000. *The Rise of the Network Society*. 2nd ed. Oxford: Blackwell
    Publishers.

Chen, Martha, et al. 1999. "Counting the Invisible Workforce: The Case of Home-based Workers," *World Development* 27 (3), 603–10.

Clean Clothes Campaign (CCC). 1999. *Almost Everything You Always Wanted to Know about Independent Monitoring.* www.cleanclothes.org/codes/monitoring1.htm

Cleeland, Nancy. 2000. "Garment Makers' Compliance with Labor Laws Slips in L.A.," *Los Angeles Times*, 21 Sept.

Compa, Lance. 2001. "Wary Allies," *American Prospect* 12 (12), 2–16.

Connor, Tim. 2001. "Still Waiting for Nike to Do It," *Global Exchange.* www.globalexchange.org

Dicken, Peter. 1998. *Global Shift: Transforming the World Economy*, 3rd ed. New York: Guilford Press.

D'Mello, Bernard. 2003. "Reebok and the Global Footwear Sweatshop," *Monthly Review* 54 (9), 26–40.

Durkee, Bob. 2003. "Fair Labor Association Board Update January 2003." www.ur.rutgers.edu/news/ACLA/flaboard2003.htm

Elliott, Kimberley, and Richard Freeman. 2001. *White Hats or Don Quixotes? Human Rights Vigilantes in the Global Economy*, NBER Working Paper 8102. Cambridge, Mass: National Bureau of Economic Research.

Fair Labor Association. 1998. *Charter of the Fair Labor Association.* Washington, DC: Fair Labor Association.

– n.d. *Changes to the FLA: A Comparison of the Old and New System.* Washington, DC: Fair Labor Association. www.fairlabor.org/html/new_fla_comparison.html

– n.d. *Monitoring Guidance.* Washington, DC: Fair Labor Association.

– n.d. *Statement of Independence and Professional Conduct, Application Form for Independent External Monitors.* Washington, DC: Fair Labor Association. www.fairlabour.org/html/accreditation/accreditation.ht.

– n.d. *Workplace Code of Conduct.* Washington, DC: Fair Labor Association. www.fairlabor.org/html/CodeOfConduct/index.html

Fung, Archon, et al. 2001. "Realizing Labor Standards," in Joshua Cohen and Joel Rogers, eds., *Can We Put an End to Sweatshops?* Boston: Beacon Press, 3–40.

Gereffi, Gary. 1994. "The Organization of Buyer-Driven Global Commodity Chains," in Gary Gereffi and Miguel Korzeniewicz, eds., *Commodity Chains and Global Capitalism.* London: Greenwood.

– 1999. "International Trade and International Upgrading in the Apparel Commodity Chain," *Journal of International Economics* 48 (1), 37–70.

Harrison, Bennett, and Maryellen Kelley. 1991. "Outsourcing and the Search for Flexibility: The Morphology of Contracting Out in US Manufacture," in Michael Storper and Allen J. Scott, eds., *Pathways to Industrialization and Regional Development in the 1990s.* New York: Routledge.

Hong Kong Christian Industrial Committee. 2003a. "Integration with the Pearl River Delta – Unfair Trade for Unfair Toys." Press Release. 10 Jan.

– 2003b. "Unfair Trade for Unfair Toys – Summary of Interviews with Hong Kong Toy Manufacturers on Buying Practices." Mimeo.

International Labour Organization. 1998. *Labour and Social Issues Relating to Export Processing Zones*. Geneva: ILO.

– 2000. *Labour Practices in the Footwear, Leather, Textiles and Clothing Industries*. Geneva: International Labour Office.

Issel, Bernardo. 2000. *Integrity of Fair Labor Association (FLA) Challenged: Sweatshop Companies Fund Nonprofit Groups of FLA*. Washington, DC: Nonprofit Watch, April.

Jeffcott, Bob, and Lynda Yanz. 2000. "Shopping for the Right Code," in Raj Thamotheram, ed., *Visions of Ethical Sourcing*. London: Financial Times–Prentice Hall.

Keck, Margaret, and Kathryn Sikkink. 1998. *Activists beyond Borders*. Ithaca, NY: Cornell University Press.

Kessler, Judith. 1999. "The North American Free Trade Agreement, Emerging Apparel Production Networks and Industrial Upgrading," *Review of International Political Economy* 6 (4), 565–608.

Klein, Naomi. 2000. *No Logo: Taking Aim at the Brand Bullies*. Toronto: Vintage Canada.

Kull, Steven. 1999. *Americans on Globalization: A Study of Public Attitudes*. College Park, Md.: Program on International Policy Attitudes, University of Maryland.

Kwan, Alice. 2000. *Report from China: Producing for Adidas and Nike*. Hong Kong: Hong Kong Christian Industrial Committee, 25 April. www.cleanclothes.org

Light, Julie. 1998. *Sweatwash: The Apparel Industry's Efforts to Co-opt Human Rights*. Oakland, Calif.: Corporate Watch, Dec.

Marymount University Center for Ethical Concerns. 1999. *The Consumers and Sweatshops*. Nov. www.marymount.edu/news/garmentstudy/overview.html

Mittelman, James. 2000. *The Globalization Syndrome*. Princeton, NJ: Princeton University Press.

O'Rourke, Dara. 2002. "Monitoring the Monitors: A Critique of Corporate Third-Party Labour Monitoring," in Rhys Jenkins et al., eds., *Corporate Responsibility and Labour Rights*. London: Earthscan.

Pearson, Ruth, and Gill Seyfang. 2002. "'I'll Tell You What I Want ...': Women Workers and Codes of Conduct," in Rhys Jenkins et al., eds., *Corporate Responsibility and Labour Rights*. London: Earthscan.

Prieto, Marina, and Jem Bendell. 2002. "If You Want to Help Us Then Start Listening to Us!" Occasional paper, New Academy of Business, Bath, England. www.new-academy.ac.uk

Ramsay, Harvie. 1997. "Solidarity at Last? International Trade Unionism Approaching the Millennium," *Economic and Industrial Democracy* 18 (4), 503–38.

Ross, J., and Anita Chan. 2002. "From North–South to South–South: The True Face of Global Competition," *Foreign Affairs* 81 (5), 8–13.

Schilling, David. 2000. "Making Codes of Conduct Credible," in Oliver Williams, ed., *Global Codes of Conduct*. Notre Dame, Ind.: University of Notre Dame Press, 221–38.

Schoenberger, Karl. 2000. *Levi's Children: Coming to Terms with Human Rights in the Global Marketplace.* New York: Atlantic Monthly Press.

Sethi, S.P. 2003. *Setting Global Labor Standards.* New York: Wiley and Sons.

Standing, Guy. 1999. *Global Labour Flexibility.* Basingstoke: Macmillan.

Sweeney, Kevin. 2000. "Voting with Their Pocketbooks," in Oliver Williams, ed., *Global Codes of Conduct.* Notre Dame, Ind.: University of Notre Dame Press, 253–64.

Tarrow, Sidney. 1998. *Power in Movement.* 2nd ed. Cambridge: Cambridge University Press.

Tsogas, George. 2001. *Labor Regulation in a Global Economy.* Armonk, NY: M.E. Sharpe.

United States Department of Labor. 1996. *The Apparel Industry and Codes of Conduct: A Solution to the International Child Labor Problem?* Washington, DC: Department of Labor.

– 2000. *Wages, Benefits, Poverty Line, and Meeting Workers' Needs in the Apparel and Footwear Industries of Selected Countries.* Washington, DC: Bureau of International Labor Affairs, Feb.

United Students Against Sweatshops (USAS). 2002. *New Changes to the FLA: Explanation and Renewed Criticism.* www.usasnet.org

Utting, Gerald. 2003. "Corporate Responsibility and Labour Issues in China," *News and Views.* New York: United Nations Research Institute for Social Development.

van Eijk, Janneke. 1998. *Keeping the Work Floor Clean: Monitoring Models in the Garment Industry.* Rev. and trans. Bart Plantenga, from *Ethiek in de Fabriek.* Amsterdam: Clean Clothes Campaign, Dec. www.cleanclothes.org

Wells, Don. 1998. "Building Transnational Coordinative Unionism," in Steve Babson and Huberto Juarez Nunez, eds., in *Confronting Change: Autoworkers and Lean Production in North America.* Detroit: Wayne State University Press.

Wick, Ingeborg. 2003. *Workers' Tool or PR Ploy? A Guide to Codes of International Labour Practice.* Bonn: Friedrich-Ebert-Stiftung.

Wilson, Jim. 2000. "From Solidarity to Convergence: International Trade Union Cooperation in the Media Sector," in Michael Gordon and Lowell Turner, eds., *Transnational Cooperation among Unions.* Ithaca, NY: Cornell University Press.

Worker Rights Consortium. 2001. *Worker Rights Consortium, Frequently Asked Questions.* www.workersrights.org

Zinn, Kenneth. 2000. "Solidarity across Borders," in Michael Gordon and Lowell Turner, eds., *Transnational Cooperation among Unions.* Ithaca, NY: Cornell University Press.

Contributors

PETER AUER is chief of the Employment Analysis and Research Unit of the Employment Strategy Department of the International Labour Organization. His interests are labour market analysis and economic and social development.

MANFRED BIENEFELD is a professor in the School of Public Policy and Administration, Carleton University, Ottawa.

DAVE BROAD is a professor of social work and a research associate of the Social Policy Research Unit at the University of Regina conducts research on globalization and on labour and social welfare issues.

TATIANA CHETVERNINA is director of the Centre for Labour Market Studies, Institute of Economics, Russian Academy of Sciences.

MARLEA CLARKE is a doctoral candidate in political science at York University and a research associate of the Labour and Enterprise Project, Institute of Development and Labour Law, Law Faculty, University of Cape Town.

CYNTHIA CRANFORD is an assistant professor of sociology at the University of Toronto. Her research focuses on the relationship between economic restructuring, labour organizing, immigration, and shifting gender relations.

GRACE-EDWARD GALABUZI is an assistant professor in the Department of Politics and Public Administration at Ryerson University and a research associate at the Centre for Social Justice in Toronto.

SANDRA SALHANI GAMBLE, formerly a researcher with the Social Policy Research Unit, University of Regina, is currently a social researcher living in London, England.

TOM GOOD recently retired as chair of the Department of Economics at St Thomas University in Fredericton, New Brunswick, and now lives in Toronto.

MICHEL GRANT is a professor of industrial relations at the Université du Québec à Montréal and has been conducting research in the garment industry for twenty years.

STEVE JEFFERYS is director of the Working Lives Research Institute at the London Metropolitan University in England.

LIANA LAKUNINA is a senior researcher at the Centre for Labour Market Studies, Institute of Economics, Russian Academy of Sciences.

STEPHANIE LUCE is an assistant professor at the University of Massachusetts – Amherst Labor Center. Her research focuses on low-wage labour markets in the United States.

MARTHA MACDONALD is professor of economics at Saint Mary's University, Halifax. She investigates gender and restructuring, serves as an associate editor of the journal *Feminist Economics*, and sits on the External Committee for the Policy Research Fund, Status of Women Canada.

DELLA MACNEIL, formerly a researcher with the Social Policy Research Unit, University of Regina, is currently a labour activist and independent researcher in Regina.

STEPHEN MCBRIDE is professor of political science and director of the Centre for Global Political Economy at Simon Fraser University.

JOAN MCFARLAND is a professor of economics and gender studies at St Thomas University in Fredericton, New Brunswick. Her current area of study is women and development projects in Kerala, India.

THOMAS PALLEY is director of the Open Society Institute's Globalization Reform Project, based in Washington, DC.

VIVIANA PATRONI is associate professor in the Division of Social Science and director of the Centre for Research on Latin America and the Caribbean, both at York University, Toronto.

MALCOLM SAWYER is professor of economics, University of Leeds, England, and managing editor of the *International Review of Applied Economics*. His research interests include post-Keynesian macroeconomics, barriers to full employment, and monetary policy.

JIM STANFORD is an economist with the Canadian Auto Workers' Union.

LEAH F. VOSKO is Canada Research Chair in Feminist Political Economy in the School of Social Sciences (Political Science), Atkinson Faculty, York University. Her research interests include precarious employment, gender and work, free trade, comparative labour and social policy, and international labour market regulation.

DON WELLS is associate professor in the Labour Studies Programme and the Political Science Department at McMaster University in Hamilton, Ontario. His research centres on economic restructuring and global labour standards.

MICHAEL JOHN WHITTALL is an Economic and Social Research Council (ESRC) fellow attached to Nottingham Trent University. His main areas of interest are European Works Councils and German labour relations.